THE
THERAPEUTIC
ENVIRONMENT

THE
THERAPEUTIC
ENVIRONMENT

Robert Langs, M.D.

NEW YORK • JASON ARONSON • LONDON

to Bernard,
and to a creative space

CLASSICAL PSYCHOANALYSIS AND ITS APPLICATIONS

A Series of Books
Edited by Robert Langs, M.D.

CONTENTS

PREFACE

This book confronts a remarkable paradox, which, stated in its essentials, is as follows: on the one hand, impingements on the therapeutic environment—the ground rules, framework, hold, and setting of the psychotherapeutic and analytic situations—evoke intense but highly predictable responses in patients, while on the other hand the delineation of this dimension of treatment generates strikingly chaotic and emotional responses in therapists and analysts. The framework has been much neglected in the analytic literature, and this too is part of a paradox in that the frame itself is undoubtedly the single most fundamental component of the analytic and therapeutic interactions. Approaches to this subject have been remarkably naive by any standards of psychoanalytic methodology, and the prevailing technical principles are similarly simplistic and poorly grounded in clinical observation. These are all signs of collective countertransference difficulties, so heavily invested as to create the possibility that the empirical efforts delineated in this book will be either summarily dismissed or ignored entirely. I can only hope that most readers will instead maintain an open-minded attitude and will, at the very least, permit the clinical observations elaborated here to call into question many accepted practices in this area; perhaps this will lead to personal reinvestigation and reconsideration.

In essence, then, this book is an attempt to apply the basic listening and validating processes (Langs 1978c) to the therapist's definition and management of the setting and ground rules of the therapeutic situation. It presents an investigation in which many basic issues related to this environment emerge in specific therapeutic interactions. Attention to these interactions permits the conscious and unconscious communications from the patient, and secondarily from the therapist, to provide us commentaries through which we may best define the analytic nature, meanings, and functions of this quite human frame. Every effort has been made to set aside personal bias and to allow these answers to unfold from the material at hand. Similarly, conclusions are not drawn until Type Two derivative validation is in evidence, and often not until such validation is repeated, not only within the given patient-therapist interaction but in other cases presented here as well.

The data accumulated in this volume and in previous investigations of the framework (see especially Langs 1975c, 1976a, 1978a) demonstrate quite clearly the basic role played by the ground rules and setting of the treatment situation. We are dealing, of course, not only with a physical spatiotemporal setting, but with a set of human management functions that in many ways defy metaphor. Still, such images as the frame or framework, the therapist's holding capacities, the establishment of a container and of a communicative therapeutic space—especially if we keep in mind their ultimate limitations—all prove serviceable up to a point and help us to discover and investigate some of the easily overlooked functions of this particular dimension. It would indeed prove difficult to conceptualize without them.

Although when secured the framework provides a silent backdrop of safety for the therapeutic interaction, impingements are extremely common; far more often than is generally realized, they become the arena for critical therapeutic work. This is a sphere in which many important actualities exist, and where the influence of these realities is considerably more powerful than any interpretive interventions related to them. Sound therapeutic work in this realm requires both management and interpretive responses. Perhaps one reason for the neglect of this particular dimension is that it contains so many actualities filled with unmistakable unconscious implications that its full comprehension would require a basic revision in how therapists and analysts conceptualize and work with the therapeutic interaction. Attention to the framework requires detailed consideration of the here and now, of the implications of the realities within the therapist and their communication to the patient, and of the admixture of fantasy and reality, transference and nontransference, in the patient's reactions.

This is but one of the possible reasons for the neglect of this topic and for the evident disregard of the patient's need for an essentially secure treatment environment. To speculate further, it may well be that what I consider inappropriate modifications in the frame have become a generally sanctioned means of expressing countertransference-based needs and defenses. Any therapist who has himself been in treatment has surely experienced a therapeutic situation in which an unneeded alteration in the framework was accepted as standard practice, and there appears to be a strong tendency toward blindly incorporating such practices into one's own efforts as a therapist. In addition, adherence to a secure frame would entail the use of techniques that might run quite contrary to those of one's own therapist or analyst.

Another factor may well be the dread in many therapists of the more regressive and psychotic parts of the personality—both their own and their patient's—aspects of which emerge only in the presence of a relatively secure framework. Then too there may well be in the analyst an unconscious envy of the patient who is held well; the analyst may feel himself poorly held by the patient, by his own therapist, or perhaps, in the past, by his mother. Another consideration involves the personal and social consequences of efforts to maintain a steady, safe, and secure environment in the face of pressures to complete insurance forms, to offer low-fee therapy, and the like. Nonetheless, while these issues are quite real and important, they do not determine clinical truth. Instead, we must establish validated clinical observations which then must be considered vis-à-vis their effects on the patient and on society at large.

In all, there is considerable evidence that each therapist and analyst enters the treatment situation with powerful needs within himself to modify the basic framework for reasons of inappropriate defense and gratification. This trend suggests a special need for caution in approaching the subject, and a need to apply rather stringent psychoanalytic criteria of validation to the formulations, managements, and interventions proposed in this realm. Such work can provide us an approach founded on sound psychoanalytic principles and essentially devoted to the therapeutic needs of the patient and, to that end, to the special needs of the therapist to function in the best possible therapeutic manner in his relationship with the patient.

Once again I am indebted to Sheila Gardner and Norma Tankenbaum for their assistance in preparing the manuscript, and in particular to Michael Farrin for his excellent editorial work. Jason Aronson continues to be steadfast in his support and it is deeply appreciated. Most of all, my indebtedness is to the trainees who participated in the seminars that constitute the substance of this volume, and who presented and discussed this clinical material with such exemplary fervor and eagerness to learn. Not enough can be said of their dedication to their patients and to the field, and we are all of us the wiser for their efforts.

As in the past, these seminars are presented essentially as they unfolded, based on the strictly sequential presentation of process-note clinical material. Some editing has been done, mainly to protect the anonymity of both patient and therapist, but also to cut down on digressions and repetitions, and to elaborate points made during the seminar that did not seem sufficiently covered. Every effort has been made to preserve the precious opportunity for clinical prediction that prevailed throughout the seminar meetings. To facilitate comprehension I have included two appendices. Appendix A offers an outline of the major dimensions of the therapeutic environment and the techniques used in this sphere, while Appendix B presents an updated glossary of terms that are used in some special way in my work.

In substance, this book constitutes an attempt to explore every possible dimension of the therapeutic environment. It is an endeavor that has long been overdue, and it is hoped that it will not only clarify this much confused area for each reader, but also that it will spawn further investigations and refinements.

Robert Langs, M.D.
March 1979
New York, New York

Chapter One

THE STANDARD ENVIRONMENT

Langs: We begin now with the second major segment of this course on the technique of psychotherapy: a study of the ground rules, their nature and functions. Having established the basis for this undertaking by developing the details of the listening process (Langs 1978c), we will be able once again to develop our conceptualizations in this particular area on an empirical basis, almost entirely through the case presentations that we will be hearing.

I will provide you with a reading list (see Langs 1976c), but I would prefer that you do your reading later, in order to permit as much of an empirical unfolding as possible—another version of entering some aspect of the psychotherapeutic experience without desire, memory, or understanding (Bion 1970). There are so many prejudices among therapists and analysts in regard to the ground rules that I want here to make every effort to allow the patients presented to us—and to some extent, the therapists as well—to be our guide as much as possible.

So we have learned how to listen, and we turn now to the basic framework of the therapeutic situation—the background or setting, the environment, which we must consider before the foreground of the patient's free associations and the therapist's interventions, which are the usual focus of treatment. In fact, before we can carefully investigate

the therapeutic relationship itself, we will find it necessary to understand the setting within which this relationship unfolds. Our work during the first ten weeks of this course (Langs 1978c) should allow us to
make this statement without prejudice, but let's nevertheless keep it in
reserve until a new patient reestablishes it as a sound dictum. Now let's
move directly into some clinical material.

Therapist: This is actually someone the rest of the seminar have
heard about in another course. She's a twenty-eight-year-old occupational therapist at a hospital in this city.

Langs: Other than this one?

Therapist: Other than this one. That specifically was her wish: to
not be treated in her own hospital.

Langs: How interesting. Is she wise, or suspicious—or both? We'll
soon find out.

Therapist: The patient . . .

Langs: Wait a moment. What is this first comment related to?

Therapist: Confidentiality.

Langs: Confidentiality. By implication, this patient may be concerned with the confidentiality of her treatment. We have just identified our first ground rule of psychotherapy, and it is probably no
coincidence that confidentiality is the first one to arise. The total confidentiality of psychotherapy, if I may identify the pure form of the
ground rule in that way, is not only among the most important of these
basic tenets, but also is one regarding which issues and infringements
arise very often these days.
      What else could be implied in her wish not to be treated in the
hospital in which she works? What other aspect of the ground rules
could be involved?

Discussant: Anonymity?

Langs: Yes. It may have to do with the anonymity of the therapist: her wish not to be in a setting where his anonymity would be under constant threat of modification, or might be altered from the outset.

So, we now have our second ground rule: the relative personal anonymity of the therapist. For the moment, we are simply cataloguing the relative constants of psychotherapy and recognizing that they come up—directly or by implication—very quickly in the course of treatment. The patient's wish to be treated in another hospital is manifest, and we do not know the context in which it arose in the session in which the patient expressed it to her present therapist. We are therefore not in a position to understand its unconscious implications for the patient, nor can we, for the moment, validate any thesis regarding these ground rules by the standards that we established in the listening part of this course. Still, it will be most interesting to see just how often references to the ground rules, and issues involving them, will arise in the course of psychotherapy and in presentations of this kind.

Now, what other ground rule is also implicit to this patient's wish to be treated outside of her own hospital? (Pause.) A very simple one: location. Another ground rule of psychotherapy pertains to the physical setting, the place in which treatment transpires.

Now, it occurs to me, as I think of how to define or use this particular tenet, that the very delineation of the ground rules, in terms of their definition and scope, is a matter of some degree of uncertainty and debate. These are issues that will have to be resolved empirically. There is little doubt that analysts and therapists would vary in identifying the nature of the essential ground rules and their specifications, just as there is considerable debate in regard to their explication. Here, as always, I will try to permit the conscious and, especially, the unconscious communications of the patient and therapist to guide me. I am certain that in addition my own prior experiences, which I have, by the way, subjected to extensive psychoanalytic validation, will also exert an influence. I will try, however, to keep that influence to a minimum.

Perhaps you will have noticed that in regard to confidentiality I set as the standard *total* confidentiality, while in regard to anonymity I alluded to *relative* anonymity and the maximal possible noncommunication of the therapist's personal feelings, responses, life history, and the like. You can see that here there also would be room for interpretation regarding some of these qualities, but we will not try to tease out this aspect for the moment, and will wait until we have some clinical material to help us.

As for the ground rule regarding the location of treatment, I would state as the ideal standard that psychotherapy—or psychoanalysis— should take place in a neutral location, a professional building and private (unshared) office, and, further, that the transactions between patient and therapist should occur within the confines of the latter's consultation room, which should remain constant.

Discussant: In one of your technique books (Langs 1973b), didn't you indicate that a therapist could have his office in his home, for example, as long as he was aware of its implications and was prepared to work with issues in that area as they came up with his patients?

Langs: How familiar: Langs quoted against Langs. As I have said before, there is a great deal that I believe to be quite sound in my early technique books (Langs 1973b, 1974), but there is much that I have revised based on my continued clinical observations and on refinement in my clinical methodology and use of the validating process.

You are quite right that the definition of the ground rule offered just now in regard to location implies differences between my present thinking and that reflected in the earlier book. However, I would prefer not to elaborate until we have a substantial body of clinical material. Let's try to keep an open mind on these issues and find our way from there, based on the presentations we will be hearing. All we know for the moment is that this therapist is about to describe a session in which an issue related to the ground rules arose, and we are already, just based on a brief introductory comment, in a position to identify several components of these relative constants. Please continue.

Therapist: Oh, there are many issues involving the ground rules. To continue: I've been seeing her for about ten months, twice a week, around the issue of a depression which followed her separation from her boyfriend, who was a young psychotherapist at a hospital clinic. (Laughter.)

Langs: That's marvelous—a surprising form of immediate, though indefinite, Type Two derivative validation. For the moment, that problem appears to be related not only to her own psychodynamics and her unconscious motives for entering treatment, but also to the ground rules. That's an interesting connection.

Discussant: Did he work at her hospital or here?

Therapist: No, at still another place.

Langs: So, we are now informed of the frequency of sessions—twice weekly. In this regard, the ground rule might best be stated in this way: there should be a set and consistent frequency of sessions. You'll notice that I am stating the ground rules in terms of absolutes, standards, ideals. This for the moment seems the best approach, since it will define the ideal setting and background of therapy as clearly as possible, and then permit discussion in regard to how consistent we should be with these rules and how definitively they should be maintained. You can see too how quickly we are identifying these tenets.

Therapist: This is the first session after my return from a one-week vacation.

Langs: How interesting. Here's another aspect of the ground rules: the matter of vacations by the therapist, and, by implication, the patient as well. To state it as a tenet and to offer a brief discussion, we could say that the sessions should be continuous except for reasonably occasional, not unduly long vacations by the therapist. In its most ideal form—once again as a standard—the patient's vacations would be expected to coincide with those of the therapist, and the patient would be responsible for both her presence and the fee—another ground rule that we have not considered yet—in respect to all sessions for which the therapist is present.

As a way of organizing these rules, I tend to place the establishment of a set fee, the frequency of sessions, the specific appointed times for each hour, and a definitive length for each session—be it forty-five or fifty minutes—as an interrelated set of tenets which are part of the *fixed frame,* a set of constants that provides a defined and steady environment.

For the moment, since you mention your vacation, I also want to point out that the therapist's right to take a vacation is actually established as one of the ground rules at the beginning of treatment.

And while most of the other ground rules are designed to stabilize the therapeutic setting and to offer it as a constant with well-defined boundaries and holding qualities, this particular tenet has a rather different effect. It is part of the basic agreement between patient and therapist, and yet it disrupts the consistency and holding qualities of the therapist's relationship to the patient; it tends to generate disturbance rather than calm. It is well to keep this point in mind, because it will lead us to expect a rather different response to the therapist's vacation, as compared, for example, to his maintenance of total confidentiality or relative anonymity.

We should hear more now, because your vacation also introduces the specific question of how you established the ground rules—if you did so—and how you handled this particular vacation. To some degree, an assumption—or even a bias—has crept into my comments: namely, that the therapist should define a set of clear-cut ground rules—an analytic or therapeutic pact, as Freud (1940) termed it—in the first session in which definitive treatment is established. Now, there are some therapists who see this as regimented and overly controlling and who prefer to leave this area quite ill-defined. We must leave room for an empirical decision in this respect; hopefully, we will have a chance to observe both types of situations and can draw our own conclusions.

Therapist: I suspect that you will be happy to hear that three weeks earlier she had returned from a two-week vacation of her own.

Langs: So, the patient went on vacation for two weeks; there followed two weeks of sessions, and then the therapist took a one-week vacation of his own. Now, how was this handled?

Therapist: Here in the clinic, it's usually not handled by us.

Langs: Who handles it?

Therapist: The secretary or receptionist.

Langs: What else would she handle?

Therapist: The fee arrangements: there is a sliding fee scale, depending on income.

Langs: Well, with this introduction, most of the major ground rules have been brought to our attention. We now have a reference to the setting of the fee, which should be stated as a basic tenet in the following way: the therapist should suggest a single fee, well within his range of usual fees, for the duration of the therapy.

It's really quite unfortunate that we are beginning our study of the ground rules with a therapy already in progress, though we will, of course, have a first hour presented to us later on. This means that in the present situation, we will not be in a position to hear the sequences of material which relate to these various ground rules and their modification—and I have by no means completed my delineation—and so we must try for the moment to use this data primarily for matters of definition. As we get into specific clinical situations in which a specific ground rule appears in the manifest transactions, we will be able to treat it as our adaptive or therapeutic context, and to organize the material from the patient around it, thereby ascertaining the meanings and functions of the particular rule involved. For now, we must settle for less.

Still, we are touching upon additional tenets. We now hear, for example, that there is a third and possibly fourth party to this therapy, in the form of a secretary and/or receptionist. This touches upon the exclusive one-to-one relationship that should exist in psychotherapy, and upon the issue of total confidentiality as well. It seems evident that the secretary must have information about the patient on which to base the fee; in addition, your comments suggest that the clinic sets the policy regarding responsibility for sessions as well. So we hear of a sliding scale which determines the fee, and that it is set by a third party rather than by the therapist.

It seems evident now that we are dealing with a clinical situation with a considerably modified frame as compared to the standards that I have been establishing. This fact is on the one hand an excellent opportunity to learn about these ground rules—since they will come to the fore at times of disturbance—and about the influence of their alteration, while on the other hand it may contribute to conditions that limit the patient's derivative and unconscious communications in this area. Since all of your presentations are from clinic patients, this will deprive us of an opportunity to observe a therapeutic interaction under conditions in which the ground rules are relatively secure, and because of this I have invited one of the staff members at this center, who is also in private practice, to present some material to us at the end of this segment of the course.

There are those who have reviewed my book, *The Bipersonal Field* (1976a), and have questioned whether any valid observations and conclusions about the ground rules can be generated by observing clinical situations in which they are considerably modified. Now, while I am well aware that alterations in the basic rules have a considerable influence on the transactions between patient and therapist or analyst (see especially Langs 1976c, chapter 16), it is nonetheless a fact that that very finding was derived through the supervision of therapies carried out under such conditions. It has always seemed evident to me, and Freud actually stated this first (1918), that we learn very little from a case that goes well—that is, from a therapy in which the ground rules are secured and soundly maintained. We learn a great deal more when things go awry. This generates adaptive and therapeutic contexts to which both patient and therapist respond, and provides us with a communicative network filled with meaning.

I suspect that this principle will quickly be borne out by this presentation, so let's return to it. We know now that we have a situation with at least one third party to treatment, in the person of a secretary or receptionist.

Therapist: This third party problem is even more complicated, because her therapy is being paid for by her hospital medical plan, except for two months at the end of the year when she has used up her benefits for that period. Then she has to be self-paying for about two months.

Langs: And at the point we're going to hear about, is she self-paying or not?

Therapist: She's back to hospital plan—it's paying.

Langs: So we have another third party issue here—we have a fourth party. We have the fact, then, that the patient is not paying her fee at all—or is she paying a certain percentage of it?

Therapist: Not a penny.

Langs: So this is, for the moment, a free therapy for this patient. It reminds me that in stating the ground rule regarding fees I believe that I left out that, ideally, the patient alone should be responsible for full payment. You can see that this implies two possible and common variations, each, I might add, with a different set of overlapping consequences: first, her payment might be made by a third party, in which case the therapist usually must participate by completing some type of form and releasing specific information to this party; and, second, situations in which a parent or spouse, and sometimes a boyfriend or girlfriend, have taken the responsibility to pay some or all of the fee. Therapists have tended, for many reasons—not the least of which are their own financial motives—to ignore the consequences of these arrangements; this is a subject to which we will most certainly return. For your information, in addition to my own writings on this topic (Langs 1975c, 1976c), there is a paper by Halpert (1972) on psychoanalysis without a fee, and his findings are quite consistent with my own—and with those that we undoubtedly are about to generate ourselves. I am torn for the moment between needing to make introductory comments and wanting to wait for specific clinical data. I will try not to overly bias our approach.

So we have now added fee arrangements to the basic ground rules. In addition, we have already experienced something about these tenets. Can anyone state it?

Discussant: They seem kind of ubiquitous. I mean, as soon as anybody does anything, they seem to crop up.

Langs: Yes, they're ubiquitous, and in addition, they're not discrete. As you can see, a third-party payer involves a modification not only in the one-to-one relationship but also, in all likelihood, in the therapist's anonymity—for example, he may be asked to reveal the patient's diagnosis or other clinical impressions. His neutrality is also altered—he becomes vital to the patient's ability to obtain the funds with which to pay the fee. In addition, the total confidentiality of treatment is probably modified, because as a rule, there are forms to be filled out and information to be released. Is this the case here?

Therapist: She's been consciously concerned about these issues at various points in her treatment.

Discussant: Aren't there some forms that you fill out?

Discussant: Yes. They usually ask for a diagnosis, which I routinely enter as emotional illness.

Therapist: Actually, I have to fill out a short form for each session, including the reason for consultation, the physical findings, and the form of treatment. I usually just enter anxiety reaction and sign it.

Langs: So, we are quickly faced with the issue of third-party payers and the alterations in the frame that usually accompany their presence. Both of you describe a common practice, by which therapists attempt a particular kind of compromise by using a routine diagnosis in completing the form—such as anxiety reaction or character disorder. To the extent that this does not accurately reflect the patient's diagnosis, this is a falsification or lie—in the nonmoral sense—that in itself has many ramifications.

   Now, I am trying to curtail my comments until we have more extensive clinical material. But let's pause and recognize that we have already introduced another important ground rule: the therapist's neutrality and his exclusive use of interventions geared toward interpretation. Having stated this tenet, we can immediately appreciate its complexities. For example, neutrality does not imply disinterest, emptiness, undue coldness, lack of empathy, or absurd deprivation. On the other hand, it does entail what I would term *physicianly concern,* the absence of direct and personal responses to the patient's communications and pressures, and a commitment to help the patient. Perhaps now we can tentatively state it this way: to be helpful by creating the essential and necessary conditions for a valid therapeutic experience, and by intervening to the greatest extent feasible without personal investment and entirely in the therapeutic interests of the patient—largely through verbal interventions geared toward interpretive responses.

   Based on this presentation, we must add to the therapist's commitment to neutrality something that I believe I have not previously stated explicitly, though it is implicit to virtually everything I have written: It is the therapist's responsibility to speak the truth and not to lie to the patient. This does not mean that he must immediately blurt out every truth that he observes, since all of the ground rules must be exercised with tact and concern. But it does mean that when he speaks he must state the truth to the best of his knowledge, and that certainly he must not knowingly communicate a lie. In light of our earlier discussion regarding the Type C field and barriers, lies, and falsifications, we might immediately sense that this particular ground rule will have considerable bearing on the nature of the communicative bipersonal field.

Two other points. First, you may begin to sense that there is a range of qualities and attributes to these ground rules, and that they are by no means all of a kind. There is the physical setting created by the therapist, which is a relative constant, and then there are the more absolute constants such as set fees, length of sessions, frequency and time of hours, the face-to-face mode or use of the couch—a ground rule that we have not as yet addressed—and total confidentiality. Each of these is readily demarcated and alterations are fairly easy to identify. And as I said before, we will refer to these factors as the *fixed frame*.

On the other hand we have the therapist's anonymity, neutrality, and the nature of his interventions, all of which are far more open to personal interpretation and spontaneous variation, and regarding which definitive deviations are somewhat more difficult to identify. I will term these factors the *variable frame*, the more human and changeable elements. Nonetheless, even though there are permissible gradations in these matters, it is essential to recognize the importance of attempting to define the particular qualities of a given response by the therapist. We must realize that at times we will be quite certain of either the clear-cut presence of anonymity or its modification, while at other times the very fact that it is difficult to ascertain the extent of possible deviation is in itself an important datum.

Second, we can see that it is not only the ground rules per se that are critical, but also the therapist's interpretation and application of them. It is probably unfortunate that Freud and others have approached these principles in terms of ground rules, a rather mechanistic concept, rather than the therapist's delineation and management of the setting, hold, and framework—to introduce some terms related to this dimension that we will consider later on. The word *rules* actually has an unfortunate penumbra of meanings, such as right or wrong, breakable or unbreakable, good or bad, conform or rebel, obey or disregard, yes or no, black or white—to name a few. They seem almost nonhuman, when in fact their very essence in the therapeutic experience is intensely human and rich in conscious and, especially, unconscious communication. I am well aware that the metaphor of the frame or framework for these tenets carries with it the unfortunate implication of such mechanical qualities, and when we find need for this means of conceptualizing the ground rules we will take considerable care not to fall into such a misuse of the concept. We need such models in order to develop the nature and functions of the ground rules—they aid our thinking. But they have distinct limitations and these must be known too.

So, we have here a clinical situation in which there are a large number of modifications of the ideal frame. These have been sufficiently identified in your introduction of this case to the point where we were able to delineate almost all the basic ground rules. In fact, I can think only of the fundamental rule of free association as having been omitted—and we will soon address that issue. Can anyone think of any other ground rule we have not included?

Discussant: The fact that her boyfriend was also a therapist.

Langs: How would you see that as an aspect of the ground rules?

Discussant: It will influence the content of her associations.

Discussant: It may imply that she's looking for a replacement for the boyfriend—a professional replacement, if not a personal replacement.

Langs: Yes, that's a good point, and it enables me to point out that we will want to distinguish issues related to the patient's—and the therapist's—motivation for entering the treatment situation, and how it influences the transactions of therapy, from issues that pertain specifically to the ground rules and setting. Incidentally, you also remind me that there are a number of implicit ground rules, such as the absence of physical contact and the goals of the relationship. The latter is a complicated issue, in that it implies a therapeutic commitment from the therapist, while, as you are suggesting, the patient may consciously or unconsciously have an outcome or method of therapy in mind that is considerably different from that intended by the therapist, who wishes to effect adaptive, structural, insightful inner change as a basis for symptom alleviation.

Finally, I would suggest that psychotherapy is based on affective-verbal exchanges, and that it precludes other forms of action and the use of medication—another tenet in need of considerable discussion.

Discussant: Coming back to the question of this patient's boyfriend, I see it as a factor that could result in a distortion of the patient's view of the need for anonymity on the part of the therapist. She may want to know him in some very special way.

Langs: Yes. Actually, you are introducing another point that we should identify explicitly: the patient, consciously and unconsciously, brings her own ground rules or framework to the treatment situation. That is, in addition to factors within the patient that influence her responses to the therapist's delineation of the ground rules, the patient herself has certain rules in mind. Often, as you are suggesting may well be the case here, the patient's frame is considerably different from that of the therapist. The framework may be designed with either of two possible goals in mind: to maintain and perpetuate the neurosis, and to gratify various pathological needs and defenses, or to create a setting in which valid therapeutic work may be carried out. As a rule, the patient's frame is weighed heavily toward the former, while the therapist's frame should of course be designed for the latter. In 1974, a French analyst named Viderman made this very point while writing on the use of interpretations in what he called "the psychoanalytic space"—a metaphor similar to my own bipersonal field concept.

So we do want to distinguish the patient's—and the therapist's—reactions to the frame from its basic structure and functions. Still, you're indicating your sense that issues related to the ground rules immediately extend into problems in the therapeutic relationship, and involve expressions of the patient's unconscious fantasies and the like. This is a good point: framework issues are often the vehicle for sound interpretive work.

Discussant: If I may come back for a moment to your ground rule regarding the fee, aren't there some therapists who believe that psychotherapy is possible even in the absence of a fee?

Langs: Yes. As you will see when you read on this topic, there are therapists who believe just about anything imaginable in regard to variations in the ground rules, and in actual practice they extend themselves quite far. Eissler (1974) has written a paper on fees, and in a rather practical way—but without psychoanalytically founded validation—he discusses a wide range of issues in this area. For now, I would simply like to state that it is indeed implicit in the ground rule related to fees, as I stated it earlier, that there should be direct compensation from the patient to the therapist. Let that be defined as the standard, and as we hear material related to this issue, we can then explore the relevant issues, hopefully resolving some of them based on the material presented us.

Now, you were going to tell us the ground rule you or the secretary had developed regarding vacations, and how it was explicated with this patient.

Therapist: She had known about this vacation for a long period of time, and earlier, I had . . .

Discussant: The patient's vacation, or yours?

Therapist: Both. I had known about my vacation for four months.

Discussant: Had you informed her of it?

Therapist: I had informed her of it.

Langs: So, quite soon we're going to have to get into the techniques related to the handling of the ground rules. How long in advance do we announce vacations? How do we do it? What is a true deviation? What is a nuance or simple variation within the basic ground rules? For example, supposing the therapist had said: You will be seen twice a week, except that I will take four vacations during the year, and I will give you advance notice. That's the ground rule. And he may have added, I will not charge you a fee while I'm absent. But within that ground rule, there may be nuances such as how much time off can be taken without seriously disturbing the therapy. Or there may be variations in how the vacation is announced or handled when allusions to it emerge in the patient's material.

Therapist: As an aside, when you talk about sessions in this clinic, people are not charged for any absence, any missed hour.

Langs: Oh. And what is the policy if she cancels sessions?

Therapist: She's not responsible for those either.

Langs: Is there any advance notice required?

Therapist: No. If you don't show, you're not charged.

Langs: All right, the rule in this therapy is: No show, no pay. We will discuss each of these policies in some detail as we go along. Okay, so that was the way the situation was structured. Please continue.

Therapist: So basically, this is the way she handled my vacation. She was also anticipating the possibility that I might leave the clinic in June, which she's aware of.

Langs: So there's another ground rule, one that is usually quite implicit. It has to do with the length of treatment. That is, in structuring treatment, the therapist implies that he has agreed to work with the patient toward symptom alleviation—and I use the term here to refer to all types of symptoms, whether psychosomatic, object related, characterological, internal or whatever—through the most constructive, insightful means available, and that the therapy will be carried out until that goal is reached. That particular standard is frequently modified in a clinic setting, often through the establishment of what is termed a *set* or *forced termination date* based on clinic policy and/or the availability of the therapist. Was this established at the outset of this therapy?

Therapist: Yes. She was told that treatment would last one year and two months.

Langs: How was this stated?

Therapist: I said that that was the duration of her hospital fee coverage, and that at that point she would have to decide if she wanted to continue, since it would then be on a self-paying basis. I promised her that I would be in the area until that time, but told her I couldn't make a promise beyond June.

Langs: You promised her your survival throughout that time.

Therapist: That I would not be gone before that time.

Langs: What I picked up on is how ground rules are stated; that has many ramifications too. I just want you to hear your words and to listen for possible unconscious communications. More broadly, we're for the moment considering how the ground rules are presented and the therapy structured, and we are attempting to maintain the listening process as we do so.

So you told her that you would be able to see her until June of this year, when her insurance runs out. You let her know that you could not assure her that after that you would be able to see her in the clinic.

Therapist: Yes. And the way she handled my going away on this vacation was to say that I wasn't going to leave town in June, although that thought had occurred to her. She said she knew I wouldn't do that to her, and that if I did she'd move to wherever I was.

Langs: Had you said anything about leaving the area to her?

Therapist: Not specifically. But she said it in a sort of narcissistic way, as an effort to deny her feelings: that if this vacation had represented any separation, it was only for a week, and it didn't symbolize either that the therapy was ending or that I might not be her therapist.

Langs: I sense that we are beginning to suffer the limitations of a nonsequential presentation, and of mixtures of actual associations and the therapist's formulations. I take this as an indication that we should move on with the direct presentation.

Therapist: So, as I say, she had responded to the anticipation of my vacation by taking a two-week vacation of her own. She then returned for two weeks before my one-week vacation, and it turned out she hadn't gone anywhere, but just hadn't come in for her sessions. She was going to go to the Caribbean, but never went.

Langs: And now we are about to hear the session that took place upon your return. As I have listened to you, two additional thoughts have occurred to me. First, the issue of commitment to see the therapy through to a point of completion served to remind me of another ground rule, implicit and seldom stated: the patient should receive the full attention of the therapist for the forty-five or fifty minutes of each session; there should be no interruptions, and that specifically includes telephone calls.

Second, in anticipating the material that you are about to present, I began to think of the extent to which this particular setting or framework—if you will, the accumulation of the ground rules—is in a state of chaos, with a host of departures from the standards I had begun to establish. It may be quite difficult to define the influence of a particular alteration in these ground rules; instead, we may be confronted with the effects of multiple modifications—utter chaos. Still, the recent issues related to the patient's and the therapist's vacations, and the anticipated forced termination, may stand out; we'll soon see. Please continue.

Therapist: The patient called five minutes before her session to say that she'd been held up at work, that a number of people were sick or on vacation or on leave of absence, and she'd been delayed. Do I have another hour for her; can she come at another time?

Langs: Stop at this point. What ground rules are involved? Let's begin to develop some principles.

Discussant: The idea that a session will take place at a given, set time.

Langs: Set time. That's one.

Discussant: The patient's responsibility for the hour.

Langs: The question of her responsibility for the hour, though here she would not be charged for the missed session. Now, let me say something that we would all probably experience, but might not register as a conscious thought. Namely, in addition to these ground rules, what else does this call alert you to?

Discussant: The relationship between the patient and the therapist.

Langs: To the relationship, but to what in particular? The obvious answer; don't restrain yourselves. We were only going to introduce specific ground rules, but we're forced to introduce something else.

Discussant: It would be more clear if she were calling to say she was upset, but there does seem to be some suggestion that the purpose of the call is to question what the patient does, and the therapist too—that is, what goes on between them, what's supposed to take place during the hour. And the work of therapy is supposed to take place during the hour and not outside of it, not on the telephone.

Langs: That is another ground rule: the therapeutic work should take place in the therapist's office, directly—not by telephone. The fact that the patient contacted you outside of the session brings up the question of the implications of any contact that occurs outside the therapist's office; that's important. But in addition, I am trying to show you that the first communication after the therapist's vacation relates to an issue pertaining to the ground rules, the ground rule aspect of the relationship. By calling him in this way, she's really asking a question about the ground rules. She's requesting what? What would you call this request? There's a general category.

Discussant: A change in the ground rules.

Langs: Yes, a change in the ground rules. What we would call a deviation in technique: the patient asks for a modification in the agreement related to the set time of the sessions. And you'll notice that it is incumbent upon the therapist to respond directly. Even if the patient had made some additional comments that would have permitted an interpretation, he would have to, by inference or directive, say yes or no. Thus we are observing a different order of intervention from the usual interpretive response, a technique that I term *management of the ground rules or framework*. It entails an actual behavioral response with implications considerably different from those conveyed by an effort to help the patient understand unconscious meanings, processes, and functions. And as an actuality and directive—it is essentially a non-neutral intervention unless it is done entirely from the patient's derivatives—we have every right to expect that it will contain major conscious and unconscious communications, and that it will have powerful effects on the patient. And while I do not want to anticipate too much at this point, allow me to suggest that this request may well have put the therapist in a quandary.

Therapist: It certainly did.

Langs: We may speculate, though of course this is open to subsequent validation, that unconsciously this telephone call and request is a reflection of the chaotic state of this therapeutic environment. It suggests that the holding qualities have been seriously damaged and that the framework itself is in a state of disrepair. The patient's call implies a wish to exploit these uncertain qualities, while on another level it may be seen as an unconscious effort to call these problems to the therapist's attention with what I would guess is a deep hope that he will secure this most unsettled therapeutic setting.

On the therapist's side, we can also immediately sense that this chaotic setting offers him an equally uncertain hold and insecure frame. Since the patient is herself poorly held—she may in addition have other difficulties in this area, outside the therapy—she in turn holds the therapist quite poorly. In a sense, then, the patient's own explication of the ground rules of therapy have an unstable quality that reflects the instability of the therapeutic hold offered her—leaving room, as I say, for her extratherapeutic problems in this area, which, by the way, would not emerge until the setting has been stabilized by the therapist. I simply want to point out for the moment that the therapist himself derives a sense of definition and safety from well-maintained ground rules and from patients who readily accept the structure offered them. Patients who hold the therapist poorly, and who create an insecure frame, usually generate some degree of anxiety and chaos in the therapist.

Discussant: You called this a request for a deviation in technique. Could you define the term for us?

Langs: Yes. In his fundamental papers on technique, Freud (1912, 1913) delineated the basic conditions of psychoanalysis, largely in the terms we have developed in today's seminar. Later, in 1940, he specifically defined what he called the "analytic pact": the basic contract between patient and therapist. In general, Freud advocated adherence to these ground rules as a means of "safeguarding the transference" and permitting its analysis, though in the reports of his case histories (1905, 1909, 1918) we find that he seldom adhered to his own tenets. I like to state it this way: Freud had the genius to identify the basic necessary background and structure for a viable analytic experience even though he himself never made use of these principles in his own analytic work.

Following Freud, there were a host of papers advocating one or another deviation in technique in the name of humanness and flexibility, though never on the basis of sound psychoanalytic validation of the proposed deviation (see Langs 1976c). In 1953, however, Eissler wrote a key paper in which he introduced the term *parameter,* which he defined as a deviation in standard technique necessitated by an ego defect or ego dysfunction in the patient. Too many analysts term all deviations parameters, and fail to follow Eissler's definition.

In brief, Eissler was well aware of the risks of parameters, in that they might replace the analysis of transference expressions and even render these so fixed as to be unanalyzable. He saw too that parameters could be erroneously invoked in place of sound interpretive technique, but felt nonetheless that if kept to the absolute minimum required they could be an important means of resolving stalemated therapeutic situations in cases of severe psychopathology. He also noted that they should be corrected or rectified as soon as possible, and that the full ramifications of the deviation and subsequent restoration of the ground rules should be analyzed with the patient. Eissler's comment that a parameter might significantly curtail analytic outcome has often been ignored by subsequent writers.

Eissler's paper inspired the International Psycho-Analytic Association to sponsor a panel on the topic of deviations in technique, the papers from which were published in 1958. In a brief but clear introduction to this panel, Greenson indicated that there was a set of ground rules for analysis (which he did not entirely define) that constituted the classical psychoanalytic framework. Within this framework, *variations* in technique are inevitable and reflect the analyst's personality, style of work, his appropriate and limited flexible responses to momentary clinical situations, and the like; these did not, he insisted, entail any alteration of the classical framework.

He then described *modifications* in the basic rules and goals, which he saw as necessary but temporary interruptions of analytic procedures and aims. Finally, he defined *deviations* as alterations in these basic procedures that lead to a permanent change in the psychoanalytic method and a renunciation of its results.

So in Greenson's terms the patient here is asking for a seemingly minor *modification* in technique: Can you see me at another time? I'm tied up at work. Okay, why don't you tell us how you handled it? We'll see if we can develop some principles for dealing with such requests.

Therapist: At that point, it was 4:55. I asked, Are you finished with work now? She said yes, and I said, It seems you could get here in a relatively short time, rather than our trying to change an hour, which I don't think would be that good. You could take a cab. She said, I'm probably ten minutes away if I do that, but I don't have enough money to take one. I then asked her if she couldn't borrow the money from someone at work, which she didn't really answer. And that was pretty much it. It seemed like that was the best thing to do at the moment.

Langs: Okay. And you hung up expecting her to get to the session at some time, in some way.

Therapist: Five or ten minutes later.

Langs: Now, this conversation brings up what other ground rule—I've mentioned it briefly. It's such a pleasure doing it like this, letting the presentation pretty much lead the way.

Discussant: He made a suggestion.

Langs: Which is related to which ground rule?

Discussant: Not making suggestions. (Laughter.)

Langs: Why don't you give it to me in a positive sense?

Discussant: Neutrality.

Langs: Yes. We're talking about the therapist's neutrality, and his use of neutral interventions geared toward interpretations. But we're also talking about interventions in another sense here. One area entails verbal interventions directed toward understanding, modified here by the therapist's suggestion. What's the other sphere involved here?

Discussant: The nonverbal.

Langs: Well actually, both verbal and nonverbal communication exist in both of the spheres I have in mind. One has to do with attempting to understand, while the other involves what? (Pause.) What is the therapist in the process of doing?

Discussant: Solving the problem.

Langs: What's the problem? I'll lead you to it.

Discussant: Finances.

Langs: Yes, but what's the broader problem, in terms of therapy?

Discussant: Maintaining the ground rules or the frame.

Langs: Yes, so he's solving a problem related to the ground rules, which is called what? What have I termed it? (Pause.) The management of the ground rules. It's so easy to overlook that part. In other words, he's doing two things: he is intervening to the patient, and non-interpretively—that's one aspect of it. The other is that he's engaged in managing the frame.
   Now, this last is a sphere of the therapist's activity that has been quite neglected. It has not been put on a par with the therapist's usual verbal interventions: his interpretations, and his related nonverbal communications. If you think of therapy and what you've been taught, I think you've been pretty much told that therapy occurs around the patient's—we haven't gotten to them yet—the patient's what? What am I approaching here?

Therapist: Perception of my role?

Langs: No, the basic material of therapy; what did we have in this phone call? (Pause.) We had some communications from the patient. Ultimately, I am referring to the patient's associations. One of the ground rules has to do with the fundamental rule, as Freud (1913) called it, of free association—the patient's associations. Here, we had an unusual form of association: the patient called the therapist and spoke to him.

Discussant: It is my understanding that there are many therapists who do not believe that it is possible to obtain free associations in psychotherapy.

Langs: To respond briefly, the term *associations* can be used in three senses. First, it may be simply a matter of the patient saying everything that comes to mind—and this is, I believe, the way in which Freud first used it. In terms of a ground rule, then, it would be stated this way: a fundamental rule of psychotherapy is the requisite that the patient communicate everything that comes to mind—thoughts, feelings, images, perceptions, and the like.

The second use of the term is more narrow, and is applied to the kinds of links between the various communications from the patient. Sometimes we speak of the patient's associating to a dream, implying that the dream is a focal or organizing point around which the other material takes on meaning. A third and related way in which the term may be used involves a particularly meaningful quality to the material, one that implies interpretability; sometimes, it is used to convey a sense of what is called psychological-mindedness—a sensitivity to intra-psychic nuances.

Now, if we adopt the first meaning, I see no inherent reason why psychotherapy cannot be structured in that way. In fact, it seems rather evident to me from the work that we did on the listening process (Langs 1978c) that it is crucial that the conditions of therapy be established in this very way, as a means of facilitating our access to neurotic, derivative communication. I suspect that those who object to this tenet or see it as unfeasible have a rather different conception of the therapeutic experience and of free associating. They are implying that

meaningful and interpretable derivatives do not emerge in psychotherapy, and I think we've already shown that they do.

For the moment, let's establish the fundamental rule as a basic
standard for both therapy and analysis, and let's consider our work
with the listening process as a global validation of its importance. But
we will not rest there: we will expect to validate the soundness of this
tenet in the presentations we are about to hear, and, further, we will
try to determine whether modifications in this ground rule serve
constructive or destructive functions.

All of this is quite relevant to how you listen. Here, the patient
makes a telephone call to the therapist and describes a problem. How
are we to treat this communication, and understand it? Should we
respond to it as a type of free association and attempt to derive its
unconscious implications? For example, should we organize it around
the adaptive context of the therapist's recent vacation, or a particular
recent alteration in the framework of which we are, for the moment,
unaware? Or should we think of it differently, as another kind of
communication? Do we attend to its manifest or its latent contents—
or both?

Discussant: It seems to me that we must think of this as associations, or we will be quite likely to miss its unconscious implications and
even respond noninterpretively.

Langs: Yes, we should treat all communications from the patient
as associations, using that term in its broadest sense. We are then in a
position to subject them to the basic listening process, regardless of how
they're framed: as a realistic problem, a fantasy, a thought, a request,
a dream, or whatever. Once we get to the material of this session, we
may be in a position to learn what happens when we fail to take a
communication from the patient as associations saturated with
unconscious meanings and functions. We must always attend to both
manifest and latent implications.

Discussant: It seems to me you are assuming the patient will be
motivated, no matter what her hostility or resistance, to continue in the
therapy.

Langs: Could you clarify your point?

Discussant: If, for example, a patient brings a problem and the therapist responds to it as an association—as in this case—the patient might well react with hostility and terminate the therapy.

Discussant: It seems to me that the question is what type of intervention is to be preferred under these conditions.

Langs: Please be clear that so far I have mainly been establishing the nature of the ground rules and have not begun to define the relevant interventions. Nor have I indicated how I would have responded to this telephone call, though I will do so in a moment.

But first I must respond to the suggestion that the absence of a direct response to this patient's telephone request could lead to hostility and termination. It is precisely this kind of thinking that is used to justify many modifications in the basic ground rules I have just delineated, and which prompts therapists to depart from the realm of unconscious communication toward so-called realistic problems, and to turn to directives and the like. In its extreme, it would entail the proposal that interpretations prompt patients to flee therapy, while manipulations and inappropriate gratifications permit its continuation.

There are many such attitudes and approaches toward the ground rules, and it will be best for us to discuss their implications when they are reflected in a therapeutic interaction under study; we may thereby determine empirically their unconscious implications and actual consequences. For the moment, the question arises as a point from a discussant, and I simply want to identify the qualities of the attitude involved.

Discussant: I thought that he was implying that if you tried to interpret something on the telephone the patient would think that you are crazy and not responding to her needs, and that she would become quite angry and want to quit. I had the feeling that you were suggesting that you would either offer an interpretation or—and perhaps this is as extreme—just hang up on her.

Langs: I did suggest that there were two resources available to the therapist: an interpretive type of response and the management of the patient's effort to modify the frame. The latter might include an interpretive intervention, though under these conditions, where we do not have extended associations and have only a very constricted communicative network, that seems quite unlikely. In fact, it is one important attribute of this patient's first deviation—the telephone call—that it creates a constricted communicative field with little meaningful data for the therapist, and yet imposes upon him an absolute necessity that he intervene. It is an effort, then, to virtually force a noninterpretive intervention from him.

On one level, you may think of this as a type of resistance, though I hasten to add that in tracing out its sources you should always look for contributions from both the therapist and the patient—it is an interactional product, an interactional resistance (Langs 1976a, c). We already have sufficient material to postulate that it is derived from the therapist's own modifications of the ground rules which are being played back to him—and exploited—in this particular form. In fact, that patient's playback through the telephone call might well lead to a more general hypothesis: that modifications in the basic ground rules tend to constrict the communicative field, the scope of the patient's derivative communication, and the therapist's opportunity for interpretive interventions. Though this seems true for this particular deviation, one might, of course, question its generalization; as we accumulate material, we will soon be able to decide that issue.

In addition, you can see why it is essential to establish a second realm of intervening in addition to neutral interventions geared toward interpretation. Without it, every direct response to an impingement on the framework would be a deviation in technique, and that hardly makes sense. All of this adds to the argument that the establishment and maintenance of the ground rules is a fundamental realm of intervening for the therapist.

But once again, my bias—which is based on many years of clinical observations and psychoanalytic validation—seems to show its face: I must leave room for us to discover empirically whether we should, when faced with impingements, modify the frame or continue to maintain it on general principle. Actually, it will be far easier to test out alterations of the frame, which I expect will be legion in these presentations, as compared to maintaining it in the face of attempts by the patient to modify it, which maintenance will in all likelihood occur less often. Therapists in general, for many reasons which we will soon consider, prefer to modify rather than maintain the ground rules under a wide range of conditions. But that too is a bit ahead of the story, although it certainly applies to this case and therefore can be derived from material already presented and can subsequently be tested as a general hypothesis.

Returning to this particular clinical situation, we have an interesting mixture: on the one hand, the therapist responded by maintaining the ground rules, by insisting that he and the patient meet at the appointed time. In fact, that was the essence of his management response, and we will take it as one adaptive context for the material that we will soon be hearing. We will then be in position to allow the patient's associations to serve as a *commentary*—a mixture of valid and invalid or fantasied responses—on that particular intervention. So we'll soon learn whether his intervention was valid, or whether instead he should have changed the hour.

But unfortunately—and isn't it so often this way in psychotherapy?—there are major complications: the therapist added a series of noninterpretive interventions to his management response. He completely modified his neutrality by telling the patient that she should take a cab and that she should borrow money; he offered a series of directives. So here is a clear-cut modification in a basic ground rule, and in listening to the session that took place we will attempt to detect its influence, and to tease this out from that of the therapist's adherence to the hour of the session. The patient's derivative response should assist us, but we do have a complicated situation. Let's get to it.

Therapist: She showed up thirty-eight minutes late.

Langs: How long was the session?

Therapist: This one went for eighteen minutes. Her usual session is fifty minutes.

Langs: So now we have a patient who is late to her session; that too is an alteration in a ground rule. Now please describe everything that happened. Give us the details.

Therapist: She arrived at the clinic and checked in at the desk. The secretary was there and buzzed me. The secretary filled out this form the patient gave her, while the patient stood at the desk. The patient then came to my office. I'm sitting there. She starts to take off her coat and says she's sorry she's late.

Langs: There's something I don't hear: was the door closed, and if so by whom?

Therapist: By her, but not immediately.

Langs: She started to speak with the door open?

Therapist: She took her coat off, started to sit down, saw that the door was still open, and walked over and closed it. It's the first time she's ever closed the door, she never closes the door herself.

Langs: You see, we're studying the components of the setting, and we'll consider all of these details. Who has the responsibility to close the door? The patient comes in, starts to take off her coat, and begins to talk: Gee, I'm sorry I'm late. You see that the door is open; what do you do?

Discussant: The therapist has the responsibility for closing the door. He is creating an interaction; he can't set up an interaction if there's access to a waiting room and to other people who may hear them. What's he going to do? It's not feasible to let the session go on and interpret it; he must do something right off.

Langs: Notice what you said: He must do something immediately in order to secure the therapeutic setting and thereby create the opportunity for a viable interaction. Instinctively we recognize that in the area of the ground rules, actualities are critical: you must establish and maintain a secure setting, for example. And such work must precede interpretations. You are in fact implying that valid interpretive work can occur only once the therapeutic environment has been secured. Let that stand as a postulate to be validated.

Does anyone have an alternative proposal as to how to handle this situation?

Discussant: The therapist could close the door himself, or suggest to the patient that the door is open, or even ask her to close the door.

Langs: Yes, as long as you recognize that it is the therapist's responsibility to secure the setting, your response would depend on the physical layout and the location of the door in respect to your position and that of the patient. If the patient has just come through the door, you might point out that she has left it open, thereby implying that she close it. If she then did not do so, you should get up and close it yourself. In principle, it is your responsibility to close the door as soon as possible, to provide the patient with an immediate and real sense of privacy, and certainly to not begin to comment yourself until the situation has been secured. In the meantime, you should make a mental note of how the patient has handled the situation; it may be possible later to interpret the relevant implications. In fact, we might even make an hypothesis in regard to this situation. Can anyone make a suggestion?

Discussant: We are obviously looking for something more than her being in a rush because she is late. Maybe it has something to do with the lack of confidentiality that we have been discussing in respect to this therapy.

Langs: Yes, you are on the right track. I think we can take it even further: Remember that the patient has just come from filling out a form with the secretary, a third party to this therapy—that is the most immediate of several pertinent adaptive contexts. Leaving the door open is an invitation to other third-party participants, and a reflection of the actual lack of privacy in this treatment situation. It therefore on the one hand expresses the patient's own wish for this modification in the framework, while on the other hand it calls this issue to the therapist's attention and may well be a means of bringing this deviation to the forefront. In any case, it is a frame-related communication and it initiates this session. As such, it is a tentative form of Type Two derivative validation of the thesis that alterations in the basic ground rules evoke strong responses in patients—they are prime adaptive contexts.

As part of our effort to define functions of the ground rules—and here we are dealing with the physical setting and the issue of privacy—it may well be that we can take the implications of this particular deviation and apply it as one quality of all modifications in the ground rules. What I mean is this: with the door open there is no privacy, no sense of total confidentiality, no sense of closure and holding, and the one-to-one relationship appears likely to be modified. The treatment has a public quality, and under those conditions we would expect the patient to be quite guarded, to curtail her comments both consciously and unconsciously, and to feel quite unsafe.

But if you think about it, the therapist too would feel exposed, under public scrutiny, and would also become defensive. The communicative properties of the bipersonal field would be severely modified and we would even expect much of the material to organize meaningfully only around the adaptive context of the damaged frame. Realities and unconscious perceptions would prevail, and distorted fantasies and pathological introjects would be secondary. In addition, you can sense that the deviation would on the one hand constitute a pathological projective identification whose specific contents and functions depend on the nature of the alteration; it would create interactional pressures for both participants. On the other hand, it would certainly effect some degree of both intrapsychic and interpersonal Type C barriers within and between patient and therapist.

As we continue, we will be in a position to identify the implications and consequences of many modifications in the ground rules and we will have an opportunity to generate a central constellation of features, to which may be appended the specific and individual implications of a particular deviation. It may well be, too, that in the material we are about to hear we will have an opportunity to validate at least a portion of this formulation because of its relevance to the present interaction.

Discussant: If the therapist picks the patient up in the waiting room, whose responsibility is it to open the door?

Langs: Well, it will be difficult for us to obtain definitive data on these questions from the therapeutic interactions that we will be studying. I will therefore simply define what I have found to be the best principles in this regard.

In general, I would expect the therapist to leave the door to a clinic office closed when going to greet the patient in the waiting room— where, by the way, he would certainly not address the patient by name. I would then expect him to open the door, allow the patient to enter first, and to then follow, closing the door behind him. In a private office, the therapist could readily leave the door to his consultation room open, and allow the patient to enter first, once again closing it behind the two of them. Much of this is covered under the principle related to the therapist's responsibility for securing the setting.

Discussant: What do you do when the patient is leaving the session?

Langs: I announce that time is up, using those words or the simple comment: Okay. I then stand up, as does the patient, who then finds his own way to the door, opening it and leaving. Some patients close the door behind them, while others leave it open. As a rule, I will close the door after them as a means of securing the framework behind the patient who is leaving, and in anticipation of seeing the next patient. My approach here is based on the belief that this process helps define the end of the hour and inherently supports the patient in his transition from his somewhat dependent position in the treatment situation to a more self-reliant role after the hour.

I suspect, based on many factors both in regard to the physical setting and the inclinations of a given therapist, that there are many valid variations in these areas. As long as they do not modify the basic ground rules we are defining today, they may well prove quite viable. The principle to keep in mind is that these procedures may serve as important adaptive and therapeutic contexts; you should apply the full listening and validating processes when the derivatives coalesce around an issue related to them. In that way you can eventually test out, clarify, rectify, and understand the unconscious implications of your own preferences in this respect.

Discussant: I've noticed that some patients like to talk to me after I have announced the end of the hour, and that some of them do so as they are leaving. Others will say, See you on Friday, or, Have a good weekend. And I have a question about how to respond: what's appropriate so that it sets a good tone between myself and the patient?

Langs: Yes. You will see many efforts to modify the basic framework at the end of sessions—and even more so during the period of termination of the therapy. Separation anxieties are legion in both patients and therapists, and such alterations, in general, constitute efforts to alleviate that anxiety through some type of modification in the framework—what I have called *framework cures* or, more precisely, *framework deviation cures*. For the moment, such comments are well ahead of our clinical data, so let me pull back a bit.

We have established that the transactions between patient and therapist should in principle occur only when they are in their agreed-upon positions in the consultation room. This implies that, ideally, the therapist should not otherwise participate in exchanges, and we will discuss the relevant techniques when we get to the end of the session being presented to us. Nonetheless, your comment about setting a tone between yourself and the patient may hint at a common attitude, namely, that any failure to answer the patient or to join in small talk will set a hostile and detrimental tone, and will generate images of the therapist as inhuman. As an alternative hypothesis, I might suggest that such kindnesses are unconsciously destructive to the secure environment of the therapy, to the necessary communicative and trusting qualities of the therapeutic bipersonal field that permit sound analytic work with the patient, and that a true analytic climate may well be reflected in nonparticipation and in later interpretations of the implications of these efforts when the material from the patient permits. We have two possibilities, then, and hopefully we will be able to decide which is the more valid therapeutically.

Discussant: Does the patient bring his coat into the consultation room?

Langs: This can vary: some therapists prefer to have a coatrack in the consultation room because of the risk of theft from the waiting room in many areas. Others keep the coatrack in the waiting room, where the patient will, as a rule, leave it. This is very much up to the patient, and variations in this regard are quite likely and have a broad range of implications and validity. Incidentally, I never tell the patient what to do with his coat; I avoid directives. This discussion also brings up another aspect of the setting that we haven't yet mentioned; can anyone think of it?

Discussant: Where you sit?

Langs: Well, yes—we're about to get to that. But what else?

Discussant: Where people wait before they come in.

Langs: The waiting room. What else?

Discussant: Whether or not the patient is allowed to smoke in the office.

Langs: Smoking, and what else?

Discussant: Seeing other patients.

Langs: Yes, and what else?

Discussant: The bathroom.

Langs: Yes. All of these details are important. The ideal office is certainly yours alone, and it would be one that has a separate exit so that there is minimal contact between patients. It would have its own bathroom and, to respond to your question, smoking would be the prerogative of the patient, though of course open to interpretation.

As you can sense, the setting is filled with unconscious meaning for both ourselves as therapists, and for the patient. When these issues appear in conjunction with some particular therapeutic and adaptive context, they are open to implicit clarification, rectification if needed, and interpretation. So, we have established the need for an exit not leading back into the waiting room. Now, what about locale? Where is the ideal office located?

Discussant: The East Side of Manhattan. (Laughter.)

Langs: Not any more. The East Side of Denver is what I hear. What else about location?

Discussant: First floor.

Langs: That might help; what else?

Discussant: Close to the subway, or other public transportation.

Langs: What other issues come up about location, though?

Discussant: A lot of them: being in an office building and close to a hospital, for example.

Discussant: Some therapists and analysts use their apartment or home.

Discussant: Neighborhood: I've had patients mugged on the way to my office.

Langs: All of these things deserve consideration. I will add this: the ideal office is in a professional building.

Discussant: When you say professional building, do you mean as opposed to a hospital?

Langs: As opposed to a hospital, your own house or apartment, or even elsewhere in your apartment building.

Discussant: I don't know of anyone who has an office in a professional building. I'm being serious.

Langs: Now you do—me. You're being stirred up now. This happens often when we get into specific ground rules or standards. I'm stating the ideal, and we will see if the specific material we hear will give us the opportunity to study the ramifications of these standards and deviations from them. Let's try to do most of this empirically.

Discussant: Can you tell us something of why you adopt these particular standards? Are you attempting to give the patient a feeling that he is involved in a therapeutic task, and coming to a doctor's office?

Langs: I am attempting to delineate the physical setting that provides the optimal conditions for psychotherapy. It is one thing to state the importance of privacy, confidentiality, and anonymity, but it is quite another matter to create the physical conditions under which they can actually be secured.

For example, I might comment at some length on the need for adequate soundproofing. We are attempting to create an atmosphere in which the therapist offers the patient his undivided attention, shares with the patient a sense of privacy and safety, establishes the greatest possible degree of anonymity and confidentiality, and thereby offers the patient the best possible conditions for the expression and analysis of his inner mental problems.

Discussant: It is my impression that many analysts in New York have their offices in apartment houses, either attached to their own apartments or in separate quarters.

Langs: There is a hint here—and I am not asking for personal confirmation—that the optimal standards I have been identifying encroach in various ways on your own personal therapeutic and analytic experiences. It is inevitable that this will be the case, and for that reason I will try to make every effort to establish the nature and function of these ground rules, and their ideal management, through the material presented to us. Little will be learned from opinions based on vague and general impressions; we must build our understanding through specific clinical data. As you can already sense, this is especially necessary when it comes to the ground rules and setting— it is an aspect of therapy that generates intense personal reactions.

Discussant: I am still not clear what you mean by a professional building.

Langs: I mean a building that has office space for doctors and dentists, or even for nonmedical professionals. It can even be a general office building. The point is to establish a neutral setting without important personal revelations.

Discussant: Are there certain qualifications about the location of the bathroom? It seems to me that it shouldn't be in the office.

Langs: Why not?

Discussant: It could interfere with therapy; it could be quite awkward. For example, the bathroom could be immediately accessible to both the therapist and the patient. Sometimes it's within the confines of the therapist's consultation room or you can only get to it by going through that room.

Langs: This, I think, creates problems, as compared to a bathroom that is accessible to the patient from the waiting room, as well as to the therapist for use on his part between sessions.

Discussant: From what you're saying, if I may change the subject for a moment, I assume that the therapist should not be drinking coffee, or eating his lunch, or even chewing gum during his sessions with the patient.

Langs: Yes, all such forms of self-gratification are modifications in the basic framework as we are defining it.

Discussant: There are some offices without a bathroom; instead there is a lavatory in the hall.

Discussant: That would be a nice place to meet your analyst. (Laughter.)

Discussant: Well, there's something disturbing about sitting in the waiting room of your therapist, and seeing a patient leave the consultation room and go to the bathroom, after which the therapist comes out and ushers you in.

Discussant: And that same patient stays in the bathroom while you begin the session. It seems bizarre and uncomfortable.

Langs: Why is that bizarre?

Discussant: It's not bizarre, but it is uncomfortable. Somehow, with another patient going into the bathroom, I get the feeling that he's almost living there.

Langs: But you see, you are now talking about the kinds of fantasies evoked by the physical arrangements of the therapist's office. Fantasy responses are inevitable, and we will soon examine them, not from your own personal associations but from the material of the therapeutic interaction. For now, we are defining the ideal setting as a standard for later considerations.

From what you are saying, you would like to have an office in which there is a separate entrance for the patient, who will sit in the waiting room, and a separate exit for the patient leaving the consultation room. In addition, you would like two bathrooms, one for the patient who is waiting and another for the patient who is leaving.

Perhaps that would be ideal, but it is really not very feasible. It is possible, instead, to have a bathroom that is outside both the waiting room and the consultation room, so that the door to the bathroom is in some type of a hallway and there is a sense of privacy. Such an arrangement also facilitates the use of hall space as a means of providing double doors that can produce adequate soundproofing, although often this must be supplemented by using a fan, humidifier, or dehumidifier to set up a background drone that muffles the sound of voices, loud noises, that sort of thing.

But notice now what is happening here in the seminar.

Discussant: We were asking a lot of questions, but it is something that we have been grappling with for some time, and we have had a great deal of difficulty in resolving many of the issues related to the ground rules.

Discussant: I experience the feeling of wanting to insulate myself.

Discussant: For me, these are concerns that we've all had, but never discussed. For some reason we have never gotten to all of this in any other seminar.

Discussant: I think that we are identifying with the patient, who wants to be protected from the other people who troop through the therapist's office, and maybe even from the therapist himself.

Discussant: I also sense a greater degree of anxiety in this discussion than we've experienced for a while.

Discussant: I would say that the anxiety is less today rather than more, in the sense that we've been able to talk about some of these issues which we've previously not dealt with at all.

Langs: Well, it seems to me to be a kind of anxiety different from the one you experienced earlier in this course. It's one that prompts a greater degree of openness of communication and even levity. I just wanted to characterize this quality because I think it is important for each of you to see that this entire area has intense emotional meaning for all of us. It has led us away from the clinical material, and since I see that our time is almost up we will have to wait until next week to hear what happened, and to draw some inferences.

Discussant: You haven't mentioned supervision in your discussion of the ground rules. Do you tell the patient at the beginning that you're going to be supervised on her case?

Langs: Again, I hope to deal with such questions once the material facilitates such a discussion. In terms of the ground rule of anonymity, we would expect the standard to be that the patient is not provided such information. However, it also implies that when the material touches on this issue, the patient's belief or fantasy that you are in supervision is handled implicitly as a valid idea, and not treated as a transference-based distortion.

Therapist: This patient knows I am in supervision.

Langs: *How* does she know that?

Therapist: Because her boyfriend is a therapist who is in training.

Langs: But have you told her specifically that *you* are being supervised?

Therapist: No, but I think she assumes it, since I am working in a clinic and am in all likelihood a trainee.

Langs: Yes. Still, there is a great deal of difference between such an assumption and the explicit revelation of supervision to the patient. Hopefully we will be able to clarify the differences later on through specific clinical material.

Discussant: I'm not clear on one point: Did you say that psychotherapy must be done face-to-face, or do you think that it is acceptable to place the patient on the couch?

Langs: That's a complicated issue, regarding which virtually no data are available. Based on my own experience as therapist and supervisor, I now believe that psychotherapy can take place under either of those conditions. There are many analysts who object to psychotherapy with the patient on the couch, largely because they believe there will be an uncontrolled regression or unanalyzable so-called transference responses, and also because they feel that one must make a sharp distinction between psychotherapy and psychoanalysis. This position is reflected in the first of my technique books (Langs 1973b), while more recently (Langs 1976c, 1978a, d), I have attempted to demonstrate that therapy and analysis are on a continuum. I would add now that placing a patient on the couch, while it certainly evokes at times intense unconscious fantasies and perceptions, need stimulate neither an uncontrolled regression nor unmanageable and uninterpretable fantasies and introjects.

I think that the matter has to be decided on an individual basis, and that in general the use of the couch is preferable since it fosters the emergence of interactional experiences and material from the patient that provides the best opportunity for analytic insight and adaptive structural change. There may well be certain borderline or schizophrenic patients for whom the absence of eye contact and the experience of lying on the couch create a threatening disequilibrium and an upsurge of primitive fantasies and the like, and who are best seen face-to-face. Nevertheless, it has become evident to me that many more patients tolerate and benefit from the use of the couch in psychotherapy than is generally acknowledged. Unfortunately, since no one I know of has adequate data, I cannot offer more extended guidelines.

I would suggest, then, that the choice of modality is an open one, subject to the kind of considerations I have just outlined. I would add, however, that a particular modality, once recommended and put into use, has become the standard for that treatment situation; thereafter, all deviations—proposed or actualized—should be analyzed and rectified if necessary or possible. Hopefully, some of you will provide the clinical studies that we need to more fully understand the issues involved.

Discussant: Do you prefer to have the patient sitting at the side of the therapist's desk, or across from him, or do you recommend the use of two comfortable chairs?

Langs: It seems that here again there are choices. The use of a desk is appropriate, as is the use of two chairs, though I do believe that some type of table could prove serviceable in establishing a physical boundary between patient and therapist. Still, even that is not vital, though all of these details should be thought out.

Discussant: Who should have the more comfortable chair? In my experience it is usually the therapist or analyst.

Langs: Yes—sometimes. There are some who use identical chairs for themselves and their patients, but I believe that this is an unconscious effort to deny important distinctions between the two participants to the therapeutic dyad. I prefer to do otherwise.

Discussant: The patient should have the better chair. He's paying for it.

Langs: Certainly both patient and therapist should be quite comfortable. Let me make just one final comment before our time is up. We have not mentioned the rule of abstinence (Freud 1915). Misunderstood by some to entail general nongratification for the patient, it is best conceived of as implying restriction of acting-out satisfactions and especially of direct and inappropriate gratifications of the patient by the therapist—often achieved through nonadherence to the other ground rules. Abstinence, then, properly refers to the therapist's nongratification of the patient's neurosis. The pathology is thereby neither sanctioned nor reinforced, nor is any unconscious suggestion conveyed that this pathology might find its counterpart within the therapist. Abstinence helps create conditions of optimal frustration that tend to motivate the patient to seek cure through insight and derivative communication—through free association and its interpretation.

This has been a fine beginning; the rest promises to be quite interesting. Thank you.

Chapter Two

SOME EFFECTS OF ALTERING THE FRAME

Langs: We should enter the seminar today without desire, memory, or understanding. This will facilitate the passive recall of last week's presentation, and will enable you to experience this type of listening. So, without further discussion, why don't you begin where you left off?

Therapist: This was the session where the patient was a half hour late. She sat down in her chair and started talking about how depressed and overwhelmed she was. At work, she said, three or four people had been absent from her section.

Langs: So her first communication is that she's depressed and overwhelmed. Who will comment? We immediately come back to the listening process; how do we listen to this material?

Discussant: It can be taken as an appeal to the therapist to desert his neutrality. If she is overwhelmed, she'll want the therapist to be more active and to do things she ordinarily would do for herself—like advise her rather than let her make decisions for herself. And from the standpoint of the ground rules it creates pressure on the neutrality of the therapist.

Langs: That may be true, but much of your formulation is based on your own subjective reaction to this initial communication. In fact, if you think about it, you are commenting in terms of the inferences that you are able to derive from this material entirely without an adaptive context. These are what I have called *Type One derivatives*. In general, you will find that validated meaning can be established only in the presence of a definitive adaptive context, and eventually our efforts at applying the listening process should allow us to reach this level—that of *Type Two derivatives*. It is interesting, however, that implicit in your remarks is the sense that you listened to this first communication from the patient in some context related to the ground rules. You were not specific, but it was evident from what you said.

So in principle we would listen to this communication in two ways: first, in a kind of open and random manner, allowing the patient's continued communications to give them shape and depth. And yet, simultaneously, we must listen to it as a *commentary* on the transactions that preceded the session—ranging from everything that took place in the previous hour (of which we know virtually nothing) to the therapist's vacation and the patient's telephone call. Incidentally, as you can see, there is something about the power of frame issues that fosters their quick recall; I find it very easy to remember now much of what took place prior to this hour. Have most of you had a similar experience?

Discussant: Yes.

Langs: I can see from your nods that this is the case. Taking this material as a commentary on the state of the ground rules and therapeutic hold, and on the recent deviations in technique—these broad adaptive contexts—what implications do you see?

Discussant: I seem to remember your predicting that there would be a sense of chaos, and this is certainly reflected in the patient's comment that she is feeling overwhelmed.

Langs: Yes, and feelings of depression are a common reaction to such chaos and to the experience of a poor holding environment. It's just the beginning, but we do have some degree of Type Two derivative validation of an aspect of our initial hypothesis about this therapeutic situation and, more broadly, about the consequences of unneeded modifications in the ground rules and their uncertain management. We will keep this in mind as we listen to additional material and seek further validation.

So in applying the listening process we begin with the adaptive context, which is virtually one or more of the therapist's recent interventions. We then generate Type Two derivatives along the me/not-me interface, which, in this case, would lead to what particular formulation?

Discussant: Well, she certainly seems to mean what she says directly, that she is feeling depressed and overwhelmed, though I guess that latent to those feelings are these disruptions in the treatment and in the ground rules. That's the "me" part of the interface, while the "not-me" part would suggest that the therapist's interventions—here I am thinking of his comments on the telephone—communicated some sense of disorganization and depression within himself.

Langs: That's an excellent formulation. If you think about it, the therapist did seem put out and confused about how to handle the patient's request for a change in her hour. In addition, he pressured the patient to keep her appointment and directly advised her as to how to go about doing it. The patient is implying that the therapist was unconsciously attempting to possess her, largely as a means of fending off a depressive response to her absence. It does all fit together rather well, and, so long as we treat it as a *silent hypothesis,* it provides us with an interesting line of thought for subsequent validation.

Discussant: I very much have the feeling that you consider any alteration in the framework an important incident in the therapy.

Langs: Yes. I am proposing that any alteration whatsoever in the ground rules will be a first-order adaptive context and therapeutic task for both patient and therapist. This is a thesis that we can test out again and again in the weeks ahead.

I want also to come back to another point implicit to the original discussion of this first association, in which you suggested that the patient was attempting to evoke a modification in the therapist's neutrality. Both Freud (1912) and Greenacre (1959) suggested that once a deviation has been invoked by the therapist or analyst the

patient will want more; unconsciously, he will endeavor to extract further modifications from the therapist. This is an issue I have addressed
in several presentations (Langs 1975c, 1976c), and we may take it as
another hypothesis to be validated. I might add here that as a rule the
therapist who deviates once will deviate again, and the patient who
alters the frame once will also do so again. Deviations create a kind of
insatiability for many reasons, which I hope to identify soon.

So, you are suggesting that the patient has an appetite for deviations and may be appealing for more. Can anyone else organize this
material around a particular deviation in technique?

Discussant: We arrived late; could you repeat her first communication?

Langs: We'll have to make an exception in this instance.

Therapist: She told me about a number of incidents at work. With
several people in her office not present, she has to work longer hours
and harder when she's there.

Langs: I hope that those of you who heard the first version of this
material at the beginning of today's seminar can recognize just how
important the specific data is to our understanding of both the patient
and the therapeutic interaction. What is most remarkable, of course, is
that the therapist has now left out the two particular qualities to the
patient's initial associations that we had been discussing, and that he
has added a number of derivatives that could also be organized around
the adaptive contexts at hand.

Therapist: She said she was depressed and overwhelmed by it all.

Langs: Can anyone offer an additional formulation?

Discussant: It seems that the patient is in some way threatened by
what has happened previously. The ground rules seem to have been
altered and she may be reacting to a shift that has already taken place
in therapy, through which she has been inappropriately gratified, and
perhaps she is now feeling guilty about it. I realize as I talk that I am
being quite speculative, but I am trying to suggest, as you had briefly

stated before, that she is depressed in some way as a reaction to the shift in the ground rules.

Langs: Yes, it's sufficient to say that she's depressed, without suggesting the presence of guilt until there is supportive evidence. Her depression could be based on many factors and we'll wait to learn what they are.

Nonetheless, you have said something quite significant when you suggest that she has reacted to these deviations by becoming depressed. That's a statement that many therapists would never make. First of all, they would not listen to the beginning of this session with the many deviations in the ground rules in mind. Some would certainly be thinking about the patient's lateness, but most would not consider at all their own modifications of the ground rules during the telephone conversation with this patient.

Most therapists do not think adaptationally, and do not maintain a consistent focus on the communicative interaction; they should consider every statement and behavior they make a potential adaptive context for the patient's subsequent material.

I won't belabor the issue, except to say that I have seen an endless number of clinical presentations, as well as cases reported in the literature in which framework issues are totally ignored. Lipton (1977a, b) has in fact suggested that many of the amenities and dimensions of the framework are essentially irrelevant to the psychoanalytic process and work—a thesis that stands in marked contrast to those I have developed here. We will put off our study of the literature until the end of the course, in order to allow these presentations to shape our thinking as much as possible; but we should know that there are those who feel that many aspects of the ground rules are of little consequence. We are here to discover the truth of the matter.

Discussant: I can understand the importance of the adaptive context, and of simply studying adaptive sequences. But I am thinking now about the listening process, and I wonder how we can determine whether her sense of depression and disorganization is appropriate or not—that is, whether it's a valid reaction to the situation or one that instead reflects some part of her own pathology.

Langs: Yes, I was just about to bring up that very issue—it is the last phase of the listening process as we defined it earlier (Langs 1978c).

We must of course await further material, but we can assume for the moment that her reaction is a mixture of (1) valid responsiveness based on realistic perceptions and introjections and (2) distortions based on her own pathological inner needs and the like. This is what I mean when I call this material a *commentary*—it requires that we sort out the valid and invalid components of her reaction.

To state this another way: we may eventually conclude that the ground rules and therapeutic situation have been handled quite well and that this response is primarily pathological and based on poor ego functioning, an undue sense of guilt, and the like. Or we may conclude instead that the situation has been handled badly, that the disorganization and depression are both appropriate and largely introjected, and that as yet we have not had an opportunity to identify her own additional intrapsychically founded contribution—largely because the problems of the therapist have covered them over for the moment.

If we begin with the adaptive context, how would you sort out this response?

Discussant: She made a request for a different hour and was turned down.

Langs: Right. That's the first and perhaps the most obvious context. We can see that an attempt to specify the adaptive context will demonstrate several overlapping precipitants. If we take this one and treat this opening association as a Type Two derivative around that context, we see a relatively nonneurotic depressive response to a rebuff of a kind, and a sense of confusion. The latter may be based on another factor; had she ever requested a different time and had her request granted?

Therapist: Yes, her hour had been changed at one point. She also didn't show for one session and didn't call, and she wasn't charged for that hour.

Langs: Was that session made up?

Therapist: No.

Langs: So, the therapist's responses do show some degree of inconsistency, and that could be a direct basis for her confusion.

Therapist: Each time she's tried to change an hour, I've tried to resist her. In that sense, she has had a lot of interest in seeing what she can get me to do or not do. But in general, she's been very accepting of the conditions of therapy, because she left two previous therapists over the same issue—paying for missed sessions. She likes it a great deal that the clinic doesn't charge her for missed sessions.

Langs: That's excellent. I've been waiting for that: consciously she liked this arrangement. Her direct reaction is: It's very nice, very good; it makes me trust you and want to have therapy with you. Such conscious responses to deviations are typical, and often they are all that the therapist will hear—though by no means all that the patient will express. However, in contrast, we will be in a position to compare her direct reaction with her indirect, relatively unconscious, derivative response.

Therapist: Those conclusions are yours, not hers. She has shown an appreciation for the clinic policy, but has not said much about wanting to do therapy in the clinic.

Langs: Yes, I am simply offering a model; my remarks are not based on material that you have presented. As such, it provides us with an important thesis and nothing more. Are there any other adaptive contexts here?

Discussant: There is the fact that on the one hand the therapist maintained the frame, while on the other he deviated.

Langs: Yes, that may make it difficult for us to sort out this material. Is she responding primarily to his adherence to the ground rules or to their modification? How did he deviate?

Discussant: He gave her directives. He told her to come in for her session, to take a cab or something like that, and I think to borrow money.

Langs: Yes, and in that light, we can consider her additional associations: the situation at work is chaotic, she is overburdened, and people have been away. How would you tie all of that to the adaptive context in the form of Type Two derivatives?

Discussant: Well, there must be a reference to the therapist's vacation and a sense of burden and disorganization that the patient is experiencing in response to it.

Langs: Yes, that threat is certainly there. For the moment, then, you are focusing on an aspect of the patient's response that is largely intrapsychically based and a reflection of her own inner pathology, prompted by an appropriate modification of the frame that occurred within the delineated therapeutic contract—the therapist's vacation. Anything else?

Therapist: This could also be a response to the telephone call and reflect the feeling on her part that I had abandoned her there too.

Langs: Yes, a reaction to your refusal to offer her an alternate hour. In addition, if we monitor this material in the adaptive context of your telephone call, and along the me/not-me interface, the patient is suggesting both that she had overburdened you with her request and that in return you may have overburdened her and felt some difficulty in handling it.

It is here that the complexities of the situation make matters quite difficult—as they so often are in the real world of psychotherapy. Your adherence to the framework may have helped you secure a segment of this therapeutic situation that has generated a fear of a therapeutic regression in this patient, one that she is concerned about being able to manage—and she may be worried as well about your ability to handle what will unfold. On the other hand, your deviations may well have overburdened the patient and reflected, in her eyes, your own difficulties in managing the framework and your own mental state, as well as hers. It may well be that the best hypothesis would be that under conditions in which the framework is partially secure and partially modified, one is faced with a great deal of confusion and difficulty in evaluating the communications from patient and therapist, and in being certain as to just what is going on.

Perhaps some further material will help us sort out these possibilities.

Therapist: She goes on a little longer, saying how horrible it is and how badly she feels. And she stops herself and says: One crazy thing did happen. She proceeds to tell me about a girl she grew up with—they often stayed together, dated the same fellow—and this girl used to take the patient's boyfriends away from her; in the past year, she had actually done this twice with men the patient had been dating. In any case, this girlfriend recently moved into the patient's building and was dating a man who was also her agent—the friend is an actress and model. When the agent dropped her, the friend was suicidal and used the patient to get some solace.

Langs: All right. How would you organize this material? How would you hear it?

Discussant: The relationship with this friend is somewhat ambivalent: she describes this friend as someone she helps in time of need, but she obviously has mixed feelings about her and sees her as a rival.

Langs: We will come back to the listening process again and again. How have you formulated this material?

Discussant: I addressed the manifest content.

Langs: Well, I think that you actually took the manifest content and derived some ready inferences—you developed some Type One derivatives plus a bit of metapsychological formulation.

Discussant: His comment was divorced from the therapeutic interaction and the prevailing adaptive contexts.

Langs: Yes, there seems to be a natural proclivity toward theorizing and formulating in isolation, a procedure that does indeed divorce the material from the ongoing interaction between the patient and the therapist. It seems difficult for you to maintain an adaptive focus and to take this material as a commentary on those precipitants. You can see too, and this is perhaps more pertinent to this part of the course, how easy it is for therapists to listen to material in isolation from issues related to the ground rules. Here these had arisen just prior to the session.

Discussant: Well, I guess I can extend my formulation by suggesting an analogy: the patient may well have the same feelings toward her friend. Now I still haven't related this to an adaptive context, but maybe it is too easy to look for a context in everything that happens.

Langs: Well, we will have to see if formulations such as the one you have just offered prove to be very meaningful, either in predicting what will happen as a session unfolds or in intervening directly to a patient. For the moment, I thought that I had adequately documented the validity of an adaptational approach in which we consistently organize our formulations around sequential adaptive contexts, and stay in tune with the unconscious communicative interaction. Certainly your approach will teach us little about the ground rules, while my methodology might teach us a great deal. Perhaps additional support for my position will accumulate as we go along.

Discussant: So you could take another step and say that perhaps the patient had these mixed feelings toward the therapist because of what had happened previously. It could be that the mixed feelings are reactions to the therapist's mixed response to the telephone call: holding steady in one area, and deviating in another. I also want to point out that there's a fairly transparent reference to the therapist's vacation: her mention of her friend's being jilted by the agent-boyfriend. I can recognize that as what you term a linear sequence, but I do believe it has some meaning.

Langs: Yes, I would agree. In fact, if the frame had been secured and maintained in steady fashion and the holding qualities well entrenched, we would be hearing material that clarifies the responses of patients to vacations—a particular modification in the framework which, as I said, lies within the basic therapeutic contract. And there is little doubt that we are hearing material of that kind, but I do believe that it is overshadowed by the patient's reaction to other ground rule issues. Can anyone add to what has already been said and provide us a more definitive bridge to these more deviant ground rule issues, and offer any formulation that might help us distinguish between the patient's reaction to the securing of the frame as compared to her response to its disruption?

Discussant: This may not be definitive, but I hear the patient saying something about losing closeness and not feeling rewarded by intimacy, and of course there is something self-destructive. But I realize that I am not organizing this around the adaptive context that we are discussing, so I guess I am somewhat lost.

Discussant: There are references to changes—changes in the conditions at work with people away, a change in where her friend is living, and changes in her friend's relationship with her boyfriend—perhaps allusions to changes in the usual setup. This could be a reference to some of the changes in the conditions of treatment, and she may be saying that this calls on her to do extra work. There's also a reference to a friend being one way for the moment and then different the next— using her or something like that. Perhaps these are commentaries on the therapist's directives during the phone conversation.

Langs: Yes, you seem a bit uncertain, but you are beginning to organize a set of coalescing derivatives around the adaptive context of the altered ground rules. True meaning comes from the coalescence of derivatives around a specific adaptive context, indirect communications that yield a series of implications, meanings, and functions—here, related to the alteration in the frame. There is a further derivative that would help clarify this discussion considerably; has anyone identified it?

Discussant: I'm not sure, but the reference to the agent-boyfriend might be what you're looking for. There might be a strong analogy between the friend's relationship with him and the patient's relationship with the therapist. In other words, either the girlfriend or the agent broke the ground rules of the work relationship by seducing the other one, and becoming involved in an affair. The agent loved her for it, but then fired her, so he had mixed feelings. Perhaps this is a commentary on the therapist's deviations, and the patient sees the therapist as seductive and loves him for it, but is also angered and is thinking of leaving.

Langs: That's excellent. You're making use of what I have called *embedded derivatives* and also allowing the derivatives to shape your selection of the critical adaptive contexts, as they should. And the patient says that a working relationship was complicated by a sexual relationship, which led to a total disruption of the relatedness, and eventually to suicidal feelings. The relationship did not remain within its initial definition and the modification led to disaster. This, then, is a remarkable form of Type Two derivative validation of our initial hypothesis about the consequences of altering the basic framework.

Here we have Type Two derivatives organized around the adaptive context of the therapist's directives during the telephone call, and around background contexts related to other deviations in these ground rules. And we hardly get a sense here that the patient is responding to the therapist's having secured the frame, thereby creating a fear of the therapeutic regression—the images do not unfold along such lines. Instead, we hear of a modified relationship and an eventual catastrophic response. I hope that this is convincing to all of you; I am trying to let the material speak for me and to avoid imposing my ideas upon the data. Remember too that everything I have learned about the ground rules, framework, and hold I have learned from patients and therapists; for me this seminar constitutes an effort to reexamine and revalidate the postulates I have derived from earlier observations of a comparable nature.

If we look at this material now as a broader commentary on the consequences of unnecessary modifications in the ground rules—framework and hold—we can recognize that the patient views these alterations as seductive; as contaminating; as a break in the boundaries; as entailing a shift in the nature and meanings of the communications and transactions between the two participants; as eventually untenable; and as having disastrous consequences—probably for both patient and therapist, if we monitor the last of that material along the me/not-me interface.

And in the specific adaptive context of the therapist's directives on the telephone, I would suggest that the patient is, indeed, unconsciously working over the implications of the introjects that she derived from this experience. She's saying that the therapist's comments altered the boundaries, modified the nature of their relationship, and had strong seductive implications. In addition, the patient may be pointing out that her own telephone call and request of the therapist was filled with seductive meaning; but in principle the therapist's errors and countertransferences must be analyzed first, and only then the patient's own pathological contributions.

You may also recall that we favored the hypothesis that these directives would indeed be experienced validly by the patient as seductive and manipulative. So we may take this sequence of associations as Type Two derivative validation. Such unconscious qualities are typical of so-called directly supportive interventions, of which this is a very good example.

Now, while I do believe that this is the overriding meaning of this material, I have no intention of overlooking other possibilities; we must extend our search for validation. I would therefore suggest that a second level of meaning of this material could derive from the patient's feeling hurt that the therapist did not change the hour, something that she experienced as a repudiation of their previously unconsciously seductive relationship, and that this has evoked a confused and depressive response. I find that particular formulation too linear for neurotic communication, but we must consider it in hearing the balance of this session.

I want to point out one other implication of my basic formulation: if it continues to be validated, it indicates that among the reasons patients become confused, disorganized, and suicidal are unneeded alterations in the basic ground rules and the therapeutic hold. I state it this way in order to hint at the power of this basic hold and the possible severity of the consequences when it is damaged. We may harm our patients not only through incorrect silences and erroneous verbal interpretations, but also through mismanagements of the framework—a consequence that I anticipated some years ago when I defined a series of iatrogenic syndromes (Langs, 1973b), the first of which was iatrogenic depression. These are matters of major consequence.

Discussant: Are you implying that the damage has been done and, because it is an actuality, there is virtually nothing the therapist can do?

Langs: Not at all. I have deliberately set aside considerations of intervening for two reasons: first, because we will deal with that subject specifically in a later part of this course, and, second, because I want first to establish the nature and functions of the ground rules before discussing the techniques we will need in handling them. All I will say for now is that because you are dealing here with actualities, it will be essential to restore the frame—to undertake *rectification*—before and along with interpreting the patient's unconscious perceptions, introjections, and fantasies. With proper therapeutic work, a great deal can be done here to afford the patient insights related to her psychopathology and to generate ego-enhancing, growth-promoting positive introjects. Are there any questions or comments before we continue with the clinical material?

Discussant: I'm not sure, but there may be a good deal of bias in what you're saying. It seems to me that the level of analysis is really what's involved here, and I think that there's much more here than you are picking up. There are other levels of meaning in this story she tells about the girlfriend.

Langs: Could you indicate specifically what you have in mind?

Discussant: I'm not sure, but there must be genetic connections for one thing, and maybe the patient is attempting to project her own feelings of hurt and depression onto this girlfriend, feelings perhaps derived from some source outside the therapeutic interaction.

Langs: Well, you are quite right: there are always multiple levels of meaning, and I think that the critical issue is to define that segment of meaning which is most immediately pertinent to the patient's adaptive efforts and unconscious communications. Here I think we need additional material in order to validate my proposal that the critical implications of this material derive from the therapeutic interaction and the adaptive contexts related to the ground rules. Your own thesis is quite linear and without adaptive focus, but beyond that we have to see if it proves to be meaningful and to have dynamic pertinence.

But for now I am considering only that level of meaning that relates to the ground rules and will continue to examine all of the material presented during this segment of the course in that particular way. I appreciate the issues you are raising, and, as I have always said, any truly meaningful debate or valid question will as a rule be answered by the subsequent material.

Therapist: But I don't think the issue is the frame at all. I think the problem is that this patient is planning to refer her girlfriend for treatment and that this is why she's bringing all of this up.

Langs: Please wait—you are actually, I believe, telling us what lies ahead in this material. In doing that, you are modifying the ground rules of this supervisory situation.

Therapist: I don't feel I've gone ahead of the material, or if I have it's because you have made a conclusion based on what you have heard to this point, and are inferring what the patient is talking about.

Langs: Let me say this: first, we are making these formulations without knowing the subsequent material in order to be in a position to predict and validate. Please allow us this methodology. Second, you should look at your own comment. To say that the issue is not related to the frame, but that she is planning to ask for a referral—that in itself is a frame issue, and refutes your own point. But we will not discuss it further until we hear it in the material at the proper point in the sequence.

Therapist: But if you make a conclusion at a point, A, and there is some other point, B, that you might just as well have stopped at, and which might include different meanings, you're saying that because of the continuity of the situation that there's a meaning at point A that might not exist at point B.

Langs: No, I believe that I'm saying that one can attempt to establish meaning at point A—in the form of a *silent hypothesis*—and that it can be then validated at point B; that meaning exists within the patient and can be detected at this point through a proper use of the listening process, and that, if it has been correctly perceived, it will be further amplified and extended at point B. I therefore believe that it is perfectly legitimate to stop at point A, and to make your silent hypothesis at that juncture, to be validated at the next point.

Therapist: You're postulating a type of associationism that I can't believe in. It is based on contiguity, whereas I believe it must be based on causality. You're taking a certain point in time and saying that certain realities exist at that moment. At a different point in time, if you take your own view of a particular session and your idea that it contains one theme, you might later state that it actually contains a different theme.

Langs: I'm afraid that there's a good deal of confusion here. I am referring to segments of associations, and to elements of a given session. I am attempting to identify various levels of meaning, and to take matters further by indicating what appears to be—based on a sensitive application of the listening process—the central meaning and implications. This does not imply that a given session contains a single theme or that I will change my opinion on that theme from time to time in some arbitrary way.

Therapist: I felt that you were insisting on the presence of one theme, and one theme alone.

Langs: Not at all. I am well aware of the dangers of systematization and premature closure. But for the moment we are concentrating on the ground rules, and the material of this session has readily coalesced around that issue. In time we may find that deviations in the basic structure and hold of treatment are of such great import to patients generally that their presence will always stimulate intense adaptive and derivative responses—that you may take as a tentative hypothesis. But as far as the listening process is concerned, one must strive to identify as many neurotic contexts as possible, and to see which best organizes the derivatives at hand; at the same time, a therapist must also be capable of listening openly to derivatives as they direct him unconsciously to unmentioned or sometimes overlooked precipitants.

Therapist: For the moment, you have completely ignored the fact that this patient has already talked about being a therapist to this woman, and how overwhelming it is. And for me, that is a very important theme and it leads her to try to make this referral.

Langs: I will not be able to respond to that last part, which I have already said I prefer not to have heard, until you reach that moment in the session. As for her being overwhelmed in her efforts to be a therapist to this woman, I would agree with you that that is an important theme and, actually, I was about to include it in my discussion.

Therapist: She's overwhelmed by it; after all, this woman has taken away her boyfriends for a long time.

Langs: And how do you evaluate that particular communication?

Therapist: I think that she's unable to handle the situation, that she's frightened because this friend is suicidal.

Langs: If I follow you, then, you are suggesting that the patient is disturbed because of the pressures in her relationship with this friend, and that you would attempt to intervene in order to help her with these anxieties.

Therapist: Yes, but along a particular line: this woman is very similar to the patient, in that what the patient is talking about is her own inability to handle her conflicts about men. That would be my ultimate interpretation.

Langs: I very much welcome an alternate hypothesis. I would like to describe its characteristics, so that we may compare it with my own formulation. Then, as we hear more material, we will attempt to determine which of the two conceptualizations receives Type Two derivative validation.

You are proposing that the adaptive context for this session and material lies outside the therapeutic relationship, in the suicidal feelings or threat of the patient's girlfriend. On that basis you are suggesting that the experience is evoking anxieties and conflicts connected to that particular relationship and to the patient's relationship with men—that is, that in part the patient is using the friend to communicate aspects of her own inner problems, as a self-representation, so to speak.

There is rather a linear quality to this particular formulation: a suicidal friend is said to represent possible suicidal feelings within the patient, and the friend who is having problems with men is thought to represent the patient's own difficulties in this area. Not only is the therapeutic relationship ignored for the moment but, in particular, no use is made of the me/not-me interface—a thought that prompts me to stress that from the therapist's side this is an intensely ''not-me'' formulation in that it totally ignores any possible reference to himself or any contribution he might have made. It also reflects the belief that intrapsychic dynamics prompted by outside relationships can be interpreted in the treatment situation in the presence of a significantly modified framework, and that such work can be both validated and helpful to the patient. It implies that the framework is often secondary, or need not be attended to at all, even in the face of such matters as the recent telephone call, the modifications in confidentiality, and the patient's lateness. The belief is that these problems are either not especially important or can be set aside in the face of an acute outside crisis. It adds to the thesis that important intrapsychic disturbances can be analyzed without linking them to the ongoing therapeutic interaction.

So this seems to me your position, which I believe is shared by many present-day therapists and analysts. Now, can anyone add to the formulation I have been developing, based on that last communication which the therapist has been emphasizing? (Pause.) Well, it looks as if no one wants to own up to the me/not-me interface, and to the "not-me" side of it—stated now in the usual way, from the vantage point of the patient.

Discussant: I think you're right: that part continues to elude us.

Langs: That's a very candid admission, and it's true for virtually every therapist. As demonstrated in the listening part of the course (Langs 1978c), it is along this interface that the valid unconscious perceptions and introjections of the therapist find their most poignant expression; it is here—for better or for worse—that we find the truth about ourselves. And so I feel it is my' responsibility to reveal this dimension as reflected in this material. It is here that the patient touches upon her own unconscious perception and introjection of the therapist's countertransferences; these perceptions and introjects on her part must be identified. To the extent that this perception is valid—and there is always some element of countertransference present—we can be certain that it is an aspect of the therapeutic experience that the patient is responding to intensely, and is communicating about.

So, viewed along the me/not-me interface, this material could allude to her unconscious perception and introjection of the therapist's difficulties in handling the sick and crazy parts of herself, particularly her own depressive and possibly even suicidal feelings. It could therefore be the therapist who she feels is overwhelmed, by herself, and the heterosexual problems could refer to other unconscious perceptions she has of the therapist. We could then link this tentatively to the therapist's management of the ground rules, and suggest that this is one basis for these unconscious perceptions and introjections. We would do this because the therapist's modifications in the framework are part of the immediate adaptive context to which the patient is responding within the therapeutic relationship.

This formulation is based on very convoluted lines of thought, on the heavily disguised derivative communications that we have identified as characteristic of the patient's neurotic associations. Here valid unconscious perceptions are intermingled with ultimate areas of distortion. This is a good example of a transversal communication. I am suggesting that this will prove to be the most meaningful level of the patient's communications for the moment, a postulate that in no way implies that this is the only level of meaning or that these same associations do not reflect important aspects of the patient's own mental world and functioning. I am simply saying that the principle of "therapist before patient" will prevail, and the meanings related to the introjective, "not-me" side of the patient's experiences must be understood, rectified, and interpreted before those related to the projective, "me" side. Still, to complete my evaluation, I would have to add that in all likelihood these unconscious perceptions and introjects are more valid than otherwise, and that they accurately represent the implications of the therapist's mismanagement of the framework, as well as difficulties he may have with interventions in other areas.

These are difficult matters to formulate and state, but as therapists we must be prepared to deal with them and with our own countertransferences as they emerge in the therapeutic interaction. To do otherwise is to turn away from the truth about both the patient and ourselves, to a form of what I have called *lie* or *barrier therapy*. Now let's have some more material.

Therapist: At that point, she tells me about an incident that happened the preceding Thursday night. She and a boyfriend the two of them share—the patient and her girlfriend—were going to go out to dinner. This is one of the boyfriends that the girlfriend had partly taken away; as I said, this woman frequently tries to take the patient's boyfriends away.

Langs: She and this woman, who was suicidal, were sharing a boyfriend. Would anyone like to comment on this particular communication?

Discussant: I wasn't clear about the telephone conversation, and I wonder if the clinic was involved.

Langs: Why do you raise that question?

Discussant: Well, the patient is describing a threesome.

Langs: Yes, exactly. There is a third party to what is usually a two-person relationship—girlfriend and boyfriend. What you have done is to have taken the adaptive context of the prevailing modifications in the framework—more specifically, the secretary who helped the patient fill out the form just before the session began—and organized this material as Type Two derivatives around that context.

But remember too that we are listening now to each association in an effort to decide which of two rather different formulations of the material accrues support and validation. We want to see whether these subsequent associations can be organized as coalescing derivatives around the adaptive context of the ground rule issues, or whether they best fit the patient's problems with men. And it's interesting that while this derivative in a quite convoluted and disguised way does allude to a basic frame issue, it also brings up problems in heterosexual relationships, though these appear rather directly, as before. It seems to me that the distinction between direct and indirect communication, between Type One and Type Two derivatives, is crucial to the evaluation as to which level of communication from this patient is more relevant to her "neurosis" for the moment.

Discussant: I am also thinking of the fact that this patient has to share the therapist with a lot of other patients.

Langs: Well, that introduces an inevitable condition of treatment to which the patient may indeed react. It has frustrating and limiting qualities, much like the therapist's vacation. Here the patient might very well be responding to this inevitability by feeling that it is because of his other patients that the therapist didn't give her a different hour.

Also, since a threesome offers greater protection against separation than does a twosome, the material might involve a further response to the therapist's vacation. It is important to see how many levels of communication can be identified in a brief segment of material.

It shows you that we cannot simply work on the basis of randomly identifying Type One and Type Two derivatives around a whole variety of adaptive contexts, but that eventually we must attempt to determine which particular context is most crucial for the patient at a given moment. Here the continuing material must be looked to, keeping in mind that convoluted derivative communication characterizes the working over of neurosis-related adaptive contexts.

Discussant: It seems to me that what was going on with that boyfriend would be more important than the fact that here's someone that the two women share.

Langs: Perhaps. But as you listen it is advantageous to try to quickly formulate each derivative as it unfolds. You should frame silent hypotheses and make efforts at silent validation before offering any intervention to the patient.

Discussant: There is also a third-party payer, which may connect to this business of threesomes.

Langs: Yes, the derivatives certainly coalesce in a typically convoluted way around various issues related to the ground rules. I think, however, based on the questions that have been raised, that we will need something from this patient that will somehow point more convincingly to the area that most concerns her for the moment.

Therapist: I am still bothered by your neglect of the similarities between herself and this girlfriend, and by the fact that this is the beginning of her talking about referring this girl, because she is telling me how crazy her girlfriend is.

Langs: I have nothing to add to that discussion for the moment. Your anticipation is quite manifest and linear, while my formulation is convoluted. I can say no more for the moment.

Discussant: I still get the feeling that this patient is trying to work over, unconsciously if you will, these ground rule issues. She had filled out the form before she came in, and this made her even later. But in addition, if the therapist participates in this sort of thing, it seems to me that the patient can't trust him to discuss it more directly, and that she has to resort to disguised communication—what you call derivative communication.

Langs: Yes, but we need something to validate these silent hypotheses.

Discussant: I would like to ask a theoretical question that's not directly related to this case at all. In terms of the ground rules, which is more important: the ground rule itself or the consistency with which it is applied? Say for example a patient says, for valid reasons, I'm not going to be able to come at the same time each week. Can you say, Okay, we'll set up the appointment from week to week—and let that be the rule?

Langs: There are those who feel you can establish many different baselines—as long as you adhere to one, that's your framework and you can do the therapeutic work from there. I haven't found this to be the case at all, empirically; and we'll eventually test that out here. In brief, I've found that there is an ideal set of ground rules and that as soon as you deviate from that ideal you do get into difficulties. You produce sectors of misalliance and bastions that don't get analyzed. And the use of a consistent, prearranged time is one of the ideal ground rules.

One of the ways I tried to prove this particular concept was through a reconsideration of Freud's case histories (Langs 1976b, 1978d, e). I took today's ground rules, as I have defined them here, and used them as a template. Every time Freud stepped out of that frame, I looked at what happened to the material. And it was especially illuminating because Freud left behind some of his daily notes from the Rat Man. And what happened then is exactly what is happening now with this patient: The Rat Man alluded to suicidal feelings in response both to Freud's feeding him and to a postcard Freud sent to him. And the Rat Man had suicidal fantasies, and spoke both of feeling seduced and of threesomes. Believe it or not. And he dreamt about a dentist who pulled the wrong tooth. All of this right after these template-measured "deviations."

Discussant: I'm not talking about deviations, but about a consistent set of ground rules that differ from, let's say, your standards.

Langs: But these are not my standards; they are the patient's. I was responding to your question by saying that I had validated a particular set of ground rules or standards, and in several ways: through Freud's case histories, through similar tests of material from the literature (see for example Lipton 1977b), and through extensive efforts at validation in my own clinical work and extensive supervisory experience. We will be able to test many of these ground rules through the presentations we will be hearing, and any specific alteration you would like to propose would have to be clinically tested in order to evaluate it. Perhaps you should hold this question until we are well into this segment of the course, and until you have had a chance to see whether your thoughts have been clarified as we move along. Please continue.

Therapist: The patient was saying that she and her girlfriends were all supposed to go out to dinner, but the girlfriend we've been hearing about goes over to the boyfriend's apartment; apparently, he lives nearby also. And the two of them don't show up to go out to dinner, and it ends up being eleven-thirty. The patient ends up very angry at everybody and the two of them finally say they'll go out, but the patient doesn't want to go with them. The next day she has a splitting headache, and talks to this girlfriend, who was angry at her for not answering the phone.

Langs: One of the hypotheses I made in *The Bipersonal Field* (Langs 1976a) was that one factor in somatic symptoms is disturbances in the ground rules and therapeutic hold. So it's interesting to hear the reference to this symptom.

Discussant: I think this links up to a lot we said earlier, things which seem to amount to saying that she's passive-aggressive. She felt she had been done an injustice and was angry at the therapist for not changing her hour. Therefore she shows up forty minutes late.

Langs: Well, you are coming back to the adaptive context issue and suggesting that the patient is responding primarily to the therapist's failure to give her a different hour. On this basis you are saying that the themes of feeling deserted, abandoned, and mistreated are related to the therapist's refusal to offer this patient an alternative session and to the deprivation involved in having to accept an abbreviated hour. These themes could also be related to the adaptive context of his vacation, but in both respects you are back to rather linear derivatives and fairly direct displacements.

So we still do not have sufficiently compelling communications to decide which particular adaptive contexts take precedence for the patient. Under such conditions, we must be prepared to allow the derivatives to direct us and to try to organize the material around each context from time to time. It is necessary also, at the very least, to monitor this material in terms of the continuing therapeutic interaction. We must avoid developing a vested interest in using formulations that leave out our possible contributions to the patient's associations and difficulties. If these tendencies are conveyed to the patient, he can easily be engaged in a bastion that seals off the deviations in technique and their repercussions, especially since the patient will characteristically communicate his reactions in this area through well-disguised derivatives.

Here, for example, we see continued allusions to people who do not meet their commitments, in response to which the patient becomes furious. And you'll notice too that the patient has just mentioned not answering the telephone—an embedded derivative related to the telephone call she had made just prior to the session. There is, indeed, a sense of betrayal, but for the moment it is difficult to establish the basis for the patient's feeling that way.

Discussant: How long was the session?

Therapist: She got a full twenty minutes.

Langs: Are your saying that you extended the session?

Therapist: Yes, I saw her an additional ten minutes.

Langs: So at some point in this material the patient will have used up her regularly scheduled hour and will begin the extended portion of the session. Please let us know that moment so we can see what follows.

Therapist: As I remember it, she looked directly at the clock at that point, but I don't know just when that occurred in respect to the material of the session. I guess we are just about at that point right now.

Langs: Then please continue.

Therapist: So, she didn't answer the phone but talked to the girlfriend the next day. It turns out she was about to leave to go to visit her parents in a distant state. And the patient ended up screaming at this friend to leave her alone, saying that no one cared about her and that she didn't want to hear from her again; she could take care of her own problems if that's the way she was going to be treated. She said the same thing to this boyfriend.

Then she went on to talk about no one caring about her needs, and how she was tired of it. At that point I said that today she had called here and had asked for a different appointment, and that I hadn't been able to arrange it. And I had been away on vacation too. I pointed out that she had gone on at length, feeling both overwhelmed about trying to deal with these problems in a friend and feeling that the friend didn't care or acknowledge what she was trying to do. And I wondered if that had something to do with how she was feeling about my not being able to change her appointment and my having gone on vacation.

Langs: So, you attempted to deal with this material in terms of her response to your vacation and to your adherence to the framework, and you set aside the deviations in technique. The positive nucleus of this intervention is that you did address certain issues related to the ground rules, while its more questionable elements entail matters of technique that cannot be discussed in any detail for the moment.

Basing my evaluation on our work with the listening process, I would suggest that you arbitrarily chose the adaptive contexts for this material, and did not allow the patient the liberty of this selection. You introduced selected experiences that the patient had not mentioned, but avoided others—at this point in the session you especially chose to ignore the fact that you were now extending her hour.

Try to enter each session without desire, memory, or understanding, and to permit the patient to put into you in scattered and derivative form all of the elements of your intervention. Permit each hour to be its own creation, and allow the patient to lead the way. We'll talk more about these problems when we get to the subject of interventions.

If you take the extension of this session as the adaptive context for this last segment of material, it's rather striking to hear the patient speak of screaming at a friend to leave her alone, rejecting the friend, and telling her that she would take care of her own problems if this is the way she was going to be treated. She mentions too that she feels no one cares about her needs—a point that some might see as contradicted by the fact that the therapist has extended the hour. Such people would consider the extension a human response, with caring and positive qualities, to a patient who had no choice but to be late. This is a very naive but all too common approach, and one that is rejected by this patient: she senses the underlying disregard for her needs for a secure frame and a consistent therapist.

We would have to predict that this intervention will not be validated, since it does not address the most disturbing and currently meaningful adaptive contexts. On the other hand, since it addresses issues related to the ground rules, it may eventually lead the patient to direct the therapist to those aspects of the situation which are really disturbing her.

Therapist: She ignored what I said, saying that what she had been talking about had nothing to do with me. She was tired of them and felt like retaliating. That's how the hour ended, and she very reluctantly left the office.

Langs: So, we're about to hear the beginning of the next session. Because of the many impingements on the ground rules, and because these deviations have not been addressed, rectified, and the patient's conscious and unconscious responses interpreted, I must predict that she will begin this hour with a frame issue or reference. If the hypotheses I have been developing with you are to receive validation from this rather chaotic material it might well come by anticipating that the framework is, indeed, so critical for this patient, and the disturbances so important, that she will continue to work them over in this hour, in the hope of prompting the therapist to move toward rectification and interpretation. Now, if these issues are really cogent, she will begin the hour with a derivative representation—some allusion to the frame.

Therapist: She doesn't wait that long—she calls me at home that very night.

Langs: Thank you. The prediction is confirmed, and through a telephone call to your home no less. How is it that she has that telephone number?

Therapist: I gave it to her when she was suicidal during an earlier phase of treatment.

Langs: Well, that's another deviation from the standard frame, though I hadn't mentioned this aspect until now. The patient should have the therapist's office number, and nothing more in that regard. Providing the patient with your home telephone has many implications. To name a few implied by the present material, it offers an opportunity for contact between the patient and other members of your family; it therefore has a seductive quality, and may modify the tenets of privacy, confidentiality, and the one-to-one relationship. It is also infantilizing, shows a lack of faith in the patient's ability to cope, and encourages the patient's dependency and reliance upon yourself. It has many of the qualities reflected in the material of the hour just presented, and is probably another adaptive context that lies behind those we have already identified. The patient brings it to our attention quite directly at this moment.

Now, you may well feel that you cannot rely on the personnel at this center to relay messages from a suicidal patient, and that the wisest choice under those conditions is the one you made. But it is important to understand that you should first attempt to repair the situation at the center so that the deviation is not needed, and should, failing that, be prepared to analyze the many consequences of this particular alteration in the framework.

So. The patient initiated this sequence through a deviation in the framework expressed in her telephone call to the therapist at his office. The therapist responded with some degree of participation in that deviation, and through added modifications in the form of departures from his neutral position. During the hour he further deviated by extending the patient's session, and now the patient contacts the therapist by telephone at home. One deviation begets another, and it is difficult to know where to place responsibility: clearly, these deviations are interactionally determined, with contributions from both participants.

Actually, this telephone call appears to validate my formulations regarding the importance of the therapist's alterations in the framework.

It is a playback of the therapist's extension of this patient's hour, and it calls to his attention the transactions of the earlier telephone conversation. All of this remains unrectified and uninterpreted. Of course, skeptics might say that this is a continued response to the therapist's vacation and his failure to change the hour, but I hope now you can see this argument as vitiated by the therapist's attempt to interpret the material using these contexts, and the patient's failure to offer a validating response. The most basic element of this telephone call is that it alters the framework. You will not as a rule find patients responding in this way after the therapist has taken a vacation if he has, as is not the case here, adequately handled the patient's reactions. I would not have made this prediction if the only issue were his having been away for a week.

Well, we are developing some evidence as to just how critical the framework is for both patient and therapist. There should be still more clarification as we go on.

Therapist: Well, on the telephone she says that this friend is really suicidal and she doesn't know what to do. She goes on to tell me a couple more details: that this friend had come back early from visiting her parents and was even more visibly agitated—crying, saying she was going to kill herself, and so on. And she didn't know what to do about it, and would I talk to her friend? I said I would, that she could call me at work tomorrow and I would try to find someone to see her.

Langs: So, one deviation begets two others—now, the introduction and acceptance of another third party to treatment. Here you respond in what appears to be a commonsense way, enabling us to recognize that such an approach to psychotherapy can only be based on a denial and disregard of unconscious communication and implications. I know you have been taught this, at least by your supervisors, though I suspect that your patients have been trying to teach you otherwise. This patient will almost certainly make similar efforts.

In addition, you are now in the untenable position of having accepted physicianly responsibility for a suicidal patient you have never seen, never evaluated, and have now tacitly recommended that she delay making contact with a physician until the following day. That in itself should enable you to sense how uncertain and chaotic the conditions of what are now two therapeutic situations are. I recognize that you said you would refer her friend, but for the moment, in the absence of another therapist, you have burdened yourself with responsibilities that are impossible to handle in any adequate fashion.

Incidentally, this is a good example of how other people—external objects—foster projection and projective identification. For the moment, the patient is not the one who is suicidal, chaotic, or agitated—or even under the immediate influence of a disturbing parental experience that on some level could be taken as a derivative of what the patient introjected from the therapist in the previous session. It is the friend who is experiencing these things and who is now sent to the therapist. One might speculate that the friend is being offered as a substitute for the patient in many ways—and you can see what this implies for the therapist's response. But let's not extend the formulation too far until we hear more material.

For the moment my emphasis is on the continued modifications in the framework, because through them both patient and therapist seem to be working toward extratherapeutic gratifications, inappropriate defenses, and both misalliances and bastions. I get a sense that both participants are attempting to repair interactional and inner damage through these deviations, an effort that approaches an attempt at *framework deviation cure*—a search for symptom alleviation through an alteration of the ground rules.

Another way of understanding the material to this point is to state that modifications in the framework evoke in patients responses of considerable affective intensity. We are finding that alterations in the ground rules are experienced as deprivations, desertions, betrayals, and occasions for feeling depressed and hopeless. This we can take as an hypothesis for later validation.

Discussant: What would you have said to this woman?

Langs: Well, I might not have had to say anything, since I believe that had the therapist maintained the framework this telephone call would not have taken place. Instead, either the friend or the patient would have called an internist or another therapist, or have come to the emergency room of this center. And that would have been my answer: that any concern about suicide is a serious matter, and that I am not in a position to evaluate the situation with her friend; she should be brought to the emergency room immediately in order to have such an evaluation.

Here, then, because of the threat of suicide in someone I have not seen and cannot evaluate, I have made a modification in the framework, and have offered a directive on the telephone. I would, in the next session, take this deviation as a major adaptive context and, entirely through leads developed from the patient, would have become involved in efforts at rectification and interpretation. I suspect that the material of the hour we are about to hear will contain such opportunities, since the patient will be in great need of such efforts.

So, in principle, I would not agree to see the friend or to talk to her by telephone the next day. I would make the referral on the telephone only in a dire emergency. If circumstances were otherwise, I would not offer to see the patient and would not make a referral until hearing the material from the patient in the next session, through which I would have a full opportunity to understand its unconscious meanings and functions. As a rule, I have found that requests for referrals are filled with inappropriate gratifications and defenses, and that patients have many other resources to call upon. The communications from patients have indicated to me again and again that referrals of friends constitute deviations in technique filled with detrimental consequences to the patient and the therapy. I know that this position, this ground rule, will evoke intense controversy, so I will not elaborate for now. I expect that here too the material that we are about to hear will offer us meaningful opportunity to understand the implications of such a request.

Returning to this telephone call, then, can you sense anything else about this patient's decision to call her therapist?

Discussant: It's asking the therapist to contain some kind of disturbance.

Langs: Yes, but what else? It's more to the surface. (Pause.) The call was unnecessary. As I said, the patient could be taking her friend to another therapist or to an emergency room. So there must be strong unconscious reasons for contacting the therapist.

Discussant: It could be taken as a gross test of how far the patient can modify the frame.

Discussant: And how far the therapist is willing to go as well.

Discussant: But in addition, Dr. Langs, you seem to be suggesting that it is a direct result of the prior deviations in the frame.

Langs: Yes, especially because they have remained unrectified and unanalyzed.

Discussant: I have difficulty with that because I think that there are other patients who themselves try to rectify a damaged frame and to tell you that you're really screwing up. She, on the other hand, seems to be trying to evoke more modifications.

Langs: Conscious efforts on the part of patients to rectify the framework are relatively rare, while unconscious efforts are virtually universal. There is, indeed, a major effort by this patient to evoke additional deviations in the framework, but I think we need the session that is about to be presented in order to understand the conscious and unconscious reasons for this.

It is well to understand that even in these efforts at exploitation there is somewhere a nucleus of curative intent—if nothing else, to impress upon the therapist through these very efforts the extent to which these deviations are getting out of hand and the impact that they are having on the patient, as well as on the therapist. It seems likely that a therapist would begin to wonder about a telephone call of this kind, and that could be the beginning of rectifying and interpretive efforts. My own guess is that the telephone call is the patient's representation and communication of the uncertain, untenable, and chaotic qualities of her own treatment situation, and of the vulnerability she is experiencing because of it. There is now virtually no sense of framework, hold, or containment, and to the extent that this emanates from the therapist it constitutes a very disruptive projective identification into the patient, who may here be attempting a relatively unmetabolized reprojection. All of this probably reinforces her own inner sense of chaos and vulnerability, and a whole series of specific ego dysfunctions, conflicts, and destructive early childhood experiences as well.

I think too that the patient is now letting us know that it is virtually impossible to help her manage her own inner state and turmoil under these conditions. I am reminded of a comment in my deviation paper (Langs 1975c) to the effect that the therapist's management of the framework is experienced by the patient as a reflection of his capacity to manage his own inner mental state, conflicts, introjects, and the like. In fact, we now arrive at a very important postulate: the management of the framework is an inherent part of the unconscious communicative interaction between patient and therapist, and is filled with unconscious meaning. That statement may seem rather obvious, but I can assure you that it has seldom been stated so explicitly and is almost never addressed by practicing therapists and analysts.

Discussant: Couldn't there be an alternative explanation? Perhaps this is an attempt by the patient to force a deviation in the frame that is not so much based on what the therapist has done, but on her own pathological needs to get into three-way relationships, like the one with the other woman and the boyfriend. Perhaps she has a need to share boyfriends and therapists for reasons of her own, and she's now setting the therapist up in the same way.

Langs: Yes, that is an alternative hypothesis, one which accounts for these behaviors entirely in terms of the patient's needs and pathology, divorced from the therapeutic interaction and the therapist. It is the usual way for a therapist to think of such interludes, and of course it disowns any responsibility or contribution on his part. Not only does it stress the intrapsychic realm; it eliminates the interactional. By contrast, my thesis began with the therapist and the therapeutic interaction, and then extended into the intrapsychic area. I indicated that the former would have to be rectified and analyzed before the latter would be available for interpretation. As long as the interactional communications reinforce the intrapsychic pathology, the latter blends into the former and thus cannot be analyzed.

But now we need some clinical material in order to see which of the two hypotheses receives psychoanalytic validation.

Discussant: I think we do need some clinical material, because this patient may very well have some sort of pathological competitive problems, and she may feel the need to modify this frame regardless of the therapist's neutrality and the correctness of his technique. For example, he may use superb technique and she might still call his house at twelve o'clock at night.

Langs: Your comment indicates the necessity of our getting back to the actual clinical situation, because this telephone call did not occur under those conditions, but in the context of modifications in neutrality and in the basic framework. Only when the therapist has maintained the frame, only when there is virtually no countertransference input, will we be in a position to concentrate on the sources of these behaviors in the patient. There is always some small measure of input from the therapist, but under these conditions the preponderant responsibility lies with the patient.

Discussant: Yes, I see.

Langs: In reality, this telephone call is an interactional product, and that is the sort of thing that has been overlooked in the literature.

Therapist: I'm really confused about how to intervene.

Langs: Well, what I'm leading up to here is that the intervention would have to include a rectification of the frame. This brings us to a whole new area of intervening: modification of your pathological inputs and the countertransferences on which they're based. And then we would finally be able to get to . . .

Therapist: Interpretive material. I see.

Langs: Yes. If you interpret this solely in terms of the patient's needs, she is going to know that you're a hypocrite, that you're denying your own contribution. And this will make her more crazy, not less.

Discussant: It seems to me from what you're saying that in the clinic you could really never get beyond the frame.

Langs: Unfortunately, that's probably right. The clinic imposes modifications in the frame that impinge upon the treatment situation throughout its duration, and this affects the patient's image of her therapist in a variety of ways. And because the framework and hold are so crucial, it is quite likely that the patient will work and rework the related issues again and again, and that any other adaptive context will in some way have to be appended to these problems.

Discussant: Well, I'm a little confused as to how you deal with the patient's psychopathology. We're dealing now with frame issues and our responses, and I don't see where the patient's pathology comes in.

Langs: Once again, you return to the prevailing intrapsychic characterization of psychopathology, divorced from interactions that include the basic conditions of a relationship—the ground rules and frame. Psychopathology has both internal and external sources, and is based on both inner fantasies and external actualities which are introjected and become part of the patient's intrapsychic world. In the development of the child, boundaries and framework issues play a critical role and they have received some attention in the literature, especially in respect to sexual overstimulation and narcissistic misuses by the parent of the child.

It is my position that the patient's psychopathology can be approached only in the context of current issues within the therapeutic interaction, and I see no problem in anticipating that you would have ample opportunity to understand and analyze the patient's psychopathology as it unfolds in response to ground rule problems. You could then produce adaptive, inner structural change, based first on rectification of the frame and an offer of a secure hold to the patient, and, second, on the cognitive insights derived from the analytic work with the patient's reactions to these impingements. This work, by the way, would address both unconscious perceptions and valid introjections, as well as distorted unconscious fantasies.

I think, however, that the issue in regard to analyzing the patient's pathology arises in still another way under these conditions. The question, as I see it, is whether these modifications in the framework create basic alterations in the communicative properties of the bipersonal field, and fundamental negative perceptions and introjects of the therapist that are harmful to the patient and create conditions under which valid analytic work cannot take place. Will you be limited to exploring only those aspects of the patient's psychopathology that relate to framework issues, or will even that work be impaired because of these breaks in the frame?

This is a far more difficult question to answer. I very much want to keep it in mind as we go along, to see what answer might be provided in the presentations we will hear. At one time, I thought that a therapist could do some valid therapeutic work with isolated issues under these conditions, but I am no longer certain of that. I think now that there are basic flaws in the entire therapeutic situation and experience at such times, and that since they are based on unmodified actualities their influence is permanent and significant. I think it creates conditions in which *lie therapy*—the development of barriers, falsifications, bastions, and misalliances—is virtually inevitable, and *truth therapy* is sacrificed, including the opportunity to get at the true unconscious basis of the patient's psychopathology in the context of the dynamics of the ongoing therapeutic interaction. But that is a very tentative hypothesis; let's try not to prejudge too much of the matter.

Well, our time is up. I would appreciate your continuing this presentation next week; there are a lot of unanswered questions.

Chapter Three

THE PATIENT'S UNCONSCIOUS
RESPONSES TO DEVIATIONS

Langs: Please begin again at the very point at which you left off. I want us to continue to experience how it feels to approach material without desire, memory, or understanding.

Therapist: Well, I will begin then with the next session. She arrived ten minutes late, and walked in and said, I'm sorry.

Discussant: That validates—now, for a second time—the hypothesis you offered last week: that she would begin this hour with a reaction to the frame and that the ground rules are important to her.

Langs: Yes, and it also reflects the chaos of the therapy under conditions of multiple deviations, a point that I have already made several times. In fact, who could offer an immediate comment concerning this lateness?

Discussant: She's giving up the ten minutes that the therapist gave her as a gift last time.

Langs: Exactly. Isn't that remarkable? In his kindness, the therapist—and you put it quite well—gave the patient a gift of ten minutes, and the patient immediately returns it. This is her own rectification of the frame, as well as her communication that there is simply no telling when sessions begin and end here.

Notice too the form that this takes: the patient does not address the issue directly. She makes and rationalizes a telephone call to the therapist's home, and she then arrives ten minutes late to the present session. The adaptive and therapeutic contexts are expressed through her behaviors, through actions—acting out and acting in, if you will— reminding us again that the therapist's deviations in the ground rules must be taken on his side as a form of acting out, as behavioral expressions of his unresolved countertransferences. As such, it invites action responses in the patient. And I say this not as an evaluation, but as a prediction that this is the evaluation the patient will give it—and with considerable perceptiveness, I must say. She has already addressed this issue and validated such a thesis, and we will soon see if she does so again.

If we are prepared to conceptualize indirect and derivative communications, whether verbal or behavioral, we can take this initial communication and permit it to direct us back to the adaptive contexts of the many alterations in this framework. Let's see what follows.

Therapist: She starts talking about how upset she still is about her girlfriend. The friend had not kept the appointment I had given her. The situation is further complicated by the fact that when the patient had called on the day of the last session to change her time, I had said that I didn't have another time between then and this hour. I had given her friend an appointment only because I thought she was suicidal; I had no one to refer her to, and that was just my feeling at the time. I didn't want to refer her to someone else without seeing her once. My decision was based on what she had said on the telephone.

Langs: Had you said this to your patient or to the friend directly?

Therapist: The friend was with her when the patient called me.

Langs: Oh, then we didn't hear the entire call last week. What I recall of it is that you had told the patient to have her friend call you the next day.

Therapist: But the friend called me that night. She told me a rather dramatic story of this boyfriend who dumped her for somebody else, and because she was so pissed off about it she dropped him as an agent, or he dropped her, it's not clear which. And she was talking about how bad she was feeling and how she had thought maybe going home would help her. So basically that was what she said. She said she had severe mood swings and was having thoughts of suicide, but she seemed to have no immediate plans to harm herself. I didn't think she was seriously suicidal for the moment.

I said to her that I thought it was something that seemed to be giving her a lot of trouble; that it was something she needed to talk to someone about, and that I would be willing to do whatever I could to help her with that, to find her a therapist. I said I thought that I needed to talk to her more in order to give her someone I could recommend, so I could look around to see who had some time. So basically I was trying to refer her to someone else.

Langs: But you did make an appointment with her.

Therapist: But that was going to be it.

Langs: If nothing else, I think that you can all see how complicated the therapeutic situation becomes when you get involved in modifications in the framework. When informing the patient that it will be necessary to adhere to the agreed-upon hour, you should not attempt to make excuses or to offer explanations; in particular, you should not tell a lie or half-lie, no matter how well intentioned.

Next, you may already sense the wisdom of not accepting friends of patients as patients of your own, even if for a single consultation. There is a valid message in the friend's failure to keep her appointment, though we will never know the details. This arrangement, of which the patient was aware, must also be considered an adaptive context for her lateness, and for the associations that unfold during this hour. In addition, you made this appointment even though, having spoken to her, you did not consider the situation an emergency. You sensed no immediate suicidal risk, and this makes your decision even more questionable—again in the patient's eyes. Also, the friend called you at home and then did not appear for the consultation—something is amiss.

Therapist: But I felt that the friend was not immediately suicidal; why should I stuff her into the emergency room on that basis?

Langs: I am alluding to the necessity of making a referral, and how I see no advantage in a consultation with you, but many disadvantages. In fact, any consultation by a therapist or analyst who is not in a position to offer ongoing treatment to the patient contains immediate modifications of the framework, and is therefore essentially destructive. I will state this as another ideal ground rule: the therapist should see patients only when he is prepared to offer therapy. To do otherwise is hurtful and destructive, and I seriously doubt that anything whatsoever is gained by it. As far as the patient is concerned, the therapeutic work takes place in the context of the therapeutic interaction, and a single consultation followed by referral is confusing and rejecting, and can do considerable damage.

Discussant: I would agree with Dr. Langs: if she's not suicidal, you could just have had her call this clinic or one nearby, and I really see no need to see her in consultation.

Langs: But just remember: when you hear of someone who is suicidal, every effort should be made to ensure a proper consultation. Beyond that, it is essential that you not ignore the dynamics of this situation as it pertains to this patient and therapist. It is no coincidence that this patient called and gave this therapist an impossible task: he could not at the time of this call evaluate the girlfriend's suicidal potential, since he had not as yet so much as spoken to her. But the patient's communication is in itself a product of the bipersonal field and the prior therapeutic interaction, including the modifications in the framework and their implications—here, to the effect that treatment is impossible under these conditions. That is a powerful commentary, but it is present in this material, and we will try to validate further as we go on. Notice that from different segments of this material we keep coming back to the same compelling implications of these extensively modified ground rules. Let's see what more we can learn about these deviations.

Therapist: Well, the friend sounded chaotic, but she had no thought disorder and wasn't imminently suicidal as far as I could tell. She seemed to be reacting to the loss of the boyfriend and I had expected her to call later in the week, and to give her the name of a therapist. But she called that night, saying that things had gotten much worse, and, even though I didn't consider her suicidal, since I didn't have time to find another therapist I agreed to see her.

Langs: Yes, your intentions were good, though I hope you can now see that they were filled with unconscious implications, many of them destructive to both the friend and your patient. Please continue with your presentation.

Therapist: The patient comes in, says she's sorry she's late, and starts talking about this friend again. She tells about this woman's visit home. She had gone to visit her parents the preceding week, the end of that week while I was away. She then said how upset her friend was getting her because she didn't know what to do with her.

And then she told me something about what her friend had told me: visiting home, and that things were horrible. She had seen the friend the night of the last session and then had talked to her the next night, supposedly after the woman had come to see me, but she never had. So she talked to her both nights, and was telling me about what this friend had said and how upset she was getting because this woman was depending on her to solve her problems. She went on: And then she didn't come. I was really angry at her. I was afraid you would be angry at me. I know you made a special time to see her and then she didn't come.

Then she says of the friend: She gets better and worse. Some of the time it's okay, I don't mind her talking to me; but other times I don't know what to say to her and I don't know what to do, and I'm always worried that she's going to do something to herself.

Langs: Since she repeats it, I want to remind you that you have to apply the me/not-me interface to these associations. The material can be considered along the me/not-me interface, as well as at the manifest level. All of it must be tied to the prevailing adaptive contexts. What can you say about this material at this point?

Therapist: On the manifest level, she's talking about how upset she is; about her friend continuing to rely on her and her feelings about how I may feel about her friend not having shown up.

Langs: Yes, but can you relate this to an adaptive context and in addition characterize its surface qualities?

Discussant: I get a sense that she's worried that the therapist will be upset with her. This seems to imply that she feels he has done her a favor, and that the friend has betrayed them both. Here the therapist went out of his way and gave the friend time to see her, and the friend didn't come; maybe he will be angry at the patient.

Langs: This is what happens when we do not begin with the adaptive context. For the moment, you are playing back the manifest content of this material, along with minimal inferences—Type One derivatives.

Discussant: It seems to me that she's discussing the friend, rather than talking about herself and her own feelings. And I have the impression that it doesn't very much illuminate the adaptive contexts—the patient's telephone call to the therapist, the call from the friend, and the therapist's way of handling the situation.

Langs: Exactly. The ground rules have been modified in the ways you have just described, to which I would add the therapist's agreeing to see the friend in consultation. Now, while I have suggested that these are powerful adaptive contexts which the material from the patient should illuminate, and found some validation in the patient's lateness, there is nevertheless something rather flat about these associations. The derivatives do not coalesce; all that they imply is that someone is upset over not obtaining the care that she needs, and that someone else is rather annoyed about it all. Now, why has this happened?

Discussant: Perhaps the therapist's interest in the patient's friend has hurt the patient, and made her feel slighted. Maybe she doesn't want to talk about herself because she feels that the therapist is more interested in the friend.

Langs: Yes, that's a rather direct inference and is well taken. But in answering my question, I had hoped that someone might say that the material is not confirming my hypotheses about the framework and that maybe the reason for its flatness is that I do not understand its implications and that I am in error in respect to the functions of the frame. That is, after all, an hypothesis we will have to consider.

There is, however, an alternative hypothesis: namely, that these extensive modifications in the framework have offended the patient, led her to mistrust the therapist, modified the communicative qualities of the bipersonal field, and caused the patient to close herself off from derivative communication. Once again, I hope that the subsequent material will help us decide which of two hypotheses is more valid.

So, while the patient may indeed be using her friend as a vehicle for projection, these associations do not deepen or coalesce. Implied here is the idea that if the therapist agreed to see her friend, this patient's therapy becomes the therapy of the friend, and not of herself. Now, we're not naive, and we know that this can serve the patient as a means of denial and as a vehicle for projection, but it is well to appreciate these qualities. Now, this is a form of resistance; where did it come from?

Discussant: From the therapist.

Discussant: She instigated it, but the therapist went along with it.

Langs: Exactly: it's an interactional product. The patient instigated it, and the therapist accepted it. Modifications in the frame can lead to *interactional resistances*—let that now stand as another thesis.

Discussant: The point I was making before was that she feels she's received a favor, something above and beyond the professional relationship, and that this was something that was personally done for her by the therapist.

Langs: Yes, that is the gift and special favor theme. Now with this element of the latent contents and functions of the adaptive context in mind, how would you see this material?

Discussant: Well, I agree that she is very distant; my guess is she's trying to protect herself from the therapist.

Langs: Yes, instead of responding with gratitude, she is erecting barriers—Type C barriers. Now, along the me/not-me interface, how do you hear this material? We have a chance here to conceptualize both projections and introjections.

Discussant: The patient talks about how both she and her friend are overwhelmed, and this could be based on an introjection of the therapist and the sense he gives of being overwhelmed.

Langs: Yes, this is a statement that the therapist has been experienced as unable to manage the situation, and that he was overwhelmed— his responses and alterations in the framework are seen as reflecting that incapacity as well as some degree of inner turmoil.

Discussant: On the projective side, the friend's difficulties with her parents and her depression after losing her boyfriend could represent something going on in the patient's life, and within the patient too.

Langs: Yes, that is indeed the projective side, and here it is also part of the "me" aspect of the me/not-me interface. We will need further associations in order to determine which side of that interface is more important for the moment, and whether both sides have some degree of validity. Remember too that after applying the interface, we must examine the communications for their truth and their distortion. These are our silent hypotheses. Let's hear more.

Therapist: She was afraid I was going to be angry at her. And then she talked about her friend getting better and worse. And what I said was, We're spending a lot of time talking about your friend and not much time talking about your feelings, about what it meant to you to refer her to me, and how you think I'm feeling about it. You started to talk about my being angry at you, but I'm not sure that we finished talking about that.

Langs: All right. Any thoughts about this intervention? How you would evaluate it? Remember, we're trying to develop principles about how we intervene when there is an issue related to the ground rules. Any comments?

Discussant: He is pointing out that she is making use of her friend as her topic of conversation rather than talking about herself. But in his comment he is not acknowledging the fact that he has, in a sense, given the okay or given permission for that to occur. So he's putting the responsibility on the patient without acknowledging his part in that development.

Discussant: No.

Langs: You disagree with that?

Discussant: Just with the emphasis. I don't think it's simply a question of shifting responsibility. The patient needs this defense.

Langs: Let's go back to basics. We want to evaluate each intervention presented in this seminar and the listening process it reflects. I think we can agree that there are *indicators* that suggest the patient's need for an intervention—her lateness, the sense of resistance, and in all likelihood the recent modifications in the framework. Now let's look at the intervention itself. We should always begin our evaluation by identifying the adaptive context. What is it here?

Discussant: The multiple alterations in the framework prior to this session, and her coming ten minutes late.

Langs: The *primary* adaptive context is usually an external stimulus from the therapist, though the patient may add *secondary* contexts. Here the primary context may be taken as the therapist's last set of interventions, to which the patient is now responding. Thus, her coming ten minutes late is not a primary adaptive context, but a secondary one, though it is a definite therapeutic context—an indicator for an intervention and what I term a *gross behavioral resistance*.

Having clarified that, I would agree that for the moment the adaptive context is a series of alterations in the framework, the most recent of which was the patient's telephone call to the therapist at his home and his agreeing to see the friend in consultation. Does this intervention attempt to deal with those contexts? And on what level is the material from the patient addressed?

Discussant: Manifest content.

Langs: Yes, this is an attempt to confront the patient with the manifest content of her associations, and to suggest, through a rather superficial Type One derivative, that the material implies an avoidance on her part of talking about herself and her anticipations of the therapist. The intervention lacks both an adaptive context and an appreciation for the therapist's contribution to the patient's resistance. It also defines the resistance in terms of manifest associations, rather than attending to the complexities of the listening process. The fact that the patient is talking about her friend may or may not constitute a major *communicative resistance*. We cannot decide the question without first identifying the adaptive context and determining whether this displaced material organizes as Type Two derivatives around the prevailing precipitant. Earlier we agreed that these derivatives were flat and did not illuminate the adaptive tasks the patient was working over; on that basis we decided that the patient was in a state of communicative resistance.

Next, the intervention does indeed place the entire responsibility for the avoidance-resistance onto the patient, and fails to treat these communications as interactional products to which the therapist has significantly contributed. It constitutes an implicit denial of the therapist's contributions, an aspect of this intervention to which I think the patient will respond quite strongly on an unconscious level.

Finally, the intervention reflects the therapist's belief that deviations in the framework are not especially pertinent to the patient's resistances and need not be rectified and analyzed before any other dimension of the therapeutic interaction. This is a very common way of thinking, and we will leave it to the patient's response to this intervention to decide whether it is valid or not.

All of this leads me to predict that, first, this intervention will not be validated by the patient through Type Two derivatives, and, second, eventually, in some disguised way, the patient will return to these frame issues in the unconscious hope of calling them to the attention of the therapist. She will work over the therapist's unconscious reasons for avoiding them as part of her own efforts to achieve the best framework possible.

You'll notice, too, in terms of the constructive nucleus contained in every erroneous intervention, that the therapist is in some sense attempting to explore the patient's reaction to his having agreed to see the friend in consultation. And while his approach tends to disregard the actual implications of this decision, and to consider only the investigation of the patient's intrapsychic responses—with some implication that they may well be primarily or entirely transference-based and distorted—it nonetheless does convey some concern on the part of the therapist about this particular frame issue. In fact, since we have a constellation of major adaptive contexts, we must be on the lookout for any tendency on the part of either patient or therapist to focus on one context in order to defend against the ramifications of another. For the moment, can anyone tell me the context that the patient has selected to focus on, and suggest another context that she may well be defending against? Then we'll see if this hypothesis is validated in the material that follows.

Discussant: Well, there were several contexts: the therapist's giving her directives, and his giving her his telephone number and revealing things about himself.

Therapist: But she's had that information since she first started in the clinic.

Langs: Yes, it is well to focus on the most recent and immediate deviations, and to then identify other alterations in the framework that are probably in the background. Nonetheless, since the patient did call you at home, this particular modification has come to the fore for the moment.

Discussant: There was also the therapist's decision to see the patient's friend.

Langs: Yes, these are all important contexts, but the situation is becoming interesting now. You're not mentioning a particular context that I think looms quite large here. The fact that you are all missing it is quite meaningful.

Discussant: Well, there are also the various third parties involved in the treatment.

Langs: Yes, but what else?

Discussant: Changing the appointment?

Langs: Well, it wasn't changed. What do you mean by changing the appointment?

Discussant: Seeing the patient past the appointed time.

Langs: Seeing the patient past the appointed time: yes. That happens to be the context I'm looking for. That's the one deviation that this patient and therapist are most likely to put into a bastion, and that's one alteration that I predict will be reflected in the derivative material. The patient will pick up on the therapist's decision to see the friend, and will use it, as she has, as a manifest theme designed to avoid what happened directly between them in the last session—his extension of the hour. Clearly, both contexts—seeing the friend and extending the hour—are of major importance, but I suspect now that the former will be used to cover over the latter.

Discussant: Why do you pick that context as the one that will be split off?

Langs: Try to answer your own question. Can you get a feeling for why?

Discussant: Well, perhaps it's more difficult for us to deal with our attempts to be nice to patients, and to realize that they're misguided so far as treatment is concerned. But there are a number of other major deviations that were mentioned.

Langs: Certainly there are a number of major fresh contexts, but I applied the listening process to the material from the patient and realized that she was prepared to work over to some extent the referral of the girlfriend, more so than the extension of her hour. Certainly, there are many unconscious responses that the patient has just begun to hint at in both of these areas, but in general the context that is most recent and most repressed will tend to have the greatest impact and the strongest implications for the patient's neurotic functioning. In addition, I strongly suspect that it was the extension of the hour that evoked both the phone call and the patient's lateness in this session.

Incidentally, the therapist's intervention includes a question, and you can see again how such an intervention directs the patient toward the surface of her thinking and away from derivative communication—the realm of expression most pertinent to her neurosis. And such derivatives would refer, as we know, not only to unconscious fantasies, but to unconscious perceptions as well—and to the introjects of the therapist to which they are related.

Discussant: In a sense, then, you're saying that this intervention actually supports the patient's resistances and even encourages her to avoid certain topics, such as the extension of the previous hour.

Langs: Yes, paradoxically, at the very moment that the therapist confronts the patient with a type of avoidance, he himself is engaged in an important form of avoidance. This is an invitation to a sector of misalliance and reinforcement of the bastions we have already identified. But in addition, when it comes to the framework, there's another aspect of intervening that hasn't been mentioned in this context and which the therapist did not at all consider. Who can identify it?

Discussant: Rectification.

Langs: Yes, rectification. A deviation in the framework is a reality filled with unconscious meanings and functions, and must be rectified in order to restore the positive image of the therapist within the patient's mind and to repair the damage done to the communicative properties of the field. The model of the therapist as simply an interpreter—and, often enough, as the interpreter of only the patient's unconscious fantasies—has to be changed, and this becomes quite evident when we discuss management of the framework. So, rectification has not been addressed here, and I hasten to add that it should always be undertaken on the basis of unconscious communications and directives from the patient. It is not a matter of arbitrarily following some principles that you believe in; the patient will lead the way, and should be allowed to.

There is yet another way of characterizing the therapist's contributions to the patient's interactional resistances: the altered frame has created a communicative field which fosters use of the Type C mode in this hour. In addition, it pushes the patient to express herself also through a Type B style of action-discharge and projective identification. Whatever the patient's own propensities, and they are probably along these particular lines, they are reinforced by the therapist's unconscious communications as expressed verbally and through his deviations in the ground rules.

Now, in terms of the patient's providing you unconscious directives as to the need for and how to rectify the frame, there is one way in which this patient began to do just that. It's a bit complex, but it will serve as a model. Can anyone identify it?

Discussant: She said, I'm sorry for being late.

Langs: Well, yes, you could sense something in that: be sorry, change your ways. But that's stretching things a bit.

Discussant: She came late.

Langs: She came late. Yes, I can see what you mean; I made a similar point earlier. She undid the gift of the extra time, which can be viewed as a form of rectification. What else?

Discussant: She mentioned that her friend didn't come for the consultation.

Langs: Yes. If this association is treated as a communication with derivative meaning, instead of a mere reflection of reality, it could be seen to express some notion that the session should not have been offered, and should not have taken place. I'm just using it as a model for the moment. You can sense it better by realizing that if this alluded to a make-up session, such as the one the patient had requested, and if the patient herself had not appeared for that hour, you could then more readily view it as a communication to the therapist that this appointment should not have been made. This would be present in addition to whatever resistances, anxieties, and unconscious fantasies and perceptions were involved in such an absence.

In principle, then, when there is an adaptive context involving an alteration in the ground rules, we listen to the material as Type Two derivatives, expecting it to contain both unconscious directives and models of rectification, as well as extensive indications of the unconscious meaning of the deviations—in terms of both valid perceptions and eventual distortions. Here we have seen two such models of rectification: one conveyed in the patient's behavior, the other in that of the friend and the patient's associations to it.

Discussant: For me, this is something that is going on in your own head, and not something that the patient is experiencing.

Langs: Well, we'll have to wait and see before deciding that point. I have tried to show you how I arrived at it by organizing this material around the specific adaptive contexts related to the framework. I am in no way suggesting that I would have intervened in this way to this patient at this time. I am sharing it with you as a silent hypothesis in need of validation and as a model for teaching. I think that we now need some more material.

Therapist: She said it was a good idea, maybe, for me to see her friend. She talked about her friend having the same problems that she has, but worse. She said: I at least know when I have a problem. She doesn't even seem to know that. And I have little problems.

Langs: This is an excellent example of the typical split in the responses of patients to deviations in the ground rules by the therapist. Consciously, she states that it was a good idea to see her friend—though she qualifies it with a maybe. Nonetheless, she accepts and appreciates it. That is the nature of her direct communications in this regard.

But then she moves on, shifting to derivative communication, and this is the part that has been missed again and again by therapists and analysts, who tend to confine themselves to the patient's conscious reactions to deviations in the framework. The patient then states that both she and her friend have the same problems, but that her friend is worse off because she doesn't even seem to know that she has them. What does this mean?

Therapist: Well, along the me/not-me interface, the patient seems to be referring to me.

Langs: Actually, she does not do it here along the me/not-me interface in the strict sense of that term, as using some communication related to herself to represent a primary meaning that pertains to you. Instead, she is doing it through displacement.

Therapist: Yes, I can sense here what you're getting at: The friend is a reference to me.

Langs: Yes, you were monitoring this material in terms of the friend serving as a self-representation for the patient, and as a means of projecting into her some of the patient's own difficulties. At this point, however, it seems evident that the friend is serving far more powerfully as a representation of yourself, as someone the patient unconsciously perceives as having difficulties similar to her own but being unaware of them.

We have made this formulation because our evaluation of your intervention, which serves as the adaptive context for these associations, was to the effect that you had failed to meaningfully identify the adaptive contexts—the alterations in the framework—to which the patient was responding, and that you had ignored the many issues in this area. We had considered your intervention essentially erroneous, a denial of your contributions both to the patient's resistances and to the problems in treatment. As I recall, I had specifically emphasized the denial of your own contributions to the patient's difficulties and had suggested that she would be especially sensitive to this aspect of your intervention. This is now borne out. And notice that this validation occurs in a form that corresponds with our definition of psychoanalytic validation: through Type Two derivative communications. Note the contrast: In terms of manifest content, the patient is supporting your deviation. But we have already established that this is not a form of psychoanalytic validation, though many therapists accept it as such. By contrast, in her derivative communications the patient is saying that your interventions reflect many serious problems of which you are unaware. Since these remarks are made in the context of a reference to a deviation, it is an unconscious commentary, in the form of Type Two derivatives, on those interventions—a commentary that for the moment appears valid.

Margaret Little stated, in 1951 I believe, that when the therapist intervenes in the service of his own countertransferences both he and the patient are alike; there is no essential distinction between them in regard to the crucial area of their psychopathology. This is exactly what this patient is stating in derivative form. So, unconsciously at least, she appears to be quite disillusioned that you are not aware of the implications of your unneeded modifications of the framework and their impact on her. Notice too that the patient is saying quite clearly, though indirectly, that these deviations are a reflection of serious psychopathology.

At this point I must apologize for being so candid and remind you that I am only translating the patient's unconscious communications into conscious statements. It is crucial that we do this, because, as you can see, this is exactly where the patient is at; it is what the patient is working over. Your problems are for the moment the main issue in this bipersonal field, and we cannot set them aside; the patient will certainly not do so.

Discussant: In her response to the therapist's intervention, it seems that she had not taken it in at all. He tried to point out to her, You're talking about your friend, rather than about yourself; but she goes right on talking about the friend.

Langs: Yes, that leads to an important point. The intervention was based on the naive notion that the manifest content of the patient's associations in and of itself is crucial and revealing in therapy. The patient won't accept that notion, and even though our evaluation of the adaptive contexts shows that up to this point in the session she had used the material about the friend to serve her need for resistance—and the therapist's—something quite different takes place after the intervention. Now the same type of manifest material—allusions to the friend— becomes the vehicle for meaningful derivative communication. Now, using the listening process we have developed, we would suggest that the patient is no longer in a state of communicative resistance, though a surface evaluation might lead to such an erroneous conclusion. Instead, you can see something about the *functional capacity* of the patient's associations: one moment a particular theme serves as a barrier to the truth, while the next moment it reflects the truth. You need the adaptive context and all of its unconscious implications—as well as a good deal of self-knowledge—to decide which is the case at any given moment.

Therapist: As part of rectifying the frame, you would make a referral to somebody else?

Discussant: Do you mean the friend or the patient?

Therapist: The friend. That was an unkind comment.

Langs: Actually it is quite possible that the ambiguity of your question reflects an awareness within yourself that the issue might well be raised as to whether this patient should be referred to another therapist in light of the extensive damage to this framework, or whether it would be preferable to secure this frame to the greatest extent possible and to continue with her on that basis. This is a question to be pondered, and one that is extremely difficult to answer.

For the moment, we have in this way at least recognized now that it is possible to so alter a therapeutic environment that both it and the therapy are beyond repair. There are deviations that cannot be entirely rectified, except for being certain to never repeat the deviation again. This means that their effects and the introjects derived from them cannot be very much modified, and this can lead to therapeutic impasses and negative therapeutic outcome. But, since we don't have a ready answer, we'll let this particular discussion stand at that for the moment.

As for the friend, yes, as I said last time, I would have immediately recommended that she be seen in an emergency room by another therapist if there were any possibility of suicide. In the absence of an acute crisis, I would not make a referral on the telephone. Based on past experience, I would expect to find that in the following session or two the patient would make it quite clear through derivative communication that the friend should find her own therapist through some other means than my making a recommendation, and that the patient was endeavoring to live out and communicate some rather disturbing underlying material in this way.

Therapist: I would never see this friend at this point, obviously. Even to make a referral, I wouldn't see her. Actually, in the intervening time, I found someone who was willing to see her.

Langs: Let's hear some more material.

Therapist: So she was talking about her friend not recognizing small, medium, or large problems. She said she was concerned about the opinion I might get of her from her friend. Maybe that would be a good idea, she said—that I get a different opinion of her. There was some sort of affect as she said, Maybe that would be a good idea—in terms of what you've been saying. And I tried to bring it back again: It seems that since I've been back from vacation a lot of things have happened here, and I think we're not looking at all of the effects they've had on your feelings about me and what you feel I'm thinking about you. I said, I think it started last session and I think it's still going on today.

Langs: I will only comment briefly at this point. Here the patient expresses a conscious concern about what the friend would reveal about her to the therapist—a communication that touches upon, but does not specify, the issue of total confidentiality. Certainly it reflects some type of worry within the patient about the conditions of her treatment and, perhaps, about the therapist's containing capacities as well.

Now, your intervention moves away from this manifest content and the context to which it is related, and shifts to the adaptive context of your vacation. It therefore offers a bastion in respect to these other contents, manifest and latent—even though you do, on the positive side, allude vaguely to "a lot of things that have happened here." In that way, you may unconsciously be attempting to afford the patient an opportunity to express herself in regard to the other deviations, but this effort is all too vague and implicit. You are intervening too quickly, directing her too much toward the surface, and introducing too many of your own associations. You are not letting the patient create the session and your interventions. Perhaps the major inappropriate thrust of your comment is to direct the patient away from the specific frame issues at hand, and I would expect her to respond to that dimension of your unconscious communications. On the one hand, you are offering interactional defenses and Type C barriers, and the patient may well accept them for a while; yet on the other hand, you leave enough room for her to get around to the frame issues, which I think she was attempting to do on her own. Let's see what happens.

Therapist: What I was trying to do was to move her away from the friend. I was feeling that the earlier discussion of her friend—while I'm sure it relates to what you said—was a replica of how she felt when she first came to therapy. I was trying to move her away from talking about the friend, because I felt that this was a reality which she would resort to in response to any intervention I might make. So I felt I had nothing that I could say to her about the friend at the moment, thinking of her as a representative of herself, as some sort of projection of the patient, which was the idea that I was working with. So I tried to exclude the friend at the moment, and I tried to get her to talk about all of the things that have been going on in the last week or so in therapy.

Langs: But much of your thinking was based on an evaluation of the manifest content, without an adaptive context and without considerations of derivative communication. In addition, in the presence of resistances the therapist should respond interpretively and not attempt to set them aside through a question. Your intervention becomes another directive to the patient, and unconsciously it also conveys a failure to understand the patient's derivative expression. Please continue.

Therapist: She starts talking about being exhausted and being at work all the time, and about that making it hard for her to get here. She knows that she doesn't talk about a lot of things, and that she has a hard time paying attention, thinking about how she is feeling, and being able to tell me about it. She said that last time—here you go—she felt I was appropriately strict about the limits I set: that I didn't give her another appointment.

Langs: Very interesting. So now she's coming back to the frame issue and in a very direct way. A striking form of validation: be appropriately strict.

Therapist: She said she felt that I was angry about her not coming on time, and she thought that I showed it in my telling her to take a cab.

Langs: So, she touches upon another deviation—your directives— and her conscious impression that they reflected your sense of anger. Isn't it interesting: once she returns to the framework issues she begins to deal with not one but two of them. It may well be that unconsciously she is feeling quite frustrated with your failure to listen to her, and to rectify and interpret the frame, so now she turns to these issues quite directly. As a result, we begin to obtain some validation of the hypotheses I have been developing about the ground rules, and while for the most part it takes a manifest form it evinces Type Two derivative qualities as well.

After all, she is now returning to certain specific framework issues, and to her direct appreciation for the limits that were set and her resentment of the directives you gave her; but she does not as yet approach the extension of the last session, or even her telephone call to you, for that matter. It's rather striking to hear her stress your adherence to the frame and to the time of the hour, as a means on the one hand of affirming the value of a secure hold, and, on the other, of blatantly denying the other deviation—the extension of her hour. It was that aspect that I had predicted she would wish to defend herself against.

Discussant: She also seems to be accepting the blame for whatever is going wrong. She says, It must be my fault. I'm tired. I'm not communicating well.

Langs: Yes, this is in part due to her own depressive propensities, and in part a result of the blame implicitly communicated by the therapist. Patients of this kind consciously accept all of the bad qualities of the therapist into themselves and berate themselves for everything, including the therapist's errors. This often goes along, as here, with some type of pathological idealization of the therapist. It is important in intervening to avoid joining the patient in such a sector of misalliance. Please continue.

Therapist: She says that she felt angry at me for giving her friend an hour that I said I didn't have for her, but she was happy that I hadn't babied her. She felt that was important.

Langs: So now she touches upon another deviation: your self-revelation about your schedule. And she comments further on your agreement to see her friend, now in terms of her own anger. But in addition she offers the first clear-cut model of rectification—don't baby her—and provide us in the process an insight into the meaning of deviations. She says it is best not to deviate because it tends to infantilize her, and as a result she will not be able to grow and resolve her problems. I would suggest that this infantilizing tendency is present in all deviations, and will attempt to validate that thesis as we proceed.

Her commentaries on your deviations have now become concentrated and quite perceptive.

Therapist: She said that it made her feel that I was kinder and more understanding in trying to help her with her friend, but she wished I had the time for her that I had given her friend, instead of having only the little time she had had on the day of her session. This was near the end of the hour, and I said, I think these issues are still very open for you and there are still a lot of feelings about what I did in giving your friend the extra hour, and not being able to change your hour when you asked for it. I think that there are other feelings that you have about the situation of calling me at home too, and I think we still need to talk about those issues.

Langs: Yes, so here you acknowledge that there are a number of unresolved frame issues, and even though you do so rather directly and based on the patient's—and your own—manifest associations, it should prove encouraging to the patient that you have become aware of the importance of these issues. In fact, I would expect her to take this last intervention, whatever its failings, as an unconscious acknowledgment on your part of the benefit of her curative efforts on your behalf toward the end of this hour. She insisted on bringing the framework issues into focus, and you have now, at long last, understood her need to work them over.

Notice, however, that you were unable to offer an interpretation, or to find meaning in the patient's derivative communications. In addition, you resorted to a directive once again, suggesting that the patient explore these areas in the next hour. You also decided to introduce the fact that the patient had called you at home as part of the unfinished business, and, much as I had predicted, you did not even allude to the extension of her previous session. Finally, not only is there no sense of interpretation as yet, but there is also no indication that you are prepared to rectify those aspects of the frame that can be corrected. Let's hear the next session.

Therapist: She comes late again, by ten minutes.

Langs: That's remarkable. She's still working over that ten-minute extension. She returns the favor twice over and this too can be taken as an unconscious directive that the framework be rectified. Perhaps the verbal material will elaborate in this direction, and if it does it will call for an intervention in which you identify the patient's unconscious communications to the effect that it is inappropriate to extend hours, after which you might indicate that you will no longer do so. So you can see that unresolved, unrectified, and unanalyzed frame issues continue to exert a major influence on this patient and her behavior. Please continue.

Therapist: She started talking about her job again, and how tired she was. This wasn't what she wanted her life to be like, she went on, and it seemed that all she was having was problems with her friends. She went on to talk for about five minutes about that same friend, about how angry she is that she's not doing anything to help herself. Then I tried to interpret to her: I said, You talked about how angry you are at your friend and how things are going so badly at the hospital; it seems that here too we've had a lot of problems. I said, I think it goes all the way back to your vacation. (She'd been on vacation the preceding month but hadn't left the city; she said she wanted to see me during those weeks, but couldn't call because she had to prove to herself that she didn't need me. That was said a month ago.) I said, I think that my going on vacation after that, and your problems with your friend, and my handling of that affair, have all brought up a lot of feelings about trusting me that I don't think we've really talked about.

Langs: Well, your heart is in the right place, and you are certainly making a noble effort to deal with the frame issues. The patient will appreciate that, though I think she will in addition be somewhat confused and dismayed by all that you have introduced on your own, without allowing her to lead the way. Certainly you have not followed the principle of allowing each session to be its own creation, and in addition you have moved way ahead of the patient in suggesting that the adaptive contexts for her unhappiness involve her vacation and yours. This shifts her away from the immediate unfinished business related to the more recent deviations.

What you said to her should have been formulated as *silent hypotheses* which should not have been imparted to the patient until supported by subsequent Type Two derivative communication and silently validated. That way you also avoid closing off certain issues and creating bastions and misalliances. You have also linked this material to the therapeutic relationship without having such a connection evident in the patient's own associations. That hypothesis should also have been maintained silently and validated before intervening. If you are right, the patient will give you relevant derivatives and will also provide you a bridge to the therapeutic relationship. Intervening prematurely generates pathological projective identifications into the patient which express your own defensive and instinctual drive needs, and now the patient will be under some pressure to work that over. Please continue.

Therapist: She starts talking about the hospital. And meanwhile, I'm getting really confused because she's not responding to what I'm saying to her.

Langs: Yes, but that's a way of experiencing how disconnected she is from your interventions—even though this is occurring on a manifest level and you have to reaffirm this impression in terms of derivative communication. Still, it should serve as a directive to reformulate, to change your way of intervening, and to discover why you're not connecting with her. It's also time to examine your countertransferences—a topic we will cover later in this course. Please continue.

Therapist: As she talked, I was feeling uncomfortable, because I felt I was trying to get her to rectify with me some of the things that have gone on in the last week, and she wasn't responding. She said she feels here like it is at the hospital when people are criticizing her. I said, I'm not aware of feeling critical of anything you've done. What I am aware of is that there are a lot of feelings brought up by this issue that I think we need to talk about.

Langs: Despite your good intentions you are having difficulty obtaining fresh derivatives related to these frame issues, largely because you are not waiting for the patient to develop the material but instead are intervening prematurely and directing her away from some of the most critical problems at hand. In addition, when a patient states that she feels criticized, it is a time for some self-analysis and a moment of extended listening. Do the indirect associations support this image she has of you, or do they suggest the presence of a distortion?

Your ready denial is, first of all, another modification in the framework, in that it is a self-revelation and a nonneutral, noninterpretive intervention. It is also a response to the manifest material, and is followed by an additional directive that the patient talk about issues that you wish her to discuss. It implies that you will accept little else. In itself, it seems to validate the patient's interventions to you about being overly critical, in that it implicitly blames the patient for resorting to avoidance, and this at a time when you yourself are significantly contributing to bastions and sectors of misalliance. Rather than understanding the conscious and unconscious implications of the patient's associations, you have responded directly to her comment and thereby shifted away from interpretive work. It is important, in attempting to rectify and interpret framework issues, that you not introduce new deviations which undermine your efforts and generate new issues in place of, or in addition to, the old ones.

Discussant: What would you have said when she said that she felt criticized?

Langs: I would have been silent and would then attempt to understand its implications through a brief period of self-analysis and through attention to the patient's continued associations. For us, the main point is that the patient began to shift away from direct framework issues to derivative communication. It may be that this would reflect major resistances and the communicative network would be unclear, but on the other hand it might have proven quite illuminating. It is rather typical, especially in the absence of rectification and interpretation, to find that the patient moves toward and away from the frame issues in alternating cycles. Let's see what happens here.

Therapist: She talks awhile about her friend again. She says that she thinks this was a bad thing that happened. If she wasn't going to come in, why did she ever get her to call me up. She herself is also concerned when she's late, worried about how I feel when I keep me waiting. I listened to that for a while. And I said something about it, which she acknowledged. At that point I was not working on what we've been talking about here, but I said something about the waiting time. That issue of time had come and gone over the last week. And I mentioned specifically that her first time back after my vacation I gave her the ten minutes that we both noticed—that she had looked at the clock at the moment the hour should have ended. And I then gave her those extra ten minutes, and there was all this other time on the phone; and then she was late for two sessions.

Langs: Again, I admire your determination to deal with the framework issues. You must have sensed something critical. However, you continue to do it at your pace, rather than the patient's.

Therapist: At that point I was more concerned about her feelings about me than about the frame per se.

Langs: But don't you see how the one is related to the other? Please do not misunderstand: I too am not concerned about the frame per se, but about how your management of the ground rules creates a setting for proper therapeutic work, and how it communicates aspects of your own inner state and functioning to which the patient will respond. In psychotherapy the frame has no meaning whatsoever as an isolated set of rules. It has meaning and function as a group of basic expressions from the therapist and, to a lesser degree, from the patient. Do not allow the framework analogy to suggest something wooden, inanimate, nonhuman, or isolated. The therapeutic framework is a very human frame filled with fluctuating unconscious communications. It is a way of holding the patient, offering him a sense of safety, creating conditions for open communication, and the like; let's keep that always in mind.

Therapist: Well, she agreed that these were all issues where time had been violated, and she continued to talk about it. I went back to it a second time, trying to get some more clarity. I don't know exactly what I said, but I mainly reiterated some of the points that I had made before and asked for more specific reactions. Oddly enough, at this time she denied that any of this was especially important, and I said, I think it is very very important. I then restated some of my remarks, though I left out the specific deviations. And she denied it again, adding that she didn't think that that was it at all. She said that she feels like she's wasting my time when she's late. And that's how the session ended.

Langs: Let's begin our discussion of this part of the material by identifying another deviation in the framework reflected in this material. Did anyone pick it up? (Pause.) Well, there was a distinct modification in neutrality. The therapist insisted that something the patient had said simply wasn't true. This is a not uncommon intervention; many therapists attempt to push aside what they believe to be denial on the part of the patient and thereby shift away from neutral interventions. However, since we do not have the specifics of what the therapist said during the last part of this session, there is little we can add for the moment. Somehow, largely by not allowing the patient to free associate and lead the way, and by imposing interventions that have qualities of pathological projective identification, the situation has become muddled. As a result the patient had virtually no opportunity to associate to the introduction of the additional deviations referred to by the therapist, and we are in no position to evaluate the extent to which his comments received validation.

After the therapist had denied feeling critical of the patient, she went on to talk about the bad thing that happened in therapy—his agreeing to the consultation with her friend. This is significant. In the adaptive context of the therapist's intervention, which included a modification in his neutrality, the patient was offering a commentary to the effect that this was a bad intervention, one that reminded her of other unneeded and destructive deviations by the therapist. That is a brief form of Type Two validation of the extent to which modifications in the ground rules do indeed have a destructive influence on the patient and the therapeutic situation.

Discussant: It's not really a deviation in the frame when an intervention is forced and is not responsive to the patient's needs.

Langs: Well, by my standards, the therapist makes use of neutral interventions geared toward interpretation and rectification based on the conscious and unconscious communications from the patient. Especially the unconscious. You are introducing the question of different types of deviations—say, those related to intervening as compared to those which involve the fixed frame. We'll clarify that distinction later on.

Discussant: For me, modifying one's neutrality means something like telling the patient something about oneself, something personal and private.

Langs: I think you are referring to anonymity rather than to neutrality. Certainly self-revelations can modify both anonymity and neutrality, but the latter is usually seen as pertaining to the nature of the therapist's interventions. And while there are questions of definition, of course, we can clarify that aspect as we go along. In the last analysis, neutrality must be defined interactionally in terms of whether an intervention from the therapist is derived as much as possible from the material from the patient—rather than from the therapist's own pathological needs—and the degree to which the patient experiences it in just that way. Much of this depends on self-knowledge, and on a monitoring of the patient's material for unconscious commentaries on your interventions.

Here, for example, the patient manifestly alluded to a modification in neutrality when she said she felt she had been criticized. Often such comments are made in derivative form and can be detected only if you are monitoring the different dimensions of the ground rules as reflected in the patient's associations and behaviors. However, beyond the inevitable gray areas in which there may be some degree of neutrality along with a bit of personal response, you can, by following the principles we are developing, readily eliminate many blatantly nonneutral interventions. Since we have a little more time, would you please present some of the next hour?

Therapist: She arrives punctually this time. But she goes to the bathroom first, so she's three or four minutes late.

Discussant: How do you know that?

Therapist: I saw her. I was out at the desk for some reason. She comes in and asks me for a prescription for pyribenzamine for her hay fever. I did not give it to her. I said, This is the first time you've asked me to write a prescription for you other than for the medication that you were taking for anxiety. (She had gotten some Valium when she first came in.) And she said, It's a pain to go to another doctor.

Langs: Let's make note: the patient began this hour with two frame issues—her lateness and a request for medication. Through the therapist's comment, we learn that the patient had received medication, from him, early in her treatment—another deviation from the standard framework. Psychotherapy is a verbal-behavioral-affective exchange, without the use of such ancillary measures as medication, hypnosis, or behavioral training.

I would suggest that it is no coincidence, in light of the many deviations in this framework, that the patient initiates hour after hour with framework issues. You can perhaps see how meaningful it is for her, and how intensely she is working over this area. I trust that you are beginning to experience some sense of validation in this regard.

In respect to her request for the medication, we have another opportunity to study a situation in which the patient attempts to modify the framework. Interactionally, this must be viewed as an outcome of the previous deviations made by the therapist and his failures at interpretation and rectification. On the patient's side, it becomes increasingly evident that repeatedly she seeks relief for her symptoms through *framework deviation cures*—efforts at symptom relief achieved through modifications in the ground rules. Of course, this too is supported by the therapist, who gave her Valium early in treatment.

Discussant: Since time is late, could you briefly summarize how you would have handled this request?

Langs: Well, here I think the therapist did all right. He neither refused nor consented, and that is the first rule: You either remain silent or suggest that the patient continue to say whatever comes to mind. That way you will soon obtain associations and derivative communications that on an unconscious level will always—I have not as yet seen an exception—direct you not to write out the prescription, thereby maintaining the framework. In addition, these communications will reveal the unconscious basis, meanings, and functions of the request for medication. You can then intervene largely by stating directly what the patient has said indirectly, and by following her implied directive not to write out the prescription.

My approach is even more neutral than that used by the therapist, who once again offered his own impressions without waiting for material from the patient. Still, in principle, he left room for the patient to associate, and that is crucial. It is most important that you not respond with a directive, and that you maintain your faith in the patient and her capacity for unconscious communication directed toward resolution of the dilemma.

Discussant: But what if the patient pressures you to write the prescription?

Langs: It depends on the context. If there have been some associations, I might be in a position to make an interpretation. If not, I can remain silent and expectant, or, if the pressure increases, I can invoke the fundamental rule. If the patient continues to press me, I might even indicate that something has evoked this request and has led her to attempt to exclude it from the flow of whatever is coming to her mind and from the therapeutic work. At worst this is a general interpretation with a mild implicit directive, and is probably the best that could be done under the circumstances. Here, the request is being used for Type B action-discharge, and there could be many reasons for that—in both patient and therapist.

Discussant: Most patients that I've come upon in these situations become quite insistent and ask for either a yes or no.

Langs: Some of that may derive from your own previous modifications in the framework. Remember too that what you are describing is a dual effort to alter the frame: first by requesting medication and second by attempting to evoke a nonneutral, direct response. It is also an effort to set aside the fundamental rule of free association. It is therefore an extremely meaningful communication, and should be treated as such. It should direct you to reevaluate the state of the framework, and to look for recent deviations or other errors in intervening which may have evoked this request and her insistence on it. Having done all of that, you can then turn to the patient and attempt to determine any additional factors in her behavior. Treat the situation as an interactional product of the bipersonal field. Here, if the adaptive context is the therapist's recent nonneutral interventions, with other deviations in the background, how would you characterize the patient's commentary?

Discussant: You have been giving me something that hasn't been helpful, so now give me something that will help.

Discussant: It is a request for a feeding.

Discussant: It's a demand of the therapist.

Langs: While this is all true, it does not capture a quality that I wish to emphasize in terms of understanding how patients perceive unneeded modifications in the framework. The patient is asking for a prescription of pyribenzamine. Does the therapist know the nature of her illness? Has he examined her? Is it appropriate for him to write such a prescription? I think the answer is obvious: he has no basis on which to prescribe for the patient, and to do so would be poor medical practice. But that's my point: as a commentary on these recent deviations, the patient is stating in derivative form that they constitute poor therapeutic practice and that they are quite inappropriate to sound therapeutic work.

Well, I see that our time is up. Thank you for your candid presentation. It certainly presented us with many deviations to consider, and I hope that it has generated some degree of conviction that the ground rules and framework are very important to your patients, and that they serve as important vehicles of unconscious communication within the bipersonal field. We still have much to learn about the nature and function of the framework, so I suggest that we next hear a first session so that we can talk about establishing the ground rules as a basis for a further consideration of their management. Thank you again.

Chapter Four

DEVIATIONS IN A FIRST SESSION

Langs: Today we will be hearing a first session. Let's get right into the material.

Therapist: This is a first hour with someone who was seen in a medical screening, in which I was a participant. I sat in on the screening, and after a discussion of the case I made an appointment to see this patient.

Langs: How interesting. In a way I take this as a commentary on the nature of psychotherapy: no aspect is uncomplicated. It turns out that there is a first session before a first session—that is, there was an initial interview before the one that you decided to present. Then let's take it from the beginning and see where it goes.

Therapist: The patient was first seen in a screening session for medical students. There were four students, a preceptor, and myself. The patient was self-referred, having called the clinic for an appointment. She was told to come in at a particular time, and I don't know if she had been prepared for a group screening or not. I think that the secretary tells the patient that she will have a screening appointment.

The patient came in and was interviewed by the preceptor in our presence. Both the medical students and I asked a few questions. The interview takes about an hour. Then the patient is asked to wait outside. She is told that it will take a little while to discuss how best to help her. There is then discussion within the group present, including myself and a social worker. In the course of the discussion, I decided that I had time available to see her; she seemed like a reasonable psychotherapy patient. So, I then went out and told her that I would like to make an appointment to see her.

Langs: You told her this in the waiting room?

Therapist: Yes. I can't remember the exact words, but I think I told her that I'd be able to meet with her—or I'd like to meet with her—and that I would like to make an appointment with her. She agreed and left. Later that week, she came at the appointed time.

Langs: Does anyone want to comment?

Discussant: What's to say? I don't think any of us like the way screenings are handled in this clinic. I don't know what else to say.

Langs: What don't you like about it?

Discussant: For starters, I don't like the fact that there's a group interview. And I don't like the fact that things are left sort of unclear.

Langs: Anything else? In terms of our approach to the study of the ground rules, and to our continued use of the listening process, can anyone add anything or offer an anticipatory comment?

Discussant: For one thing, no ground rules have been established as yet.

Discussant: I expect to hear something from the patient that refers to the group nature of the interview, in terms of the lack of confidentiality and of a one-to-one relationship—the violation of the very private relationship with the therapist.

Therapist: That's what I was trying to say about this interview. I think it's implicit that when somebody calls a psychiatric clinic they expect to be seen by a therapist in a one-to-one situation, with some privacy. And what happens is that patients come in and they are seen by several people, and there's an exposure involved in that; and of course, it's the only way a person can get into the clinic.

Langs: I think of Searles's paper (1959) on the efforts to drive the other person crazy: that very much characterizes the clinic policies at most psychiatric and therapeutic centers. Still, in terms of the ideal standards of the framework, this initial interview violated the canons of the one-to-one relationship, privacy and total confidentiality, and neutrality—this is, after all, a situation in which the therapist personally selected the patient as her own. And if we put all of your comments together as a kind of prediction, you are suggesting as a group that we will hear responses to these adaptive contexts in the material we are about to hear.

This will prove helpful in respect both to the framework and to the listening process as it is carried out in the first hour. You will perhaps be able to see that even in an initial session, so often thought of nondynamically and as a matter of formal history-taking and evaluation, the patient is responding already to sequential adaptive contexts and is communicating dynamically in the context of the therapeutic interaction. And if we are right that patients are extremely sensitive to the basic hold and framework, then we would expect this patient to respond, both directly and through derivatives, very intensely in this area.

Discussant: Another aspect to this is that the initial interview was carried out primarily by a person other than the one who is now going to be the treating therapist. After all, even if there are other people present in an interview, it's possible for a patient to have a certain feeling of relatedness to the person who is most involved with her. So this too is another adaptive context. The attachment that the patient may have developed to the initial interviewer is shattered, and she has to begin again with someone else.

Langs: Yes. We are attempting in advance of this hour to identify various unconscious communications inherent in the format of that first session. These are different dimensions of the primary adaptive task confronting the patient, and should prove useful in organizing and understanding the material we are about to hear.

Discussant: In terms of latent material, I would think that the patient might have some feelings about the fact there was a group of doctors sitting around. And of all those doctors, you are the one who has chosen her. It lends itself to all sorts of fantasies that they were fighting over her, but that you specifically chose her for your own. You fought to get her as your patient.

Discussant: It could be the opposite too, though. She could fantasize that the therapist got her through default.

Therapist: Also, I was the only woman in the room. I don't know if that will be pertinent, but it might be. It could give all of this a homosexual tinge.

Langs: Yes, and we must add another break in privacy and confidentiality: the therapist arranged this appointment in a public place, the waiting room. Now, two questions: can anyone add to this characterization of this adaptive context—this first contact—and which of these dimensions do you think will have the greatest impact on the patient?

Discussant: Well, she must have known right away that they were going to be discussing her.

Langs: Yes, and that is an excellent means of evoking what I have termed *iatrogenic paranoia* (Langs 1974).

Discussant: Her presence in the group interview was a kind of exhibitionistic display that could have gratified certain unconscious needs and defenses of the patient.

Langs: Yes, but notice: as we go on surmising, we are paying less and less attention to the other side of the situation.

Discussant: Do you mean the patient's feeling of shame or her rage at being exposed?

Langs: Well, that's more about the patient. I'll ask it directly: what about the therapist? (Pause.) It's voyeurism—the therapist's voyeuristic needs.

Discussant: The patient was on display. In addition she had no say as to who her therapist would be.

Langs: Yes, she was placed in a totally helpless position: accept the therapist or else. Not that she was told this directly, but it's quite implicit to the transaction involved. You can imagine the pressure that the patient felt, finding herself in a group interview, dealing with a therapist who selects her, and—what else?

Discussant: The fact that she was seen by students.

Therapist: I can't remember how they introduced themselves— they may have said student or doctor—but because of their age the patient may have sensed something in that regard.

Discussant: Even before she was seen, she has to fill out a financial statement and the fee is set by a secretary.

Therapist: Yes, she did fill out a form with the secretary.

Discussant: It seems to me that the presence of third parties to treatment and that discussion in the hall will have the greatest effect on the patient.

Langs: Yes, that's quite perceptive. I suspect that the patient would be able to forgive a great deal, but the fact that the therapist, at the very first moment of the one-to-one relationship, initiates therapy in a public setting will leave an intense residual effect. This is now the therapist expressing herself, and it will be quite important to the patient.

Discussant: But at this clinic we never really have a clean first session with the patient. The procedure is for someone else to screen him and for the contact to begin with a secretary.

Langs: Yes, and these policies have never been examined carefully, because there has been little serious consideration accorded the nature and functions of the framework of treatment.

Discussant: Do you accept every patient that you see in consultation into treatment?

Langs: Yes, every patient who wants to enter therapy or analysis with me. In general, the fee is not an issue since virtually every patient I see can afford at least one session a week. I do not see a patient in consultation with the attitude that, depending on what I hear, I may or may not accept him or her into treatment. As I told you before, I offer a consultation only when I have open time. As a physician, I feel a commitment to treat whoever seeks my help; I believe that is a standard that should be maintained. Deviations in this regard generate negative introjects and very destructive images of therapists, which have detrimental effects on patients at a time when they are often in great need, quite confused, and filled with mixed feelings—positive and negative—about going into therapy.

Discussant: How do you handle a call from a personal friend; do you see him in consultation first?

Langs: Definitely not. I keep such conversations as brief as possible, call someone I feel to be a competent colleague to see if he has time available, and then call back the friend with a specific recommendation.

Discussant: Is there any understanding about what you will or will not tell the person you're referring them to; what sort and amount of information you will pass on?

Langs: I will give no information. I'll simply tell the colleague that I have a friend who wants to be seen in consultation. Period. I don't let friends in such circumstances tell me about their problems to begin with. If they start to, I say, Look, don't; it's not necessary and it won't be constructive. You tell me that you need help; that's all I have to know.

On a related topic I have touched on already, I very much prefer that referring physicians and therapists simply give me the name of a potential patient; no other information at all. It is sometimes difficult to train colleagues to adhere to such a policy, especially other therapists and analysts, but you should really not be a party to modifications in the confidential relationship between the patient and the referring physician; in addition, having prior information about a patient modifies the basic frame at the outset. Sometimes it means having secrets, knowing things the patient does not know you know, and this not only is a burden but may also contribute to a poor hold.

Discussant: I sense you would not accept a referral from one of your patients. To my knowledge, that is common practice among therapists.

Langs: Yes, while I have not done a survey, I share your impression. And of course you are right. When patients suggest such referrals I analyze them and uniformly find them filled with unconscious meanings that could sabotage both therapies were the referral accepted. The same applies to referrals from a former patient since there, first, you are not in a position to analyze the meanings of the referral in terms of its unconscious implications and functions, and, second, you are dealing with an important residual therapist-introject which could take on a very destructive coloring if such a referral were accepted.

Discussant: While we're on this subject, I gather that in principle we should not take notes during sessions or make use of a tape recorder.

Langs: Yes, such practices modify the frame in detrimental ways. They imply breaches in privacy and confidentiality, and we will soon learn more about the consequences of such deviations.

Discussant: I think that you mentioned in one of your papers that you do not make use of your own clinical work in the books and papers that you write.

Langs: Well, I can see from these many questions that there are an almost endless number of potential modifications in the framework, and I appreciate your need to clarify some of the seemingly finer points. I have indeed taken such a position and do maintain, in every sense of the concept, total confidentiality in regard to my work with patients. That is one of the reasons for recording these sessions: since you are making this material public, in the professional sense, as part of your efforts to learn, I feel that once I disguise such material it is not unreasonable for me to make use of it in order to teach a broader audience. As I have said before, only your own therapy or analysis and the need to present material in order to learn how to do psychotherapy can be a sound basis for modifying the ground rule of total confidentiality—and in each of those cases, even though the alteration in the framework is justified, it will have some detrimental effect.

I must tell you that there are many analysts who do not understand why I will not present my own clinical work. Perhaps once they read this, my position will make sense to them, because their mistrust of me and their confusion is based on a failure to understand the implications of the framework and my commitment in that regard.

Discussant: Wouldn't you modify the framework when there's a threat of suicide or homicide?

Langs: Well, now you are getting to an issue that has recently been brought up in the courts and that has, I believe, led to laws that force such deviations in the framework—at least under conditions of homicidal threat. Clearly the law does not understand the nature and functions of the framework, or attorneys and judges would recognize that under such conditions the most destructive measure that a therapist can take would be to modify the total confidentiality of the therapy. The same applies to situations in which a patient is suicidal; deviations under these conditions can be disastrous.

At times, of course, you can be faced with a terrible dilemma, especially when the risk of suicide or homicide is great. However, in my experience, this will almost never happen in a treatment situation where the framework has been held secure. There is a point at which the framework has to be sacrificed in order to maintain the life of the patient, but even then there will be disturbing consequences. Since you do not have specific material related to these issues, let's not attempt to pursue them further for now, and reserve additional questions for moments when the clinical material directs us to them.

Discussant: I would like to ask one more question: When the patient asks directly if I am in supervision, should I indicate that I am?

Langs: Here too we should be working from clinical material. That way you would see the kind of adaptive context that evokes such a question, and could discover that it most often is a response to other deviations in the framework. In such a situation, the analyst should not respond directly, should maintain an analytic approach, and should interpret the implications of the question in the proper adaptive context. This should be done in a manner that implicitly accepts the existence of supervision rather than denying it. It is also important not to attempt to assure a patient who is being supervised of the total confidentiality of the therapy; I've seen that done with disastrous consequences, because it is a blatant lie. With patients who become preoccupied with the presence of a supervisor—often because the therapist has acknowledged this fact—I think it best to discontinue the supervision and thereby offer the patient the opportunity for a therapeutic setting not inherently and grossly disrupted.

Discussant: I would expect to lose many referral sources if I didn't call them back after seeing a patient and tell them briefly something about the consultation, or at the very least, my conclusions about the patient.

Langs: Well, I think that there you must make a choice between your commitment to your patient, who needs a situation of total confidentiality and privacy, and your own need to cater to the inappropriate needs of your colleagues as a means of building a practice. Patients suffer considerably from coincidental comments from an internist, for example, based on what he has heard as feedback from a treating psychiatrist; often this can seriously damage the framework and the therapeutic hold.

You are quite right, of course. There are many physicians who have a great need to know their patient's secrets and to be in control of both their patients and those to whom they refer them; they will not tolerate the absence of feedback. I make every effort to educate potential referral sources, but there is no doubt that in terms of present-day practice my approach is quite unusual; it evokes considerable suspicion and resentment. Still, my first commitment is to my patients, and I really will not compromise. I will try to explain myself to a colleague, but I will not exploit a patient.

Discussant: So you do not call back a referring physician after seeing a patient?

Langs: No. I tell him in advance that if a patient calls me he can be certain that I will see the patient in consultation (assuming that I have time available, which is the only basis on which I would accept the referral), and that he can be assured that the best possible disposition has been made. If he is so curious about whether the patient has come into therapy, he can ask the patient rather than me. In fact, such queries are very reassuring to the patient since through them he can begin to sense that he does indeed have a therapeutic setting in which total confidentiality is assured. And I can tell you that I learned all this from patients whose therapy I supervised and from my own patients—both through Type Two derivative validation based on interventions in keeping with these principles and from supervised work that disregarded them. But I sense again that we are too distant from the clinical material, and I would like to get to this first hour that isn't really a first hour.

Discussant: Well, if I may say this, we have been taught that in situations where a patient has been admitted to the psychiatric service at this center, it is vital to call the therapist who has been treating the patient outside the hospital, whether in our clinic or privately. On principle we ask the patient's permission, and uniformly it is granted. What do you think of that?

Langs: Look, I'm afraid that you will really learn very little from this type of discussion. There is a characteristic split in the attitude of patients toward deviations: consciously, they are quite accepting, while unconsciously they are furious. The detrimental implications are legion. So if you were to present the material from a session that followed such a request, we would expect to find a host of derivatives which contain the patient's unconscious response to the deviations—not unlike those we have already anticipated for this particular situation. Allow us then to develop some specific clinical observations as to how patients respond to violations of confidentiality and the like; then you will be in a position to decide for yourself, based on a full application of the listening process, whether it is better for the patient and the therapy to adhere to the frame, or to make selected deviations based on the patient's conscious consent.

I'll just add this: I think that it is a myth that information from other therapists have any value whatsoever for your treatment of a patient. As I have tried to demonstrate, there is only one critical fulcrum for the therapeutic process: the present therapeutic interaction and its extensive unconscious implications. I am well aware of many rationalizations for such deviations, but once you have learned that a secure frame is far more crucial than any bit of historical or clinical data, you will respond differently to such situations.

Now please allow us to hear this presentation. The prediction is that frame issues will be quite crucial for this patient in this session and that we will be hearing a rather strong derivative response. Please continue.

Therapist: Okay. She's a twenty-six-year-old white female, Catholic, single, the second of five children, and a student in her first year of training at another teaching center. She is learning to be an occupational therapist. She is the first patient that I had in the outpatient department, and she is still with me. (Laughter.)

Langs: We can only hope that she doesn't pick that up too quickly.

Therapist: She came into my office at the appointed time. Besides my own I have two chairs in the office, one next to my desk and the other at the far end of the room. She sat down in the one at the far end of the room.

Langs: That's an interesting commentary; who will briefly formulate the implications of this particular behavior?

Discussant: It reflects a lack of trust.

Langs: How quickly you move to Type One derivatives, rather than beginning with an adaptive context and attempting to develop more specific implications and Type Two derivatives.

Discussant: Well, based on that whole experience of the screening, and the way it was handled, the patient may have felt angry and in need of some distance, or mistrustful.

Discussant: Perhaps this is the patient's response to the therapist's failure to observe total confidentiality; she became mistrustful of the therapist.

Langs: Yes, but try to be even more specific. (Pause.) Well, we take the patient's decision to distance herself from the therapist as a commentary on the specific modifications that already exist in this framework, and their unconscious implications. She is saying that in general when the therapist modifies the frame the patient needs distance and appears mistrustful and fearful. We will, of course, have to validate these initial silent hypotheses in the cognitive material, but we should be free to experience such impressions as long as we plan to validate them.

I have several additional associations, as I would term them, to this behavior. First, this is the first session in which there is a one-to-one relationship and relative privacy. The patient seems fearful, and may have some sort of unconscious perception of the therapist's anxieties as well. The presence of third parties to that first interview could justify such perceptions, and for all we know the therapist may indeed have conveyed some of her own anxiety since this is the first outpatient she has treated in this clinic.

Second, I think back to our comments concerning the therapist's decision to select this patient for therapy. I suggested at the time that the patient might find something seductive in this approach, and that this would evoke a need for distance. The actuality of choosing a patient as your own is in some sense an acting out by the therapist, an action that evokes an action response in the patient. This is a principle that we identified during the first presentation and that is quickly validated here. With both these formulations, we will need the verbal associations for additional validation. For the moment, the best hypothesis seems to be that the patient has responded to multiple modifications of the framework with a kind of modification of her own—choosing to sit at a distance from the therapist rather than being next to her desk, which would be the expected position. Please continue.

Therapist: She began by asking me if I were a resident.

Discussant: Well, that's a frame issue.

Langs: Yes, so it is. Had this not been a first hour—or sort of, at any rate—I might have predicted, as I did with the previous case, that once again, because of the many deviations, this hour would begin with a frame reference. In a sense, I have learned something new: that frame issues take precedence over virtually everything else, including the initiation of treatment through the presentation of the patient's complaints. This should serve as a reminder that when a patient begins the session with a reference to the frame or an impingement upon it, it is in all likelihood his way of telling you that there is a significant frame issue outstanding. Here you have one of the most significant blind spots among analysts and therapists. It is, in a sense, a sanctioned channel for countertransference expression, and I suspect that much of this is based on the fact that, almost without exception, analysts and therapists themselves obtain treatment in a therapeutic environment with significant modifications in the frame. But let's not wander too far from this clinical material. Who would like to attempt to formulate this first verbal communication from the patient?

Discussant: Well, there seems to be little doubt that the adaptive context, or series of contexts, relates to the many deviations in the framework that took place in that screening interview. Perhaps the patient is now expressing some of her doubts about the therapist in response to that experience.

Discussant: She's also asking the therapist to immediately modify her anonymity.

Therapist: In addition, she really put it to me. I felt very helpless and quite uncomfortable.

Langs: Yes, this is all quite pertinent. Let me organize it a bit. With just this single verbal communication, there is much that we can develop in the way of silent hypotheses. In addition we can sense a number of qualities of the framework that we have not yet identified— though here too, we may have to state these as tentative formulations.

To begin with the therapist's comment to us just now, I think we have some initial cognitive evidence to verify the therapist's subjective experience that the patient was creating interactional pressures, projective identifications, through which she was placing into the therapist her own sense of uncertainty, anxiety, and undue pressure. But these efforts did not begin with the patient; rather, they were initiated by the therapist and her associates when they exerted such interactional pressures on the patient in that first hour. So we have here a sequence of unanalyzed projective identifications, beginning with those in which the therapist participated, and evidence that the patient introjected that first experience in terms of a predominantly hostile interactional projection which she was unable to metabolize insightfully, and which she almost immediately reprojected into the therapist. And while we still need cognitive validation from the patient's material, this is an attractive hypothesis that is also in keeping with the material of the first presentation.

So if I may generalize this tentative finding in terms of the framework, this material suggests that deviations in the ground rules constitute pathological projective identifications, into the patient, of aggressive and erotic contents, and that in addition they constitute an essentially disruptive, pressured projective identification which evokes considerable anxiety. To state this a bit differently, deviations significantly impair the therapist's containing functions, and/or arise from such impairments, so that the patient feels frustrated in respect to her own needs to have her projective identifications contained and metabolized. In addition, these alterations in the ground rules create conditions under which the patient herself is used by the therapist as a pathological container. Deviations in the framework very powerfully impair the therapist's hold of the patient and reflect countertransference-based disruptions of the therapist's holding capacities. Here, in a single association, the patient expresses her own sense of being held quite poorly and feeling threatened, and she in turn responds with a disturbance in her own hold of the therapist. Thus, rather than beginning this session in a cooperative manner that in some way implicitly supports the therapist, the patient refuses to maintain a sense of hold in response to the previous deviation. Instead, she refutes these implied wishes of the therapist and, as a result, the latter feels quite disturbed.

So, we have here a communication which tells us something of the nature and functions of the framework, and the consequences of its disruption. We also have Type Two derivative validation of our earlier hypotheses regarding the prior deviations. Characteristically, the patient does not address them through direct comments, but indirectly, by raising another frame issue. Here too we have a rather characteristic response to alterations in the ground rules by the therapist: patients often ask direct questions under such conditions, attempting to evoke not only modifications in anonymity, but nonneutral interventions as well. You can see too, as with the previous presentation, that modifications in the framework significantly disturb the *therapeutic alliance*. And this is so despite the fact that many therapists invoke deviations with the conscious intention of furthering the alliance.

Finally, you can see how this initial, seemingly hostile question is an interactional product, and in part an introject of the therapist's own inadvertent, hostile, and seductive approach to the patient. If you think of this as a resistance, it is an interactional resistance, and as an interactional product it conveys the very toxic qualities of what the patient herself had experienced earlier.

Discussant: Is it your impression that the patient is attempting to draw the frame issues to the therapist's attention? I would think so. I also wonder if this is not an effort to give the therapist a dose of her own medicine, by showing her just how it feels to experience these deviations in the ground rules. It also occurs to me that the patient might be trying to find some kind of relief by getting rid of her own tension, by placing it into the therapist.

Langs: Those are all excellent silent hypotheses. It may well be that this is, in part, the initiation of an unconscious effort to cure the therapist and, in addition, to evoke a framework deviation cure for the patient. I am quite impressed with the richness of the formulations we have been able to generate under these conditions. That too is a tribute to the power and deep implications of the ground rules—the frame. Please continue.

Therapist: I did not record whether I answered her question was I a resident, but my best guess is that I probably said, Yes, I am. Then she asked if I was in analysis.

Langs: So, you acknowledged that you are in training and thereby specifically modified your anonymity. Clearly you were under a great deal of pressure and I think that we can all both sympathize and empathize with you—this is quite a dramatic beginning to your career as a therapist treating outpatients. Then the gratification of one deviation stimulated the wish for another: the question as to whether you are in therapy. This too, however provocative, may well contain an unconscious communication regarding the patient's appreciation of your need for help, and it may be followed by unconscious therapeutic efforts on her part.

Under conditions of this kind, patients can, in derivative and direct ways, be extremely hurtful and disturbing. We must remember that this is in large part based on an introject of the unconscious communications conveyed in your own participation in the screening interview. The patient is deeply embroiled in a disruptive spiraling communicative interaction, even though you yourself might like to disown its more destructive attributes. These are painful confrontations, but I think that they can be the foundation for a far better perspective on the nature and function of the ground rules, and this can perhaps lead to a far more sensitive and nontraumatic approach to patients in clinic settings. There are major conflicts of interest in having to teach medical students and residents, while having to maintain a basic therapeutic commitment to patients who are suffering and in need of help. It is really beyond the scope of this discussion to propose reasonable compromises, but this patient makes it incumbent upon us to recognize the issues and to address rather than ignore them.

Discussant: You made the comment that the therapist had modified the ground rules regarding her anonymity. However, the ground rules haven't been established yet, so how can this be viewed as a deviation?

Langs: There are two answers to your question: First, that these are ground rules that will soon be established, and to have modified them in advance of their definition is essentially disruptive. But, second, I have proposed the thesis that the ground rules are not of the therapist's making but rather are an expression of the patient's conscious and unconscious therapeutic needs. On this basis I have proposed that there is an implicit set of ground rules that is best for all patients. On some unconscious level this patient very much senses that this is the case. Remember too that the ground rules are conveyed not only through explicit statements, but implicitly as well, through your actual behaviors and responses, including your reactions to pressures from the patient to deviate.

Discussant: Is there anything we can read as background for what we are discovering clinically?

Langs: The literature is summarized in my 1975 paper on deviations in technique (Langs 1975c) and updated in chapter 16 of *The Therapeutic Interaction,* Volume II (Langs 1976c). Since much of it involves my own work, I would prefer that you wait several more weeks before pursuing these studies and their historical antecedents. I would, however, like to mention a paper by Viderman, written in 1974, entitled "Interpretation in the Analytic Space." His use of a spatial metaphor for the analytic situation, comparable to the bipersonal field concept, sensitized him to the boundaries of that space and therefore to the frame. He explicitly stated that every patient brings his own framework into treatment, based on a variety of unconscious needs and fantasies as to how he wishes to be—or not to be—cured. Much of this framework is infused with the patient's psychopathology and its past history, and with wishes for noninsightful symptom relief through misalliances and bastions. And you will find it rather characteristic for the opening phase to include impingements by the patient on the therapist's framework, as well as efforts to introduce his own deviant frame. Proper management and interpretation of these attempts provide the patient constructive introjects and cognitive insights. This is by far the best means of establishing a sound therapeutic alliance. I have found that often the patient's frame is designed to avoid the experience of, and analytic work with, the psychotic part of the personality. The patient dreads the necessary therapeutic regression, and there is a good deal of evidence that analysts and therapists are similarly motivated in respect to making unneeded deviations.

Returning to the immediate clinical situation, the therapist herself—partly for reasons beyond her control—has created a deviant structure for the initiation of this treatment, and now the patient tries to modify the framework even more. They both seem now to be experiencing the disturbed therapeutic environment. We may view the patient's questions—Are you a resident? Are you in analysis?—as an unconscious effort to exploit and extend the therapist's deviations; as an interactional product it contains important inputs from both patient and therapist. Under these conditions there would be some difficulty in sorting out and analyzing the patient's own needs for a modified frame. Nonetheless, in principle it is best to respond to these initial questions with silence or, if pressured by the patient, with a brief explanation of the fundamental rule of free association. You should indicate to the patient that you may not answer her direct questions, and could then add that it will be helpful for her to say whatever comes to mind so that the two of you can begin to understand what she is feeling and thinking.

In general, when a patient begins a session by talking about emotional difficulties and shows a ready capacity to free associate, I do not indulge in such explanations and clarifications. If they are called for by the communications from the patient, I make them as brief as possible. Very rarely do I repeat or clarify them. My basic attitude is to allow the patient to create the session, and I respond even in a first hour with as much of an interpretive approach as seems necessary or possible.

But the patient's opening questions have another source, I suspect, that we have not specifically mentioned. Based on what we heard of the evaluation session, I suspect that the patient was asked a multitude of questions, many of which she experienced as discordant with her own therapeutic needs.

Discussant: Yes, as I remember that meeting, a number of people did ask her a variety of questions.

Langs: So, the patient immediately conveys the qualities of disturbance and pressure that these questions created for her. Let's state that as a tentative hypothesis.

Therapist: I didn't know how to handle questions like this and felt very confused. I felt that answering her questions would be a modification in the framework, and I certainly didn't want to offer her, right off the bat, an implicit model—a faulty one—of how I wanted to work. At the same time, I felt that the patient is entitled to know who I am in terms of my professional qualifications. Perhaps they are implicit in my working in a clinic situation, but I did feel confused and experienced a dilemma.

Langs: Yes, and it is a dilemma that many therapists experience. But I think that today this patient will help you to move a long way toward resolving it, through an extensive commentary on your decision to answer her questions directly rather than having treated them as derivatives to be organized and understood around a particular adaptive context. After that, of course, you could have then decided on the best possible intervention. It is my belief that statements regarding your qualifications would have little direct meaning to this patient, and would entail disruptive self-revelations. Your actual management of the therapeutic situation and interpretations of the material from the patient will implicitly and explicitly convey to her everything she needs to know about your capabilities. This implies too that maintaining the frame and an interpretive approach is far more in the interests of the patient and her therapeutic needs than your informing her of your training status or whether you are or are not in treatment. As you yourself said, letting her know implicitly that this will be an interpretive psychotherapy and that everything will be listened to as material for eventual interpretation will—with extremely few exceptions—provide the patient something far more helpful than beginning this hour with further deviations in the framework. These remove you even more from the interpretive approach and from providing the patient the secure hold needed in order for you to do insight psychotherapy.

Remember too, in light of our earlier discussion regarding the opening moments of this session, that these are, on one level, projective identifications from the patient; she has a strong and immediate need to test out and experience your containing capacities. Can you handle her interactional projections, metabolize them toward insight, or do you respond with uninsightful projective identifications of your own, thereby continuing this rather vicious circle of projective identifications and projective counteridentifications (Grinberg 1962)?

On the object relational level, the patient is attempting to evoke devalued images of yourself and will be sensitive to your processing in that regard. Cognitively, the issue is whether this material will be handled symbolically and processed toward interpretations, or whether it will be answered noninterpretively, thereby shifting the therapeutic work into another modality. So you can see there are no innocuous questions in psychotherapy. Your handling of framework issues communicates a great deal about yourself, generates complex introjects, but also can be taken as an opportunity for insightful therapeutic work.

Discussant: But supposing the patient pressured you to respond?

Langs: Supervisees often ask that question, while patients very rarely create such pressures. As I said before, my initial intervention would be silence. If the patient pressed me, I would invoke the fundamental rule and ask her to continue to say what comes to mind. If there were further pressures, I would point out that she should indeed ask questions or communicate whatever her thoughts and feelings might be, but that she will find that I may not respond directly to her questions. If the pressure continued even further, I would shift to the best interpretive intervention that I could offer, to the effect that the patient seems to be under a great deal of pressure, that perhaps something has set this off, and that it would be well, as a means of attempting to understand these pressing queries, to see where her thoughts and feelings go. In this way I convey something of the implicit and explicit ground rules concerning how we will work, and am already attempting to rectify the framework, which has been so badly damaged in the evaluation session. Based on my clinical experience, the patient would respond positively to such efforts, and might herself rather quickly shift from a Type B communicative mode to a Type A. The main exception here would be Type B patients, who are more interested in destroying rather than creating a sound therapeutic situation; they would prove quite refractory to such an approach because it involves confronting the terrible, psychotic part of their personalities. But notice that long before you directly structure treatment toward the end of a typical consultation session, you are already deeply involved in delineating the framework.

Discussant: How do you state the fundamental rule?

Langs: For the patient who is speaking freely, I will not state it explicitly. Here, where the patient very quickly deviates from the fundamental rule of free association, I would simply suggest to her that she say whatever comes to mind—that this is how we will do our therapeutic work. Keep explanations to a minimum in your delineation of the ground rules; excessive verbiage is bound to be self-revealing and nonneutral. Later, as the material permits, we might offer an occasional interpretation related to efforts by the patient to modify the framework, especially where there have been deviations to which the patient is responding.

So I would stick to the basic principles of intervening and if possible wait for an adaptive context to be represented before commenting, although I might play back derivatives in the absence of an allusion to a powerful context of which both the patient and myself could be aware. Here, under continued pressure from the patient, another possible intervention would be to point out to the patient that she has begun this hour by raising questions about your background and qualifications, and then waiting for an answer. You might add that she seems quite concerned and that something must have evoked this. You'll notice that here I am playing back the sparse derivatives available from this material and hinting at the presence of an adaptive context—in this situation, we have postulated that they pertain to the many deviations that occurred in the evaluation interview. If we are correct, the patient would soon get to them on some level.

Discussant: In a sense, these aren't ground rules. I would reserve that term for rules that are stated explicitly at the very beginning of treatment. Right now you are involved not in making direct statements, specific delineations, but in demonstrating these rules through your behaviors and interventions. They seem to be implicit axioms of therapy rather than ground rules.

Langs: It is important that you not think of these rules in terms of their formal delineation; rather, you should recognize that they are conveyed both directly and indirectly. We can call them ground rules, axioms of therapy, the framework, the setting, the means by which a therapeutic space is created, the holding environment, the background of safety, or whatever. By any name, they are a dimension of the therapist's communications which creates an atmosphere—a set of conditions, boundaries, and rules—which define the nature of the transactions that will take place in the treatment setting. They are a set of relative constants—a background—which may come to the foreground from time to time, as they have here, and which offer an important means of effecting inner structural change when managed and interpreted properly.

The manner in which they are explicated unfolds in the course of the therapeutic interaction, especially in the first session and in the opening phase. Some ground rules need never be stated, while others must be carefully defined. We will cover this last aspect of the framework when we approach the end of the present therapeutic hour. If there are no further questions, it would be well to hear a bit more of this session.

Discussant: I think that there are a lot of important issues here. If we think of these tenets as ground rules, might we not, if the patient asks us, Are you a resident, respond in some sensitive way, such as by saying something like, While you may expect that I am going to answer all of your questions, I actually will not do so.

Langs: I think the point here is to not think so exclusively in terms of rules. Once you do that, you are likely to believe that flexibility is best and that the patient is far more important than the rule. While the latter statement is certainly true, there need not be any opposition between the patient's needs and your therapeutic approach. Approaching the framework in terms of dos and don'ts is somewhat manipulative and rather flat. Instead, recognize that these aspects of intervening are a basis for a therapeutic hold, a means of establishing a space or setting in which the patient can safely communicate the derivatives of her neurosis as a basis for its analytic resolution. You are endeavoring to provide the environment within which implicit positive introjective identifications will take place: first, on the basis of the very management of the framework; and, second, through the therapist's valid interventions, a part of whose validity consists in their not being contradicted by modifications in the basic setting.

Discussant: It seems to me that to respond initially with silence would run the risk of infuriating the patient, so that it might make the situation even more threatening.

Langs: Well, we are moving more and more away from clinical data and into speculations based on imagined manifest contents and the therapist's inner needs. It is here that we must return to clinical material and allow the patient to answer these questions; otherwise it becomes a matter of arbitrary debate. I sense too that the frustrations inherent to these ground rules are creating difficulties for you. Stated as a principle to be validated, it is well to be as indirect as possible early in a first session, and to become explicit only as the patient expresses a need for clarification by blocking further communications and associations.

The therapist thereby has ample opportunity to hear derivative communications from the patient, and to enable these seemingly innocuous or surface questions to be revealed as filled with unconscious meanings. Such work also quickly reveals many conscious and unconscious fantasies within the patient as to the nature of the framework he prefers, as well as his view of the process of therapy or cure. Remember: direct answers to questions tend to acknowledge the importance of manifest over latent content, and to cut off the patient's further communications in terms of the unconscious meanings of the pressures being directed toward you. The patient quickly shifts to responding to the new adaptive contexts you are offering through your noninterpretive intervention, and the situation becomes complicated and difficult to sort out. Think too of maternal care: sometimes appropriate frustration is vital to growth and is therefore the only truly human response.

Discussant: But if a patient comes in and asks a direct question and you don't answer it or at least clarify the basis for your failing to do so, it seems to me that you are responding in a hostile way to the patient. After all, the patient knows that therapy is different from what takes place outside, but doesn't know in what way. For him it's an entirely new situation. And I think that the therapist therefore has a responsibility to explain the differences.

Langs: This is what happens when we develop a discussion without material from the patient. For example, I do not share your impression that patients know that therapy will be different from outside relationships, for two reasons: first, because patients wish to make therapy similar to the outside in order to protect themselves and maintain their neurosis, and, second, because in the hands of many therapists the differences that you vaguely allude to are not defined and actualized.

Please do not misunderstand. I am proposing an approach that begins with silence and then, with patients who need it, extends into a clarification of a particular ground rule, often in a manner that promotes exploration and a definition of the treatment situation in which insight, the search for the unconscious truths within the patient, assumes top priority. You must, as therapists, be sensitive to the patient's needs, but you must also distinguish their conscious demands from therapeutic requisites. It is not a hostile act to attempt to create a sound therapeutic setting and approach, nor is it destructive to be appropriately frustrating. These are delicate matters, to be handled with utmost sensitivity. Certainly insensitive adherence to ground rules can be an expression of countertransference-based aggression, but we must remember that surface kindness can also serve countertransference needs.

Perhaps I can clarify this by pointing out that under these conditions the issue is often not only whether the patient is working over previous deviations by the therapist—as is the case here—but also, and more fundamental, whether truth therapy or lie therapy is to take place. The patient is quite divided in this regard and, all too often, the therapist is as well. As a result the patient would like to create her own set of ground rules and transactions as a means of avoiding disturbing inner truths. To the extent that the therapist shares such anxieties she will be inclined to enter into a sector of misalliance and permit an implicit definition of the treatment situation that detracts from the unfolding of derivative communication and responsive interpretive work. It is important to appreciate these underlying issues, and they take on meaning as the patient continues to associate and, in her own derivative language, addresses such issues. We follow the lead of the patient, but we do so in a manner that understands these clues in depth.

Discussant: I am not clear on one point: I take it that you don't attempt to explain to the patient something about how therapy itself works.

Langs: You're right; I don't. Such explanations are actually a rather extended projection by the therapist, and really have no substantial meaning since the answer lies in the actual unfolding of the transactions between patient and therapist. I attempt to keep all explanations to a minimum, and to eliminate those that have no true function in defining the therapeutic situation. On this basis the patient develops a secure therapeutic alliance and a sense of trust, while explanations and self-revelations only create mistrust and sectors of misalliance. But, once again, we need some clinical validation of these principles.

Discussant: There seems to be considerable difference between pointing out to the patient that something has prompted her to ask a lot of questions, and explaining the ground rules, including the fact that you will not be answering all of her questions.

Langs: But you see, this is an unusual first session. We already have strong evidence of powerful adaptive contexts that the patient has not as yet mentioned, and you are in a unique position this early in treatment to intervene with a form of playing back derivatives around those adaptive contexts in an effort to have the patient become more and more aware of the fact—and I believe this will indeed turn out to be a fact—that she is responding to these earlier deviations.

In consultations that have not been contaminated, this would not likely be the first communication from the patient. If it is, I would quickly review the framework—the nature of the consultation, the first telephone call from the patient, and other possible countertransference-based contributions—and only then would I attempt to understand the basis within the patient—paranoid trends, for instance—for this type of opening communication. My approach is far kinder to the patient, in that it does not immediately hold her entirely responsible for these questions, nor does it view them as a grave indication of necessarily severe pathology, though it leaves this open as a possibility. With a patient I had never seen before, it is extremely unlikely that I would know the hidden adaptive context, and I would therefore have no choice but to respond with some clarification of the related ground rules.

In principle, even in the first hour, interpretive intervention is to be preferred to a clarification of the ground rules when the patient is communicating in a manner that seems both internally and inter-actionally meaningful. This is another aspect of setting the tone of treatment. But you do so with tact and sensitivity, and with full recognition of the limitations of the available material.

I keep trying to come back to this session. For the moment I am thinking of the patient's second question, as to whether the therapist is in treatment. This could be a derivative of the initial screening inter-view, and the patient's continued anxieties that her therapy would be made public and would lack total confidentiality. If you respond directly to the manifest question, you are suppressing and devaluing the derivative communications contained in this query. As you can see, the way in which you respond will contribute to the conditions of treatment and to the nature of the communicative interaction.

Discussant: Some patients make a major issue of your failure to answer their questions.

Langs: A manifest issue, one that has led to many noninterpretive responses and blind alleys. I am attempting to show you that in this session these questions are associations with particular functional capacities and latent contents. Next week, when we hear further material, we may have an opportunity to validate my formulations and for you to see how deeply meaningful these questions actually were. If you treat these questions as manifest content without an adaptive context and fail to apply the full listening process to them, you are left without interpretive recourse—you don't understand the unconscious level of communication. This is a very common failure in listening and understanding in therapists who work with borderline and psychotic patients, who focus on the patient's conscious demands and see them as a reflection of their ego dysfunctions, and who do not approach such material in terms of Type Two derivatives organized around specific, interactional adaptive contexts.

And you can see from your questions that, in general, therapists are invested in noninterpretive work and surface listening, and that we have to overcome a major sense of resistance if we are to learn to listen in depth and to develop the skills through which we can create a truly valid therapeutic setting. Inherently, we prefer to gratify directly and even inappropriately, rather than limit, frustrate, and create a sound therapeutic alliance and environment. As therapists, there is much we must work through to do this kind of therapeutic work.

Well, I see that our time is up. We will continue with this session next week.

Chapter Five

A SHIFT FROM AN INSECURE TO A SECURE ENVIRONMENT

Langs: We begin today without desire, memory, or understanding. In that regard, it occurs to me that it is quite unlikely that anyone in this seminar would fail to almost immediately recall the segment of this session that was presented to us last week. As we get ready to listen, is there anyone who does not remember the presentation? (Pause.) So it is unanimous—we all remember something.

Discussant: For a moment my mind was blank, but now it's coming back to me.

Langs: Well, without alluding to it until we hear more of the session today, this gives me an opportunity to point out that your recall of the previous session is influenced by the patient, the nature of the material, and factors within yourself. In this case, the patient has made such a powerful impingement that I doubt anyone would fail to remember it. I usually enter a teaching seminar such as this virtually blank in terms of the material of the previous week, and recollections develop as I listen to the new material. Here, as soon as I began to speak, I could remember the opening of the session that we are hearing. So, please continue now from where you had left off.

Therapist: I'll just start with the beginning of the sentence, because I didn't really complete the sentence.

Langs: Okay, we're not going to be purists about it. (Laughter.)

Discussant: But suppose we don't remember the previous session?

Langs: Then take that as an interactional block and attempt to sort out the factors in its development. The stress is on passive as compared to active recall, and on the search for the unknown in lieu of being wedded to what is already known.

Discussant: In that case, does it really matter what happened in the session before? I mean, is there any importance to continuity or, if not to continuity, to knowing what happened in the previous hour?

Langs: It is remarkable to see how confusing a new clinical principle can be. It distracts us from the central focus of this part of the course, but I will briefly state this much. Entering a session without desire, memory, or understanding (Bion 1970, Langs 1978a) is a matter of approaching each hour with the openness and attitude which will best serve both therapist and patient in the pursuit of the unknown—new truths about the patient's unconscious conflicts, fantasies, and the like.

As such, this principle implies neither that the transactions of the previous hour are unimportant nor that there is a lack of continuity to the therapeutic experience. All of this is accepted as present, but the stress is on a more passive form of recall in which the links to the past hour unfold through a silent working over of the patient's present associations, rather than through deliberate rote memory. This gives you an opportunity to experience the degree of continuity or discontinuity, and to allow each session to be its own creation. It is not a disregard for the conscious and unconscious actualities of the transactions of the previous hour, but an attempt to open oneself to new and unexpected qualities that may have been missed in the previous hour or that emerge in the present.

Discussant: To know the adaptive context for the patient, which is virtually always the therapist's last significant intervention, you would have to know something about the previous session.

Langs: Yes, but we would like that realization to unfold at the behest of the patient's present associations. Allow them to shape your memory, to generate reasons to intervene that are based on the patient's therapeutic needs rather than on your own idiosyncratic wishes. Allow them to provide you new elements of understanding.

We keep veering away from this clinical material. I suspect that that too is a reaction to the intensity of the pressures this patient has created on the therapist and on the members of this seminar. Still, it is time to hear more.

Therapist: The patient wanted to know if I was in analysis. And I believe I asked her why she wanted to know, though I'm not sure of this. She said that if I was in analysis, it would make me more sensitive to understanding her feelings and also the countertransferences involved. She was also concerned that I might be leaving the clinic in one or two years. I said . . .

Langs: Before we hear your intervention, are there any further thoughts about this material?

Discussant: In itself, I find this very unusual. I can't remember a patient whom I've seen here who spontaneously asked me if I'm going to leave in one or two years.

Discussant: Or if I'm in analysis.

Discussant: Or refer to my countertransferences.

Langs: What would you postulate to account for this?

Discussant: We talked about it last week. And I think this adds to our discussion of how her questions were related to this patient's feelings regarding the initial encounter in the waiting room.

Discussant: I think that's one factor. I think there's also the variable that she's obviously much more psychologically minded than the average patient.

Discussant: Not necessarily; this could reflect a lot of intellectualization as well.

Discussant: Or it could be that there were so many deviations already. So now she's asking, How many more are there going to be?

Discussant: She's concerned about her therapy, and how she's going to be treated. She may also have reason to be concerned about the therapist's countertransferences—given what she experienced previously.

Discussant: These questions could follow from a psych course. A lot of referrals of students follow such courses.

Discussant: What I mean by psychologically minded is someone who is familiar with psychiatry or psychology.

Langs: Well, there have been many comments and I will try to clarify several of them. First, regarding psychological mindedness, this is usually meant to imply someone who is inclined toward self-awareness and self-reflection. It also is used to suggest that someone can work well in therapy because he is inclined to think things out and explore them, rather than acting blindly.

Now, in evaluating these particular associations, it may well be that there are extraneous factors, such as having attended some sort of psychology course or knowing someone in the field. And while these possibilities should be taken into account, they should not substitute for more dynamic considerations, such as those related to the unfolding therapeutic interaction. I would tend to agree with those who view these continued questions and comments as, in part, further efforts to create anxiety and pressure within the therapist, and to evoke further deviations through self-revelations. In addition, they are designed to clarify the nature of the framework. They are derived from unknown factors within the patient, and partly known factors from the therapist, among which her participation in several deviations of the basic standards of therapy loom large.

This patient is remarkably focused, both manifestly and latently, on framework issues. She wants to know if the therapist is in analysis, implying concerns about confidentiality and about the therapist's capacity to manage this treatment and her own countertransferences. By implication she is suggesting that the therapist is in need of such treatment, and it will be easier for us to discuss this aspect here since many of the deviations were not the therapist's responsibility, but the result of clinic policy. But let me emphasize two things: first, therapists can exploit such policies for their own countertransferences, as when this therapist arranged treatment with this patient in the waiting room; second, in your work with your patients, you must accept full responsibility for these policies and must not attempt to "split the transference," as it has been termed, laying off onto the clinic the destructiveness implied in these deviations and presenting yourself as blameless. This kind of good-bad split interferes with the communicative properties of the field, the patient's opportunity to work through these issues, and a great deal more.

This patient wants to be understood and wants to be securely held. She seems to have some knowledge of clinic policies, and anticipates a forced termination that will further disregard her needs. So, while I would not answer personal questions, I would eventually clarify the framework of this treatment, and this would include a specific statement as to its duration if indeed this has been predetermined. I have seen many presentations in which this was not done, and it evokes intense rage and paranoid responses far more destructive than a patient's reactions to time-limited treatment—which itself has significant detrimental consequences.

We now have considerable evidence that the patient is responding quite intensely to the earlier deviations in the hypothetical ideal framework—which may now seem to you far more real than theoretical, considering the extensive needs of your patients. For now, I would continue to listen and hope that the patient will in some direct or derivative way get around to the specific adaptive context of one or more of the previous deviations, at which time I would be in a position to interpret her unconscious perceptions, and perhaps fantasies, in terms of Type Two derivatives around each precipitant. In this very specific way you would be dealing with early resistances: first, by ceasing to contribute to them; second, by securing a new holding environment; and, third, by interpreting the implications of the prior deviations. A sound therapeutic alliance is likely to follow. She could begin to trust both you and the setting.

Notice too that my initial silent hypotheses regarding the patient's reactions to the modifications in the frame are being supported by the patient's continuing associations; I suspect that we will have even more validation as we continue. Incidentally, her question about whether the therapist is in treatment, and the remarks about her counter-transferences, implies another concern within this patient. Can anyone identify it?

Discussant: The question of how much is coming from the thera-pist's own treatment and how much from herself. This would be similar to the patient's attempt to sort out how much is coming from clinic policy and how much from the therapist's own problems.

Langs: Yes, exactly.

Discussant: Some of this could perhaps be heard as her having been threatened by the interaction that had taken place the previous week. I'm just wondering if she's not trying somehow to put the therapist in a sort of one-down position: Look, let's get it straight. You're a patient also, if you're in analysis. And you have problems as well. She may have felt in a very vulnerable position last time, being put through all of that. And now she wants to turn the tables and put the therapist in that position.

Langs: Yes, here you are formulating what could be the therapist's metabolization of introjective identifications that the patient is now projectively identifying into her. You also imply efforts by the patient at role and image evocation. Some would see this as an attempt to turn a passive threatening experience into an active attack, and view it as an identification with the aggressor. You might also consider this as an attempt to evoke an empathic response in the therapist by showing her just how it feels to be assaulted in this way.

There is still more here: the patient also wants to know if the therapist can contain, metabolize, and interpret these pressures, and thereby maintain a state of what Bion (1970) has termed *reverie*. Finally, we can again state that the patient has experienced a very inadequate and traumatic hold, and that she is, in turn, refusing to provide the therapist an adequate hold; instead, she is offering a disruptive hold of her own. The material also implies a lack of trust, a disrupted thera-peutic alliance, and an absence of any background of safety.

In all, then, while you can identify various aggressive and protec-tive motives in these questions, I think that you can also readily see unconscious efforts at cure, at properly defining the framework, and at assisting the therapist to establish a secure and safe frame. It is important to appreciate the underlying positive intentions—which I hope to validate as we go on—especially since the therapist is bound to feel threatened and even angry in response to these apparently hostile and embarrassing questions. That very feeling of anger should be processed as an interactional product and traced out for sources within the patient and yourself. The use of the me/not-me interface could help you understand something of the patient's sense of anger, and could lead you to trace out its sources as well.

Therapist: I am mindful of how I selected this patient, and on one level I felt that she was now putting me through a kind of selection process. It helped me see that there was something provocative in what I had done.

Langs: Yes, by treating this material along the me/not-me interface, and in terms of therapist introjects, you can accept these communications as some type of unconscious confrontation and interpretation. While there are undoubtedly projective aspects as well, you must consider the introjective side first. It is essential to apply the full listening process to this material and to understand it in depth in terms of the prevailing adaptive context. It is important that you not shift to the manifest level, either in understanding or in intervening. Incidentally, another way of maintaining a perspective on this material is to recognize how on one level there is indeed a sense of attack, while on another the patient provides you a number of alternatives. Implicit to the question as to whether you will see her for just a year or two and then leave is the idea that you are, after all, in training, and that much of what is happening is the fault of your instructors and of clinic policy. In a sense, then, she covers the gamut of immediate possibilities: your behaviors and deviations last time could have been based on countertransferences, poor instruction, or insensitive clinic rules—probably all three.

Discussant: In addition to the quality of making the therapist feel what the patient was feeling, I thought of these first associations as an effort to punish the therapist.

Therapist: You may be right: I certainly experienced interactional pressures very strongly.

Discussant: I experienced a catch-22 type of situation when the patient asked if the therapist was in analysis. If the therapist says yes, then the patient can claim that the therapist has her own problems to work out. If she says no, the patient can claim that people who are in analysis are much more sensitive. There is no safe answer, and the therapist is on the spot whichever way she goes—unless, I suppose, she can find a way to offer an interpretation.

Langs: Yes, these associations are difficult to interpret, and they tell you something of the communicative field when the frame is modified. But in addition, this very active and sensitive discussion enables us to identify many of the qualities of the patient's experience under conditions of an altered frame: nothing is certain, no one is safe, everyone is under pressure, and there is even doubt as to how to handle what is being expressed. The deviations constitute countertransference-based projective identifications and, as I have noted, disturb any sense of a secure hold.

And isn't it rather striking that you are all able to quite readily identify many of these qualities by empathizing with both the patient and the therapist? This material is strongly evocative of sensitive responses that are far more readily identified than the complexities of the usual listening process and how to intervene. There is something immediate about all of this and quite fundamental. That too tells you something about the framework itself.

I believe that it will be possible to show you that there are elements of this kind inherent to every deviation in the framework. Although the blatancy of these deviations and their being connected with the initiation of therapy account for much of the intensity of this patient's responses, I nonetheless postulate that patients universally react strongly to all deviations—major or minor—at any point in treatment whatsoever.

Discussant: For me, this experience has provided real insight into the meaning of projective identification. I can experience how those earlier deviations placed something powerful and disruptive into the patient, who is now attempting to put it back into the therapist. And

I think that the patient's verbal associations confirm my subjective experience, in that they reflect her considerable doubt concerning the competency of her therapist and the definition of the framework.

Langs: Yes, but I must add that I would prefer more definitive cognitive validation before feeling that an interactional formulation such as the one you just offered has been confirmed. We want to hear something about someone attempting to disturb the patient or someone else, something about disruptive pressures, and the like. But for the moment these communications are largely being enacted, to some extent on both sides.

Discussant: Since you are attempting to generalize from this experience, I think it should be pointed out that this group of deviations was overtly humiliating and constituted a major invasion of the patient's privacy and need for confidentiality. Most deviations do not reach these proportions or have these qualities; more typical are situations where a session is extended or the patient is given an extra hour. This is therefore an extreme situation.

Langs: It is, however, from these extremes that we learn a great deal about the more subtle deviations. But there is another point: already we have an opportunity to see that there are certain meanings, functions, and effects that are probably shared by all modifications in the ground rules, but that in addition there are highly specific effects consequent to each type of deviation and to its emergence in a particular therapeutic interaction.

Our experience in this seminar confirms this point. The deviations we saw in the previous presentation (chapters 1–3)—the telephone conversation, the directives, the third parties to treatment, the extension of an hour, the offer to see a friend of the patient—created a sense of chaos, pressure, and helplessness in both participants, effects that are in some ways comparable to those we are observing here. These are the general effects.

On the other hand, the extension of the hour had seductive and infantalizing qualities, while the directives to the patient on the telephone were hostile and manipulative in addition. These are examples of the effects specific to *types* of deviation. The use of the present patient for teaching purposes, with its violations of confidentiality and privacy, appears to have the same seductive, hostile, and infantalizing qualities, and seems to have certain additional features in common with the first therapist's decision to see his patient's friend, as well as with the presence of the secretary. In each instance the patient sensed the lack of privacy, and felt used and betrayed. There is in these two cases some similarity in these more specific effects, because the deviations are similar in kind; but each case has in addition its own very singular qualities related to the ongoing communicative interaction.

We have seen too that deviations in general appear to reflect pathological projective identifications into the patient, as well as impairments in holding and containing capacities, and serve as a means of limiting and disturbing the communicative qualities of the bipersonal field and blurring the boundaries between patient and therapist. In the first case we saw, the deviations seem to have been a major dimension of the ongoing therapeutic interaction, with their own highly specific features, and to have become a vehicle for countertransference-based expression undoubtedly related to the specific meanings of the therapist's relationship with his patient. In the present case, however, the deviations are embedded in an interaction in which teaching needs are placed above those of the patient, and the therapist's need for a first patient became an important factor. In addition, the therapist's relative inexperience, which led her to speak to the patient in the waiting room, also looms large. These, then, are deviations exhibiting the rather more general qualities pertaining to types.

So, in summary, the effects of deviations group themselves in three classes, which I list in order of their increasing specificity: those shared by all deviations; those characteristic of a specific type of deviation; and those stemming from the fact that every deviation is part of a particular therapeutic and communicative interaction between patient and therapist. As we go along, we will attempt to sort out these three levels, since they each infuence in a somewhat different way your management of the framework and your interventions in this area. In time, through the presentations in this seminar and through your own clinical experiences, which you are now in a far better position to understand, you will be able to develop your own catalogue of the effects of various deviations. But in addition to these broader effects, you should always remain open to the specific implications of the deviation at a given moment in each unique treatment experience.

When we turn to consider the patient's responses to deviations, here too we will find a certain commonality of reactions in all patients—a first level of reaction. Then there will be a second level, determined by the specific nature of the deviation and the particular resources and psychopathology, present circumstances and past history, and other individual factors within the patient. And, third, there will be a group of determinants definitively related to the patient's experience of the current and past therapeutic interaction; these derive from an intermixture of countertransference and noncountertransference inputs from the therapist, and lead to both transference and nontransference reactions in the patient.

This last classification leaves room for valid conscious and unconscious perceptions and reactions within the patient to a particular deviation in the framework. At the same time it enables us to consider a given patient's special sensitivity to a deviation, his personal interpretation of its unconscious meanings, and the presence of possible distortions in his reactions—these based on his psychopathology.

For example, in this situation another patient might come to this first hour with the therapist and be profoundly depressed. She would have taken in all of the badness as introjects with which she became identified, and have turned all of the rage and hostility against herself. In general, patients and all human beings have two choices in this respect: introjective or projective, depressive or paranoid, self-castigating or attacking. Beyond that, another patient might exploit the unconscious sexual qualities of the situation and begin with intense conscious or unconscious homosexual fantasies, or be in a homosexual panic in response to the violations of her confidentiality and the relative lack of boundaries between herself and the therapist.

Still, in each of these reactions there would be elements of truth and valid unconscious perception and introjection, as well as elements of psychopathology—e.g., distortion and projection. However, in accordance with the principles we have been developing, we must first know the nature of the unconscious communications contained in the deviations, and thereby trace out the patient's valid and appropriate unconscious and behavioral responses; after that we can attempt to comprehend and interpret the pathological elements.

You can see now the complexities of the spiraling interaction between patient and therapist, with inputs from each, with evocations and responses that have to be sorted out, and with complex unconscious communications. We need to apply the listening process quite carefully and to test many silent hypotheses under these conditions before we can arrive at a balanced appreciation of the actualities and distortions on both sides. And the management of the ground rules is a central element of this interaction.

Now, returning to the session being presented, it appears that many of the initial deviations were imposed on the patient, and that she did little to evoke them. The therapist, then, did a great deal to stimulate the patient's first communications in this session. The patient herself uses the deviations as an opportunity for threats and pathological projective identifications into the therapist, but also attempts to generate an interaction in which rectification and interpretation related to framework issues can occur. We deal always with interactional and intrapsychic amalgams. All right, let's hear some more.

Therapist: I don't feel like going on. (Laughter.)

Langs: But this material is taken from a therapy that you conducted when you were very young and inexperienced.

Therapist: I told her that I would be here all of this year.

Langs: Well, it might have been better to say simply that you *plan* to be here all of this year, rather than putting it in a way that tries to guarantee the future. But in general you acted correctly in defining the time limits of treatment as they existed. I must add, however, that in principle I seldom do this in response to a direct question and without first affording the patient the opportunity to continue to free associate and to provide us material that can reveal the unconscious implications of the question. I do this even with a question that I plan to answer and that appears quite realistic and valid on the surface. We are attempting to create conditions under which the patient's unconscious fantasies, introjects, defenses, processes, and the like can be explored and interpreted, and there should be no exception to this approach. A question can be answered in the context of an interpretation if it is called for, or can be responded to after exploratory work has clarified its unconscious implications for both patient and therapist.

Discussant: I see this response as the therapist choosing to defend herself, which is understandable. She was being assaulted, punished, and put under pressure, and in defense she says, Well, I'll be here for the rest of the year.

Discussant: Why not view it as giving the patient some information, a statement of fact?

Discussant: Well, as Dr. Langs has pointed out, such an approach does not permit exploration and understanding. It denies unconscious meaning.

Discussant: The way she put it she was emphasizing the sense of continuity, rather than the time limit and the ultimate destruction of treatment.

Discussant: It seems to me that there is no question that the patient had put the therapist under attack. This question is part of that attack, and usually there are elaborate fantasies behind such threats. I can see now that, in addition, there can be powerful realities filled with unconscious meaning behind an attack like this, such as the framework deviations we have been discussing. But if the therapist immediately responds and defines the length of treatment through a blunt reply, it cuts off any revelation of the source of these questions and of what underlies the attack—reality or fantasy.

Langs: In terms of the listening process, such a reply deals with the material at what level?

Discussant: Manifest content.

Langs: Yes, and you are all quite right: when a therapist feels attacked and under pressure, she may often respond either defensively or through counterattack, rather than through an effort to understand the adaptive context and the Type Two derivatives contained in the patient's communications. These pressures make it quite difficult to maintain neutrality and lead many therapists to rationalize, almost as a reflex, their nonneutral interventions. And as we have been seeing, therapists have a need to express themselves in nonneutral ways, although I am quite pleased to see that the discussion here is already shifting somewhat away from efforts to justify unnecessary deviations in technique toward attempts to formulate sound reasons for maintaining the frame.

Here, then, is another situation in which you will be implicitly expressing and shaping the nature of the transactions between yourself and the patient, especially through maintenance of the fundamental rule of free association and the use of neutral, interpretive responses. Eventually you will show the patient that certain questions must be answered since the basic therapeutic situation must after all be defined; but you will also be showing her that this is done only in rare instances, and even then after exploration. I would say that only questions about time limits on treatment, the frequency of visits, your fee, and your vacation schedule merit direct response. I can think of little else that would call for a definitive answer even after exploration; most other questions are to be taken as free associations to be understood and interpreted. And all questions should be subjected to the listening process without exception.

Technically then, the therapist could be silent initially. If the patient continues to press the issue, you might invoke the fundamental rule by explaining that it is best for the patient to continue to say whatever comes to mind before you proceed to clarify this aspect of treatment. Under further pressure, it might be possible to interpret the patient's concern about the boundaries and definition of treatment, linking this to the adaptive context of the initial deviations. Under unrelenting pressure, after having attempted the best possible interpretations, I would clarify this aspect of treatment for the patient.

So it is in regard not just to resistances in general, but to frame issues in particular, that interpretive and management responses are likely to occur in the first hour. We might now state another rule of thumb in addition to reality before fantasy and therapist before patient: namely, frame before content, ground rules before anything else. Not because I say so, but because patients say so. It is this that the patient being presented is telling us. The frame must be rectified and the repercussions of these deviations interpreted before a sound therapeutic experience can be initiated. Frame first: let's not forget that lesson.

Discussant: You could get into violent conflagrations in initial sessions, and it seems to me that that should be avoided. I have found that patients can become very angry at interpretations very early on in therapy, especially in respect to what they view as concrete issues. I agree that you shouldn't close it off. Supposing the therapist were simply to point out that the patient is just starting treatment and is already asking about the limits of therapy, about how long it's going to be; you could then add that the patient has obviously thought about this a lot and ask what is going on in her mind. The patient might conceivably come back and say, You know, you jerk, this is the first session, and I ask you a concrete question and you turn it back on me. The therapist can run into a lot of difficulty in situations like this.

Langs: Well, we are back to advocating noninterpretive interventions and to viewing manifest content as manifest content and nothing more. Your suggestion reflects poor technique, but beyond that it fails to recognize that patients who wish to remain on a concrete level are usually expressing a wish to deny unconscious processes and meanings, and to avoid what I call truth therapy. Such patients are often quite difficult to engage in therapy.

Once you begin to recognize the crucial issues that underlie such attitudes, you will tend to sit back and to attempt to develop an associative and interpretive approach, and to do so quite carefully and sensitively. These patients are quite defensive and will attempt to establish their own deviant frame in the therapeutic interaction. Some of them wish to exploit you and to use you, even as a therapist, as a pathological container; they have virtually no interest in insight. You must proceed with them slowly and carefully, and yet you must adhere to the basic framework as much as possible.

The type of response you have proposed for the therapist has a kind of antagonistic and insensitive quality; it addresses the manifest content and asks for conscious associations. In the listening part of the course (Langs 1978c) we found that such questions tend not to evoke meaningful derivatives, but to generate resistances and defenses that would reinforce in the patient the very attitudes you have described. The interventions that I propose are carried out in the context of understanding the patient's unconscious investment in deviations of her own, and show an appreciation for the factors in both therapist and patient that have evoked these questions.

Incidentally, I have always been struck by how the hypothetical examples made up by trainees tend to be antagonistic to insight-oriented therapy and sound principles of technique. Some of this comes from clinical experiences I'm sure you've had, in which you felt that your intervention was quite sound and that the patient's hostile response to it was based not on your own unconscious communications but on the patient's anger and destructiveness. We cannot judge the matter. In general, however, it is important to take every response from a patient as an interactional product, and as a commentary, with valid and distorted elements, on your intervention. In this way, your patients will unconsciously teach you the techniques you need, but you must have mastery of the listening process in order to hear their message.

Discussant: I have a silent hypothesis; I don't have an intervention. I think we assume that people who come to therapy are in some kind of crisis and are seeking help from the therapist. Certainly the screening interview that initiated treatment in this case wasn't helpful, so surely there must be feelings concerning dependency and frustrated needs, anger about what happened, as well as some hope that the situation can be improved. I think some of the patient's effort here is aimed at determining how realistic this hope is, and how dependent she can become on the therapist. So I think that her questions reflect some of the dynamics of this patient, rather than a projective identification.

Langs: Your point is well taken. But we know that meaning on one level—for example, the cognitive or object relational—does not preclude meaning on another—here, that of projective identification. The same communication functions in all three spheres.

You're pointing out that the patient's needs were probably almost totally disregarded in the evaluation interview, and that this would be particularly disturbing if she is in some state of crisis. You see these initial associations as a response to that neglect, and as a reflection of the patient's level of anxiety and her need for a secure situation in which her dynamics and concerns can meaningfully unfold and be interpreted.

Your comments are a variation on remarks made earlier regarding the patient's unconscious efforts to rectify the framework, to define the therapeutic situation, and to create a sound therapeutic alliance. All of this can be maintained as a silent hypothesis, and elements of it can be used when you decide to intervene. For instance, concerns about dependency are only implicit in this material; they are not as yet cognitively represented, nor do you consider them in terms of the unconscious therapeutic interaction. Still, this may be a sensitive hunch based on a Type One derivative reading of the material. Hold on to it, and we will see if it is validated and if, in addition, it is given specific meaning in the context of this therapeutic interaction and the patient's own inner conflicts.

Discussant: My silent hypothesis would be—and here we all agree—that the patient was upset about the interaction the week before. We can disagree about the reasons, but obviously the patient was upset by it. I think we need a way to intervene other than simply saying, You must have been upset by last week, or even, Did you have any feelings about our interaction last week? I think either of these can lead to denial by the patient. She might continue to punish the therapist and say, No, you're absolutely wrong; I don't have any feelings about last week. Or, perhaps worse, she might answer with a simple no. I think the best way to phrase the intervention would be to say, What were your feelings about last week?

Langs: The best way to phrase it is to be silent and allow the patient to say it. Here you respond with a question and even introduce the transactions of the previous week. I have already suggested that, empirically, such questions tend to manipulate the patient and to direct her toward the surface of her thoughts and feelings, away from derivative communication. I would permit the patient to direct the unfolding of this session; we could then see whether she gets around to the previous week or not. So I would be silent, allowing the patient to continue and waiting for some representation of the specific adaptive context for this hour and for a bridge to treatment. At that point I would be far more prepared to intervene than at present. In fact, I could then use the specific adaptive context she touches upon and show her how this material is related to it. For example, if she alludes to her needing help and how this was ignored last week, or to having felt exposed, I could then point out that these initial experiences clearly raised all kinds of questions in her mind about me as her therapist, about the nature and conditions of the therapy, and about the way things might unfold in treatment. I could add that all this seems to have evoked questions about my qualifications as a therapist and a sense of considerable disturbance. In this way, I would be offering a general interpretation based on an adaptive context and Type Two derivatives, and as the associations become more specific I could be even more definitive.

Discussant: What you just formulated for us as an intervention is, I gather, something that you are holding in abeyance until the material will allow you to communicate it to the patient.

Langs: Yes, exactly. In this course, we state aloud the nature of our silent hypotheses and preparatory interventions. This enables us to see whether they are validated and supported by the patient's continuing associations, and to make revisions or elaborations as necessary. This is the phase of listening freely and attempting to synthesize, breaking it all down again, resynthesizing, and so on. None of this is offered to the patient until we have obtained *silent validation,* a proper bridge to therapy which facilitates intervening, and until we are fairly certain an intervention is necessary. In this session, there is a powerful indicator for an intervention—namely, the therapist's participation in a number of significant deviations in the framework. In principle, all deviations are strong indicators for intervention, and we then interpret or play back derivatives, and manage the framework, as the material permits and when conditions are such that a sound intervention can be offered.

Discussant: One question: if the patient never got to any reference to the first session, would you remain silent as far as interpreting this material is concerned?

Langs: The decision to intervene is always a very complex question. In the context of a powerful indicator, which we have here, and of strong derivatives related to the framework, I would probably play back the derivatives in a way that hints at the likelihood that the deviations of the previous week had served to evoke these reactions within the patient. The precise nature of my intervention will become clearer as we hear this session out, but since you seem to need a specific model, I will propose one.

Based on the material to this point, I might formulate a tentative intervention along these lines: You have begun your individual sessions with me with expressions of great concern regarding the conditions of your therapy, my qualifications, its length, and how it will unfold. There is great evidence of a need on your part to define the boundaries and nature of this situation, and it may well be that something has very strongly set off these concerns.

Here, I am creating a *preconception* (Bion 1962)—a state of unfulfilled tension—that could be made into a *conception* through the realization that the major precipitant for these communications is the previous modifications in the framework. Such an intervention could well lead the patient to directly comment on her experiences during the evaluation interview, and to then communicate further derivatives related to her unconscious perceptions and fantasies. In fact, only through such a route can you eventually reach the distorted, transference-based elements in this patient's response.

By the way, while I would very much experience the interactional pressures being developed by this patient, I would also see this as a positive communicative sign, in that she begins this first session with the frame issues. It suggests to me that she will help me quickly work over the many hurtful deviations in which I had participated the previous week, and I would anticipate a workable, though difficult, session. I sense the potential for a Type A communicative style, in addition to the evident Type B mode.

Discussant: Dr. Langs, I think it's terrific if you are able to do this. We're always assaulted seeing patients with this degree of sophistication; they do bombard you with questions. The thing is, I know I haven't that knack; I've never been able to finesse these questions. I've always answered them directly, because I do feel I should; though, on the other hand, maybe I just don't know what else to do. But I also feel inexperienced, put on the spot, and it's very difficult. It's been hard for me to deal with this sort of material.

Langs: Yes, I can understand that. It all comes back to the listening process and understanding the material; if you are able to quickly recognize the unconscious basis for an assault by a patient, you have a sense of potential mastery. You can begin to prepare an interpretive intervention, rather than a direct answer or a defensive response. You can experience a sense of sympathy with, and empathy for, the patient, and you have a feeling of perspective. That's one of the goals of this course: to provide you with a capacity to listen, understand, and intervene that can support your ability to develop a secure framework and an interpretive mode of treatment. But notice you are stressing the degree of sophistication in this patient as the central factor in these opening questions, while I have emphasized the therapist's deviations. We have contrasting silent hypotheses here, and you are showing me that we need additional material to decide which of these positions is the more valid.

Discussant: Does the patient ever, ethically, deserve an answer? For example, has the patient the right to know whether you are an analyst or not, or whether you're in treatment, or that you're a Sullivanian as opposed to a strict Freudian?

Langs: I really can't answer such questions in the abstract, in the absence of pertinent clinical material. As far as we know, the therapist responded with some degree of self-revelation here, and the patient's subsequent associations and behaviors should help us to answer these questions. What ethics require is the securing of a sound therapeutic situation and a capacity to respond interpretively to the best of your ability. On this basis, some deviations are, indeed, unethical, but my approach has been to detail the manner in which they disrupt treatment, disturb the patient, and reflect the psychopathology of the therapist. The creation of a sound therapeutic environment is your most important obligation to the patient, and the patient's therapeutic needs must always dictate the nature of your interventions. Adherence to neutrality and anonymity are the best standards, and the patient will learn about you as a therapist in the most meaningful way from the manner in which you explicate the ground rules and handle the material. But beyond that, it is essential to take all communications from the patient on both the manifest and the latent level, without exception; you must treat them as derivatives and search for their adaptive context. To ignore this is to turn away from insight psychotherapy, from truth therapy. I might add that there are holding and containing issues here as well, and that direct answers tend to reflect failures in these functions.

Discussant: But patients often put you in a position where you really feel bombarded. And you sense that they're doing things in a bullying way, that they don't want to give you time to think. In such situations containing becomes very difficult. That's the hard part.

Langs: Of course, but that's where the listening process can serve you so well. Remember that therapists tend to rather quickly identify the nasty and malicious things that patients do to them. Some of this stems from their own sensitivities, and some from the actualities of the patient's intentions. This malicious aspect is stressed because it is often more obvious and manifest. But by applying the listening process we can take the same material and recognize indications that this patient is attempting to help her therapist, to cure her rather quickly of some rather poor therapeutic practices. In a sense, the patient is doing the job of this course: she is letting the therapist know that deviations in the ground rules of the kind that she experienced in the previous week are totally destructive of the treatment process, and raise serious issues concerning the therapeutic setting and the therapist's counter-transferences. This is unconscious supervision at its best: direct and very much to the point. Yes, it is rather aggressive and the tone is hostile, but that quality should be viewed as an interactional product of the patient's experiences in the evaluation interview, whatever unresolved aggressive feelings she may be displacing onto therapy from earlier life experiences.

If you can resolve your unconscious countertransferences to the point where you can properly manage the framework and keep counter-transference inputs to a minimum, your work as a therapist will be more peaceful and easier to manage. The people who come to us are emo-tionally ill and disturbed, and there will always be pressures and some degree of assault. But in general these will be less massive, better understood, and easier to contain and metabolize if you have developed the cognitive tools and are undergoing some adequate therapy or analysis of your own. Remember, I am not suggesting that I would not feel a sense of pressure under these conditions. I am merely stating that I would be in a position to better understand them, that if I had had any say the antecedents of these pressures would not have occurred, and that I am prepared to appreciate both the hostile and the constructive aspects of what the patient is doing. The chances are that I could better metabolize these pressures and translate them into interpretive interven-tions and rectifications of the frame.

Therapist: I remember having a feeling that I wanted to fight back—I guess to attack her in return.

Langs: Yes, and you should take that as an interactionally produced subjective experience, apply the me/not-me interface, and attempt to understand both yourself and the patient in that context.

Discussant: I realize now that I have been screening people in the clinic, and taking on extra patients with a view to eventually taking them into private practice. This is done by many of us, and obviously there are countertransference issues involved, but I do have my needs. Then, when I experience pressures like this, I start to think that I will lose the patient if I don't answer directly, that they will just walk out.

Langs: Certainly a policy of selecting patients with an eye toward taking them with you into private practice will create many complications for a given therapy, and is a particular deviation in the framework. And it is a problem that won't go away once you are in private practice; even then many therapists feel that they must give in to the direct demands of their patients or they will lose them. But such feelings are directly reactive and based on manifest content, and often cover a dread of truth therapy, of derivative communication, of unconscious processes and contents, and, ultimately, of the sick and psychotic parts of the personality of both patient and therapist.

In actuality, if you do give in to the patient's direct demands, you alter the conditions of the treatment situation, and you lose the patient at that very moment. For some time I have realized that many patients do not wish to be patients in the true sense of that term. We will define this more extensively when we explore the therapeutic relationship, but to be a patient implies a wish to communicate verbally and behaviorally in a form that lends itself to understanding the inner truth underlying one's emotional illness or characterological problems. But many patients are involved in a mere pretense of therapeutic work. If you respond to them by modifying the framework and accepting their frame, you then accept their role as nonpatient—a pretending patient, a liar in Bion's nonmoral sense (1970)—and also forgo your own role as therapist—as truth therapist, if you will. Under these conditions some patients will stay in treatment all right, but only because the Type C barriers and falsifications serve certain pathological needs and defenses; but other patients will terminate, because it is really their wish to have insight or truth therapy.

By maintaining the frame you are in a position to hear meaningful derivatives through which you can interpret the patient's efforts to have you deviate. If you modify the framework, such communications do not emerge as clearly; in addition, the patient will not trust your interventions. The situation is considerably more chaotic and quite unpredictable—even with respect to the practical issue of whether you will have a patient or not. It is here that entering sessions with intense desires becomes distorting and disruptive, ultimately defeating both patient and therapist.

Discussant: It becomes difficult when you enjoy working with a particular patient and really want her to continue with you. I also begin to wonder whether the framework deviations created by the clinic destroys any hope of sound therapy, or whether we can work in selected areas in an effective manner and offer the patient some type of positive and insightful experience.

Langs: Yes, we touched upon this issue earlier, and perhaps we can return to it toward the end of this section of the course after we have heard a number of presentations based on work with clinic patients. One thing is clear for the moment: if you ignore these frame issues, they will seriously undermine therapeutic work in any other sector. Such an approach would probably limit you to symptom alleviation through Type C barriers, lies, and falsifications, and ruptures of interpersonal and intrapsychic links—a type of misalliance cure. It may well be that viable work in a clinic setting will center almost always on framework issues, from the presence of a secretary to the imposition of an arbitrary time limit termination date. Certainly, if you can rectify aspects of this frame—for example, by accepting the fee yourself rather than leaving that to a secretary—you would provide an important interlude for positive introjective identification and insightful therapeutic work.

Discussant: When a time limit is imposed on a treatment, we sometimes experience a sense of relief to know that we will be able to stop with certain patients at the end of a year. With patients who put us under all sorts of pressure, we use the time limit as a sort of safety device. I am becoming aware of how that helps us sidestep many important therapeutic issues with these patients, and how it would become a barrier to meaningful therapeutic work.

Discussant: I understand what you're saying, Dr. Langs, but let's say, for example in this case, we don't know what's going to happen for the rest of the session. We have our silent hypothesis that this is somehow related to what had gone on the week before. Let's say that for the rest of the session the patient continues to assault the therapist, continues to say things like, You know, you don't seem very experienced, or you don't seem this or that. And you make your intervention: Well, I get the feeling you're coming on strong—or you're attacking me—or however you want to put it. Would it be wrong to also acknowledge the deviations in the framework the week before, by introducing them and asking the patient if she has any feelings about what happened last week?

Langs: I trust that we can all sense how pressured the members of this seminar feel. There are many questions, and they are good ones, and while I think they are helping to clarify important framework issues, at the same time they are keeping us from getting on with the material—from hearing the patient, who ultimately must answer these questions. I have already answered this particular query by indicating that I would not simply address the manifest content here, or directly suggest to her that she has been harassing or attacking me, and that I would prefer also to not arbitrarily introduce the events of the prior week. I would like the patient to lead the way, and would let her move closer and closer to those transactions; I would wait for her to allude to them in some relatively direct form. Lacking that, and in the context of these intense interactional pressures and a basic need to clarify and rectify the framework, I have already indicated I would select the best derivatives available and play them back to the patient, organizing them around the adaptive context of the prior deviations. In that way, I would unconsciously communicate my sensitivity to these issues, and would thereby appear a bit safer to the patient, a bit more sensitive and understanding, and a bit more capable of managing my counter-transferences. On the basis of these introjects, as well as the cognitive qualities of my intervention and my demonstrated capacity to contain and metabolize these projective identifications and to manage the role and image evocations, this patient would very likely move more directly to a working over of the deviations and to her many anxieties, perceptions, and fantasies related to the framework of this treatment.

Now, had the hour we are looking at begun in the fashion I have just outlined, it is quite unlikely that the patient would have harassed or attacked the therapist, or would have failed to shift to other levels of derivative communication. I have much more faith in the patient and her wish to communicate and get well than you have for now, and I guess that this stems from a bit of faith in my own ability to manage and understand these communications. But for the moment, at least, it appears that we all agree that rectification of this framework and inter-pretation of the patient's unconscious perceptions and fantasies in this area is the first therapeutic task that faces this therapist in this treat-ment situation.

Discussant: Suppose you're dealing with a patient who asks these very specific questions. Say, it's a borderline patient who has a good deal of underlying rage, and with whom you're not misperceiving, not distorting the rage—it's actually there. And you deal with the next question in this manner, which I agree is probably technically correct. Don't you run the risk of losing the patient in the very first session?

Langs: We will find that borderline and psychotic patients need a well-defined frame, almost desperately. And they will respond accord-ingly, so long as you handle the situation with tact and sensitivity. I outlined a range of responses beginning with silence, extending into a variety of interventions, and ending with selective answers to questions that appropriately require clarification. But I must add that with most of these patients you will seldom find yourself under these pressures unless you yourself have modified the frame or, as is more often the case these days, they have been in previous therapy in which the frame was extensively modified and damaged. In such a situation, you must continue to distinguish between manifest and latent content, and the patient's conscious attitudes and unconscious therapeutic needs. It is here that the split that I identified earlier as characteristic of the patient's attitude toward frame issues appears in a particular form: consciously, the patient demands deviations, while, unconsciously, his derivative communications direct you to maintain the frame and to contain and metabolize the pressured projective identifications they are generating.

But all this is becoming far too abstract; we need definitive clinical data. I will then be able to show you how the underlying issues relate to truth versus lie therapy—to experiencing and resolving the disturbed parts of the patient's personality or avoiding them, and to the therapist's expressing his concern and humanness by following the unconscious directives of the patient to secure and maintain the frame or by presenting the patient a deliberately false image of goodness, filled with underlying destructiveness.

So once again we are letting these issues become matters for abstract discussion and debate, rather than turning to our clinical presentations for the answers we need. I sense a need on your part to move away from the clinical material and to justify a wide range of deviations, in the face of two presentations that seem to speak quite clearly for the importance of securing the frame and maintaining it. Is it possible that we as therapists experience some type of anxiety and fear in respect to a secured therapeutic framework and hold? I offer this as a thesis, not only on the basis of your questions in this seminar, but also based on the observations of the two therapists who have presented case material to us. It is a thesis well worth keeping in mind, and perhaps we will find it confirmed as we proceed.

Discussant: I sense some type of anxiety, that's true. But you hear patients tell you that they left a particular therapist because he gave them no feedback, he said very little during the session. That is a very common thing.

Langs: You are proving my point: without clinical material, anything and everything is possible. Here you offer me evidence in the form of manifest content, with no possible opportunity for validation through Type Two derivatives. But don't you see, this is the type of clinical evidence to which you are accustomed. The type of validation that I have defined as psychoanalytic is more difficult to master, more demanding in a sense, and yet far more meaningful. You could be referring to a therapist who never made a correct intervention during an entire treatment; there is no way of knowing. And furthermore, in terms of the listening process, such comments probably relate to a traumatic adaptive context within the patient's immediate therapeutic interaction with yourself. Their most pertinent meaning probably lies in the present, rather than in the past, but the point is, there is no telling, and you are not citing psychoanalytically meaningful evidence. We are too far from the material, so let's hear more at this point.

Therapist: So after I told her I would be here all year, she wanted to know about what kind of therapy this would be: psychoanalytic, behavior modification, or what?

Langs: So, she continues in the same vein, trying to define the situation, to evoke noninterpretive responses, and to elicit answers that will essentially be without meaning. That is, specifying for her the type of treatment you are offering is to say very little; we have clichés on the one hand, and her unknown fantasies and beliefs on the other. I suspect now that the patient is trying very hard to move away from the contents of her own inner mental world; further, she is trying to create a therapeutic situation in which Type C barriers—lies, falsifications, and broken links—will prevail. And while this expresses some very definite needs within this patient, it is also a commentary on the initial framework deviations and on the therapist's present noninterpretive interventions: they serve as Type C barriers against underlying chaotic truths, about both patient and therapist, and also about the therapeutic situation.

Remember that the therapist has already answered several of these questions. And what has happened? The patient became insatiable, as Freud (1912) suggested she would. He stated that when the analyst becomes involved in modifications of anonymity, the patient will want more and more, and the analysis will soon become that of the analyst rather than that of the patient. Greenacre (1959) made comparable comments, and I have been able to validate this thesis repeatedly (Langs 1975c, 1976a).

So through the patient's commentary on these nonneutral interventions and direct responses, we discover that they promote a situation in which the focus is shifted more and more onto the therapist; communications seem restricted to their manifest meanings, and the patient continues her extensive projective identifications and efforts to create Type C barriers. Thus the patient unconsciously exploits these deviations to in effect remove herself from treatment. The communicative properties of the bipersonal field have been disturbed, and the patient attempts to disrupt them further and to maintain a form of lie therapy. Here the effort to maintain bastions, sectors of misalliance, is more prominent than the wish to rectify the situation and cure the therapist. There is, however, some effort exerted in that more positive direction, as the patient continues her attempts at defining the therapeutic situation and its framework.

But there is more: this material is quite rich. Can anyone characterize what the patient is now doing and relate it to our earlier discussions of the frame?

Discussant: She's provoking more deviations, and punishing the therapist in an almost harassing manner.

Langs: Yes, but can you add anything to that?

Discussant: She's putting the therapist on the spot, and continues to interrogate her just as she was questioned the week before, in the screening interview.

Langs: Yes, but there is still more. The patient is indeed attempting to evoke further deviations and to exploit the modified frame. It is as if she's saying: If the treatment is going to be public, there will be no therapy; I don't have to reveal what's inside of myself, and that's fine with me. You do the free associating, and I will listen. The modified frame will help the patient avoid the most disturbing parts of her personality—a thesis I hope soon to validate.

Discussant: Would you say that this stems almost entirely from those original deviations?

Langs: Well, that's the point I was about to develop. At this juncture, I am impressed with the patient's own need for a modified framework, every bit as much as I am with the effects of these early deviations. We have here an interactional product with powerful contributions from both participants. All of which suggests another insight: These deviations, which presented the patient an opportunity to split off, repress, and deny the sick part of her personality, fit extremely well with the patient's defensive style: denying of her own inner problems, projecting them into others, in this case the therapist, and attempting to focus on the disturbance and problems of others rather than on her own.

So alterations in the ground rules reflect particular types of defenses and pathological gratifications, and often these coincide with those within the patient to create an especially intense sector of misalliance. In the present instance, I would wonder if the patient did not obtain some type of masochistic gratification from the destructive qualities of those earlier deviations. Now she uses them as a kind of license for her own pathological aggressiveness and tries to make the therapist suffer. All of this gets lived out without insight, and continues the spiraling interchange of pathological projective identifications.

To state this point in terms of a postulate: deviations in the ground rules express the therapist's pathological defenses, superego expressions, and gratifications, which will often in some way correspond to pathological mechanisms within the patient. They therefore constitute an aspect of a neurotic vicious circle of the type described by Strachey (1934) and Racker (1957), in which there is a correspondence and reinforcement of the pathology of the patient through that of the therapist. Such unconscious behavioral reinforcements of the patient's psychopathology will, of course, preclude its analytic modification regardless of the nature of the therapist's interpretive interventions. By implication, deviations in the framework repeat some aspect of the patient's pathogenic past and reinforce his present pathological inner world and the etiological factors that helped create it. As a result, deviations will consistently take on specific unconscious meanings for each individual patient in keeping with some aspect of the history and nature of his emotional illness.

I think you can sense more strongly now that this patient offers her therapist no sense of security, that in fact there is a kind of violent refusal to hold. Therapists, despite their own needs to be held, must be prepared for moments like this, moments when the patient not only refuses to hold the therapist, but violently antagonizes him. The therapist must be capable of experiencing this subjectively, of tolerating the absence of support from the patient, and of processing this experience toward an interpretive intervention. Still, the intensity of this repudiation of the patient's holding functions suggests significant psychopathology in this regard.

Finally, these communications point to another hypothesis that has a particular representation in this initial hour: When the frame has been altered, the only meaningful Type Two derivatives that will be available in the communicative field will relate to the deviations. The patient will not give you meaningful interpretable material in any other area, and the derivative communication will concentrate on the implications of the altered framework for both patient and therapist, as experienced by the patient in terms of unconscious perceptions and fantasies, valid introjects and distortions. It is clear that for the moment no other adaptive context exists, and there is no other level of meaningful communication. This hypothesis is supported by our observations of the first presentation, and we can now keep it in mind for further validation.

Discussant: It's reassuring to hear you say that a patient can be sick also.

Langs: Yes, as a strict empiricist, I too am glad to have had an experience where, in the course of a case presentation, the psychopathology of the patient begins to loom larger than that of the therapist. The situation we are considering especially lends itself to such a formulation, since a number of these deviations were not in the service of the immediate pathological needs of the therapist. In addition, what began as a relatively valid response to the pathological inputs from the therapist and her colleagues has now shaded into an exploitation by the patient and a primary expression of her own pathology in the context of the disturbing inputs she has experienced.

I try to apply the listening process in a fair-minded way, I think with some success. I really have no bias in this respect, and in fact, once you secure the framework, learn to listen, and begin to intervene with sound management and interpretive responses, you will be able to see with your own patients that the psychopathology of the patient will indeed loom larger and larger. Too many of my critics say I favor the patient and see him as the healthy one in the therapeutic interaction. They view me as overly critical of therapists, and say I am preoccupied with their pathology. But what these critics fail to recognize is that in pointing up the therapist's psychopathology I am not attempting to picture anything essential to the therapeutic interaction, some inherent and irreparable flaw. Quite the reverse. I am simply trying to offer and illustrate a clinically valid methodology—the listening process—and to apply it to see what it reveals. And if it reveals—as it does—the ubiquity of countertransference and the therapist's pathology, well then it also offers the means by which these countertransferences can be managed and their influence minimized. It should hardly be surprising to find that, you, as trainees having experienced little adequate personal therapy or analysis, will often put your own psychopathology into the field. But as you put these techniques together, you will more and more be able to lessen your own pathological inputs and to observe bipersonal fields in which the psychopathology of the patient clearly predominates.

Please continue.

Therapist: Well, I said something to her. (Laughter.) I asked her what her thoughts were about the therapy that she will be receiving.

Langs: Any brief comments?

Discussant: Well, it's a response on the manifest level. It also invites the patient to move away from the question of whether the therapist is in treatment and a trainee, toward speculations about the type of treatment.

Discussant: It could have been worse: she could have said that it was going to be a psychoanalysis. (Laughter.)

Langs: In terms of what this therapist has been taught, this is undoubtedly a rather typical response: to ask for further direct associations. In the listening part of this course, we discovered that this seldom prompts derivative response, and that it often serves the defenses of the therapist and leads to sectors of misalliance. The point is therefore well taken that it may move the patient away from more personal questions into a rumination about the type of therapy that she anticipates: it would therefore constitute an invitation for an interactional obsessive defense and Type C barrier. In terms of creating the therapeutic environment, you are demonstrating to the patient that under pressure you will respond with questions of your own and ask for surface associations. But notice something else: In asking the patient about the type of treatment she expects, you communicate a failure to understand that she is already, herself, implicitly conveying to you the type of therapy she wants—a therapy in which she can place you under pressure, direct questions at you, and avoid as much as possible any communications related to her own inner feelings, life history, or symptoms. The patient implicitly demonstrates to the therapist her own model of therapy, and in that context her derivative communications will reveal her unconscious fantasies about treatment—always a mixture of appropriate and inappropriate elements. Her conscious thoughts will be the least revealing in this respect, while her derivative communications have already given you a rich image.

In terms of communicative fields, the patient is endeavoring now to maintain a Type C field, using the questions she asks about you as barriers to the chaotic truths within herself. Whatever the initial constructive underlying intentions, the barrier function becomes more and more impressive. Your response is that of a Type C therapist; it attempts in turn to create barriers to the inner chaos the patient is evoking within you, as well as to the chaos within her that prompted her to behave in this way. As I have noted repeatedly, some of this chaos has come from the deviations in the framework, and that too is being avoided. But it is through this type of interactional reinforcement that the Type C field is created and often maintained for very long periods of so-called therapy. We can very much sympathize with the pressure that you were under, and understand your recourse to a question and Type C barriers. This is turning out to be a therapeutic situation from which we can learn a great deal. Please continue.

Therapist: She said that she felt that she wanted analytically oriented therapy. And I agreed. (Laughter.) Then I made an intervention. I told her that I appreciated that this was a new situation and very difficult for her. And the rewards involved were not always immediately apparent, but that we should try to work together.

Langs: Okay. That's termed a direct appeal to the therapeutic alliance. What is its unconscious function?

Discussant: To stave off the patient, to tell her to cool it.

Langs: And to whom is the therapist alluding?

Discussant: Herself—her own anxiety about starting the therapy.

Langs: Yes. Let me begin with the positive core to these non-neutral interventions: it appears that the therapist is attempting to reassure the patient that she will offer some type of insightful and more neutral treatment. Here she is responding to the patient's indirect communications about the previous deviations. And perhaps because she had not consciously recognized the implications of this material, and yet had sensed something, she responds with this particular intervention about offering analytically oriented therapy—rather than with a sound interpretation. The second part of her comment elaborates upon this approach: rather than interpreting the nature of these transactions, the therapist makes an appeal for patience and tolerance.

I suspect that this will have a mixed effect: on the one hand, it should be a bit reassuring, but on the other hand, as a less traumatic but nonetheless specific deviation in technique, it will evoke continued concern, and probably exploitation, on the part of the patient.

Your characterizing your second remark as an intervention leads me to point out that through the listening process, we learn that every communication from the therapist—from his silences to his managements of the framework to his verbal comments—are to be taken as interventions, and studied for their unconscious communications and for the patient's commentary and validating responses. Therapists tend to think of their efforts at interpretation as their sole interventions, and to very much disregard the many other comments and behaviors which actually serve as significant adaptive contexts for the patient. A great deal is missed and misunderstood in that way.

Certainly, your comment about the difficulties of therapy and the delays and rewards are as much a conscious effort to reassure the patient as it is an unconscious attempt to reassure yourself. This is your first outpatient, and you are getting a lot of flak. In fact, this is a really disturbing initiation into the field for you, but one that can serve you well—and, I might add, one that will turn out to be far less atypical than you might imagine. Your comment has aspects of both projection and projective identification: attributing to the patient the concerns about whether it's worth getting involved in therapy is the projection, a response to which she readily lends herself; while the projective identification is an effort to place into the patient some type of positive introject. I should caution you, however, that such efforts, as Strachey (1934) pointed out in one of the first papers on this subject, are unconsciously experienced and introjected by the patient as destructive and as covertly reflecting a negative introject. The surface is positive, but the depths are not. We may have a chance to validate this thesis when we consider this patient's response.

It is, of course, quite understandable that, having experienced some rather nasty and destructive projective identifications, you would attempt to modify the situation with a more benign interactional projection. Among the possible erroneous responses to these inter-actional pressures, this is undoubtedly one of the kindest available. Still, we must face the fact that it falls short of an interpretive process-ing and will generate within the patient neither cognitive insight nor truly positive introjects.

Finally, in terms of the ground rules, the patient seems to have created a situation where your own free associations—if I may call them that—are for the moment more meaningful in depth than hers. For now, you are joining her in implicitly structuring the situation in this way. So, despite your good intentions, there can be rather signif-icant detrimental consequences to this approach. But as a first effort it has many positive attributes that I very much believe can eventually be shaped into sound interpretive work. Please continue.

Therapist: She mentions that she had thought of private therapy and then dismissed it.

Langs: See how the derivatives keep accumulating? Private therapy: a nice way of putting it. Go ahead.

Therapist: Then she moved from the chair she had been sitting in—way across the room—to one closer to me.

Langs: Isn't that interesting: a positive effect did result from the benign qualities of the projective identification. Under these condi-tions, the positive nucleus must have been quite important to this patient, in light of how traumatized she had been in that first interview. She rather interestingly counterbalances this particular behavior with the derivative about wanting private therapy. So we learn that noninterpretive intervention, under a very specific set of circumstances in which there have been extensive and hurtful deviations in the framework, can have a constructive effect in modifying earlier negative introjects. I suspect, however, that an appropriate interpretation would have led to the same move and to extensive cognitive validation as well.

Discussant: The patient probably realizes that the therapist is able to tolerate her assault and is not attacking her back.

Discussant: In a way, the patient may be saying she's sorry.

Langs: As I have said, among the various responses to the disruptive pathological projective identifications and role and image pressures, the therapist's particular comment shows some capacity to detoxify the harmful qualities, though it lacks a sense of processing toward interpretation. Now, let's notice another aspect of this material: Into what realm does this patient's response fall?

Discussant: Action-discharge.

Langs: Yes, that is the mode, though it certainly has a constructive quality to it. But the behavioral response also falls into the realm of the framework: she now moves into the chair in which she was expected to sit. She rectifies one of her own modifications of the framework. In the adaptive context of the therapist's last intervention, which on the surface was less self-revealing and certainly less defensive than her previous comments, the patient may have been able to distinguish the therapist from her colleagues who participated in the evaluation interview. Clearly, she now feels safer and has a renewed hope of rectifying the framework; she now approaches these efforts in a far less destructive and threatening manner. There is as yet no cognitive insight, but there seems to be preliminary movement on the part of both patient and therapist in the direction of constructing a communicative field within which that might occur. Without conscious or spoken realization, some of the more destructive introjects and images of the therapist appear to have been modified.

Discussant: I am struck with how the therapist was able to control herself, to manage how upset and attacked she must have felt, and to respond in a way that avoided lashing out in revenge at the patient or reflecting an intense sense of offense. It's as if the therapist were saying, Despite all of your hostility, I would still like to treat you and to approach it by endeavoring to achieve insight. And the patient seems to appreciate this response. Perhaps, in the terms of our discussion, she appreciates the therapist's capacity to hold her when she's kicking and screaming, and to contain her assaults.

Langs: Yes, those appear to be sound inferences open to validation from the subsequent material. After all, the therapist has now created a private setting and an individual treatment situation, and has shown an ability to define at least some elements of a sound therapeutic relationship. Previously, as a participant in a group interview, she must have loomed as a threatening figure who was quite unpredictable and who could not be trusted. Please continue.

Therapist: When she changed chairs, she said that the noise (which was present all along) made it difficult for her to hear.

Discussant: Where was the noise coming from?

Therapist: I think it was probably from outside the building, because it was hot and the window was open.

Discussant: There are also frequent noises and discussions coming from the hallway.

Discussant: In the adaptive context of the deviations that we were discussing and the hints at rectification, I would postulate that the altered framework creates noise and distraction, making it impossible to do therapy. In response to that last intervention, the patient now wants to be able to hear the therapist and understand her.

Therapist: Then she began talking about her relationship with Fred, an older Jewish attorney. She said that he had been married before, for several years, and had been divorced for a few years. He has a young son and daughter and sees them about once a week. When she met his children there were a lot of problems.

Langs: Notice how the entire tone of the session has changed: the patient now begins to talk about her own difficulties, rather than focusing manifestly on the therapist and the frame. For the moment, we must recognize that the therapist's responses were not disruptive and that they facilitated this development. We will continue to listen to these associations as derivatives related to the prevailing adaptive contexts within the therapeutic relationship, but we are now experiencing a different type of communication. Much of this stems from the therapist's last intervention and the qualities that we have already identified.

Therapist: She went on: she said the children would be very provocative when Fred wasn't looking, and she felt that his son saw himself as a prince and felt that everyone should cater to him. She described one episode in particular when they took the children away with them for the weekend; there were many arguments between her and Fred. She felt the children needed more discipline. She also noted that the son had a twitch. Then she said, As I became looser, the children were more receptive.

Langs: There is so much here now: the field has clearly shifted from a predominantly Type B mode to Type A, and certainly the patient is communicating in that way for the moment. Any comments?

Discussant: I hear something about a situation in which several people are involved, and there are children in need of discipline.

Discussant: There is also something about becoming more receptive as the patient became looser. I'm not sure, but that sounds like an introjective identification with the therapist after her last intervention.

Langs: Yes, that's excellent. We are now dealing with Type Two derivatives—unconscious fantasies and perceptions—related to the deviations, and with additional derivatives related to the therapist's last intervention. As you can see, the manner in which the patient presents her chief complaint is actually shaped by the therapeutic interaction, and, in addition, by the realistic task of communicating her problems. There is such a strong tendency to think of first sessions in terms of surface communications that this unusual first hour has provided us a rather dramatic opportunity to realize in exaggerated form something that is true of every consultation session. Clearly, the more powerful the adaptive contexts within treatment, the more intensely will the material from the patient relate to the therapeutic interaction. And even in situations where there are no dramatic adaptive stimuli from the therapist, the very way in which he shapes the consultation and begins to define the treatment setting will serve as strong adaptive stimuli for the patient's associations.

Here, the reference to the unruly children, who expect selfishly only to have their needs gratified, is in part an unconscious perception of the therapist, who participates in a group interview. The deviations reflect a lack of discipline according to the patient, and there is, she adds, a strong need for discipline. This communication is a type of unconscious directive I mentioned earlier, through which the patient, quite indirectly, unconsciously communicates the need to rectify the frame. This could be done quite implicitly toward the end of this hour through a proper structuring of the therapeutic setting. On the other hand, if the patient provided a bridge back to therapy and some allusion to the earlier deviations, it would be essential to indicate interpretively—that is, explicitly—to the patient that she had in fact been reacting to the undisciplined and nonprivate qualities of the first consultation, and that she viewed it as a situation in which she was being used to cater to the needs of the therapist and the other members of that group. She is now indicating that what was needed was a far more disciplined and private situation, and on that basis, you could add, it seems wise now to define the ground rules.

There would, by the way, be little need to refer to the patient's unconscious perception of the therapist's becoming looser and her own response in the form of increased receptivity and communication. This is a positive, implicit introject that needs no conscious acknowledgment for the moment. We now have Type Two derivative validation of some of our earlier hypotheses about the frame and therapeutic interaction. Let's hear a bit more.

Therapist: She then felt more receptive and the children's problems quieted down. She admitted to being very jealous of them and very angry.

Langs: So you see, she can now acknowledge some of her own inappropriate responses. Both she and the children—she and the therapist—have problems, and as the frame becomes more secure she can acknowledge her own difficulties. Well, I see that our time is up. We will attempt next week to complete our work with this session.

Chapter Six
ESTABLISHING THE
THERAPEUTIC ENVIRONMENT

Langs: We have now an excellent opportunity to begin this seminar without desire, memory, or understanding. So, without further comment, please continue from where you left off.

Therapist: Okay. She was talking about Fred's two children and his visiting them on weekends. She had spoken of how his son was very provocative and how there were a lot of problems with him. He behaved like a prince and everyone would cater to him. She described one weekend in particular when they took the children away with them, and there were many arguments between her and Fred. She felt that the children needed more discipline. The son had a twitch. But as she became looser, Fred was more receptive and problems quieted down. She admitted to feeling jealous and angry. She had never met Fred's ex-wife. (I think I asked her if she had met her, though I'm not entirely certain.) She went on to say that she didn't want to be chummy with her.

Langs: Well, once you intervene, we must comment. Any thoughts?

Discussant: The therapist asked a question, once again directing the patient to the surface of her thoughts. In addition, I'm not clear why she asked this particular question at all.

Discussant: There is selectivity there and it might be considered a nonneutral intervention.

Discussant: It also moves away from frame issues, and from acknowledging that the patient is reacting to these issues. It also takes the therapist away from defining and rectifying the frame.

Langs: Yes, that's excellent. There is an important issue here: Can the therapist begin to develop an exploratory psychotherapy without first addressing and rectifying the existing deviations in the framework? In this course we do not want to prejudge such questions; instead, we hope to allow the material from the patient and the therapist— especially the patient—to provide the answers. And as I will show you in a moment, I think that this patient gives us an important clue. The frame has to be dealt with before sound therapeutic work can take place in any other area. By this I mean that both interpretation and rectification, based on leads from the patient, will prove necessary. And here, quite characteristically, when the patient begins manifestly to discuss her own problems, the therapist responds in a manner that suggests, first, that this material was not subjected to the listening process in its fullest sense, in terms of arriving at Type Two derivatives in response to the prevailing adaptive contexts; and, second, that the therapist has some notion that you can begin right in with direct exploration of the patient's difficulties without securing the frame.

Much of this takes place because the therapist has responded to the manifest content of this material, and I think that the patient quickly responds to this. After all, if you examine the unconscious communications reflected in this intervention, you can see they reflect a special interest on the part of the therapist in relationships between two women, or in ex-wives, in particular—threats or intruders to the patient's relationship with this fellow Fred. Unconsciously, this is undoubtedly a derivative of the therapist's concern with her relationship with the patient. And all things considered, it certainly is not a neutral intervention. It selects a particular segment of the material for focus, based on some arbitrary need of the therapist rather than on the patient's need for an interpretive intervention.

I think that the patient senses this and that this is reflected in her next association, about not wanting to get too chummy with the ex-wife. In the adaptive context of the therapist's last intervention, this commentary, studied along the me/not-me interface, suggests an unconscious perception and introjection of the therapist as becoming too chummy—too seductive. The patient's response, once again, is to push the therapist off, both on a manifest and a latent level. This suggests too that the deviations have in general been experienced as seductive, and that they have aroused unconscious homosexual anxieties and fantasies in the patient, who defends herself with distancing and barrier efforts. It also sheds additional light on the initial pressures that the patient placed on the therapist and on a particular motivating factor in that regard. Remember, though, that this is not just simply the patient's defenses against her own unconscious homosexual fantasies about the therapist—transference fantasies, if you will—but that it also reflects an unconscious perception of the therapist's own unconscious homosexual conflicts and fantasies, a perception that therefore has a nontransference component as well.

For us, this response has importance not only because it is non-validating, but also because it reflects something of the seductive quality of a nonneutral intervention—a deviation in the framework. In addition, it may be taken to reinforce my point that the frame must be established first, and the boundaries of the therapeutic relationship made clear, before other types of therapeutic work can be undertaken. This inference is far more tentative, but perhaps it will be more clearly stated in derivative form by the patient as we proceed.

In any case, the patient's comment that she does not want to get too chummy is another one of those unconscious directives communicated to the therapist as a means of guiding her toward rectification of the framework. The patient is saying, Don't deviate; don't ask nonneutral questions; don't begin to blur the boundaries between us; don't get too chummy. Rectify that bit of seductiveness and (I suspect, along with that) rectify the other alterations in the framework.

In respect to technique, I might add that I would not attempt to verbalize or interpret this material for the moment, but would take it as an unconscious directive that would lead me to review my last intervention and to rectify the frame by not repeating comments of that kind. I think it would be a bit much to suggest to the patient that she has perceived my last comment as somewhat seductive, and that she is suggesting that I should keep my distance. I don't think the patient could really make use of that particular insight at the moment, nor do I feel that it could be meaningfully imparted to her. Instead, I would resort to the important technical principle of making silent use of the patient's unconscious supervision and efforts at cure, and of demonstrating in my next viable intervention that I have benefited from her endeavors. Quite often, especially in situations with more minor technical errors, this is all the patient needs.

Discussant: I can see now what you mean by the term *commentary*. You are not taking this material simply as fantasy, but attempting to sort out valid perceptions and actualities in the therapeutic interaction from the patient's fantasies. And I can see how the two seem to intermix, and how we must learn to sort them out.

Langs: Yes, to state that in other terms: every communication has *transversal* qualities—it spans reality and fantasy, transference and nontransference, validity and distortion. We are always sorting out opposing elements.

Discussant: What do we do if the patient directly points us to the framework? I've had that happen with my patients. It's extraordinary.

Langs: Oh, it happens. It will happen particularly in a very noisy situation with a lot of contaminants. Can you elaborate?

Discussant: I mean, you're talking about the implicit acknowledgment of deviations. But when you're confronted by what's really a very apt statement by the patient that there's some degree of error, or something that's inappropriate, I don't know how else you would handle that other than to acknowledge it directly to the patient.

Langs: Can you be more specific?

Discussant: Yes. This was a biggie. I had decided I was going to terminate with a patient, and the patient had been asking me whether she would be able to continue. And because of the countertransference, a tremendous amount of guilt on my part—I knew I was going to do a fellowship next year, or thought I might be—instead of handling it appropriately what I said was: Look, I don't know about the fellowship yet (which was true), but you're having difficulty paying the fees in the clinic as is, and I don't think it will work in private practice; I don't think the two of us should continue. I said this because it was almost as if there were some collusion between the two of us, a denial of the fact that we were going to terminate. And she said to me four months later, You know, that was really an inappropriate thing for you to say, because it really is up to me. If you don't want to continue with me, that's one thing, but if it's an issue of money, you're taking away my independence by telling me I can't continue because of a money issue. She was pointing out a countertransference problem. She was legitimately alluding to an area of countertransference, and to where I had acted inappropriately. But it's also a very personal sort of thing that she was doing with me.

Langs: Personal in what sense?

Discussant: Well, there's also a little bit of role reversal going on elsewhere in the treatment. This isn't the first time that she's made comments of this sort to me.

Langs: Without specific material from the session you're referring to, my response can only be brief and general. In principle, it is important to remember that direct acknowledgment of errors constitutes a modification in both anonymity and neutrality. Because of this, under most circumstances, implicit acknowledgment serves the needs of the patient far better than an explicit statement. The key is to accept the patient's valid perceptions of your erroneous interventions as essentially nondistorted and to intervene accordingly. In this way, the patient's constructive ego functioning is accepted and reinforced, including his reality testing and helpful efforts on your behalf. But remember too that such acceptance also implies that you will attempt to correct the underlying source of your error and that you will respond differently in the future—that you will benefit from the patient's corrective and curative efforts.

Now there are certain errors, such as your failing to remember a session or arriving quite late, in which explicit acknowledgment is inevitable. I'm not proposing that we avoid such acknowledgments, though I am suggesting that we offer them only under rather blatant circumstances. A judicious application of these principles based on an understanding of the negative consequences that follow upon explicit acknowledgment of an error, even when it is necessary, provides a perspective on these situations which can guide your interventions and help you anticipate the patient's subsequent reactions. These principles, as you will see, are based—in accordance with our general methodology—entirely on commentaries from patients.

Technically, it is essential that you recognize that in referring to the patient's criticism of your earlier intervention as it appeared in the later session, you are alluding to a manifest communication. While I agree that it evidently is a statement of a solid truth, we must recognize that at that particular point in treatment and in that session, its most critical function lies in its use as a derivative of some unconscious fantasy and perception related to an immediate adaptive context. From the material, it seems likely that you had made another error which had brought up your earlier mistake, but of course we have no data from which to validate that thesis.

Therapists shift far too readily to work with manifest contents, and they do so very often when dealing with the complexities of their own mistakes. Because of the likelihood that the derivative function of this comment is more revealing of the patient's psychotherapy than are its surface qualities, an explicit acknowledgment of the type you suggest could unconsciously serve an immediate defensive function for both you and the patient; it could become the means of creating a bastion within which the current frame issue that I am hypothesizing would be sealed off.

Under these circumstances, I would prefer to implicitly accept as valid the patient's comment about your earlier mistake, and to work with the present adaptive context and derivatives. In principle, I would have no special objection to a brief acknowledgment of the accuracy of the patient's view of your mistake, though this might not be the best time for it. For the moment, I would be concerned that this material has many unconscious meanings for the patient of which you are quite unaware, and which might never appear in direct and derivative form for analytic work if you simply agree with her at this time. It is difficult for us to keep our technique geared to the needs of the patient rather than to our own inappropriate needs. Here, for example, the therapist's guilt might prompt a confession or an inappropriate apology. Implicit acknowledgments are not inhuman, and can be conveyed in a sensitive manner that the patient can comprehend and benefit from, especially since a proper therapeutic environment is maintained. Incidentally, as I hope you can sense, I am suggesting here something that we discussed in the listening part of the course (Langs 1978a): the same manifest material varies in its *functional capacity* and Type Two derivative meaning from session to session, depending upon the prevailing adaptive context. These are important clinical issues, and we will discuss them further as new material calls for it. Please continue.

Therapist: It's interesting for me to go over this session again. I was supervised with this case, and, as I recall, most of the issues we have discussed here were not discussed with my supervisor. Almost no attention was paid to the frame.

Langs: Yes, that's typical.

Therapist: To continue: Here, I asked the patient about Fred's thoughts about her therapy.

Langs: We will confine our discussion to issues related to the framework; who will offer a comment?

Therapist: I'm introducing a third party to treatment.

Langs: Well, we can make the distinction between asking a question about a third party—a psychological invitation—and actually inviting him into the session, or the patient's disussing her treatment with him. Still, you seem to sense something about this intervention that is inappropriate.

Discussant: Well, this is not an interpretation, and I believe it is a nonneutral intervention.

Langs: Yes. In the listening part of this course we found reason to discard questions as an intervention in psychotherapy. Now, in the framework part, we find additional reason; I'm afraid we—or more precisely, our patients—really have it in for the use of questions. It would seem that there are many reasons to avoid their use and few signs that they can be constructively applied. But we will not close out the matter until we study interventions specifically.

So it can be said that, communicatively, the therapist had a need to introduce the presence of the boyfriend into treatment. More broadly, we see that her technique during this part of the session has shifted to the use of scattered and seemingly arbitrary questions, a style that is bound to reflect countertransference factors. And this is true even though this is a first session; this is an aspect of this approach often overlooked by those who turn to it. But this is not to say that questions need be avoided entirely in a first hour. My point is that they should not be used unless there is clear indication of a manifest block, and that they should be directed toward the elaboration of the specific communications from the patient and in terms of her continuing associations.

Getting back to the material, what we have here is a symbolic introduction of a third party to therapy, and on some level it will disturb the therapeutic relationship in its communicative qualities. We also can see how interventions like this tend to reflect patterns within the therapist. The first question was about the ex-wife, and now the therapist wonders about Fred. The unconscious communications conveyed here, their specific meanings as a reflection of a biased kind of curiosity, will be worked over unconsciously by the patient. If this type of intervention becomes pervasive, it could become a serious pathological input to the bipersonal field. For the moment, it needn't be too disruptive if you realize that the patient's responses are not especially illuminating or validating, and you rectify this propensity. Modifications in neutrality entail a certain level of self-revelation. Go on.

Therapist: She said that Fred had been in analysis some years ago, and that he had some passing thoughts about her getting into treatment. In the main, he felt that she was too healthy. But when he saw her act out, he would point out how erratic her behavior had become and he then encouraged her to seek treatment. Here again—and I realize that I do tend to ask a lot of questions which, as I review them, do not seem especially constructive—I asked a question.

Discussant: When a therapist becomes this active, does it tend to encourage acting out?

Discussant: Someone else is pointing out to her that her behavior is inappropriate, and that might be an indication of what she wants to do in therapy.

Therapist: Or what I want her to do. Along the me/not-me interface I realize now that these associations could refer to me and my erratic behavior—my scattered questions. So I guess that once again, she's encouraging me to seek therapy. She had hoped that I would be healthy, but begins to have questions about it. I can see that level much more clearly now. I had never realized that patients could communicate unconsciously with such intensity in a first hour. The possibility had never been discussed with me in any of my supervision.

Discussant: I would agree. It seems to me that these particular associations tend to validate your formulation about the countertransference factors in these questions. I had been skeptical, since we all tend to use questions a great deal—in almost every session and certainly in first hours. It's remarkable to be able to hear the patient's unconscious commentary on such practices. It's especially striking since the patient had raised the question of the therapist's therapy earlier in the session, when responding to the prior deviations in the framework. Now she comes back to these issues as the therapist's technique begins to be somewhat disruptive, modifying the frame a bit, and suggesting the likelihood of countertransference. The message is: When you act out, you need therapy, and these questions constitute a form of acting out.

Langs: That's quite excellent. Modifications in neutrality are, indeed, a form of acting out by the therapist, and they call for self-analysis or formal treatment—in addition to rectification within the treatment situation and an interpretation of the patient's unconscious responses.

I am, of course, very pleased to see the extent to which the members of this group are beginning to use the listening process in a very sensitive way. It is reassuring to me to hear you detect in the communications from the patient the unconscious expression of some basic principles of technique—her unconscious supervision. I have stated countless times that I have learned virtually everything I know of technique from the unconscious communications of my own patients and those whose treatments I have supervised. I learned a bit more from the unconscious communications from myself and my supervisees as I subjected them to in-depth analysis, and, in all frankness, the least constructive experiences have been characterized by conscious and direct criticisms.

Discussant: I would like to offer another formulation. An additional unconscious meaning of this material may be to the effect that the patient is warning the therapist that she should not think that she—the patient—is so healthy that the therapist can get away with all this crap that the therapist is doing to her. She might act out because of it.

Langs: Yes, along the mc/not-me interface, we find this material richly meaningful in terms of its derivative qualities and unanticipated meaning. These are all justified silent hypotheses, and the patient's subsequent associations should coalesce around one or two of them, thereby indicating the most pertinent level of meaning for the moment.

So, along the me/not-me interface, there is strong reason to believe that this material refers to both the patient and the therapist. It implies that at this moment the two are alike in important ways and that rectification of the therapist's nonneutral interventions is essential if the distinction between the two of them is to be established or reestablished.

The patient's associations now suggest a renewed sense of pathological projective identification, especially role and image evocations, perhaps based on her feeling that you are pushing her toward the sexual area and the details of her affair. On another level, this material implies another principle: that under conditions of a modified frame, since action is always an element, there are unconscious pressures on the patient to act out, to live out, rather than to contain her impulses and inappropriate needs. It seems likely too, that when the therapist's hold of the patient is impaired there will be a greater tendency toward acting out, and somatization.

There is also the offer here of an unconscious model for the therapist, and a directive toward the rectification of the frame. Fred is pointing out the patient's problems to her, and suggesting that she get some help with them. There is an implication of a more constructive therapeutic approach in that communication. In any case, you can see the extent to which the therapeutic situation is best characterized as a spiraling unconscious communicative interaction, shifting from moment to moment depending upon the inputs from both patient and therapist. Please continue.

Therapist: I then asked her another question, about what her family's response was to therapy. And she said that she had not told them; they would disapprove. When she was in high school, an aunt she was close to disappeared; much later, she found out what had happened.

She said, When I found out all the family secrets, I learned that she was in a mental hospital. I also have a cousin who hit rock bottom, and she began seeing a psychiatrist in a very hushed way. My family just wanted to know when she would stop. She stopped this week.

Langs: Any comments?

Discussant: I hear the theme of secrets, dangerous secrets, and I wonder if it has something to do with this therapist's revealing so much of herself.

Langs: Yes, in the adaptive context of these somewhat self-revealing questions and the previous deviations in the framework, the patient returns now to the dangerous qualities of the therapeutic space. In a setting in which there is, by implication, no essential background of safety, disturbing actualities—and their meanings—must be kept secret, obliterated and placed behind intense Type C barriers. This is a further characterization of the bipersonal field under the conditions of an altered frame.

In addition, the family discussions may well be a derivative of the initial group consultation with its public qualities. All of these deviations make it risky to be in treatment, and might lead to a wish to discontinue. Notice too that the fear of being or going crazy is introduced here. In the adaptive context of the deviations and monitored along the me/not-me interface, we would consider this an unconscious perception of the therapeutic situation and the therapist and, in addition, a representation of some fear within the patient that is intensified under these conditions. As a commentary on the altered frame, the patient is saying that the situation becomes confusing, secretive, crazy, and that the only protection is in flight. We therefore have additional representations of the chaos engendered within the bipersonal field and both participants when the framework is modified. The fear here is that either or both of them will turn out to be crazy. And while some of this certainly comes from the patient, the other significant vector comes from the therapist and her mismanagement of the frame. And all of this is, I would submit, far more important for the moment than any historical details that might be teased out by this approach. Sound psychotherapy does not unfold through the identification of specific and detailed facts about the patient's life, but as a part of an unconscious communicative interaction to which these details are appended and through which they take on ever-changing unconscious meaning. Please continue.

Therapist: She then mentioned that she had realized she had some problems when she found that in talking about her father she would blush intensely. She asked if I had observed that. I replied, No, I had not seen it.

If I may comment, I now, of course, hear the patient unconsciously pointing out that I am probably not a good observer and that I am missing some important aspects of her pathology. And I must say that reading this now is like hearing this material for the first time. I suddenly have a sense of depth, where before I had simply listened to the manifest content; there was a flatness about my listening.

Langs: Yes, you have an entirely different experience as a therapist when you begin to apply the full range of the listening process. But in addition I think that you are learning a great deal from the errors that you made, and from the patient's unconscious responses to them— things you couldn't appreciate as long as you confined yourself to manifest content.

Therapist: She went on and said that sometimes she developed an intense allergic reaction, with sneezing and even a rash.

Langs: If we continue to focus on this material as a commentary on the therapist's management of the framework and its implications, how would you understand these last associations?

Therapist: Well, something is not contained; there is an eruption. To put it more broadly, you get sick.

Discussant: Yes. The patient is unable to contain her impulses and fantasies, but doesn't feel that it's safe to express them verbally. So she somatizes.

Langs: I had suggested earlier that alterations in the framework disrupt the therapeutic hold and reflect poor containing capacities. And the introjects that the patient derives from such experiences appear to interfere not only with the patient's own hold and containment of the therapist, and of others as well, but in addition—and this is what emerges here—of themselves. We are learning, then, that the altered framework promotes acting out, somatization, and behavioral expression, and that it interferes with symbolic, verbal communication.

Discussant: You are therefore implying that there can be no Type A field with a modified frame.

Langs: Yes, but I would refine your comment just a bit. With an altered framework, there is a pressure toward the Type B and Type C communicative modes. However, we have seen empirical evidence— and this patient has provided us some of that—that it is still possible for the patient to make use of the Type A mode around the frame issue itself, though not around any other conflict or problem. In this context, what do you think the prevailing communicative field is in this session?

Discussant: Type B.

Discussant: Types B and C.

Langs: Yes, I think we have a rather striking mixture at this point. I would say that the patient has shifted about, beginning the hour with the Type B mode in response to what probably was a Type B style on the part of the various interviewers in the consultation session. She then shifted to a Type A mode, though entirely around the issues related to the framework, and continued to use that mode in response to the therapist's demonstrated capacity to contain and hold her. However, once the therapist began to ask her questions—which quite evidently served as both Type B projective identifications and Type C barriers against the underlying truths within patient, therapist, and environment—the patient responded with the Type B and C modes herself. Here we can see quite clearly the extent to which the framework and the therapist's management of it can influence the patient's communicative style.

Despite the Type B and C qualities, the patient continues to communicate Type Two derivatives around the adaptive contexts that we have identified, and maintains to some degree the Type A mode. Communicative styles are, of course, not absolute, and will vary from time to time within a given patient. What is particularly fascinating is to see this patient so readily shift from one mode to the other, and it may well be that, in addition to patients who are overridingly predisposed to a particular communicative style, there is a fourth group who tend to shift about. Somatization often serves as a means of action-discharge or as a communicative medium with patients who use Type C barriers in the verbal realm. In all, then, this patient is offering Type Two derivative validation of a number of basic hypotheses related to the nature and function of the framework.

This material leads me to stress again the function of the frame in securing a communicative interaction in which symbolic expression can prevail, including the derivatives of the patient's unconscious transference fantasies and, I would add, valid nontransference-based unconscious perceptions. Classical psychoanalysts, beginning with Freud (1912, 1913, 1915), have advanced the notion that the ground rules and boundaries of analysis "safeguard the transference" (Greenacre 1954, 1959, Greenson 1967) and permit its illusory and analyzable expression. Milner (1952) stated this tenet exquisitely, indicating that, as is true with the frame of a painting, the ground rules set off the analytic space from the rest of reality, and is essential in affording the analytic or therapeutic situation its unique and illusory qualities.

More recently, Bleger (1967), Viderman (1974), and I (1975b, 1976c) agreed with this point of view, and elaborated it in a number of directions. Based on our work here with the listening process, we have been able to state this as a principle: a secure frame is essential for a Type A communicative field, and for the expression of analyzable derivatives of the patient's unconscious transference and non-transference fantasies and perceptions. It occurs to me at this moment to offer as an addendum something I don't recall having previously made explicit: when the frame is secure, the material will tend to center around the patient's unconscious transference fantasies. By contrast, when there are significant deviations in the ground rules the material will reflect primarily the patient's valid unconscious nontransference perceptions, fantasies, and introjects based on the behaviors and communicated pathology of the therapist.

Discussant: By that criterion, it seems to me that most of the psychotherapy practiced today works in the realm of nontransference far more than transference.

Discussant: And most analyses as well.

Langs: Well, I certainly don't have the data we need to make such statements, but your comments are in keeping with my impressions from presentations made to me throughout this country and Canada, and from my review of the literature.

Discussant: In respect to your earlier comments, doesn't a somatic symptom have some type of unconscious meaning?

Langs: Yes, it certainly does. That is, it has a symbolic meaning. I would agree with that, and it would lead me to stress the distinction between verbal and somatic symbolization. Acting out also has a symbolic communicative function, so we could add behavioral symbolization to our list. In the Type A field, we are dealing with verbal and affective symbolic communication, as distinguished from failures at symbolic representation or symbolic expressions in a distinctly different mode.

Discussant: Isn't the therapist's answer to the patient's question, her telling the patient that she didn't notice the blushing or the rash, a form of self-revelation?

Langs: Yes, it constitutes yet another modification in the framework. Every error by the therapist modifies the frame in some manner, and that is why I earlier suggested dividing the ground rules into those that are relatively constant elements of the setting, and those that are relatively changeable and reflected in the therapist's verbal interventions. Perhaps in time, we will discover distinctive implications for each of these groups, in addition to the considerable number of shared characteristics that I am stressing for the moment. Please continue.

Therapist: She said she felt that her father objected to the therapeutic relationship, and that his feelings were very strong, since he would not discuss it at all. When she and Fred went away for a weekend to the mountains, her mother cried hysterically the night before. You know, now that I think about it, she may have said that her father objected to the relationship with Fred, rather than to her being in therapy; I'm no longer certain.

Langs: Here is a good opportunity to demonstrate that the manifest content is itself very important, despite our primary interest in derivative communication; it must be accurately registered if we are to understand the latent content and the various mechanisms that have shaped the surface derivatives. As you can see, if the patient is talking directly about her father's objections to treatment, we might sense a defensiveness characterized by projection and displacement. That is, the patient may be talking here of her own objections to the therapeutic relationship as it is now unfolding, and displacing and projecting these objections onto her father. Along the me/not-me interface, this would also represent a thinly disguised introject of the therapist's unconscious struggle against being a therapist, based on the patient's unconscious reading of underlying factors in these interventions.

On the other hand, if the patient is saying that the father objected to the patient's relationship with her boyfriend, this would be a derivative far more remote from the therapeutic relationship, one in which the level of defensiveness is considerably greater. Interestingly enough, the mechanisms would be no different in this instance, since the defenses would still involve displacement and projection; here, however, their use would be more intense and would include an additional displacement—from the therapist onto the boyfriend. Please continue.

Therapist: She went away with Fred that morning and her father prayed that there would be a flood or that the car would break down. Initially, she had brought Fred to a family gathering, and her father liked him. They still don't know she's living with him, which she has been for nearly a year, and they call her at her old roommate's apartment. They also don't know that he's divorced. I might add that some of these details may have come in response to further questions.

Then I asked her about her family's reaction to her dating someone Jewish. She said they could be more upset only by her dating a black man, and that her father was particularly upset. Then she mentioned that her father is a union organizer who has to deal with jewelry manufacturers, and that she had never gone out with a Jewish man before; she didn't initially encourage the relationship. She said that Fred practices his religion more than she does hers; he goes to the synagogue on a few high holidays, but he wouldn't want to raise any children that they had as Jewish. She said it would be okay for him to be the one to give the children religious training. I said it must mean that she felt negatively about Catholicism, and she agreed. I feel very embarrassed reading this; I see so much more now.

Langs: Learning is often disquieting. But I do think you'll long remember what you are discovering today.

Therapist: Then, I think about the middle of the session, I asked about the other people in her family—who they were. She said she has a sister, named Alice, who is very close to her mother and is in college in the South. The patient is also very close to this sister, talks to her often on the telephone, and has told her about Fred. Then there's another sister, Betty, with whom she's not especially close, and who is living with a man. Then there's a brother who is in high school and plays football, while another sister is working.

Langs: Any comments?

Therapist: I can see how I promoted a Type C field—the patient is offering a lot of details and I can detect little underlying meaning.

Langs: Yes, that is quite true. In addition, you can see how your questions have made it virtually impossible for us to see how the patient herself, based on her own unconscious fantasies and needs, would have structured the treatment situation and her communications to you. Questions do not enhance our understanding of the patient but limit it, often quite severely. And we can say this despite the fact that this is a relatively innocuous question often asked by therapists who attempt to get detailed histories in the first hour. We'll soon have a lot of information, most of it quite dead. It will be nondynamic, with little bearing on the patient's unconscious conflicts and psychopathology, and even less relevance to the unfolding unconscious communicative interaction. The only function it will serve is to destroy communicative meaning within the therapeutic bipersonal field.

To state this as a broader principle related to the framework, non-neutral interventions can generate a Type C field. Here this occurs because the patient believes it is no longer safe to offer threatening and meaningful symbolic communications; the therapist has indicated unconsciously that she is unable to manage them. Also the therapist has insisted upon functionally meaningless details, which are characteristic of the Type C communicative style. In that regard, one might almost suspect Type C therapists of having designed the usual intake interview; its popularity certainly suggests that there are many such therapists at work today. I trust you can all sense that the material we are hearing has become flat and dry—we have here an interactional resistance produced by both patient and therapist.

Discussant: Why did you say that the material dried up? I was trying to listen to this as Langs would, and I could envision the therapist's relationship with the patient being represented by and recapitulating the patient's relationship with Fred.

Langs: Oh, I was referring to the therapist's questions about the family, not the earlier material. You may have found some meaning to the earlier derivatives, and I would gladly accept that as listening as Langs would if you would simply organize it around a particular adaptive context.

Discussant: Yes, I was doing just that, thinking of how there may be some questions about the patient's relationship with Fred, and its framework, and that there may be a parallel between those issues and the deviations in the frame of therapy.

Discussant: I also heard the theme of the patient having a secret relationship with Fred, and something about a sister who was also living with a man. The family didn't know about it and the image was mixed: maybe on the one hand it was none of their business, but on the other the patient was deceiving and lying to them.

Discussant: It's something like that initial interview. For the patient, it was like a family gathering and everybody was nosy, wanting to know what's going on in the patient's life, even between the patient and her therapist.

Langs: Yes, that's quite good. I'll add this: You've mentioned the reference to lying to the family. How does this tie into our discussion of the modifications in the framework and the type of communicative field it promotes?

Discussant: Lies and deceptions are characteristic of the Type C field.

Langs: Exactly. It is no coincidence that the patient mentioned these deceptions. When the framework is modified, the therapist cannot be trusted and patients often feel that they must deceive him. To put this in new terms, an altered frame creates the conditions for *lie therapy*—the truth is set aside. You'll be quite surprised to see how often themes of deception emerge under such conditions.

Remember too that in the initial interview the therapist participated in a familylike setting that violated the patient's sense of safety, privacy, and confidentiality, and her response is to close off the truth and become involved in deceptions. Perhaps the patient is telling us that deviations are really a lie from the therapist, who proposes to do insight psychotherapy but creates conditions that make this impossible. Deviations certainly serve as barriers to the truth, and the patient is letting the therapist know something along these lines. In addition, the patient's own use of a lie is in evidence, whatever its underlying intrapsychic and interactional basis.

We are approaching the end of this session. Would anyone have intervened yet, and if so how?

Therapist: Since I hadn't intervened in a positive sense, I might be able to allude to a number of the deviations and to her responses to them.

Langs: Yes, your response should fall into one area: the need to offer an interpretive and frame management intervention if at all possible. But you should ask yourself: has the patient put such an intervention into you; has she alluded to the deviations in this session?

Therapist: No, she hasn't. I don't think that I allowed her to make a bridge; my questions may have prevented it.

Langs: Yes, there are strong reasons to intervene in this hour, but the patient has represented the adaptive context largely in derivative form, though she has done so in part through allusions to yourself and therapy; there is the link you need. I would suggest the following as a sound principle for use in circumstances of this kind: in the presence of a powerful adaptive context that has not been mentioned directly by the patient, it is best to play back selected, coalescing derivatives around that context in an effort to have the patient fill in the critical missing element, and to then discover the rich unconscious implications—fantasies and perceptions—of her associations.

A brief illustration: you might have pointed out that in this initial session the patient has shown a great deal of concern about yourself, your background, and your training; you would thereby be beginning with the representations of the adaptive context and the specific link to the therapeutic relationship. And you could continue by pointing out that in this context the patient has been talking about family gatherings, how her father pries into her affairs, how she has to resort to lies and secrets, and how disturbed she is over a lack of privacy and confidentiality.

Now, I am not attempting here to offer a complete intervention, since our extended discussion makes it almost impossible for me to go back and capture all of the derivatives. I'm simply offering this as a model, and if the patient picked up on the deviations more specifically and added some more relevant material, I would then attempt to focus on her unconscious directives toward rectification. Further, in defining the ground rules of treatment—in structuring the therapy—I would do so in a manner that shows an implicit appreciation for the patient's wishes for maximal privacy, confidentiality, neutrality, and anonymity. In that context, I would allude to such derivatives as a reference to Fred's children needing limits and her view of her father's prying as quite inappropriate.

Discussant: In other words, you would refer to the patient's discussion of how she prefers her relationship with Fred to be private, without intrusions from her family, and state that it sounds like it's important to her that her relationships have a sense of privacy.

Langs: Yes, you are approaching the rectification of the frame in that way. However, proper timing is important.

Therapist: It seems to me that this would have been a good time to do something like that. If I had become too specific, she would have remained focused in one area; but had I played back a variety of derivatives, she could then have picked up on what was most important to her.

Langs: Yes, I think this is best conceptualized in Bion's terms (1962): the proper playback creates a *preconception*, an unsaturated tension state, that can be fulfilled only by the missing adaptive context. This would be conceived of as the development of a *conception* —a saturated realization in the form of a selected fact that gives new and specific meaning and unity to the previously disconnected derivatives. Accept that for what you can get from it; we will study those processes later in the course.

You can see now how your many questions served as a Type C barrier designed to seal off the chaos related to the unresolved issues involving the ground rules. I would anticipate that the patient's need to clarify and rectify that aspect of the treatment situation will lead her to respond to your questions only briefly with the details you requested. Sooner or later, perhaps before this hour is at an end, I would expect her to come back to the frame issues in some derivative way, or perhaps even more directly. I think that this will occur for another reason, one related to the second type of intervention that I earlier suggested would be needed around this point in the session. Can anyone identify it?

Discussant: I think it had to do with the formal statement of the ground rules.

Langs: Yes, that's exactly it. Should the therapist fail to establish the framework, I would predict intense repercussions in the following hour and even the risk of immediate premature termination. It would undo all of the positive nuclei in the therapist's efforts in this session, and conjure up once again for this patient the chaos and dangers that she has been experiencing in this insecure and threatening setting. Let's try now to hear the balance of this session.

Therapist: Before I begin, do I understand you to be suggesting that, ideally, we would not keep charts or records?

Langs: Yes, that is clearly part of the optimal conditions for insight psychotherapy. Note-taking implies fixity, the capture of the patient, the possibility of violations in confidentiality, and the like. I am aware that there are laws to the contrary, but I do not know the details, though I do know that they are destructive of a proper therapeutic atmosphere. I am expressing our commitment to offer the best possible therapy to the patient, and all other considerations must be secondary.

Discussant: I would be afraid of a malpractice suit.

Langs: It is my belief that such suits arise when therapists compromise and modify the framework, and create actualities destructive of the treatment process and damaging to the patient. It would be difficult for me to conceive of such a suit in response to a therapist dedicated to the therapeutic needs of his patients, and capable of offering a secure therapeutic hold.

Time is short, so I must be brief even though there are many important issues here. Most of them do not pertain to the immediate clinical material, and therefore can be dealt with only through rather general, undocumented comments. But you see, if your concern is malpractice and you are self-serving, your efforts will be directed more toward your own anxieties and therapeutic needs, and less toward those of the patient. While I can appreciate your anxiety in the light of the recent increase in malpractice suits, I must also say that I truly believe that your implication that we must compromise our principles in order to protect ourselves from outside parties is one of the ways in which psychoanalysts and psychotherapists are destroying their own integrity and work. As therapists, we must begin by delineating the conditions under which the patient can best be helped, and must do so through the thorough application of the listening process, not through some superficial and naive approach. For some, the social consequences will then loom large, and I will leave it to them to clarify that area and to deal with the issues that are bound to arise. However, no outside need or pressure should dictate our conception of the truth and our therapeutic practices; in essence, as I have tried to demonstrate, they should stem from the patient's unconscious communications.

Therapist: Then you would not accept a patient who would insist upon your completing an insurance form?

Langs: I would not accept such a form as an inherent part of the framework, or as a precondition for therapy. I would simply establish treatment on the basis of the patient's total responsibility for the fee, and offer a totally confidential treatment setting. I would then analyze any wish by the patient to modify that framework with those conditions established. I neither directly refuse or agree. I simply convey an implicit aspect of the ground rules; namely, that I will set up a rather simple and basic framework, and that any deviations should be decided upon on the basis of analytic work. And I can assure you that the derivative material has, in every situation I have observed in my own therapeutic and supervisory work, made it absolutely clear that a deviation of this type destroys the possibility of what I have termed *truth therapy*. Your patient, in her own way, said just that a little while ago. Take that as my Type Two derivative validation for the moment, since we do not at present have material more clearly related to that issue. Let's not belabor the point; instead, please finish out this session.

Therapist: She went on to describe her other siblings, and each of their schools. Her youngest brother has become quite rebellious of late, and has been calling the patient more often than he had before. He is not as intelligent as the other kids.

Langs: There is a commentary on the process of symptom allevia-tion in psychotherapy here. The patient began this hour somewhat paranoid-like (because of the inputs from the deviations, we don't know how much of this is iatrogenic paranoia, and how much her own psychopathology) and hysterical, while at this point in the hour, she is an overcontrolled obsessive. How did this change occur? Well, it seems to have developed in at least three ways: through the therapist's capac-ity to contain the patient's disruptive and pathological projective identifications, through her ability to secure a small piece of the frame, and through her offer of interactional obsessive defenses by means of raising these detailed questions. The patient's communicative style changed from a Type B to a Type C, and this makes her appear calmer and less grossly disturbed, though the underlying issues were never interpreted or even touched upon. Noninsightful symptom alleviation can, indeed, occur on such a basis, but you can be quite certain that the danger of new and repetitive eruptions is considerable. Please go on.

Therapist: She then mentioned a younger sister and brother who are both still in grammar school. Then she spoke about having to be a model for the younger children, and her deciding not to tell them about her relationship with Fred.

Langs: Yes, there is a need for a constructive model and for a certain type of confidentiality. Even within the constraints that you have placed upon her, she is attempting to get back to the framework. With the hour drawing to an end, she is quite right in pointing to the need for definition.

Therapist: She said that she feels very guilty about not sharing more with her parents. She feels angry and is unclear how to express it.

Langs: I will just quickly link this to the framework. She may well be feeling some anger now that you have not more clearly defined the therapeutic situation, and through Type Two derivatives she suggests that she will therefore not be able to share more with you. This will evoke within her a sense of guilt, but along the me/not-me interface the patient is also saying that perhaps you are angry with her and for that reason have not defined the therapeutic situation; she adds that you either should feel guilty for not doing so or that the failure is based on some type of unresolved guilt.

Therapist: Then at the end, she asked how often she would be seeing me.

Langs: She is now functioning as your unconscious supervisor, and through a nice derivative she addresses your failure to define the framework of the therapy.

Therapist: So I told her that I would like to see her twice a week. We arranged definite hours, and she seemed happy when I said twice weekly.

Langs: Before we discuss the definition of the ground rules in the first session, can you tell us how the next session began? It should include a frame issue I believe; there is still a great deal that is unresolved in that area.

Therapist: She came into the next session with a book, and I asked her what she was reading. She said that she was reading Menninger's *Love and Hate*. (Laughter.)

Langs: Thank you. In a way, that is of course a modification in the framework: an attempt at understanding through reading rather than through free associating within the session. Your own response was a further modification in the framework—another nonneutral question. Unfortunately, time will not permit hearing more of that hour; we must briefly discuss the technique of establishing the treatment situation in the first hour. Can anyone help us with that?

Discussant: Well, it seems to me that toward the end of the session we should say something about the frequency of the sessions and arrange specific hours. This patient seemed to be talking rather freely, so perhaps we would not have to tell her that she should say whatever comes to mind—or we could mention it in passing. Then there is the problem of telling the patient how long treatment will last in the clinic, but that had been dealt with earlier. I can't think of anything else.

Discussant: We might want to say something about how often we will be on vacation, though on the other hand, that might wait until the therapist actually plans to be away.

Langs: Since time is short, allow me to complete the picture. Somewhere about three-quarters of the way through the first session, I think that it is essential to define the explicit ground rules of therapy. If certain aspects have been covered earlier in the hour because of the material from the patient, they need not be repeated again. As a rule, with a patient who is already saying whatever comes to mind, that ground rule may not be mentioned at all or may be addressed in passing—with a comment such as, We'll work much as we have done today, with your saying whatever comes to mind and allowing things to unfold from there.

In general, the establishment of the framework should begin with a brief expression of a therapeutic commitment on your part, something like: It seems quite clear that you need to be in therapy and I very much believe that I can be of help. Make it brief and to the point. From there, you proceed to define the constants: the fee, the frequency of sessions, the length of sessions, and the specific hours. For example, here, even though the fee was set by the clinic secretary, I would go on to say, As you know, the fee will be five dollars a session and I will expect you to pay me on a weekly basis. I put it that way, because, as I understand it, that is clinic policy. In fact, I should have said that the patient should have been paying the secretary on a weekly basis, but I guess I couldn't bear putting it that way.

Actually, the ideal approach is to simply ask the patient to keep track of the sessions, and to pay at the beginning of each month for the sessions of the previous month. As a standard, it is probably the best method possible, since it avoids handing the patient a bill to keep and possess as part of yourself. If for any reason you give the patient a bill, it should be written by hand by you, and no one else should be involved in any way.

Once a patient has agreed to a fee, you should then establish the frequency of the sessions. Here, you can only advise the patient that, optimally, treatment should be twice a week—or whatever seems called for. The patient may have some questions in this regard, and by and large it is appropriate to offer a general response to the effect that it is necessary to maintain a certain frequency of visits in order to accomplish, in a reasonable period of time, the goals the patient has set for the therapy. Often, the patient will ask about how long treatment will be, and the response must be vague—something to the effect that the patient should think of it in terms of years rather than weeks or months— since there is in an initial interview no sound basis for such an evaluation. Here, of course, in a situation in which there is a time limit to treatment, the patient should be told that treatment with you in the clinic will last until such and such a time. And while questions about this aspect should be subjected to free association and analysis, it may at times be necessary to simply indicate to the patient that this is based on clinic policy.

So we mention the fee, the frequency of visits, the time limit if there is one, and then we move on to arranging specific hours. In doing that, it should be made clear to the patient that the hours are set aside for him and that he is responsible for this time. I offer no elaborations, such as telling the patient that he will have to pay for his sessions if he takes a unilateral vacation or is sick. I state the ground rule directly and simply, and allow matters to unfold from there. Should the patient question this ground rule, I would simply reiterate the principle, and suggest that any further questions be subjected to exploration. I am aware that in this clinic such responsibility is not established, and I will not comment on that deviation for the moment. Based on my accumulated clinical observations, I see no valid exception to this tenet—

despite my comments to the contrary in the technique book (Langs 1973b). It is inappropriate for the therapist to accept any loss of fee because of even inadvertent life circumstances of the patient. We could discuss this in some detail, but since time is short, I must move on.

As a rule, I tell my patients of my vacation plans if at all possible—something to the effect that they can expect that I will be away for a week in the spring and for all of August. If you already know the specific dates of your vacation, the patient should be informed of them. Often it is helpful to add a comment to the effect that other than that, and for major legal holidays, you expect to be in the office and the work of therapy to continue.

Finally, in regard to the face-to-face modality or use of the couch, if you plan to continue to see the patient face-to-face, there is no need for comment in this area. On the other hand, if you believe that it is best for the patient to be on the couch, you would inform the patient that he will be working on the couch in order to facilitate the treatment process. If the patient asks questions here, I would simply reiterate that this particular modality is the best means of achieving the goals of therapy; beyond that, exploration is indicated. As you can imagine, patients have intense conscious and unconscious fantasies about lying on the couch, and these can quite meaningfully be subjected to analysis based on the patient's free associations and behaviors.

Sometimes the patient will make a request that raises the issue of total confidentiality. For example, the patient may mention in the first hour that she has insurance and that she would like you to fill out forms. To that I would respond by indicating that I propose to create a therapeutic situation in which total confidentiality is a basic element, and that any wish to modify that aspect of treatment would have to be explored in detail. As I said before, I neither agree nor refuse to fill out the form; I simply and briefly indicate that this is a request that will have to be analyzed. Sometimes a parent of an adolescent will call to make the first appointment. You should tell them on the telephone to have their child call instead. Here too, on seeing the patient you might indicate that treatment will be totally confidential. In most situations, however, your relative anonymity, total confidentiality, use of neutral interventions, the absence of physical contact, and the like will not be directly defined for the patient, but will become apparent in the course of the therapeutic experience. The same applies to the one-to-one relationship and privacy, as well as to the need to explore major life decisions before enacting them (a rule I had not identified previously): if an issue has arisen, the ground rule can be defined; if not, nothing need be said for the moment.

Discussant: Suppose a patient says he can't afford treatment without insurance; then what do you do?

Langs: I would establish a fee that the patient can afford and a realistic frequency of sessions on that basis—even if this is once a week. In this regard, I want to mention that I maintain a range of fees and that I ask for my usual fee—which is my maximum fee as well—in all situations except those where there is clear evidence of financial difficulty. In that case, I offer my lowest fee, one that I feel is still in keeping with my level of experience and expertise. In principle, once I have suggested a fee, I adhere to it. If the patient responds to my usual fee by asking if it can be reduced, I again indicate that treatment should begin on the basis of that particular fee, and add that we could then explore the possibility of a reduction. I will then make use of the patient's derivative communications and manifest comments as a basis for establishing, first, the reality of the need for a lesser fee and, second, the implications of such a reduction. Clinical data indicate that reduced fees have self-sacrificing, seductive, and infantilizing attributes that undermine the therapeutic process—often with disastrous consequences. Almost without exception, it will turn out that the patient can afford the stated fee and that a reduction is, on one level, an unconscious effort to destroy the communicative properties of the field and the potential for truth therapy. The same is true of patients who insist upon a commitment to complete the insurance forms long before they permit an analysis of their direct and derivative associations.

To avoid any uncertainty, let me mention again that the framework precludes note-taking both in the session and afterward. Psychotherapy becomes a spontaneous relationship that unfolds without constraint and in a sound communicative medium. The boundaries and limits necessary to such a setting stem from the therapist's interventions, and not from artificial devices. This implies too that there is but a single therapist for a given patient. Even with a potentially suicidal patient, the goal is to work through such issues as separation reactions to planned vacations by the therapist so that a third party—a substitute therapist—is not introduced. While it is, indeed, necessary to have another therapist cover your practice while you are away, that coverage should essentially be designed for prospective patients and only dire emergencies with present patients. With sound interpretive work, there should be virtually no need to introduce third parties to treatment in any capacity.

Well, I see that our time is up. Many of these principles are spelled out in my paper on the therapeutic relationship and deviations in technique (Langs 1975c), which I hope you will read sometime during the next few weeks. However, some of what I am presenting here is quite new, and based on observations and clarifications made in the last year or so. I want to thank our presenting therapist for a most candid and illuminating presentation. We will begin with a new therapeutic pairing next time.

Chapter Seven

SOME MAJOR ALTERATIONS
IN THE SETTING

Langs: Why don't you begin right off?

Therapist: Okay. This is a session from about the eighth month of therapy with a patient seen twice a week in the clinic. By way of basic description, the patient is a thirty-year-old single homosexual, who happens to be a student at this center—a graduate student. I started with him after he'd been in treatment with another therapist in the clinic, who had left the program the summer before. He actually transferred the patient to me, so I'm his second therapist, and this is about eight months later. I can start with the session I want to present, or do you want me to say something about the previous session?

Langs: Give us a brief summary of the previous session so we have an orientation.

Therapist: I think so, because otherwise you're right in the middle of things. I'll begin with one statement about the prior eight months. A lot of the material from the patient revolved around his relationship to me, almost constantly for the whole eight months. There was a desire to be closer to me, even to the level—as I say, he's a homosexual, so, speaking frankly—of being sexually attracted to me.

Langs: Let's develop an hypothesis using the introduction we just heard, and then we'll try to validate it. Can anybody help me?

Discussant: Can I ask one question? Who was his former therapist?

Langs: Do you mean by name? We can't do that, but we can tell you whether it was a he or a she.

Therapist: It was a he.

Langs: Why do you want to know that?

Discussant: Frankly, I was wondering whether the previous therapist was homosexually inclined.

Langs: How would that lead to a frame hypothesis?

Discussant: There have been, I believe, overt homosexual therapists who have worked in this clinic, and a number who have had strong latent homosexual tendencies. I guess that I am wondering about what the patient knew about his former therapist—the question of self-revelation.

Langs: Yes. You are wondering if there had been some overt or covert revelation by the previous therapist that had modified his neutrality and anonymity. You are implying, then, that on that basis the patient became preoccupied with the present therapist and sexually attracted to him. Now, we should identify something very interesting about that first formulation. Can anyone characterize it?

Discussant: It was defensive; it was projective.

Discussant: There was denial.

Langs: Denial of what?

Discussant: Of contempt and anger.

Langs: Anyone else?

Discussant: Denial of the role of the present therapist.

Discussant: I was simply saying that the report we heard is that the patient is preoccupied with his relationship with the present therapist. And what I actually had in mind is that I think that part of that came from the forced termination, and from the prior therapist.

Langs: Yes, there is some logic to your approach. Perhaps it is well to begin with possible factors in the prior treatment, though we must be careful from the outset to not use such formulations as a denial of possible or actual contributions from the present therapist. It is true that a forced termination can evoke what I would term *iatrogenic homosexuality* (Langs 1974)—it could intensify the patient's conscious homosexual fantasies and wishes toward the present therapist as a response to the traumatic loss of the first therapist. In addition, other modifications in the framework of the first treatment experience, and the nature of the therapist's errors—elements related to unconscious perceptions of the therapist's homosexuality—could also be factors. But we must be prepared to extend these formulations with hypotheses related to the present treatment situation, so the past does not serve as a defense against the present, a barrier to more pressing and disturbing current truths. You will notice that it is far more difficult to raise questions about the sexuality of the present therapist than to raise such issues about the former therapist. If psychotherapy is characterized as a search for the ultimate truth about the patient and his neurosis—and, secondarily, about the therapist as it relates to those truths—such questions must be raised, hypotheses generated, and then subjected to the validating process.

Discussant: Hopefully, in the direction of nonvalidation for once.

Therapist: I just sat with the patient in our session and tried to do my job.

Langs: Yes, and we will soon see something of how you carried it out, consciously and unconsciously. I trust that you understand that I am not attempting to get personal or to pry. Such matters are inherently anxiety provoking, but they must be dealt with quite directly if one is to do sound therapy. Take the model as one of self-questioning:

if a patient's homosexuality intensifies, or if he becomes intensely preoccupied with homosexual desire for us, let's not put the responsibility entirely on the previous therapist or on the patient's psychopathology. Let's treat it as an interactional product as we would any other symptom or communication, and explore it for our own contributions as well as those from the patient and from others. If you can be honest with yourself, and if you can tolerate the truth, then you will be able to offer it sensitively to the patient and help him to tolerate it as well—all in the service of enabling him to resolve his symptoms.

It has been suggested that a modification in the framework, such as a lack of neutrality or anonymity, by the past therapist or, in particular, by the present therapist, could manifestly or covertly communicate conscious or unconscious homosexual conflicts and needs in one or both of the therapists, which could in turn intensify the patient's sexual interest in the present therapist. That, then, is a frame hypothesis related to the patient's preoccupation with the therapist, directly and homosexually, stated with all candidness and openness to validation, and mentioned as one among many possibilities. Can anyone offer another proposition?

Therapist: I'm almost tempted to go back to another session.

Discussant: Or to another case. (Laughter.)

Therapist: To another session quite early in treatment where he was pressing me to disclose exactly that kind of information.

Discussant: I would just like to be clear: you are not implying that the therapist is responsible entirely for this patient's homosexual preoccupation with him. I am trying to understand your concept of an interactional symptom, for example. We know that this patient was homosexual before he entered treatment and, on that basis alone, shouldn't we anticipate that he would become involved in sexual fantasies about, and wishes toward, the therapist?

Langs: Yes, as I have said repeatedly, it may well be that much of this derives from the psychopathology of the patient. The bipersonal field concept leads us to recognize that this is never entirely so, and that there will be contributions from the therapist, however small the degree.

No therapist is ever free of countertransference, and with this patient all errors and deviations in the frame, however minor, will intensify his homosexual needs and wishes—often those directed toward the therapist.

For the moment, all I am attempting to do is to postulate possible contributions from the therapist. Of course, we could have waited to see whether any significant frame issues would arise, and we then could have attempted to determine their contribution to this preoccupation. But on the basis of the two presentations we have already heard, I thought we might be able to generate a couple of hypotheses—silent hypotheses—and subject them to the validating process. I prefer a predictive methodology, since I think it tends to be more convincing. I am well aware of the dangers of creating a biased set, but I do believe that our careful application of the validating process serves as a relative guarantee that we will be open to nonvalidation and to other possibilities.

So, can anyone offer another hypothesis?

Discussant: Yes. I propose that this sort of pressure is going to make a beginning therapist quite uncomfortable, not only because of the manifest seductiveness, but because this patient is someone who is actively intruding on the therapist's covert impulses.

Langs: Could you state that in terms of the framework?

Discussant: I am suggesting that it has probably been difficult for the therapist to maintain his neutrality and to respond with good interpretive interventions. He may also have shown his anxiety and thereby modified his anonymity. Beyond that, there may have been some type of latent response that revealed his discomfort—some sort of self-revelation.

Discussant: I think there is another factor, namely, that this patient is a graduate student at this center. On that basis there could be a lot of uncertainty about the boundaries of the therapeutic relationship, and there could be some type of personal exposure of the therapist. For example, they might meet in the hall or the patient might hear something about the therapist. With a patient of this kind, I can think of many possible ways in which the standard framework, as you term it, might have been modified.

Langs: Yes, that's excellent. As a silent hypothesis, we could state that the fact that this patient works at the same center as the therapist creates the likelihood of infringements of the therapist's anonymity and neutrality, and of the privacy of the therapy. It could also evoke realistic concerns about the total confidentiality of the therapy—that is, the patient could be well aware of the presence of records, secretaries, and the like. He could be worried about being seen by others in the waiting room, and there could be a significant alteration in the one-to-one quality of this treatment setting. In addition, the patient could specifically know of the therapist's trainee status.

Discussant: In a way, the patient's wish to have a homosexual experience with the therapist is an effort to involve him in a major modification of the framework. This would be a way of having the therapist further modify his anonymity and neutrality, as well as a reflection of the lack of clear-cut boundaries between the patient and the therapist.

Langs: Exactly. This patient's particular symptom impinges upon the framework, in that it is an attempt on some level to seduce the therapist and involve him in sexual activity. It is an attempt to modify the frame in a major way, and while it may stem from very serious psychopathology within the patient, who himself lacks a sense of boundaries and perspective—an internally based framework—we have reason to hypothesize that a second factor may exist: the many alterations in the standard framework that we already know to be present in this treatment situation.

This hypothesis implies, first, that deviations in the framework will, on some level with all patients and in a major way with patients suffering from perversions and other sexual disturbances, lead to an intensification of erotic fantasies and wishes toward the therapist. Second, such deviations so impair the communicative qualities of the bipersonal field that the patient may have serious difficulty distinguishing fantasy from actuality, likely transactions from those that are unlikely. In this way, then, his own difficulties in maintaining the boundaries between fantasy and reality, wishful thought and effort at actualization, are seriously impaired. A wish that within a secure framework is experienced as a dream or fantasy tends, within an altered frame, to be experienced as an immediate desire, or even as a real possibility. This is one type of chaos that we have seen now with each presentation. Deviations communicate pathological inputs from the therapist which as a rule are perceived unconsciously by the patient; deviations also create uncertainties about the therapist's intentions and reliability.

The distinction between fantasy and action also suffers. Once the therapist has modified the framework, the patient is no longer certain of the limits of his fantasies or of the possibilities of actualizing them. If the frame is not rectified and if in fact there are countertransference-based interventions, these problems will only intensify. And as already noted, the presence of one deviation will evoke wishes for yet another— and expectations of fulfillment as well.

In this context I must also propose an hypothesis related to the so-called erotized transference, of which this is an example. Without delving into the literature, which we will do in the next part of the course (see, however, Langs 1974, 1976c), I would propose that an extremely common contribution to a patient's wishes for direct sexual gratification from his therapist is made through unneeded deviations in the framework and through other countertransference-based errors by the therapist. We already have indications that, in general, modifications in the framework tend to heighten both erotic and aggressive fantasies and wishes, and to push their expression in the direction of seeking direct gratification. Indications are that they lead to frank expressions of such wishes in certain types of patients who are themselves inclined toward erotization and acting out.

I trust that you recognize that I am suggesting that this type of supposed transference—actually, a mixture of transference and nontransference—will stem from factors in both patient and therapist, in proportions to be determined. For the moment, our investigation of the frame has already suggested that deviations can play a role in this type of symptomatology, and the material available here suggests a firm hypothesis along these lines. If you wish to turn this around even before we obtain validation, let's at least recognize the implication that rectification of the frame and establishment of a secure setting will be essential, not only as a means of helping the patient better control and modulate these inclinations, but also as the only basis upon which the underlying factors in these tendencies within the patient could be analyzed.

These formulations are in keeping with another proposition we have stated: that the framework serves to support and enhance ego functioning and the management of pathological instinctual drive expressions—it reinforces healthy defenses. Impairments of the frame, on the other hand, are disruptive of these defenses and in addition probably heighten pathological instinctual drive expressions and needs. I very much suspect that we will be able to validate much of this once we get into the clinical material.

Therapist: I can tell you one or two fairly pertinent things relating to the transition, and things that I know the previous therapist did.

Langs: Well, as long as they're prior to this point, you may do it briefly.

Therapist: The first therapist was attending a seminar here which the patient also was attending as a part of his training, so they would see each other from time to time in this other context.

Discussant: What course was it?

Therapist: It had nothing to do with sex.

Langs: The *latent* content was human sexuality and the loss of boundaries. But, you know, what's fortunate about this, I must say, is that it's not the present therapist; we can therefore state all of this and not feel too uncomfortable. The patient had extratherapeutic contact with his former therapist. You can sense the lack of boundaries and seductiveness, the loss of anonymity and the exposure of the therapist. If we turn it around, we can experience how the frame helps both patient and therapist to maintain an adequate degree of separateness and privacy, and how its fragmentation is bound to overstimulate the both of them.

On this level, the patient's wish to go to bed with you is a derivative of his actual experience with the previous therapist, and is based too on an introjection of the unconscious implications of the deviations in the previous treatment. Hopefully, since this is such a critical area, the material we are about to hear will enable us to validate some of these ideas; if not, accept them as models which are not unlike the models we were able to derive from the previous presentations. The correspondence of such models is another level of validation; while it falls short of the Type Two derivative confirmation that is the hallmark of psychoanalytic work, it is nonetheless helpful. Please go on.

Therapist: When he presented the termination to the patient and told him I would be the therapist, he also told him he was leaving this center and exactly where he was going after he left. And he also made a statement like, Your new therapist will be a second-year resident. He also said something like this: On the one hand, he may not be as experienced as I am, but, on the other, you have to realize that he'll be in a position to make a commitment to treating you for two full years.

Discussant: That's awful.

Langs: Unfortunately, the deviations in the framework that you describe are so powerful that we will have to discuss them even though we may not be in a position to validate our comments. Such remarks are not all that uncommon, either. But first, can anyone suggest how the present therapist might protect himself against this introduction?

Discussant: He would have to show the patient that he was actually quite capable.

Langs: But something could precede that.

Discussant: He might have to interpret the patient's suspicion about the adequacy of the previous therapist.

Langs: No, you are now responding in terms of the content of the material and running the risk of projecting and blaming.

Discussant: I suspect that you are looking for some type of rectification of the frame, but I cannot think of how it could be done.

Langs: Yes, can anyone else help us out? (Pause.) It would be essential that you, in reality, disconnect yourself from the previous therapist, and you could do this only by not engaging in any discussion with him about the patient and seeing to it that you had no prior information whatsoever. If you could maintain that aspect of the frame, and convey it implicitly in your interventions, it could form a nucleus out of which the patient could begin to realize not only that you yourself are capable of establishing and maintaining a sound framework, but also that you are distinctly different from his previous therapist.

I am reminded of *The Bipersonal Field* (Langs 1976a), which begins with a conversation between a patient and a therapist in the hallway, a modification in the framework that, as I recall, I discussed rather extensively. On the basis of that initial communication—and it was between a second therapist and his patient, as they approached their first session together—I believe that I predicted that there had been some type of frame issue in the previous treatment. And in that context, I discussed the importance of total confidentiality, and my deep conviction that prior information about the patient is not only valueless but is actually destructive of the therapeutic interaction.

I cannot agree with those who suggest that this kind of modification of the framework occurs only with inexperienced therapists. I already have considerable evidence that such modifications are quite common with experienced analysts, and in fact, as some of you may know, Stone (1961), in his important monograph on the psychoanalytic situation, actually advocates limited self-revelations to the patient under judicious conditions. He includes among these permissable revelations such things as telling the patient where he is going on a vacation, or the nature of his interests and hobbies. And though he does stress the importance of prior analytic work on the therapist's part, he too easily concludes that on that basis such bits of information, far from proving detrimental to the therapeutic process, will actually enhance it. Kanzer (1963), in his review of *The Psychoanalytic Situation,* took issue with this position, and, as you can see, it stands in marked contrast to the principles that I have been developing with you and to the clinical data that we have heard. These deviations have a consistently strong influence on the patient, though they can be readily overlooked by the therapist as long as he does not consider the subsequent material as Type Two derivatives in the adaptive context of the deviation.

In a way, we have here a unique, tentative type of validation: the formulation of an hypothesis regarding significant deviations in the framework of the prior treatment, and validation through the retrospective report of specific alterations in the framework of which we were unaware. As I said earlier, we will supplement this effort with a careful exploration of the framework of the present therapeutic situation, but we already have a bridge to this therapist; implicit in his comments is the probability that he discussed this patient with the previous therapist, read the notes, and fully accepted the heritage handed down to him by the first therapist.

Therapist: Unfortunately, you are quite right. At the time, I had no idea what I was getting myself into.

Langs: So, the previous therapist engaged in multiple deviations in the framework, including a number of self-revelations. In addition, he modified your anonymity and actively demeaned your capabilities. And you were also presented as the one who set the time limit for the treatment. I strongly suspect that all of this contributed significantly to the blatant seductiveness that you were quickly faced with in this case, and there is in addition some likelihood that even at this late date there will be echoes of these issues in the material from the patient.

Maybe now you can all see why it is best not to accept information from a consulting or previous therapist; you have absolutely no way of knowing just how destructive and disruptive he has been. You could be accepting Pandora's Box; once the patient opens it up for you, it will prove difficult to separate yourself from the chaos. You would have a near impossible job of rectification, and it would be far easier if you had not been party to the deviations. Here, in a situation where the patient undoubtedly is consciously aware of your involvement with the previous therapist, it serves to reinforce his conscious and unconscious perceptions and introjection of you as homosexually inclined. In fact, the very discussion of this patient between yourself and the first therapist constitutes an unconscious homosexual interaction, which would only serve to intensify the patient's wishes for a similar experience. It would also reinforce his own homosexuality and the unconscious basis for it; the distinction between yourself and the patient in this regard will be seriously blurred.

Therapist: Well, he had some concerns, initially—this is going back earlier in the therapy—as to whether things he said would get back to the other therapist; it was the central issue of a couple of sessions.

Langs: You can see where it came from.

Therapist: In actuality, he needn't have worried, because the other therapist never bothered to dictate any notes, and I actually didn't have much by way of prior information. He had talked to me only once about the patient.

Langs: Once is enough. Let's now turn to your brief summary of the session just before the one you want to focus on. I have already offered my guarantee that these issues will appear in some form in the material we are about to hear. This is based on the hypothesis that when the framework of therapy is modified, damaged, and disturbed to this extent, the patient will continue to work it over until the end of his days, let alone to the end of this treatment. He will also return to it again and again until the present therapist offers as much in the way of rectification as possible, and a series of sound interpretations of the relevant unconscious perceptions and fantasies.

In these days when so many patients go from therapist to therapist, this type of therapeutic experience leaves permanent damaging residua. Much of it centers around the issue of lie versus truth therapy. Under these conditions, the patient could only have experienced lie and barrier therapy, with extensive sectors of misalliance and bastions. As a result of the pathological defenses and gratifications involved, he will have strong resistances to a form of truth therapy in which he will ultimately experience his own inner chaos and pathology—even though it promises him a singular opportunity for lasting adaptive structural change.

These are matters that simply cannot be taken lightly. Remember too, that this patient has continued with a second therapist in this clinic. There are many ill-gotten gains for him under these conditions, and I suspect that the patient will, in derivative form, tell us something of why he has remained in a blatantly destructive treatment situation. Based on the material that we have heard to this point, there is a likelihood that one factor is that the sickness outside of himself is greater than the sickness inside, and the former reinforces and justifies the latter. Please continue.

Therapist: So this is the preceding session. In this section, uh, session—that's a slip that he once made—he started out with a comment about the fact that recently he had been coming to sessions with a can of soda, which he would drink during his hour.

Langs: Well, I trust that everyone knows that I did not stage this presentation. The therapist actually picked a different session to focus on, and this is his introduction. And where does it begin?

Discussant: With a frame issue. I must say that I am not sure how to classify this one, though.

Langs: Yes, as I continue my study of the frame I find that patients and therapists are full of unexpected surprises. Actually, this would fall under the rubric of the rule of abstinence, a tenet that we have not discussed to any degree as yet. It is rather interesting and pertinent to recall that Freud first defined this aspect in writing of the expressions of the patient's transference love (Freud 1915), and her demands that it be gratified by the analyst. Freud specifically stated that these needs and longings must be allowed to persist as a means of maintaining the patient's motivation for insightful structural change through analytic work. He indicated that direct gratification of these claims would enable the patient to achieve her ends, though the analyst would not achieve his—implying that the patient was seeking a form of misalliance or lie cure rather than the insightful truth cure offered by the analyst.

In this course, we have alluded to abstinence in reference to the analyst's neutrality, the absence of physical contact, and the maintenance of his anonymity. As you can see, abstinence is a complex concept that is a factor in almost all of the other ground rules. In general, deviations in the framework gratify the pathological needs of the patient, and thereby alter the rule of abstinence.

As you may know, some analysts misconstrued this rule, extending it beyond the therapeutic dyad to prohibit their patients a variety of gratifications, sexual and otherwise, in their everyday lives. Not only was intercourse interdicted, but marriage as well. To this day some analysts forbid marriage during the course of treatment.

Actually, the issues are quite complex since there is probably some degree of pathological gratification when a patient marries in the course of an analysis or therapy, but I would still insist that there is no need for an interdiction. We should simply adhere to the principle of analyzing before acting, and allowing the patient's material— the derivative communications—to tell us the unconscious functions of the proposed marriage and exactly how it should be handled in the therapeutic situation.

So abstinence is the attempt to secure a therapeutic situation in which the patient does not receive pathological gratification. It implies, then, adherence to the other basic ground rules, and it also calls for a distinction between appropriate and inappropriate gratifications in the treatment situation (see Langs 1976c). Thus, we should recognize that the patient is entitled to and should obtain a range of appropriate gratifications in the course of treatment, especially those derived from the security of the therapeutic hold and framework, and from the insights and inevitable positive introjects that stem from sound interpretive work.

So this patient begins with a modification in the framework in the form of an inappropriate self-gratification. We will soon see how his verbal associations illuminate the unconscious meanings and functions of this behavior. In light of our earlier discussion, we can see already that this behavior serves to validate the thesis that disruptions in the framework continue on as powerful adaptive contexts for long periods of time—though we must accept that confirmation quite tentatively since we do not know the events of the hour immediately previous. In addition, the specific form—that of an alteration in the rule of abstinence—is in part based on an introject of the unconscious nature of the deviations that we have already had described to us. Inappropriate gratifications played a significant role in those particular modifications of the framework. So in addition to sources within the patient—and I am sure that there are important contributions from that realm—there is a significant input from the alterations in the framework. In fact, I would like to stress the evidence that it is an alteration in the frame rather than erroneous efforts at interpretation that contribute to a behavior of this kind. This is a bit of acting in, and it is based in part on the acting-in qualities of the prior deviations. Furthermore, the self-gratification is based, first, on an introjection of the previous therapist's misuse of the patient for self-gratifying reasons, and, second, on possible misuses by the present therapist as well. In light of the damage to this framework, this self-gratification is also a defense against, and a representation of, a likely dread of actual physical contact or some other form of pathological gratification in the relationship with the therapist. The level of anxiety and the fear of actualization is quite high, and I must stress again that this stems from factors within both the patient and the therapeutic situation, including the altered frame.

Therapist: In a previous session, I had said something about the soda, inquiring what that was about. I also introduced the idea (and I don't recall exactly what I said) that this was behavior that we should be interested in understanding.

Langs: That was before this course. I trust that now you wouldn't ask the question or make the confrontation. You would just ask it *silently*, and wait for the derivatives to unfold for you to interpret to him.

Therapist: In this session, he had just sort of jokingly said, Well, I've still got my soda. Then the bulk of this preceding session was involved with the fact that for a few months, he had been involved with a homosexual lover he had met sometime after we started therapy. And this relationship had very quickly developed into one where there was no actual sex. The lover was someone he kept complaining about; he was promiscuous and would get his sexual gratification through casual encounters in toilets and things like that, but would never be sexually interested in the patient. It was unclear whether the lover was impotent, or simply preferred sex with anonymous people rather than with him, even though the two of them still, supposedly, loved each other. And he was occupied with trying to get help for this lover. Another thing about the lover was that the lover was Jewish. The patient is Spanish. I obviously am Jewish. And he had been asking me for a couple of sessions to provide him with referrals so that his lover could go into therapy.

Langs: Here again is an impingement on the frame. Now, how would it be handled? This material dictates a principle that I think is true as a generalization. What would happen if you did make such a referral?

Discussant: It would play out what has already happened in this treatment: a seductive therapist referred the patient to this therapist, and now this therapist would get involved in referring the patient's lover to someone. It is like a chain of homosexual gratifications. It seems pretty clear to me that it would have strong homosexual implications, even though the therapist was not involved in any explicit homosexual way.

Langs: Yes, what you are touching on here is a concept that many analysts and therapists have had difficulty understanding: the actual behaviors of the therapist have valid and real unconscious meanings that have a great impact upon the patient. Therapists tend to consider only the surface of their own behaviors and their manifest intentions, and fail to recognize the rich unconscious communications they contain. The patient, on the other hand, tends to react primarily to these unconscious communications, and only secondarily to the manifest intentions. A great deal of valid therapeutic work centers on the rectification of pathological unconscious communications contained within the therapist's interventions, and on an analysis of the patient's responses—nontransference first, transference distortions second.

Incidentally, that this request is loaded with unconscious meaning far more than realistic need is seen in the fact that this therapist is working in a clinic. The patient is quite familiar with the resources here, and yet he sets aside his own capacities and seizes this particular moment as an opportunity to evoke a further deviation in the framework—undoubtedly in part as a means of calling this issue to the therapist's attention, partly as an effort at continued inappropriate gratification and misalliance, and partly in the hope of rectification and ultimately gaining analytic insight. For the moment, the material suggests a major investment in pathological homosexual gratification, though there is some allusion to hoping to cure the friend—a representation, along the me/not-me interface, of both the patient and the therapist.

With a focus on the framework issues with which we are familiar, can anyone offer a brief formulation of the material to this point in this session?

Discussant: Well, we could take the deviations as the adaptive context, including the patient's drinking of the soda.

Discussant: Isn't that a therapeutic rather than adaptive context?

Langs: Yes, there is a tendency to confuse the therapeutic and adaptive contexts, partly because they sometimes are identical. This is not the case here. Since we know nothing of the previous session, we are limiting ourselves to viewing this material as a commentary on the deviations we do know about. We would therefore consider those alterations in the framework as the adaptive context, and the soda drinking is a therapeutic context related to the adaptive context in rather evident ways. It is a secondary organizer of the material.

Discussant: As a commentary, the patient is saying that these deviations have led him to see the therapist as a homosexual lover, and as someone who is promiscuous and out of control. I am not sure how much of that is valid, and how much is distortion.

Langs: Yes, your point is well taken. It is a question that we can legitimately ask of the subsequent material, even though we have reason to believe that there is much that is judicious in this commentary.

In your formulation, you use a *transversal* tone that encompasses both the previous and the present therapist, and we should recognize that there is little doubt that this material alludes to the first therapist; in addition, it must in some compelling way refer to the present therapist as well. In terms of the deviations in the framework on the part of the first therapist, you are quite right in emphasizing that, despite the absence of actual sexual contact, he had behaved in an unconsciously seductive and homosexual manner, had been promiscuous and insensitive, and had made the referral to the present therapist in a seductive fashion.

Beyond that, we could monitor this material along the me/not-me interface and develop a view of both patient and therapist, and actually generate a silent hypothesis that, in some way, this therapist has continued to modify the framework through measures that carry with them many of the implications of the earlier deviations. On this basis we could suspect that the adaptive context for the drinking of the soda— the therapeutic context—takes the form of modifications in the framework of which we are unaware. At the very least, it could pertain to the presence of the clinic secretary, the fact that the treatment is still taking place at a center where the patient is a student, and the likelihood of modifications in anonymity and abstinence in the present therapeutic relationship. Since we know nothing of the previous hour, let's leave it at that, and hear more material.

Therapist: In discussing the sessions leading up to this one, I recall my supervision from an able supervisor. We had done some work on the request for the referral of the boyfriend, and we saw it in terms of the patient's effort to displace his own concerns and anxieties onto the boyfriend. We formulated that in this way he was trying to get help for himself and his own sexuality, but absolutely nothing was said about the ground rules and framework. We eventually made the decision to give him the referral, so in the session I am describing here I had responded to this material by giving him the names of some therapists.

Langs: It seems now that there is some confusion about the sequence: could you clarify the exact point at which you intervened? After all, you are now describing what we will term a modification in the standard framework, and it is quite important to hear the material in sequence. In that way, we can understand the material on which you based your intervention, and the patient's responsive associations as well.

In the supervision that you described briefly for us, the approach was entirely in terms of unconscious dynamics within the patient. There was no allusion to the therapeutic interaction, and possible countertransference-based inputs were thereby ignored. In particular, the many frame issues were neglected. The formulation shapes up as what I have already termed a psychoanalytic cliché; if I am correct, it will be designed to serve as a Type C barrier to the chaos that exists in the framework area. Here, by the way, is the kernel of truth in your formulation: there is an unconscious effort at cure being undertaken by this patient, but it refers to both yourself and the patient, and to the need to establish a secure therapeutic situation in particular. Incidentally—and we need not pursue it here—it is difficult for me to follow how your own formulation that the patient was attempting to get help for himself through his friend led you to offer the referral. It would seem to dictate instead an interpretive and nongratifying response. But instead of pursuing that question, could you please clarify the sequence of the session?

Therapist: Well, I gave you the material pretty much in sequence. It was at the point where he was talking again about wanting to get help for his lover and asked me specifically, What about the referral? It was at that point that I gave him the names. Oh, by the way, in the last session we had discussed changing an appointment time at his request.

Langs: You can see how lightly we take framework issues; even in a presentation related to the ground rules, you forgot to mention that.

Therapist: Yes, I can see that now. As best as I can recall, I told him at the beginning of the session that I could change the hour as he had requested.

Langs: Through this experience, we can see too how material in and of itself, divorced from the actualities of the therapeutic interaction, has little meaning. Now that we know how the session actually began, the derivatives come to light and the session takes on many implications unavailable to us previously. However, I think that silent hypotheses can be framed and validated, even in the absence of an identified adaptive context, if we have learned how to monitor material sensitively in terms of Type One derivatives. I refer here to my suggestion that in all likelihood the therapist had himself recently altered the framework of this treatment situation. It now turns out that he had done so at the very beginning of this session, and this provides us again that unusual form of validation I have termed *retrospective validation.*

So in the background of this session is the patient's request to change his hour and his expectation of a response in this session. He then begins the session by drinking from a can of soda, his own alteration of the frame. The therapist, without waiting for the patient to begin to communicate and set the tone of the material, without waiting for additional behaviors and associations through which he might clarify the unconscious meanings of the patient's request and obtain derivative directives of how it should be handled, announces that the time can indeed be changed. The patient gratifies himself; the therapist inappropriately gratifies the patient; and possibly, the therapist inappropriately gratifies himself. And the material that follows is the patient's commentary on these transactions.

You might ask why I assume that the change in hour is inappropriate. First, we have our established standards and that includes set time. In principle, there is no reason to change a single hour, though under unusual circumstances, such as a job change, it might be necessary to change the set time on a permanent basis. Such a shift should be preceded by a full analytic exploration.

But in addition, there is a second basis for my comment: this clinical material. We are told of no exploratory work in this regard. But in addition, now that I know the immediate adaptive context, in one quick moment I can organize the session that we have just heard around it and discover the patient's commentary. Can anyone do that for us?

Discussant: As I remember it, the patient's first response was to talk about a homosexual lover he was involved with, though without actual sex, and who was promiscuous and impotent. If we take that as a commentary on the changed hour, it is a pretty clear way of saying that the therapist has now become unconsciously homosexually involved with the patient. It also sees the changed hour as a reflection of something indiscriminate and of the therapist's impotence.

Langs: Yes, that's quite good. Treating this material as a commentary on the deviation, we must be reminded that there are elements of reality and fantasy, and contributions to the patient's perceptions from both himself and the therapist. Since the patient is homosexual, there is a marked stress on the homosexual implications of the deviation. These are always present, but would be brought out in bold relief by this type of patient. Such deviations do indeed unconsciously gratify the therapist's countertransferences, among other factors. And of course, this patient is likely to be extremely sensitive to that aspect, to which he will add his own homosexual fantasies and a propensity to experience interactions in sexual terms. Based on the material at hand, it would be quite difficult to sort out the contributions from each participant here; what is important for us is to recognize the need to do so.

So we learn again that it is the impotent therapist who modifies the frame, a therapist who is indiscriminate and who manages his own sexuality—his inner impulses of all kinds—quite poorly. Deviations entail inappropriate instinctual drive gratifications and create critical sectors of misalliance. On another level, they constitute pathological sexual projective identifications which some patients will find more gratifying than threatening, while others will, of course, be more threatened than gratified. Here, we sense such a mixture, and it has a large measure of gratification which then leads the patient to seek out more by asking for a referral for his lover.

Incidentally, as long as the therapist is involved in this type of misalliance, in which shared unconscious pathological gratifications play a major role, it seems likely that the patient will continue to drink soda during his session. Certainly, too, efforts at verbal interpretive work in some area other than the framework, such as implying that the patient has voracious oral needs or something of that sort, would have little influence on his behavior. Can you now be specific about the rest of the session?

Therapist: Well, he had gone on about his lover in the way I have described, and then he had asked for the referral. I responded by asking him to clarify what he was asking for in terms of the referral. And the patient said that his lover had asked him several times whether I had said anything about a therapist for him. He went on to describe how much the lover really wants to go into therapy. He knows his promiscuity is a problem and he wants to change it.

Langs: Any comments?

Therapist: He's saying that he is not the only one who is disturbed, there are others, and I guess, viewed along the me/not-me interface, that includes me.

Langs: Yes, I'm really sorry that it's unfolding this way, but our patients often have very painful messages for us—especially when we modify the frame. And a homosexual patient is certainly going to stir up your own unresolved homosexuality, partly for his own defensive needs and partly because he must help you secure those counter-transferences if you are going to be in any position to help him.

You apparently approached this problem on the surface, with a question, thereby showing your disinclination to work with the unconscious implications of his request. Therapists often do this when asked a direct and realistic question, especially one that seems to call for an ultimate answer. They forget that in psychotherapy, properly structured, they have a very special type of communicative field; while there are, indeed, realities, a therapeutic process relies on derivative communication, with everything else in its service.

And yet, despite your efforts to shift to the surface, the patient manages to find a means of derivative expression: the lover's promiscuity is a problem and he wants to change it. In the adaptive context of the change in the hour—the deviation—he returns to the problem of uncontrolled sexual gratification and the need for rectification. If this session had been approached with a greater eye toward derivative communication, it seems quite clear now that the therapist would be in a position to interpret the patient's unconscious perception of his offer of a changed hour as a form of homosexual collusion—the patient too is gratified homosexually by the change—a reflection of impotency and a kind of indiscriminate and destructive form of sexual gratification. He could then go on to point out that the patient had stressed the need to change such behaviors which, in the context of the offer of the different

hour, can mean only that the schedule should be left intact and a different session not arranged. The therapist could even add that the
patient is clearly implying that it is only on the basis of maintaining the
schedule as it now exists and not becoming involved in indiscriminate
changes in the time of the session that the patient would have the
necessary conditions of treatment in which he could effect his own
hopes for insightful relief of his symptoms.

It seems now that the current prevailing meaning of his wish to
get the lover into treatment is twofold: first, it expresses the patient's
wish for a secure treatment situation of his own and for a valid
therapeutic opportunity which, in terms of his perceptions—we are not
as yet in a position to evaluate their validity—has not been offered him;
and, second, it expresses the unconscious wish to cure the therapist,
and probably, since he has failed to do this, for the therapist to get
himself into treatment.

It is these unconscious meanings that must be understood rather
than gratified through a referral, and certainly you can see on this basis
that the referral would greatly modify the rule of abstinence and would
actually preclude the analytic resolution of the intrapsychic consequences of this entire situation for the patient. Instead of offering a
referral for the lover, the therapist should have become involved in a
reexamination of the nature of the present treatment situation and his
own valid capacities and countertransferences, and should have made
renewed efforts to offer a sound therapeutic experience to this patient.
This would include securing the frame in whatever way necessary,
and interpreting this material around the prevailing adaptive contexts,
including the patient's own efforts to modify the framework. As you
can see, there would be an entirely different outcome on such a
basis—for both patient and therapist. Offering the referral creates a
sector of misalliance and a bastion, and denies the many unconscious
meanings being communicated in the patient's derivatives—both
perceptions and fantasies.

I can only hope that the richness of the unconscious implications of
this request has convinced you that it is not indifference, coldness, or
rigidity that has led me to develop this particular standard, but the
realization of the extensive unconscious implications of such a request,
and an understanding of the type of setting that promotes their analyzable expression. This patient is attempting to teach the therapist these
very principles; let's all learn from them, and let's recognize that

this is exactly what the patient is working over—the deviation and its reflection of countertransferences within the therapist. And because this is so, it is here that the therapist must have his understanding and intervene, and it is in this very painful area that we must address our comments in this conference. If we wish to deal with the truth, there can be no other way. Well, enough of sermonizing; please go on.

Therapist: The lover had just been given the name of some community counseling center, and the patient said, I really don't know what that place is like, so I'd really like to get some referral from you. I think I asked some other question like, You asked me for private referrals, is that what Mark—the lover—wants or is prepared to get into? And he said, He's really uptight about money. To tell you the truth, he was planning to come to a clinic and lie about how much he makes.

Langs: Are there any comments at this point?

Discussant: I heard the reference to a lie, and thought of the Type C field and what you are now calling "lie therapy." I'm trying to put that together with the deviations. Does this material imply that the change in the hour creates a Type C—lie—field?

Langs: Yes, I believe that's exactly what the patient is trying to tell the therapist. If we now attempt to put together our experiences with deviations in this respect, we can see that with some consistency patients indicate that deviations in the framework lessen the Type A qualities of the therapeutic bipersonal field, and increase the Type B aspects of projective identification and action-discharge and the Type C qualities of barriers, lies, and falsification. It would be very easy to miss the links between the change in the hour and lying at a clinic if one did not adhere to the principle of taking each deviation as the adaptive context for all of the associations in the session.

On another level, the patient is also indicating that the technique of asking questions and directing the patient to the surface of his thoughts is an effort to develop lies and barriers to underlying, more disturbing truths. There is something very telling in this material. The friend plans to come to a clinic and lie about his income, thereby creating a fundamental condition to the treatment in which a lie and deception is a component. This is a striking commentary on alterations in the framework and the type of communicative medium they create. Here again, based on the patient's own unconscious propensities and the nature of the therapist's interventions, there is a stress on the quality of deception and falsification in a field whose frame is not secure. But we already have other evidence that indicates that this is a general truth, one that may be especially prominent with certain patients and therapists. Deviations in the framework destroy truth therapy; it could not have been stated more clearly.

Another principle that I have stated earlier is illustrated here. Once again, in the situation of an alteration of the framework, the only meaningfully coalescing derivatives organize around the frame issue—and nothing else. These are Type Two derivatives in the adaptive context of the change in the hour, and they reflect an introject of the therapist related to his mismanagement of the frame and the patient's unconscious understanding of how this affects the conditions of treatment. He acknowledges that he himself needs lies and barriers, but he makes clear that the therapist has such needs as well—these are powerful transversal communications. Let's hear more.

Therapist: The patient was saying that Mark was planning to go to a clinic and lie about how much he makes, but the patient tells him, Mark, that's not going to get therapy off on the right foot.

Langs: What do we have here?

Discussant: A model of a rectification.

Langs: Exactly. The tone of the session has shifted toward unconscious curative efforts. Here, the patient offers you another directive to rectify the frame.

Discussant: Would you have intervened at this point?

Langs: For the moment, I do not have a sense of where we are in the session as far as time is concerned. If we are about halfway through the hour, I would maintain an attitude of listening in respect to the request for the referral of the lover, and hope to get a derivative that will bridge both that request and my actually having changed the hour—at which point I would intervene. Much of this material may well stem from the patient's expectation that the referral will be forthcoming—a point I haven't emphasized.

As you can see, I began with a silent hypothesis which has been silently validated; at this point, I am, indeed, preparing a silent intervention. I have already outlined that for you, and now have another component: these deviations do not get therapy off on the right foot. If the patient does not provide a clear link between these derivatives and the two modifications in the framework at hand, I would still intervene because of the importance of these therapeutic contexts and the clear-cut need for a rectification of the framework. At almost any point in the session, I could begin an intervention by pointing out to the patient that the hour began with my informing him that I could change the session that he had asked me to shift, and that he had spent a good deal of the hour asking, in addition, for me to refer his lover to a private therapist. Much of what he has been saying is a very perceptive commentary on these requests, and especially on my decision to offer an alternate hour. Quite indirectly, he is making it clear that this constitutes a form of underlying homosexual gratification. I won't repeat what I have already said, though I will stress that I would end the intervention with the two references to the need for rectification, and conclude by indicating that the patient has made quite clear that both changing his hour and giving him the name of a therapist for Mark undermines treatment, creates an atmosphere of lying, and interferes with the establishment of a sound basis for his own therapeutic experience. Please continue.

Therapist: Then he said, At least I'd like him to have a good interview. He meant consultation. Around this point I gave him the names I had gotten from my supervisor and said something like, Well, you can call any one (I think there were two or three) of these private practitioners, or go to any one of the clinics in town, as I had said before. So he took them, and he asked me whether these therapists were associated with this center or what. He then asked me something about their level of experience. And I again said that they were in practice and that they're on the attending staff. So, he took the names and pocketed them.

Langs: Any comments?

Discussant: I hear something that I experience as rather odd: the patient is arranging for treatment for his friend with a more experienced therapist. This must say something about his feelings about his own treatment, though I'm not sure what it is.

Discussant: Now that the therapist has deviated, the patient asks for more in his questions. Also, would you consider as another deviation the fact that the therapist wrote down these names on a piece of paper and gave it to the patient?

Langs: Yes, I would indeed. It modifies the therapist's use of neutral interventions geared toward interpretation, which implies confining himself to the verbal sphere, and it also alters the rule of abstinence. The entire deviation has been undertaken with a focus on manifest content, and with nonneutral responses filled with unconscious implications that are, for the moment, being ignored by both patient and therapist. I expect that the patient will soon, in derivative form, work over additional unconscious implications of this transaction.

But already you can see the characteristic split that I described to you earlier in a patient's responses to alterations in the framework: consciously, he requests the change in hour and the name of a private therapist for his friend, and expresses appreciation directly—though in addition, he begins to raise questions which hint at reservations on his part. On the other hand, the derivative material has to do with homosexual gratification and promiscuity, impotency, lie therapy, and destroying the basic foundation of treatment. As Type Two derivatives in the adaptive context of the deviations, they are powerful communications. Still, most therapists would not listen in that way and would totally deny the links between the derivative material and the deviations. That's why I wanted to not only demonstrate their existence, but also to predict their presence and nature.

Discussant: But isn't the therapist's giving the names on a piece of paper quite similar to his handing the patient a bill?

Langs: Well, I said earlier that the ideal frame includes allowing the patient to keep track of the number of sessions in each month and to be responsible on that basis. There is some inappropriate gratification for the patient in receiving a bill from the therapist, and as we review this issue I see even less reason to justify this practice as a necessary component of the treatment situation than I had previously allowed. But nonetheless, the additional piece of paper with the names of the therapists on it extends the pathological elements in such a practice, and provides the patient with a special piece of the therapist for him to possess—a measure that will have extensive unconscious meaning for both therapist and patient, and to which both, especially the latter, will respond.

Discussant: The patient has another real gratification in connection with the bill because he gets money back from the government at the end of the year by deducting his treatment as a medical expense.

Langs: Yes, but there at least the therapist is not actively participating. His role is far more explicit when he completes an insurance form, a step that provides the patient with considerable extra-therapeutic gratification while also modifying the standard of total privacy and confidentiality.

At this point in the session, with the transfer of the piece of paper, I would postulate a buildup of a *preconception* (Bion 1962), a tension state that will evoke an intense search for a realization that would saturate and resolve the preconception, and provide a sense of closure in the form of a *conception*. The only realization or selected fact that could satisfy this buildup is, I believe, a working over of the frame issues. With that in mind, let's see what happens.

Therapist: So, he pocketed the paper and then he said, Okay, I guess now the session begins. I guess it has already. I really feel that Mark will get help, and he should have it even if I don't stay with him. I have a feeling that things won't go well with the relationship now, sort of a foreboding. You never know.

Langs: He now has a foreboding: two requests for deviations in the framework have been granted, and he responds first with a comment that reflects the way in which the therapist and the patient are splitting off aspects of the session, although he adds that this should not be done. He then alludes to his conscious expectation that all of this will be helpful, but next he experiences a foreboding—things are not going to go well now. When the frame is altered, we know that chaos will follow, and it seems likely that the patient is beginning to experience or anticipate the detrimental consequences of the deviations.

Therapist: Then he told me about two people. He has a friend, a woman, who is also a graduate student here. He said, Anne told me about a couple of her friends (they have nothing to do with this center) named Frank and Susan. Frank is gay, but the two of them fell in love and they lived together. It was a man and a woman. And Frank was impotent. So he saw a therapist. And it was eight months of hell, he said smilingly.

Langs: I am learning that many therapists get involved in one deviation after another—I don't think we've had a presentation yet where this has not been the case. In one way, it makes it difficult to organize the material because each segment should be developed around a specific, single deviation—adaptive context—and then around the total accumulation of effects. Here, for example we have a continued commentary on the first two modifications in the framework, but its most intense precipitant is what?

Discussant: Handing the patient the piece of paper.

Langs: Yes, actually, that deviation is twofold: the offer of a referral for Mark, and the gift of the piece of paper. And what do you hear?

Discussant: The eight months of hell is certainly one element. It shows that the reference to therapy as hell is connected to his own treatment.

Langs: Yes, and for once, to his treatment with his present therapist. And I think that this is his emphasis now because of the weight of the current deviations. What else?

Discussant: The therapist has been destructive.

Discussant: I think that there's a lot of gratification to the idea that the therapist is going to help the patient get a perfect lover, but the therapist is not going to be his lover himself.

Langs: Yes, here you allude to another possible unconscious meaning of the referral, though I would recommend your maintaining it as a silent hypothesis until the patient's derivatives support your formulation. It is well stated, however, and demonstrates how each deviation contains specific unconscious and dynamic meanings and functions.

Discussant: It seems to me that the patient is trying to create a situation where he can live out rather than work through his problems, such as his oral conflicts as reflected in his drinking the soda and getting direct gratification from the therapist.

Langs: Yes, that is a factor, but I think that you are losing sight of the principles of the listening process. We want to formulate the material from the session in terms of the actual unfolding spiraling interaction. We have the adaptive context of the piece of paper with the names of the therapists on it and a set of associations which serve as a commentary on that particular intervention. We should therefore maintain that particular organizer and approach these derivatives as Type Two expressions with unconscious perceptions and fantasies contained within them.

Discussant: He's saying that there have been eight months of hell and nothing changed. More immediately, then, he's saying that these deviations create a hell rather than a place of cure—if that's his idea of heaven.

Discussant: He's also saying, along the me/not-me interface, that the therapist seemed to be setting up an appropriate relationship, but then was impotent.

Langs: Yes, you are now selecting Type Two derivatives around the adaptive context of this intervention. The patient pockets the paper and this is where his thoughts go. There is a matter of falling in love and living together—itself a representation of the meaning of possessing a piece of paper from the therapist. And the man was impotent—a theme that has now been mentioned twice. And what is the patient telling the therapist? That these modifications in the framework are an expression of love that seems appropriate, but is not. That instead of conveying the therapist's sense of strength and true therapist-love (if I may use that term), they are undertaken out of his sense of weakness and impotence. Furthermore, he is saying that the bipersonal field is now a hell. And all of this despite your good intentions and well-meant efforts.

These are the patient's commentaries, and we have simply translated them into direct language. The material also includes a reference to someone else who is at this center—a more disguised derivative related to the complications in this therapeutic relationship that result from therapist and patient being involved at the same center. So, simply listen to your patients, especially to their derivative communications, and they will tell you the implications of alterations in the framework. If you respect their unconscious perceptiveness and the validity of their unconscious directives, I think you will want very much to maintain the framework and provide the patient a bipersonal field other than the seductive, frustrating, provocative hell described here. Please continue.

Therapist: He continues to talk about these two people, Frank and Susan. Frank saw a therapist and it was eight months of hell, especially for Susan. But finally he became potent and they're really having a fantastic relationship. (Pause.)

Langs: I very much hope that somebody was about to say that these associations seem to contradict my hypothesis. The patient is saying that in the long run such practices do produce potency. So we must now entertain an alternate hypothesis: deviations create strengths. We will allow the patient to clarify, but I suspect he is alluding to some type of misalliance cure based on something like the following: I better get potent if I am to escape this hell and this therapist. But, there may be something about a disruptive frame that we have yet to learn; let's see where it goes.

Therapist: He said, Especially for Susan, I guess. Because I identify with her, in that I love a man who is not potent, a gay man at that; I'm hoping that he'll become potent through therapy, too. Mark has got his problems. He and I went to Philadelphia for the holiday weekend just past. He paid my ticket one way. We were on the subway there and it cost twenty-five cents, and we had to return to the hotel. And he said, One of us should stay in the station while the other gets our bag, so we can save twenty-five cents. The patient cited that as an example of Mark's being very cheap, part of his personality, and then said, And I wanted to buy another puppy. Mark already has one. I was going to the dog show, and he wanted me to wait till 5 P.M. Sunday to go there to get the puppy, so they would have lowered their prices—to get one of the dogs that is unsold. Finally I decided I would go on Saturday if I wanted, and then I felt immediately better.

Langs: Can anyone offer a comment on this material? (Pause.) Yes, his associations do become confusing and fragmented. However, I had indicated that we now had to hear this material as a commentary on the patient's concept of how a modified framework produces potency. And I think that he has done just that: He is saying that in the presence of someone who is impotent, cheap, and petty he mobilizes his own resources and feels more potent. And this is one means of uninsightful misalliance cure that is not uncommon in the presence of a relatively incompetent therapist.

Now, we don't know if this applies in a valid way to the present therapist, but we do know that this is the patient's unconscious perception of him based on these deviations. The patient is stating something of the absurdity of your position, and I think he is now showing you why he decided to continue in the clinic in the face of the horrendous experiences that he had with the first therapist. It certainly is misalliance cures of this type that keep patients with many incompetent and destructive therapists, and it is through an avoidance of a proper use of the listening process that these therapists are able to continue such practices without insight into their implications.

I know I'm getting a bit rough in my comments, but I think that all I have said is very much implied in these associations. And I must state my message as clearly as possible, because each of you is here in order to learn to do therapy on a sound and truthful basis rather than through the use of misalliances, bastions, lies, and barriers. It is at moments such as this that I am reminded of just how difficult and painful the lessons of psychotherapy can be. But it is the patient who is asking that they be learned, and quickly, or there will be no hope for a valid cure for him.

So, the material becomes diffuse in the face of the most recent deviation, and that too is a commentary on the alterations in the frame: among its many ways of disturbing the communicative properties of the bipersonal field, it leads the patient to communicate in fragmented rather than coalescing derivatives. He'll fade off for a while, and undoubtedly come back to the frame issues. Let's see what happens.

Therapist: He said, I had a dream while in Philadelphia, that I had adopted three girls. Two were babies, I mean about two years old. And the third was like nine or ten. I told it to Mark, and he said, You mean, those two little girls are the puppies and the nine-year-old is me? I said, Mark, I think you're right. (Laughter.)

Discussant: This sounds to me like we have developed a Type C field.

Discussant: It sounds to me like the transference, I mean, the therapeutic relationship, both transference and nontransference. I don't know why it's coming up now, but I somehow see it as related to the change of therapist. In that adaptive context, the patient is saying something about being adopted by the new therapist.

Discussant: I think we laughed because this seems to be a parody of the type of therapy this patient is receiving.

Langs: Well, to maintain our particular focus, the dream occurred in anticipation of obtaining both a change in the hour of the session and a referral for Mark. And while I would agree that the material is not coalescing well and that even with the report of the dream it begins to take on Type C qualities, there remain certain fragments of Type A communication. In the two contexts just mentioned, we learn that it is the patient's unconscious perception that the therapist's deviations are an expression of a parental role—a way of adopting the patient. We learn too, by implication, that the deviations create a parody of therapy, lie therapy rather than truth therapy. There is also a modification in the framework on the part of the patient in his telling the dream to his lover.

Perhaps the most important communication, then, in terms of the functions of deviations in the framework is that it shifts the therapist's actual role from that of an interpreter to that of a substitute parent. This is, in part, a function of the alteration in the rule of abstinence, since it relates to the nontherapeutic gratifications offered to the patient in these ways. Incidentally, the friend's intervention is typical of Type C therapists who offer their own speculations based on the manifest content of the dream as a barrier to underlying dynamic and inter-actional truths. The deviations do appear to be reinforcing the patient's own tendencies toward the Type C mode of communication. Please continue.

Therapist: The patient then said that he had seen an exhibit at a museum in Philadelphia in which the replication of cell systems was involved. He went on: I felt very excited and thought of doing something like that. I have the necessary scientific background in histology and culture media, and it's an interest that goes back to my early childhood, so I was on the right track.

Langs: Can anyone tie this material to the framework?

Discussant: Isn't he talking about the conditions of growth?

Langs: Yes, he's talking about growth-promoting media and his wish to have one available for himself. In derivative form, he makes a rather exquisite commentary on the consequences of deviations in the ground rules: they disturb the medium and interfere with growth. By contrast, a sound therapeutic hold is growth-promoting and filled with promise. How beautifully stated; how much he longs for it.

Therapist: He said, I really shouldn't be in nuclear physics. I feel like I'd like to save the world that way. Something like that. I was very polite and idealistic when I graduated from high school; I'd go to church and I really wanted to do things like that. Then he said (and I believe this is something that had also come up before), I feel like I'd like to go into analysis.

Langs: Right. So now he comes back to the frame, to therapy, to wanting something else.

Therapist: He says, I have a lot of feelings I can sort out and learn from. There no one will interrupt my thoughts. This all refers to things that have gone on in previous sessions. At one point, he was very angry at me for not answering his questions. But more recently, he complained in one session that my comments or questions interrupted his thoughts and derailed his associations.

Langs: Just try to remember that you are now alluding to manifest content, rather than the Type Two derivative meaning of those complaints. What is interrupting his thoughts right now? Someone try to answer, and I'll suggest this much: begin with the adaptive contexts of this session.

Discussant: He perceives structure in some situations and not in others.

Langs: Well, that's a rather isolated statement offered without a context.

Discussant: It seems to me that the context is that the patient is wondering whether or not the therapist is providing a gratifying, seductive homosexual quality to the interaction.

Langs: I see you are having some difficulty doing this in a systematic manner. Let's do it step by step, rather than through isolated comments, since the more organized your ultimate listening, the clearer will be your response. What, then, is the adaptive context?

Discussant: Giving him the piece of paper with the referral on it.

Discussant: And giving him the change in the hour.

Langs: Yes, and now how would you organize this material as Type Two derivatives around those contexts?

Discussant: He's saying that it doesn't work, that he should give up and change therapy.

Langs: Yes, but let me translate these derivatives into another exquisite statement about modifications in the frame. The patient is saying that under such conditions, there can be no growth; his thoughts are disturbed and he cannot be rescued from his neurosis. He cannot be saved and therapy really shouldn't be done this way. It destroys his capacity to think and to express himself through analyzable Type Two derivatives and the Type A mode. It creates conditions under which analysis is impossible; and he very definitely expresses wishes for an analytic situation.

It's all there and it's really quite poignant. The interaction becomes filled with Type C barriers or develops into exchanges of projective identifications. So, in his own way, he's saying that the frame functions to create the conditions under which the patient will have thoughts he can communicate through derivatives—in short, under which he is analyzable. It determines the communicative medium and the communicative mode. And now he says that that is exactly what he wants, representing it in terms of wanting to get into analysis. Whatever its other meanings, he is suggesting that he needs a different type of framework. And I must add there is every evidence that he is right.

Therapist: There's just a little more to the session. He said: There were two times that I felt that way, that I'd like to go into analysis. Around the time that I stopped with my other therapist and started treatment with you, and in this situation with Mark. I intervened again and asked him, What was there about those two times? There was a long pause and then he said, Well, in both instances the distance from the love object was such as to cause me pain.

Langs: You see how little therapists think about the frame? The patient's thoughts about analysis occurred at the time of the forced termination, and the allusion to the situation with Mark must refer on a latent level to the present therapeutic experience—especially the deviations. But rather than thinking in terms of adaptive contexts and derivatives, you address the surface with a question and you obtain a Type C response: a psychoanalytic cliché. We have to realize that he has therefore also been saying that interventions of this kind destroy his capacity to think and to express himself symbolically.

Discussant: I know that I have wondered for some time whether there aren't really a number of different ways to do therapy. It seems quite clear that you believe that there really is this one correct way, and I do recognize that you have based this on what the patients have been saying unconsciously, in derivatives and the like. I just want to say that I am becoming convinced of the soundness of your position, because

every time we move away from it, the patient unconsciously com-
plains, and even becomes depressed.

Langs: One basic format, with many variations in keeping with the
pathology and assets of the patient.

Discussant: I know I'm cutting you off, but I want to ask you
something. There are so many deviant conditions in the clinic—at this
point I'm really convinced of this—that it makes it impossible to work
here. But sometimes it's hard to know how to rectify all this. What happened with this patient happened to me in a very similar way last night.
The change in the frame was that the patient now has the option of
going into private therapy with me. Okay. And she would have to be
paying me more money, and it will be an economic crunch. That's all
secondary to the change in office that's involved, and we talked about
an awful lot of stuff. And when she said to me at one point in the
therapy—I don't exactly know why it happened—when she was talking
in derivatives again after I had made some interpretations around these
frame issues, she suddenly said, I wish we could talk like this again, but
we can't. As if just being in the clinic interfered with that. She said,
There won't be another opportunity until we start privately.

Langs: Well, it sounds quite moving, but we're really not in a position to fully comprehend the implications of an excerpt like this. But
you are implying that many deviant clinical practices must be rectified,
so that you write your own bills, collect the fees yourself, write no notes
except possibly for a final summary, and then in a quite general way. If
you secure the situation as best you can, the patient will have a more
open communicative medium than presently exists.

Discussant: Yes, I begin to realize that the bipersonal field is different under these conditions, and it can't be changed unless we secure
the frame. We seem to begin to get into important issues, and then
somehow the patient blocks. I know it's hard to decide on the factors
involved, but I'm beginning to see that allusions to the deviant
framework often appear at such moments.

Langs: Yes, and for that reason I will later have a therapist present
to us here a few sessions from a patient in private treatment (see

chapters 13 and 14). Perhaps then we can define the differences between the communicative fields engendered by the two situations, including, perhaps, irreducible differences. Is that how the session ended?

Therapist: Yes, that's the end of the hour.

Langs: So, it ends with this kind of commentary: The therapist's distance is causing the patient pain. Well, you can sense how much unfinished business presently exists in this treatment situation. In the next hour, we can expect many significant derivatives related to the disturbances in this frame. It's becoming monotonous now, but there is a good possibility that the patient will begin once again with a frame issue. I won't state it as a firm prediction since, unconsciously, the therapist has attempted quite powerfully to shift the patient away from the frame issues. Despite that, it is on that kind of note that the patient ends the hour. And if he doesn't begin with this area immediately, I predict that he will get into it quite soon.

One final comment: as this course unfolds, I feel a greater need to distinguish between the ground rules that reflect relative constants, and those that involve more variable responses, such as qualities of the therapist's verbal interventions. I say this because I have begun to realize that infringements on these relatively fixed aspects of the frame are in many ways a more powerful stimulus than nonneutral verbal interventions. Both are important, but I do think that if we try to separate the two into different categories, we will find certain differences in the way patients work them over. I thought of this distinction in this session, where the patient is clearly working over the alterations in the constants and yet is responding to the therapist's nonneutral interventions with less intensity and clarity. In general, I think that you will find that the former type of deviation is far more readily represented in the patient's material and more easily analyzed than erroneous but well-intended interventions. Let's keep that thesis in mind for further discussion.

Thank you for a most illuminating presentation. We'll continue with this patient next week.

Chapter Eight

SOME CONSEQUENCES
OF DEVIATIONS
FOR PATIENT AND THERAPIST

Langs: Let's begin without desire, memory, or understanding. Please start where you left off.

Therapist: The session began with something I had to communicate to the patient. Shortly before this session, someone—the receptionist, I guess—told me that the accounts office at the clinic was confused as to the patient's status. They had to speak with him and asked me to tell him to get in touch with them. Technically, since he's here at the center, he's not really supposed to pay anything for his therapy, but somehow they were muddled about that. So at the outset of the session, before anything else happened, I gave the patient this message, that he was requested by the clinic to stop down at the accounts office at some point.

Langs: In terms of the framework, how is this an impingement?

Discussant: It's an adaptive context.

Discussant: It puts a third party in on the treatment.

Discussant: Since the therapist began the hour, wouldn't this also be a modification in neutrality?

Langs: Yes, each of these answers is quite to the point. First, it is an adaptive context to which the patient will now respond, both directly and indirectly. Second, it announces, with the therapist's participation, the presence of a third party to treatment. And, third, by not permitting the patient to shape the course of the session, it interferes both with the therapist's neutrality and with the fundamental rule of free association.

In this last respect, as a matter of technique, even on those rare occasions where you have an announcement to make to the patient—for example, that you will be taking a vacation—it is best to allow the patient to initiate the hour, and to find some point about midway to introduce the contaminant. You should also allow yourself sufficient time in advance of the event, whenever possible, so that you might postpone mentioning it in a particular session, if the patient is under duress or there is an important interpretation to make, validate, and have the patient work through.

So here again, we begin an hour in which we can expect the patient to teach us something about the nature and functions of the framework, and the consequences of its modification. Having entered this session without desire, memory, or understanding, I am led now, by the therapist's intervention, to recollect the previous hour and the many alterations in the framework. Under more usual circumstances, we would have had an opportunity, each of us, to experience the extent to which the patient's material would foster such recollections. As a matter of fact, I now remember suggesting last week that there was a strong possibility that the patient would begin this particular session with an allusion to the framework; I hadn't quite anticipated—and based on our experiences at this clinic, I might have—that the therapist would do so instead. (Laughter.) So we will now listen adaptively, and I expect, learn more about the frame.

Discussant: So you might say that the therapist entered the session with some type of desire.

Langs: Yes, this will occur from time to time, as, for example, when you are planning to take a vacation. It will then shape the session to some extent, though if the patient has something that he has a need to work over, he will in most situations find a way of working it in. This type of desire might not bias our listening, while other needs would tend to do so more strongly.

Therapist: Well, I don't think I'm entering the session in that way, but I have compromised my capacity for free-floating attention and neutrality. I have to get his financial status ironed out. I don't know what they're going to tell him, or how it's going to affect things. But I realize I have set the tone of things.

Langs: Yes, this particular desire has been placed into you by clinic personnel. And you are aware that you have now given the patient a directive and introduced the first theme in the hour, thereby modifying your neutrality. There is also an element of self-revelation, in that you are conveying your own inability to deal with his fee, and possibly, some ignorance on this matter. We also want to make note of the fact that this patient is in treatment without a fee. Since your message brings up the no-fee issue, it can be taken as a specific adaptive context and we can expect that the patient will offer us a commentary on this particular deviation, along with his responses to the other alterations in the ground rules. Remember, the standard frame includes the patient's direct responsibility for payment of an appropriate fee.

Discussant: I was just thinking that what the therapist does for the clinic has implications in terms of his functioning as a go-between, a relayer of messages for the clinic. In a sense, he is being given directives by this administrator, or whomever, which may have certain meanings to the patient. He's no longer functioning independently as a therapist; he himself is being given directives. He was told, You have to tell the patient something. It puts him in a submissive position.

Langs: Yes; can you identify what you have just done?

Discussant: Well, let's see, I guess I'm trying to identify some of the implications of this particular deviation, the latent content of the adaptive context.

Langs: Yes. If you were the therapist, this would be part of your own subjective monitoring of the unconscious communications contained in your intervention. This is an important foundation for the listening process, though it must not bias you to the point where you are no longer open to receiving the patient's own unconscious perceptions and the unconscious meanings that he particularly attributes to your intervention. This, then, is your way of indicating that specific adaptive contexts have extensive latent contents, functions, and meanings, and that they serve as critical vehicles for unconscious communication—here, from the therapist in the form of modifying the frame. And we could add to our silent hypothesis regarding the unconscious communications contained in this initial intervention. Who can help us?

Discussant: Well, the therapist is putting his needs before those of the patient.

Langs: Yes, that is quite true, and it could serve as an unconscious model of a need for immediate discharge, and of a narcissistic bias: self before others. With cues even as seemingly subtle as this one, the patient himself could become involved in acting out and in pathological projective identifications. Now, some of this may be modified by the fact that this particular intervention is offered in respect to the patient's need for therapy and to clarify and settle his fee; still, the timing and manner in which the intervention was made will have important unconscious implications.

So, this hour begins with an adaptive context, filled with unconscious communications. It is a modification of several dimensions of the framework and impinges upon the aspect of the frame that I have conceptualized as the fixed or constant dimension, and upon the fundamental rule of free association, the set fee, the one-to-one relationship, and total confidentiality. That's quite a package. In addition, it impinges upon the more variable aspects of the framework, the therapist's neutrality and anonymity. It will be interesting to see which aspect the patient works over and which parts he tends to set aside.

So I am predicting once again that these deviations, as actual transactions and qualities of the spiraling communicative interaction, will be filled with unconscious meaning and function, and that the analysis of the implications of these actualities in terms of the patient's perceptions and fantasies will provide a very meaningful therapeutic experience for the patient—if indeed this analysis is carried out. But I am also predicting that such work may be compromised because of the influence that these deviations will have on the communicative proper-ties of the bipersonal field and on the relationship between patient and therapist. While these are therefore not the optimal conditions for such analytic work, it would nonetheless constitute a very important means of generating insight and positive introjects for the patient—all at a critical time when noninsightful and negative introjective transactions prevail in the therapy.

Again I am suggesting that psychotherapy is not a simple matter of interpreting associational derivatives—words, affects, and the like—projected in some isolated fashion from the patient's psyche, but that it takes place around meaningful adaptive contexts, actualities imbued with unconscious functions and implications, constellations that are extremely pertinent to the patient's neurosis. Sound therapeutic and analytic work takes place around these actualities and their un conscious implications, and includes an analysis of the fantasies and perceptions which they evoke, along with their genetic implications. That is the basic medium of therapy, and you can sense from this how important it is to maintain sound communicative properties in the bipersonal field. The very substance of the treatment effort is modified and even disfigured when deviations are brought into play. By con-trast, with the frame secure, the communicative medium open and clear, and the relationship trustworthy and safe, the patient can experi-ence the here and now, perceive and communicate his responses to its unconscious implications, convey his unconscious fantasies and perceptions, touch upon their genetic connections, and ultimately relate it to his neurosis—thereby providing a meaningful avenue for sound interpretive response.

Well, I had wanted to mention something about the type of therapeutic approach that develops from a grounding of psychotherapy in the adaptational-interactional viewpoint, because it is a dimension of my work that I have been trying to clarify of late. I find that I make my discoveries empirically and that it then takes some time before it is possible to state the approach in terms of a generalization and a basic theory of technique. Once defined in that way, it provides a broad perspective that permits in turn further empirically based refinements. Enough of that for now. Let's see what unfolds in this hour.

Therapist: I don't have a written record of any overt, direct response to my comment. I think he just said okay and laughed, and he probably muttered something about the bureaucracy of the clinic; he often does that. Then he said, Well, I have one question that I've wanted to ask you. Do you think that you've been effective? (Laughter.) Shall I go on?

Langs: I think that you will be better able to go on once you take that as a commentary on the adaptive context that we have just identified for this session. At least in that way you will sense an opportunity to learn, and it will temper your discomfort.

The patient's first commentary on these deviations is that it raises a question in his mind about your effectiveness—he has doubts about it. And, perhaps not so very strangely, we've heard this before. Can anyone remember what prompted it the last time it came up?

Discussant: It came up with my patient, in response to that initial group intake interview, with all of its modifications in the ideal frame.

Langs: Yes, exactly. This is now a repetitive commentary: in the adaptive context of major deviations in the framework—and I suspect especially when they impinge upon the relative constants of the treatment situation—the patient experiences serious doubt about the effectiveness of the therapist and of treatment. As I have said before, it is only because therapists in the past have tended to disconnect the patient's material (his associations and the like) from their own modifications in the framework—from the crucial adaptive context to which it was a response—that consequences of this kind in response to alterations in the framework have been overlooked.

Now, there's another quality to this first association. Can anyone identify it?

Discussant: Well, once again, it feels familiar to me. I think that the therapist might be experiencing a bit of the pressure that I felt when the patient began her first session with me after that group intake by asking me that whole series of questions about myself and my capabilities.

Langs: Yes, this question has the quality of a pathological projective identification. It creates interactional pressure, and in addition it's an effort to evoke an ineffectual self-image. And you can see something of the source of this pressure. On the one hand it must derive from some hostility, some propensity toward projective identification and self-doubt within the patient. But, on the other hand, there are major inputs from the therapist: his deviation in the framework and poor holding of the patient; his directive, which treated the patient as relatively ineffectual and which conveyed in actuality some of the shortcomings of the therapist himself; the therapist's own pathological projective identification into the patient of the pressures he was experiencing from the clinic administration, pressures reflected in the manner in which the message was conveyed; and, especially, his need to begin the hour with that communication. So, as always, we are dealing with an interactional product and find significant inputs from the therapist which must be rectified and interpreted. I am beginning to realize that there is a fascinating interplay between these two realms of intervention, but we will cover much of that later on.

Who can take this further? What else does this opening communication tell us about the functions of the frame?

Discussant: In the first place, it is in itself something of an attempt at modifying the frame, asking the therapist a direct question that he wants him to comment on.

Langs: Right. So, it's seeking out a direct response, another modification of the frame: the search for a nonneutral intervention.

Discussant: It has a subjective quality beyond those already mentioned: of putting the pressure on the therapist and making him feel bad, uncomfortable, maybe that he's failed, guilty. It's persecutory in a sense.

Langs: Yes, I'm glad you said it first. Seitz (1978), one of the reviewers of *The Bipersonal Field,* called me paranoid-like for alluding to the patient's efforts to harm the therapist—apparently not knowing that Freud himself (1912, 1915), Searles (1965), and Bird (1972), among others, identified such efforts and wrote of their implications. Patients wish to get well, but they also wish to both harm and help us. The latter has been even more overlooked (for exceptions, see Searles 1975, Langs 1975b, c, 1978a). Somehow, that reviewer responded to my comments regarding the patient's harmful intentions, while completely overlooking the many references to the patient's curative endeavors on the therapist's behalf.

For us, what is important is that you have identified another subjective quality to the pathological projective identification, the role and image evocation involved in this initial association. We will, of course, treat it as a silent hypothesis in need of validation, especially from the cognitive material to follow. But for the moment I think that we can agree that this question does, indeed, have a persecutory quality. On that basis, we can make a tentative formulation in keeping with our other hypotheses regarding the functions of the frame: a secure frame is nonpersecutory and offers a safe and helpful hold; by contrast, a modified frame is persecutory, attacking, and harmful. We are postulating an exchange of pathological projective identifications, and learning something about the implications of the therapist's deviations as mirrored in the meanings of the patient's effort to modify the framework. The altered frame creates an atmosphere of doubt and uncertainty, a lack of security, a sense of hard-to-manage pressures, and an impaired hold. Much of this is tentatively validated now through features shared by the three deviation-dominated presentations we have heard.

As you know, for some time, based on observations of this kind, I proposed that this type of unneeded modification in the framework is a reflection of poor therapeutic practices. Here, in one stroke, the patient says exactly that, though, as always, quite by implication. And let's be clear how we arrived at this: we identified the adaptive context, heard the manifest associations, generated first- and second-order themes, took them as Type Two derivatives along the me/not-me interface, and tentatively decided that this is a valid statement of incompetence in the therapist—whatever else it says about the patient and whatever distortions it may contain.

Discussant: This first association brought me back to parts of the last session that I hadn't recalled immediately—issues involving the competence of the therapist.

Langs: Yes, this initial derivative might serve to stimulate the recall of the adaptive context of the prior hour, as well as of other aspects of that session that related to the framework. We must be careful not to miss the fact that this opening intervention from the therapist serves as the immediate context; on the other hand, we must be prepared to link the present context to those that arose in the prior hour. The patient himself, then, based on both sets of unresolved contexts, begins the hour with an effort to evoke a self-revelation from the therapist—at which point, I trust, most of you would remember much of the prior hour, which, of course, centered around self-revelations and deviations. For me, what the therapist's first intervention did not help me recall, the patient's first association did.

Discussant: But you need the memory of the previous session in order to know what you are on the lookout for in terms of the adaptive context. Without that, you would have difficulty postulating the meaning of the material in this session and would have to treat it as Type One derivatives or even manifest content. You yourself have made it clear that the recollection of the adaptive context is essential for proper listening.

Langs: Yes, but once again you are overlooking my stress on the difference between active and passive recall. In stating that you should enter the session without desire, memory, or understanding, I do not mean to imply that you should remain in such a state throughout the hour—at least not in regard to memory and understanding. Not at all. The rule stresses the importance of passive recall in an effort to discover what is new, but it does not neglect the need to identify aspects of the material without which you might be unable to intervene.

If you find in a session that you are unable to recall your intervention in the prior hour, and cannot identify the prevailing adaptive context, you then have to sort out several factors: those within yourself that are blocking passive memory, and those in the patient's material that do not facilitate your recollection. Here, for the moment, we have quite the opposite situation: communications from both therapist and patient greatly facilitate recall of the previous hour, and even suggest that both will be working over framework issues in this session. In general, you will find that frame issues tend to evoke interrelated communications from the patient from session to session, and to greatly facilitate your own recall—another tribute to the power of the frame.

Discussant: You wait to see what comes to you. While I often sit in my office before the patient comes in, trying to think of the last session in some detail, you are now saying that it is better not to do so, to just leave it open and see what happens. In that way you kind of recall the previous sessions secondarily, somewhat shaped by the associations from the patient in that hour and somewhat, of course, from what is going on within yourself.

Discussant: I am in good shape. Often I can't remember anything. (Laughter.)

Langs: That's a different concept; that's called exploiting the theory. (Laughter.)

Therapist: I must make a note not to take any more notes in sessions.

Langs: Yes, note-taking is really disruptive of the therapeutic process in many ways. It not only interferes with the discovery of what is new, but it disturbs your empathic, intuitive, and cognitive efforts. In addition, it implies violations of confidentiality and the one-to-one relationship.

Discussant: You are also talking about note-taking after a session, and suggesting that we not jot down anything even then.

Langs: Yes, I'm glad this is now registering with you. It takes several reworkings, and probably, in addition, a specific example, like the one of the previous hour, where the therapist wrote something on a piece of paper for the patient. While that is not exactly what we are talking about for the moment, it is related to it in a way and may have facilitated the working through of your confusion regarding this particular ground rule. Let's hear more.

Therapist: So, anyhow, I responded, Obviously you have been questioning that lately—me and my effectiveness.

Langs: Very briefly, let's analyze this intervention.

Discussant: It's kind of a why-do-you-ask type of question.

Discussant: It seems to bring up other issues from past sessions, and to be rather vague.

Langs: Well, in analyzing an intervention you should always begin by identifying whether it makes use of the adaptive context, and the level of listening on which it is addressed.

Discussant: This is a response to the manifest content and certainly lacks an adaptive context.

Langs: Yes, and what is its main unconscious function?

Therapist: Well, I would have to say now that it avoids the immediate adaptive context of my opening comment.

Langs: Yes, it directs the patient to stay away from the chaos in yourself and in the therapeutic interaction, even though it is well meaning. It addresses the manifest content and ignores the adaptive context—it therefore offers an interactional defense, one that is likely to be obsessional. The best intervention here would, of course, have been the use of silence. There is even a nonneutral quality, in that you are attempting quite quickly to move away from the immediate context.

Discussant: It is directing the patient where to go. It is insisting that he talk about this, and almost focuses on it.

Therapist: But that needn't prevent things from developing; it needn't really crimp his associations that much.

Langs: Don't overlook the unconscious communications contained in even the most seemingly innocuous intervention. You are not allowing the patient the freedom of free associating and show little interest in indirect material, in derivatives. You are asking the patient to stay fixed in this area, to communicate his immediate and direct thoughts about it, and to create a bastion in respect both to your announcement at the beginning of the hour and to the powerful adaptive contexts of the previous session. While it is certainly possible that the patient himself will connect his concerns about your work to those contexts, it is far more likely that he will not do so consciously, and that it is only possible for him to do so in derivative fashion. Remember: the question is also a commentary on your well-meaning deviations in the previous hour—you must leave the field open in that respect.

Discussant: I think too that this is an effort to push the patient into pleasing the therapist. There are many patients who are concerned about doing a nice job in their sessions, and the slightest suggestion from the therapist will lead them to search for whatever you are hinting at, and often to tell you just what you want to hear.

Langs: Yes, that's one level, but there are usually far more complicated issues involved. I don't like this type of explanatory hypothesis, because it ignores the specific unconscious communications contained in an intervention of this kind, as well as its functions in terms of the ongoing communicative interaction. It also stresses the patient's conscious desires and simply doesn't address the complex unconscious underpinnings.

Therapist: He said, Well, I've been thinking again that what I really want to do is go into analysis. I feel that the thoughts I have and the things that come up just need to be explored fully, and I really want to understand myself.

Langs: We hear again the patient's appeal for a sound communicative bipersonal field and relationship, and his wish that the therapist would treat his associations analytically. He wants a Type A field where there is a search for understanding, and as long as he provides Type Two derivatives he means exactly what he says. As a commentary on these deviations, the patient is saying that analytic understanding is not feasible when the frame is altered and as a result he must seek it elsewhere.

You will find that in some derivative way, every patient truly interested in insight therapy will find an indirect means of asking for a secure frame and interpretations. Unconsciously, they somehow know that this is what genuine help consists of, and they want you to know that. We must search for the general implications of each specific communication from this patient in the context of these last deviations.

Therapist: He said, And I want to explore all of these things slowly, and I want to understand myself without this discontinuous effect of waiting three days for the next session.

Langs: So, even though he comes close to a direct criticism of your work, we discover that he is actually making use of considerable derivative communication. The adaptive context is the alterations in the framework, and the patient makes use of a related derivative—the time between sessions—as a means of representing it in disguised form, complaining about an aspect of the secure frame at a time when we are hypothesizing that he is responding to unmentioned modifications. This is a silent hypothesis that needs validation, though there is good reason to make it.

Discussant: I begin to see what you mean by listening—the manifest complaint is about the frequency of sessions, but you are suggesting that the latent complaint is about the deviations in the frame. Here, my association is to the fact that the therapist recommended a private therapist for this patient's lover. I would suspect that the patient thinks of that therapist as an analyst, and is quite envious. In any case, in some way this must be a response to that adaptive context as well.

Langs: Yes, that too is an excellent silent hypothesis. It is shaped quite nicely by the derivatives in this session, and now needs validation.

Therapist: It seems to me that many supervisors would accept this patient's manifest complaint about therapy, see him as capable of being analyzed, and on that basis consider a referral, perhaps to an analytic clinic.

Langs: Yes, that may be true, but that's where I take a different position. The critical communications in psychotherapy are not conscious but unconscious, and are to be organized around specific adaptive contexts. This approach leads to considerably different formulations, interventions, and conclusions than might otherwise be made. The payoff lies, however, in the failure to obtain true psychoanalytic validation—or insightful symptom relief—on the other basis, and on the ability to validate the type of formulations and understanding that I have been teaching you.

Discussant: It certainly seems obvious that the patient turned to a frame issue to represent his complaint about the altered framework.

Therapist: I can also see now that these derivatives relate to the immediate adaptive context. He is telling me that my opening the session with that directive created a great sense of discontinuity between last session and this, and what he has been working over. I know that it is all connected to framework issues, but it's like he is telling me that I had interrupted him.

Langs: Yes, the patient's associations are a form of preliminary Type Two derivative validation of our initial formulations of some of the unconscious implications of your initial intervention in this session. This is quite perceptive, and I hope you are experiencing quite directly the kind of sensitivity that the approach to listening and formulating we are developing here is beginning to give you.

Therapist: Yes, I am well aware that I am hearing many things now that I haven't heard before. It is more troublesome, but it is quite exciting. To continue, he went on like this, saying that he would like a situation where there would not be the discontinuous effect of waiting three days for the next session, without having his train of thought interrupted.

Langs: Yes, so he now becomes more specific in alluding to the influence of your having begun the hour. First, we must take this as a general commentary on alterations in the framework: they interrupt the patient's train of thought and therefore are quite disruptive. But, second, we must take it as a specific commentary on your decision to initiate this particular session; such a step has a disruptive effect and interferes with the patient's free associations. He is saying that he resents it, and that he would prefer to leave such a treatment situation. He is staking a claim to his right to initiate the hour and at least the opening course of each session. And it is so important to recognize that the patient is saying exactly this in derivative form, and that he is making a valid point.

Therapist: Would you make an intervention at this juncture?

Langs: Well, my silent hypotheses are beginning to be validated, and I am shifting into the stage of preparing a silent intervention. There is a strong indicator, in that the therapist has modified the frame in this and the last hour, and it is more than evident that this creates a strong need within the patient for an intervention—rectification and interpretation, if feasible. We know the adaptive context, and the patient has alluded to it in derivative form by mentioning the gap between sessions. I would hope to have a clearer link to the immediate alterations in the framework, so I would continue to listen, but I could intervene with what is already available. The associational complex, the derivatives, seem to be coalescing in a Type Two manner around the adaptive context of the deviations in the frame, so I have a good deal of what I need to make a sound intervention. Finally, there is an additional indicator: the patient is threatening a premature termination to his therapy. He requires an intervention, and I am preparing one along the lines we have already discussed.

In general, in deciding on intervening we identify the intensity of the indicators and turn next to the communicative network. We identify the adaptive context, determine how it is represented, explore the relevant derivative network, and then ascertain the presence of links and bridges to the therapist and the specific context at hand. Now, I know that this model is quite complex, and I offer it now in abbreviated form so that we can discuss intervening in regard to framework issues in a somewhat systematic way. We will not, however, work this over in any great detail, since we will have ample opportunity to do so in the part of the course that deals with intervening.

In this situation, I would especially like to hear the patient allude to the previous modifications in the framework, as well as to those with which the therapist began this hour. I would like to be able to deal with both adaptive contexts, and to have meaningful derivatives related to both.

Discussant: Could you just briefly describe the intervention you are preparing?

Langs: Well, if I were the therapist in this situation I would be thinking of starting with the adaptive context of sending the patient to a third party to discuss his fee, and I would hope to be able to link that up to the referral I made in the previous hour and the paper I had given him. I would probably want to begin with the therapeutic context of his thoughts about leaving therapy, and would then point out that I had begun the hour with the accounting-office directive and had made other modifications in the previous session. The specifics of much of this would depend on what the patient directly and indirectly represents, since I will allude only to deviations that the patient on some level identifies. I would go on to suggest that in response, he perceives me as not being very helpful, has doubts about therapy with me, is experiencing a sense of disruption and discontinuity, and feels that under these conditions he cannot get to understand himself.

Discussant: What's odd about that is that it almost makes sense for the patient to want to quit under those circumstances.

Langs: Yes, that's what I call a rock-bottom truth. The patient's problem is not in wanting to terminate therapy under such conditions, but in his inability to consciously identify the basis for his wish, as well as in some of the more distorted responses that are undoubtedly associated with these deviant conditions—material that we have not as yet heard, which would demonstrate his own neurotic and inappropriate exploitation of the situation, and something of its genetic meaning for him. But when we understand the adaptive context and recognize that this material is based primarily on valid unconscious perceptions, we get a far more constructive picture than we would otherwise obtain. Most therapists immediately assume that patients who wish to terminate treatment prematurely are acting out their own psychopathology and their own internal resistances to therapy. They insist that such a response is inherently destructive, and fail at times to recognize its true unconscious meanings and implications.

Discussant: I can see the shape of your interpretation, but you did not include any effort at rectification. How then are you going to correct the frame here?

Langs: Well, for one thing, there are aspects of this modified frame that cannot be rectified, and the best that I could do under those circumstances is to make every effort to not further alter the frame or repeat these particular deviations. For example, you could try to obtain permission to handle the fee yourself, and you could secure the frame later on when—and I say "when" because it seems inevitable—when the patient attempts to have you modify it in the future.

For the moment, the patient is hinting at rectification by attempting in some derivative way to identify the conditions under which he could have an insight-oriented therapy. He might lead us to aspects of the frame that can indeed be rectified; and remember, we will only do so when the patient's derivative material points us in this direction. Still, within these limits, you can do some interpretive work with the patient's responsive unconscious perceptions, introjects, and fantasies, and at least show him that you have, despite your destructiveness in some respects, constructive qualities as well. In addition, you would of course be offering him some cognitive insight into the effects of this deviation on himself and its implications for his neurosis. In that way his view of you as ineffectual, disruptive, or whatever could be modified, and he could obtain some understanding of the unconscious implications of his associations. We are approaching here the limitations of clinic treatment, and perhaps now we should hear more material.

Therapist: First, may I ask why you would not introduce very specifically the qualities of my opening intervention, and point out the different types of deviations involved?

Langs: There are many reasons: first, I allow the patient to put the intervention into me, and I analyze the defenses which account for whatever is missing. That, of course, is a basic principle: we analyze defenses before contents, and there are massive defenses here in the form of repression, perhaps denial, and certainly displacement. He has obliterated your announcement for the moment, though he is responding to it unconsciously. Our intervention should either include some comment regarding that obliteration—which I would do only in the presence of strong derivative representations of it—or should stress the playback of related derivatives so that the patient himself could provide the missing context. On that basis, his continuing associations might provide a means through which we could interpret the unconscious motives and factors in his avoidance—addressing both our own contribution and that of the patient to this particular defense and resistance. It is important, then, not to bypass defenses, but to help the patient modify them and eventually understand their unconscious basis, within himself and within the therapeutic interaction.

Discussant: Aren't you saying, then, that if you don't approach the defenses first, and analyze them, an interpretation in which you introduced the adaptive context would not be accepted because the same defenses would still be there? He would still need to deny your interpretation because his defenses have not been understood and altered.

Langs: Yes, that's part of it. However, when you offer a correct but premature intervention, you will find that you will usually obtain islands of validation, along with defensive and negative responses based on the prematurity of the intervention and the therapist's need to force the issue.

Discussant: I would just like to add that it seems to me that you are implying that it is harmful for the therapist to introduce his own associations and connections, not only because they could be wrong, but also because it sets the therapist up as the powerful or capable one and suggests that the patient is not capable of arriving at an interpretation on his own, or even of providing the therapist the derivatives needed for an interpretation.

Langs: Winnicott (1965) has written of the uselessness of the therapist's being ahead of the patient, and here I am suggesting that it can be destructive as well, filled with error, a reflection of poor therapeutic principles that lead you to bypass rather than analyze defenses, and that it often serves the therapist's need for cleverness and inappropriate gratification far more than the therapeutic needs of the patient. Premature interventions are often experienced as pathological projective identifications, rather than as a sound basis for cognitive understanding and positive introjective response. Patients do expect us to make the interpretations that they are unable to generate consciously, but we must wait for our patients and allow them to put the necessary derivatives into us.

Discussant: I could sense how the patient would feel hopelessly incompetent with a therapist who is trying to be clever and brilliant. After all, correct interpretations often entail narcissistic injuries to the patient, and premature interventions would only aggravate the wounds.

Langs: It's time for some discipline; let's get back to this session and the framework.

Therapist: The patient was saying, I feel that the thoughts I had and the things that have come up just need to be explored fully and I really want to understand myself, without this discontinuous effect of waiting three days for the next session, without having my train of thought interrupted, without even seeing a facial response in the therapist. No matter how good you are, you're going to show some response.

Langs: That's beautiful. What does that tell you about this and all modifications of the frame?

Discussant: They are self-revelations.

Langs: Thank you. Deviations entail self-revelations that are detrimental to insight therapy. In the adaptive context of the deviations, this is the unconscious, derivative communication, and on that level it is quite valid.

Discussant: Could this patient also be saying that treatment is really not possible with this therapist, in this clinic?

Langs: Yes, I had already alluded to that possibility, and it appears now that the patient is unconsciously attempting to indicate why this may well be the case. Based on this session, it appears that the best that we can say about this difficult issue is that under deviant environmental conditions in which rectification is not feasible, it may well be that therapy along insightful lines is also not feasible. With rectification, there will be some residuals of the earlier damage, but a greater chance of generating a sound therapeutic hold and communicative field, and of doing some reasonably insightful work.

Discussant: How do we know that this is not an expression of the patient's resistances, rather than a statement of truth about the treatment situation?

Langs: Well, we have been listening to this material around the prevailing adaptive context—the initial deviations in this session. We then obtained a Type Two derivative, and of course we must evaluate the extent to which it is valid and the degree to which it is distorted and defensive. This decision depends on our self-knowledge, our understanding of the unconscious communications contained in our intervention—the adaptive context—and our further analysis of the material from the patient.

On this basis, there are many reasons to feel that this patient's statements contain a great deal of truth, and that they are, in addition, in keeping with the statements of other patients under similar conditions. Yes, he may be using all of this defensively, but we must first understand the truth before we can discover what is inappropriate. All we know for now is there have been a series of deviations in the framework, and that the patient is convinced that insight therapy is not feasible under such conditions. That's a compelling message, and I see nothing as yet in this material to suggest that it is anything but a valid commentary. Still, we can take my position and yours as contrasting silent hypotheses, and allow the patient to provide us with further clarification.

Therapist: He went on: No matter how good you are, you are going to show some response, whether it is a widening of the eyes, a raised eyebrow, a twitch of the lip, or whatever. He said, That time I went through that whole transference neurosis with you—that's his term entirely—that was really a time I had a lot I wanted to understand and could have understood.

Langs: If that's a reference to something you and the patient share and understand, we're entitled to know it. I want to clarify it because it may be tied to another principle I want to develop. Please tell everybody, briefly, what this all refers to.

Therapist: It refers to the first couple months of therapy when I first inherited this patient, and he was perpetually on the verge of terminating therapy, of walking out. He kept pressing me to reveal, to tell him whether I'm straight or gay. He wanted to know this and made it sort of a sine qua non of therapy, justifying it with all kinds of rationalizations.

Discussant: Which way was he going to stay?

Therapist: Well, that was unclear too. Manifestly, he said he would stay with a gay therapist. Then, finally, at one point he said he was leaving therapy. Then he came back to therapy and spoke about an enormous erotic transference that he had toward me. And he said he thought of terminating therapy because he felt—he had the idea or the conviction—that I was attracted to him also, and that I'd then be able to be involved with him, since I no longer would be bound by any professional relationship.

Discussant: I think that we can see that this patient was pretty panicky—I guess you would call it a homosexual panic—because of the uncertainties about the ground rules, based on his experiences with his first therapist and on some of the things that the present therapist was doing.

Langs: Yes, once again we can feel the sense of chaos—here, erotized chaos caused in part by the lack of structure. But we are not in a position to understand the factors involved, with one exception: the patient refers to that particular period in this session. And that's why I wanted to characterize the earlier period, and found validation for my hunch that the patient was referring to a time when the framework was severely damaged, the boundaries unclear, and the therapeutic hold disrupted. And you can see that the patient was attempting to invoke what I have termed a *framework deviation cure* by terminating and taking flight from a chaotic treatment situation. His associations at that time revealed his uncertainty about the boundaries and nature of the therapeutic relationship, and this shows that frame issues were quite important during that period, as they are at the moment in therapy we are now hearing about.

The principle I had in mind was that at times of deviations the patient will tend to recall other such periods. He does so in part because in many ways the two interludes are identical, and in part as a means of attempting to communicate and represent the unconscious meanings of the current situation—here, in terms of certain more obvious implications related to the earlier period.

Remember what the patient said: he went through what he called an enormous transference neurosis—what I would term a mixture of transference and nontransference, with a large portion of the latter, expressed through conscious thoughts and fantasies about the therapist. He is probably misusing the term *transference*—which actually alludes to distorted *unconscious* fantasies and perceptions related to the therapist—in a manner not unlike that of many therapists and analysts.

Still, he wanted to understand himself—and, I would add, the therapist—at that time, but failed to do so. This is an important commentary on the earlier and present alterations of the framework, and on deviations in general. When the frame is not secure, understanding is impossible and the whole experience, which is filled with constructive potential, becomes a waste since no understanding is imparted. Now, I realize that part of this may have been the case because the therapist had been unable to interpret the patient's material, but you can be certain that this was also a consequence of the modified framework.

And the patient implies a second consequence of the altered frame: the so-called transference illusion cannot exist or be maintained. I have already referred to Milner's comment (1952) that the framework of treatment, much as the frame of a painting, is essential to the unique conditions within the frame. The production of analyzable material, the communication of feelings, perceptions, and fantasies that the patient somehow experiences as real and yet knows to be in part based on his present intrapsychic pathology and past pathogenic interactions—the entire experience of an analyzable transference constellation requires a secure frame as its basic foundation. Without it, there is no transference illusion, but instead the threat of the actualization of the patient's unconscious and conscious fantasies, and often of validation of what would otherwise be transference: the patient's pathological fantasies and introjects are confirmed in the actual unconscious implications of the therapist's behavior.

I will state the implications of this material for alterations in the framework in still another related way: when the frame is modified, it is impossible to distinguish between reality and fantasy, between what is valid and what is distorted. The truth cannot be determined, either about the patient or the therapist. This is another factor in the resulting chaos and in the actual uncertainty that the patient experienced about the therapist. The frame kept changing, there was no sense of stability, and the patient vacillated and felt totally confused.

Now, don't be deceived by the likelihood that this patient is suffering from borderline pathology; this should not lead you to believe that these consequences occur only with severely disturbed patients, but not with those who are more integrated. This material reflects meanings and implications of an altered framework for every patient, and we can benefit from the unfortunately exaggerated responses of this patient and thereby learn something about the needs every patient has. This can also help answer a question that is often raised: whether the frame need be secured for more severely disturbed patients who suffer from borderline and psychotic syndromes. This patient's answer is unmistakable: the more disturbed the patient's ego functioning and sense of self, the more essential it is that the standard frame be secured and maintained. Well-meaning deviations unconsciously communicate dysfunctions in the therapist that undermine the functioning of such patients. Such measures are often the cause of nontherapeutic regressions (Langs 1976a) for which the average therapist has no explanation.

Therapist: So he said, That time I went through that whole transference neurosis with you, that was really a time I had a lot I wanted to understand and could have. Even now there are things that come up that I could never even begin to get into here. Like the other day I was going to a dinner party. I didn't know that someone I knew was going to be there. Here he said something about a male aide who works at this center, a man who had once made homosexual advances. And then he said something about another employee—a trainee too— who also had made homosexual advances toward the patient, and then had told other people that the patient had spurned him.

Langs: Do you hear now another function of the frame? What happens when the frame is modified and there is the kind of alteration that we're dealing with in this session?

Discussant: The patient feels rejected.

Langs: Rejected and what else?

Discussant: Seduced.

Langs: Seduced, yes. What else? (Pause.) Publicly exposed: "He then had told other people." And just look at all the allusions to boundaries: the unexpected guest and meeting someone from the center at a dinner party. A male aide and a trainee who work at this center who have made homosexual advances to the patient. All of this has, of course, a great deal to do with the patient's unconscious perceptions of the therapist and the current treatment situation, and it is all conveyed in the adaptive context of the recent deviations in this framework. In addition, we can once again see the presence of distortions: the therapist has not been overtly seductive as far as we know, he is not homosexual, but nonetheless on some level he has been seductive and has exposed the patient publicly. These are, then, transversal communications that touch upon both reality and fantasy, and the two will have to be sorted out.

So we hear more and more in derivative form about alterations in the framework. And so far, with I think just one exception, we have heard a multitude of consequences and functions of deviations in the frame, and virtually every one of them is detrimental, destructive to the treatment of the patient, and a reflection of significant countertransferences within the therapist. The themes are becoming repetitious and quite distressing; there is no sense of constructive potential or hope. And this too is the atmosphere when the frame is modified.

Unneeded alterations in the framework reject the patient, seduce him, expose him, and reflect unresolved countertransferences of the therapist. Deviations are an unconscious sexual exploitation of the patient. And while distortions have additional important elements, it is critical to sense how uncertain this patient is within an altered framework in regard to the possibility of actual homosexual contact. Under the usual environmental conditions, the therapist may make an error in interpreting filled with latent unconscious sexual wishes, but the secure frame provides the patient a basis for relative certainty that the therapist will not proceed with an actual seduction or with more blatant though disguised efforts at unconscious homosexual gratification.

Clearly there are gradations, and the security of the framework serves as an implicit guarantee to the patient—and, I might add, to the therapist as well—that more direct forms of inappropriate gratification will not take place. Under these conditions he is relatively safe to react, to express himself, to convey his own unconscious perceptions, and to go beyond them and indicate his responsive distortions and pathology. So the secured frame permits not only expression of the patient's unconscious transference fantasies, but also communication of the patient's unconscious perceptions of the therapist—and his conscious perceptions as well.

For the therapist too, the framework helps with his appropriate defenses and controls, his management capacities. It provides him a safe setting in which he need not feel unreasonably endangered by the patient's impulses, sexual or aggressive. It is my impression that situations in which patients have assaulted or otherwise blatantly violated the usual boundaries of the therapeutic relationship are characterized by major modifications of the framework.

Moving back toward this material, the patient is indicating that your sending him to a third party, and perhaps the absence of a fee as well, is a homosexual exploitation. That is a transversal communication or commentary with both validity and distortion.

Discussant: But why are you calling it a homosexual exploitation?

Langs: Because that is how the patient was experiencing it, and we should not simply write off this claim by stating that it stems entirely from his own homosexual conflicts. Perhaps it is fortunate that some of this is based on a clinic directive, but we must suspect that other deviations have stemmed from the therapist's own unconscious needs, though probably in a wider environment that has encouraged such practices.

In any case, we have heard before that modifications in the framework have unconscious sexual and aggressive meanings and functions, and that they are an actual means of unconsciously gratifying pathological unconscious sexual and aggressive fantasies. For the moment, we really can't sort out how true this is for the present therapist, though the therapist himself should take associations such as this, place them in the light of the prevailing adaptive context, and become engaged in self-analysis in order to determine, as best he can, the extent to which there are kernels of truth in the patient's unconscious perceptions.

Now, I know that this is very difficult for someone who is not in analysis or insight therapy, but the patient requires this of you—it is fundamental to your therapeutic commitment to him. You therefore must do this as best you can, in the hope of becoming sufficiently insightful to rectify the frame and perhaps get under a bit better control the unconscious homosexual conflicts and fantasies that are contributing to your mismanagements of the framework. It is here, of course, that you are bound to experience the limitations of your cognitive understanding and the impact of your own underlying psychopathology. But you are the instrument of therapy, and this is the means through which you can best strive to maintain your work on a level that serves the therapeutic needs of the patient to the greatest extent possible.

Remember: if the patient behaved in this way, you would expect to analyze it for its unconscious homosexual meanings. Many therapists have felt that this is unnecessary when it comes to their own behaviors, which should be understood simply in terms of their manifest expressions. But that constitutes a denial of unconscious meaning and communication, and the patient will almost never share that denial. This material indicates that under conditions in which you modify the frame in this way by exposing the patient, introducing third parties to treatment, giving them gifts, and the rest, it will be virtually impossible to insightfully resolve his homosexuality. It is possible that he might become so appalled by the introjection of your own unconscious homosexual exploitation of him that he would repudiate his homosexuality in an unconscious effort to offer you a constructive model, and as a means of justifying the discontinuation of therapy; but here at least, that is an unlikely outcome. As the therapeutic situation now stands, it justifies this patient's homosexuality, mirrors and reinforces it, and undoubtedly supports it in ways that the patient's earlier environment supported it. The deviations have created what both Strachey (1934) and Racker (1957) have termed "a neurotic vicious circle"—an actuality that leaves the patient no way out.

In this way, you can see that the question in this session, Have you been effective? and the question in his first sessions, Are you homosexual? are equivalent in important ways. A homosexual or latent homosexually gratifying therapist cannot cure a patient's homosexual problems.

I hope that by now you are beginning to experience the impact of modifications in the framework, as actualities filled with unconscious communications and implications for both the treatment and the patient. It is the basic background, and if it corresponds with and reinforces the patient's pathology, effective therapy, truth therapy, is impossible. Its sound management is a basis for experiencing the therapist as different from both the patient himself and his past pathogenic figures, in addition to providing the patient a sense of safety and an adequate therapeutic hold. As you can see, deviations in the framework serve to reinforce the patient's psychopathology and preclude its analysis in several ways.

Discussant: Is it possible for you to offer some type of systematic classification of the effects of modifying the frame? I am becoming aware of many detrimental consequences but am having difficulty organizing them.

Langs: Yes, I share that feeling. Of course, this means that deviations actually disrupt virtually every dimension of the therapeutic experience. I think this is why there could be many systems of classification. Does anyone have any thoughts on this matter? (Pause.) Yes, it is difficult to conceptualize. I will simply list whatever effects occur to me, and perhaps a categorization will suggest itself.

1. The influence on the patient: a modified frame shifts the implications of his expressions away from transference, distortion, and pathological unconscious fantasy representations toward nontransference—the introjection and working over of essentially valid unconscious perceptions of the therapist based on the deviation, often with extensions ultimately into the transference sphere.

Now let me list some subcategories under the effects on the patient:

There is an ego disrupting effect, with disturbances in reality testing, defensive functioning, and internal management capacities.

In the object relational sphere, there is an uncertainty in regard to the nature of the therapeutic relationship and its boundaries. It becomes unclear as to whether impulses and fantasies directed toward the therapist manifestly or in derivative form will be directly gratified or treated as material for interpretation. In addition, there is considerable uncertainty as to whether the therapist's response will be interpretive or a counterresponse in which he gratifies his own inappropriate needs.

Symbolic communication and expression is impaired, and pressure is created toward the use of projective identification and action discharge, as well as of Type C barriers.

By and large, modifications in the framework reflect superego pathology in that they invite sectors of misalliance and collusion, noninterpretive therapeutic work, and in some nonmoral sense serves to corrupt the therapeutic situation. These deviations therefore reinforce the patient's superego pathology, rather than offering constructive models for introjective identification that could provide healthy nuclei for the development of an essentially nonpathological superego. These deviations also generate compromised ego ideals that reinforce the patient's disturbances in this area and, along with that, his self-image.

Deviations in technique promote the gratification of pathological and inappropriate instinctual drive needs.

Deviations also impair the patient's sense of trust, safety, being held, and containment.

For the patient, these deviations also constitute on some level actual repetitions of the past pathogenic interactions responsible for the development of his psychopathology, and in addition confirm current pathological introjects and dimensions of the patient's psychopathology since they in some way unconsciously express similar propensities.

Deviations produce negative introjects of the therapist which reinforce pathology—a point related to the previous one and a much overlooked factor in the etiology of emotional disturbances.

So we can offer some classification of the detrimental effects of deviations in the framework on the patient. This categorization can supplement our earlier scheme in regard to the positive functions of the secure framework. Now let's look at the implications of alterations in the framework for the therapist.

2. Alterations in the framework reflect the therapist's difficulty in managing his own inner world—conflicts, anxieties, psychopathology, and the like—and constitute a significant expression of his unconscious countertransference fantasies and needs.

They reflect ego dysfunctions within the therapist, his superego psychopathology, and an attempt on some level to gratify his pathological instinctual drive needs, both seductive and aggressive.

They constitute a form of projective identification and action discharge, and often, in addition, a desire to create Type C barriers designed to seal off the chaotic parts of the patient's personality, the therapist's own personality, and the treatment situation itself. They therefore reflect, too, the therapist's difficulty in utilizing symbolic communication.

Deviations constitute failures to provide a safe holding environment, and to function as an appropriate container for the patient's pathological projective identifications. In the object relationship sphere, they are a reflection of significant psychopathology whose specific nature depends upon factors in the patient, the therapist, and their prevailing therapeutic interaction.

Please accept this as a first attempt at classification. It indicates that modifications in the framework influence the therapeutic interaction, the nature of the transactions between the two participants, the intrapsychic state of both, and, ultimately, whether there is any possibility of insightful cure. Let's now return to the clinical material.

Therapist: He says, I was waiting for Mark the other day. (I think I mentioned this last time: Mark is his homosexual boyfriend.)

Langs: When asked when I might intervene in this session, I suggested that I would wait until we had some clear-cut derivatives that would link this material to the therapist's modifications in the framework and, in addition, definitive bridges back to the treatment situation. Can anyone make use of this last association and the previous segment of material to identify such links and bridges?

Therapist: Well, the reference to Mark certainly brings me back to the previous session and the patient's request for a referral for him, which I had provided by giving out the names of therapists who work outside of the clinic. Mark was asking for therapy.

Discussant: Well, he also mentioned a trainee at this center, and a male aide. They must represent the therapist.

Langs: Yes, the bridges and links are still somewhat disguised, but he is moving closer to their direct representation. It would certainly be relatively easy to point out that the patient is referring to people at this center who have exposed and betrayed him, and to use the material about Mark as an organizer for the playback of derivatives related to the deviations of the previous hour. However, since the patient is coming closer and closer to more specifically representing the adaptive context, I would wait a bit longer before intervening.

Therapist: So he said, While I was waiting for Mark the other day, I was having thoughts I used to have long ago, of not being small enough to fit into my mother's womb.

Langs: Thank you. Thank you. That's why this session is just so beautiful. What does this tell you?

Therapist: The container? He is not being contained.

Langs: The container, and what else? (Pause.) The adaptive context is a series of modifications in the framework, and this is a continuation of the patient's derivative responses: first, it conjures up an image of waiting for his homosexual lover. But then there is an image of not being small enough to fit into his mother's womb. The patient represents the frame, the hold, the container, the background of safety in terms of the maternal womb. It's a remarkable allusion to the framework as managed by the therapist, and here it represents the patient's longing that somehow he could have that protection once again—in therapy. The therapeutic hold is modeled on the maternal hold.

Discussant: With a strong emphasis on basic security.

Langs: Yes, the safe, protected container. So, he has been talking about the destructive side of the deviations, and now he comes to an expression of the longings of what he would like to have—another level that is related to his comments about wishing for analysis.

Therapist: He said, I thought of this again when I didn't feel like getting out of bed in the morning. That's always been a problem of mine.

Langs: Bed, sleep, safety, no impingements. That's what you're supposed to create for the patient, that kind of atmosphere. Then you can take it from there—in therapy a necessary therapeutic regression should follow. But it won't take place without a secure therapeutic hold first. Please continue.

Therapist: He said, I was thinking again about it, and kept it in mind during the entire day, through six hours of classes and while concentrating on my work—that I wasn't big enough to come into my mother's womb. And then he started laughing, and realized that he had made a slip of the tongue. He started laughing and said, Big enough to go in, come in. And he started remembering what he said, which was he wasn't big enough to come into his mother's womb. I said to him, You're laughing. He said, Well, because I had the thought that at least my ass is big enough for my father to get into me. And then he started laughing again.

Discussant: It's almost like, first he's talking about desiring the frame and the womb, and then he turns it into a homosexual wish.

Langs: But he's saying that he becomes the container. He's seeing another side of the situation. I think that he's implying that the homosexuality provides him with security that he doesn't get under healthier circumstances. Perhaps we can validate that impression.

Discussant: With regard to the incestuous quality, doesn't that refer to the therapist and his deviations?

Langs: Oh, yes. The incestuous sexual qualities are further representations of the deviations, and their homosexually assaultive aspects yet another transversal communication. And here too, perhaps, there is something about why this patient stays in treatment: he allows himself to be penetrated, attacked, and homosexually gratified, and he can think of himself as holding the therapist.

He has now also illustrated my comments regarding how a specific modification in the framework can repeat a version of past pathogenic interactions and reinforce the patient's psychopathology. For this patient, it represents his mother's failure to provide him with a secure womb and early maternal hold, and his father's probably unconscious homosexual assaults as well. Still, it may well be that his father compensated in some way for his mother's inadequacies. The genetic links of these deviations for the patient begin to emerge, and now it may be possible to include them when intervening.

Therapist: I made an intervention. I said, I would have thought that being big enough could have other connotations.

Langs: Well, that was made a long time ago when you knew nothing about adaptive contexts, the importance of the framework, and the like. You therefore addressed the manifest level of this material, invited further rumination, and treated the material as isolated contents. Let's not belabor this evaluation but instead hear more material.

Therapist: So he said, Well, general ones you mean. I don't think that as an infant you're aware of those connotations, of not being big enough. He picked up on my implication that the slip was not being big enough to go in his mother's womb, so he said, Genital connotations, you mean. I don't think that as an infant you're aware of those. He was saying that this is a thought that he's had since infancy, since childhood. He said, I don't think as an infant you're aware of that, of not being big enough. Look, I first had homosexual fantasies of having intercourse with a man when I was three or four years old. I can remember them clearly. Maybe not the actual mechanics of it. I didn't know those. But I'd be sitting on my basement steps and the oil burner would go on, and I had those thoughts, with the feelings in the right areas and everything.

Langs: Here we must hypothesize that the genetics are connected to the deviations, and to the actualities of the therapeutic interaction. This material is, of course, a commentary on the therapist's intervention, which the patient experienced as a form of homosexual play perhaps, with some hint of the potential for things possibly getting out of control. But, in intervening, it would be important not to isolate these genetic aspects, but to tie them to the various dimensions of the therapeutic interaction. Please go on.

Therapist: Then he sort of stops that train of thought and says, Anyhow, in answer to my initial question, have you something to say? You don't have to answer it. Not that you were going to. Have you been effective? Well, yes you have.

Langs: Yes, as if to validate my hypotheses, he comes back to the present therapeutic situation now. Let's see where he goes.

Therapist: He continued: But I really want more. I want to be in analysis five times a week. I feel I can do it. It's a real commitment. I don't know what they pay now. He had been talking about applying to one of those low-cost clinics, so he said, I don't know what they pay now. About twenty-five dollars a week, which would be about a thousand dollars a year. I think I can swing it with a student loan, but I don't want to waste time. There may be a waiting list. I figure I'll give it two more sessions and then I think I'm going to apply. He meant two more sessions, I think, in the sense that he's willing to explore it with me.

So look, he went on, we'll talk about it a bit longer, but I'm definitely going to make up my mind one way or another. I think I'm going to apply. I think there are one or two clinics in this area—and he sort of trails off. Then he says, But then there's the thing of leaving you. Will you be crushed? This patient is great. He said sort of playfully: You'll just curl up into a little ball and roll under your desk. (Laughter.)

Langs: And create your own frame, your own place of safety. He's holding you, he feels, which has more truth to it than poetry. And he's going to hurt you by taking away his hold, because you've been doing that to him.

Therapist: So he said, And roll under your desk. And then I'll have to say to you: Come out—here he used my first name—don't be crushed. Now he's appropriating my first name.

Langs: Yes, he becomes more personal, social. Don't be crushed: modifications in the frame are crushing.

Therapist: I said to him, What thoughts do you have about that, the effects on me? And he said, Well, I want to discuss it. You won't let me go until we've discussed it all. For another three months at least. I'm sure there is a lot that could be said, but what the heck, I'll be in analysis anyway. Then he mentions the prior therapist, who used to say, You're not ready for analysis. But, he adds, I feel I'm ready now. Apparently he had first raised the idea of going into analysis when he was ending his first therapy.

Langs: Yes, he goes back to the other doctor and his modifications— his nonneutral interventions. But he's still talking of everything but what has happened in this situation today.

Therapist: He said, So I feel I'm ready now. That was the time he was terminating with me, and he had one line: You'd not be losing a therapist, you'd be gaining an analyst. So this guy had apparently said to him, You're dealing with losing me by saying you want to get an analyst.

Langs: Right, but you have to realize that he's playing back a cliché, which is a commentary on your interventions. It's easy to forget that part, but it's there.

Therapist: He said, I thought I'd rather have an analyst than start with a new resident. Analysis will be great. No soda or cigarettes of course.

Langs: He brings up the soda again. Now in terms of what appears to be a model of rectification and, I suppose, renunciation.

Therapist: He came in with a can of soda last time; I don't think he had any this time. Then I said, You see that as a possible change; then why do you do here what you feel ought to be banned in analysis? Bringing in the soda. He answered by saying that the other therapist had said it was okay for him to smoke. Another thing: on the front door of my office there was a sign, which had been there even before me, but which I left there, asking patients not to smoke. So he said, He said it was okay for me to smoke. It makes me more relaxed. But I don't know if that's good, for me to be relaxed in sessions. Maybe not. I'd like you to refer me to an institute. I wonder if you're at one of those institutes yourself. (Laughter.)

Langs: So he is actually compromising, and looking for another contaminated situation at the very moment that he is hoping for a secure frame. And now, of course, he wants a referral for himself—and you—just as you offered one for Mark. It becomes clear that on some level both are tantamount to the end of insight therapy with you— maybe. The degree of uncertainty about virtually everything is one of the most striking aspects of this communicative field.

I was pleased to see that you made some effort to deal with the frame issue. It shows that you sensed that there was something inappropriate being communicated there, though unfortunately there were several problems with your intervention. We have time for a brief comment.

Discussant: The therapist's remark sounded critical to me. This means that it was not a neutral intervention at all.

Discussant: The therapist is referring to a deviation that the patient made in the previous session, and ignores his own deviations.

Langs: Yes, that comes from listening on a manifest level, rather than in terms of an immediate adaptive context and derivative responses. The intervention is an effort to inquire into a frame issue and almost a directive to rectify the frame that is, unfortunately, not derived from the material from the patient. And it is expressed in a nonneutral, somewhat critical manner, which is contradictory to the announced intention to secure the setting. Your intentions are uncertain, as are the patient's, and as is this bipersonal field. Notice too how the patient alludes to a framework deviation cure through drinking soda and smoking during his sessions—a cure through direct gratification. And he contrasts it and sees it as an alternative to insight therapy, which as he so perceptively points out, requires certain types of abstinence and renunciation. Please finish up now.

Therapist: I can run through it: it's pretty straightforward. He said: I wonder if you would be at one of those institutes. The doctor there could be a resident too. Are you? I'm wondering if I'd like you as my analyst. It would be both good and bad. I don't know if you're into analysis. I don't know what you do. He meant, what kind of therapy. (Laughter.)

Langs: We'll take your word for it.

Therapist: But then again, he said, I was surprised to hear that you came from Tulane. Another thing: he had once asked me where I went to medical school, which I had never told him. But apparently, somehow—I never found out how—he found out which medical school I went to. He went on: So I don't know what to expect; you might be. I said, I wonder whether my giving you referrals for Mark has anything to do with your thinking of analysis?

Langs: Yes, you are trying; you are really trying.

Discussant: But the therapist has introduced the referrals for Mark, not the patient.

Langs: Yes, I think that as a function of the compromised communicative qualities of this bipersonal field, the patient approaches representing the adaptive context rather clearly, only to pull back and obscure rather than further clarify. You will find that this happens quite often in the presence of modifications in the framework. So, even without an understanding of listening in terms of adaptive context and Type Two derivatives, the therapist senses that there are important framework issues here. He seems to have taken his cue now from the

reference to the personal information that the patient had learned
about the therapist from other sources—probably another consequence
of the two of them being present in the same center. But he doesn't
really have the necessary links to the specific contexts, so he introduces
them himself. And despite its limitations, this intervention is an
acknowledgment of the therapist's contribution to the patient's
apparent resistance—his thoughts of terminating his therapy here and
seeking analysis. And as such, it should evoke some type of positive
derivative response. Despite its limitations, this is the therapist's best intervention in this hour—it certainly moves in the right
direction.

Therapist: He said, Yes, that might be bringing it up at this point,
but it was there anyway. So I'll have my two puppies and an analyst.
What more can I want, he said sort of half-humorously. Then he
started talking about Mark's needing to have his male cat spayed. He's
starting to mount a female cat the patient took care of while another
friend was away. He said, She's too young yet. I will let you know what
happens with Mark. He'll probably go to some low-cost clinic somewhere. But I'll keep you informed. I really do love him, Mark. Isn't
that something? And that was the end of the session.

Langs: The beginning of the next session, just the opening lines?

Therapist: He said, I want to get back to the subject of analysis.
I've been thinking about whether I would feel better if I started talking
about the time commitment of getting into analysis.

Langs: Well, I don't see much in the way of positive introjects,
although he does talk about his love for Mark. He also manages to get a
heterosexual image in through the reference to the male cat mounting
the female, though it certainly has a number of probably pathological
implications. In the main, however, the material has become more difficult to organize around the adaptive context of the deviations, and it
seems to have reached its peak when the patient expressed his longings
for a safe womb.

Discussant: Can you tell us now when you might have intervened?

Langs: Probably at the point where the patient alluded to his wish for a womb. I would have felt that this is a session with a strong therapeutic context, and that the patient had expressed a distinct need for intervention and rectification. I would not be in a position to rectify immediately, but I could at least interpret, or approach an interpretation. I would have said something like this: You are talking now about wishing for a safe place, a womb, as you earlier had expressed your wish for a therapeutic situation in which you could come to understand yourself. You referred just a moment ago to a trainee and aide at this center who had attempted to seduce you and who had betrayed you and exposed you publicly. Now while you don't explicitly connect this to my announcement at the beginning of this session—here, I think the material would justify such a reference along with some mention of the patient's avoidance of it (the resistance aspect)—I began the hour by telling you that it was necessary for you to go to the accounts office in the clinic to straighten out your fee. And notice that you went on to speak about analysis. You questioned my effectiveness, stated a wish for understanding and continuity, said something about my exposing myself and about your former homosexual fantasies about me, and then spoke of the workers here who have made advances to you, betrayed you, and exposed you. Then you mentioned waiting for Mark. All of this conveys something of the implications of my sending you to the accounts people and their involvement in your treatment.

As you can see, I have made a transversal interpretation, without attempting for the moment to distinguish between unconscious fantasies and perceptions, leaving room for both. I think that the patient would have validated such an intervention with a significant selected fact, and that his additional associations would have helped us to sort out reality and fantasy. I think, too, that with that particular intervention the patient would probably have gotten back to the deviations in the prior hour in a very meaningful way, and that in addition he would have offered in derivative form directives related to the necessary rectifications in the framework. I might then have been in a position, based entirely on his associations and their implications, to suggest that he not go to the accounts office, and that I would make some effort to be the one to establish and collect his fee if there were to be one.

I think that in the main it is because of the absence of any hint from you in regard to rectification that your relatively crude but well-meaning interventions regarding the framework received little validation. For the moment, we have as a result a session in which we have learned a great deal about the unconscious meanings and functions of the framework, but have not been able to validate our formulations psychoanalytically. Still, we see a weaker form of validation in our ability to predict aspects of the material accurately and to find many areas of agreement with the derivative communications we have heard from other patients subjected to alterations in the ground rules.

Thank you for a very interesting presentation. We will begin with another patient next week.

Chapter Nine

MEDICATION AND THE FRAME

Langs: Why don't we get right into the material.

Therapist: Do you want anything about the patient?

Langs: Yes, very briefly orient us about the patient, the therapy, and anything about the frame that took place prior to where you're going to begin.

Therapist: Okay. This is a twenty-seven-year-old graduate student here at the same medical center, whom I started working with about a year ago, when he was in his second year of graduate school. His presenting problem was—well, he came after his midyear exams and complained that he had failed many examinations in graduate school despite the fact that he had always been a very good student, never had any problems before.

Just a little background in terms of framework. When I started seeing him, he was quite upset, markedly anxious, and not sleeping. Initially I dealt with the case as though it were a sort of crisis situation, and I was quite active in the treatment for the first several months—less analytical, and more directly supportive, more giving in the sessions. When we started working after his first year, after a break for the summer, I adopted a much more analytic stance in the sessions.

Langs: There are many myths about so-called crisis and supportive therapy, and perhaps some of the material that we will be hearing will harken back to that phase of the therapy. But already we have two frame issues: an initial noninterpretive approach, and the fact that both of you work at this center and are, in a sense, in training here. That guarantees us frame-related material, to be sure.

Therapist: Let me just say, because it will provide some background, that these sessions are from a few months ago. But nearly a year earlier, near the beginning of therapy, two obvious framework issues arose: one, I had given him a prescription for some Librium; and two, right before a major battery of examinations and the presentation of a thesis, I gave him my home phone number over the weekend because he was extremely anxious—and he did call me once. So that will provide the background.

Langs: So, we have another multideviant therapeutic situation, and some of the alterations in the framework took place almost a year ago. Let's maintain them as background adaptive contexts, and see if, even at this time, the patient is still reacting to their implications.

Therapist: I'll mention one other frame issue. I had been seeing him twice a week in treatment, and about six months ago the problem came up in our schedules, when he got into his major research and class responsibilities. And what had to be done was I changed therapy from two forty-five minute sessions to one half-hour session and one forty-five minute session.

Langs: And now he walks with a limp? (Laughter.) That is a new wrinkle, a new kind of uneven hold. We'll see what its effects are.

Therapist: He started off the session I want to present in a characteristic way for him, talking about . . .

Langs: First, do you remember anything of the session previous to the one you're about to present?

Therapist: Yes, he was sort of talking about a relationship that he's having with a girl and something about her coming from a wealthy family. It led into a discussion about how he feels about wealth. He had had a discussion with another graduate student about some of these doctors who drive around in fancy cars and are making all sorts of money. And he was sitting around with this friend figuring out how much different doctors that they knew must be pulling in each year, and how much top scientists in their own field earn—which is a lot too—and this one must be making at least two hundred thousand, and this surgeon is making even more. How it doesn't pay to just teach, and how much you can earn in private industry, and with your own corporation. And he said somehow he wonders if in some way he was having so much difficulty in school with his work and exams because he felt guilty about someday becoming a rich scientist. He has a connection with a large firm that manufactures specialized medical equipment and he expects to do quite well.

Langs: You summarized the session without a word from yourself in it. The word *discussion* suggests that you perhaps spoke; did you?

Therapist: I didn't say very much, except near the end of the session. I made some comment about the fact that his parents had always spoken very negatively of wealthy people who had turned around and treated them as though they were looking down their noses at them—his parents. And I added something like, Perhaps the idea of becoming a wealthy scientist had implications in terms of becoming one of them, with all this background that his parents had given him about what happens to people when they come into money.

Langs: So you are a typical classical psychoanalytic psychotherapist, working without an adaptive context, and making use of genetic interventions that are disconnected from the therapeutic relationship. Was there a validating response?

Therapist: No, he just ruminated about my intervention a bit, and the session ended.

Langs: Well, we have no idea of the adaptive context of the session that you just briefly summarized, but it has helped to orient us in respect to the session we are about to hear.

Therapist: Well, he begins this session by saying that he is extremely anxious about some upcoming exams, including some work in the very field that he hopes to get into industrially. He feels quite angry at some of his teachers and professors because they seem to be making life very difficult for him: they are really pouring on the work and they don't seem to give much consideration to the fact that there seems to be a policy in this graduate school to bunch all of the exams together. He was in the elevator with one of his professors, who teaches one of his courses, and the professor made some sort of snide remark about how many people in his group were not going to pass the exam, that it was going to be a tough one. And this got him very angry, this attitude.

Langs: Is this a thirty or a forty-five minute session?

Therapist: This is a full session, forty-five minutes.

Langs: Well, let's see if we can develop some hypotheses related to the framework. Did anyone hear an embedded derivative related to the ground rules?

Discussant: Something about things being bunched together and not being given enough consideration. I don't know exactly what the words were, but he seemed to be relating it to the scheduling.

Langs: Right. This could be a derivative related to the scheduling problem. What else?

Discussant: The proximity of working in the same institution with the therapist. He was in the elevator with his professor.

Langs: Yes, we see here an allusion to the relative lack of secure boundaries. And what is the quality of the associative network in which these derivatives are embedded? And, even before that, who can identify the type of exercise that we are engaged in?

Discussant: I don't think it is clear. In a way, we don't have a specific adaptive context related to the frame, so we are monitoring this material in terms of Type One derivatives related to the therapeutic relationship, and to the ground rules. On the other hand, we do have what I think you have termed background frame issues such as the unequal sessions and the fact that both the patient and the therapist are in training here.

Langs: Yes, you put it quite well. We are dealing with a mixture of Type One and Type Two derivatives, and we do lack a critical immediate adaptive context. Even so, the material organizes quite meaningfully around the two deviations in standard technique that we have already identified.

Discussant: You asked about the character of the associations, and I would say that they are quite unpleasant. In fact, the patient is saying, indirectly of course, that these arrangements make life difficult for him, create work for him, lead to extraneous remarks, and provoke and infuriate him.

Langs: Exactly. There is a distinctly distressing tone to these derivatives, which you have monitored along the me/not-me interface to some extent, though not entirely since you have not suggested the additional possibility that the patient unconsciously perceives the therapist as under pressure and angry. After all, that too may relate to the patient's perceptions of these alterations in the framework, and we should at least identify it as a silent hypothesis.

So, for once, there are no blatant immediate alterations in the framework and we can see that the session begins somewhat less dramatically than those that we have studied earlier. Incidentally, the reference to being in the elevator with the professor may also touch upon—which particular deviation that we heard about in the introduction of this case?

Discussant: The therapist's decision to give the patient his telephone number.

Langs: Yes, it's a distant derivative, but it does relate to a way in which the therapist created an uncomfortable proximity between himself and the patient—to a degree, a lack of boundaries.

Therapist: He said that he is having a lot of trouble sleeping. He is sleeping very poorly and feels very tense. And then, sort of in passing, he said, I'm wondering, well, if maybe I should ask you for some Librium.

Langs: Well, I hope that convinces the skeptics. We had developed some rather tentative silent hypotheses that the patient was at least in part unconsciously working over a number of unconscious frame issues in this particular session—for immediate reasons of which we were unaware. We were even able to link these associations to a very early deviation in which the therapist gave the patient his home telephone number. And now the patient himself gets around to a second specific major deviation characterizing the early phase of this therapy: the use of medication.

I trust that you can all see that this would constitute Type Two derivative validation of our initial silent hypothesis. Through derivative communication, the patient is stating that the framework is indeed on his mind. It is rather comforting to obtain this kind of Type Two validation in respect to a framework issue. Since there is little reflection of efforts at rectification and even interpretation in the material being presented to us, we will have little chance to study more definitive validation within the context of sound therapeutic work related to the frame—although, as I said, I do plan to invite someone in private practice to present at least one instance of rectification to us at the end of this segment of the course. As a result, it would be important for us to make as many early predictions as possible in order to obtain our own Type Two validation of the ideas we are developing; this type of confirmation has appeared a number of times in our work with the previous cases. Now let's hear more.

Therapist: He was saying how difficult it is for him to concentrate on his studying, and that he's starting to have the music come back into his head. This was sort of obsessive: one of his problems in the past was that musical tunes and commercials would come into his head while he was trying to study. And he couldn't get them out of his head, something that he had heard on the radio. Eventually he got rid of his stereo and his T.V. set. He sent them home.

Langs: Any comments? Let's stick to the frame.

Discussant: Well, there is a sense of being poorly held: he is sleeping very poorly and feels tense. Also, something is intruding into his mind—perhaps things are not being contained very well. This may have something to do with the lack of a secure framework.

Discussant: But he is asking for medication. How does that fit in? If he is suffering from an insecure frame, why would he want to alter it some more?

Discussant: Perhaps he feels that's the only way he can get better. Is this what you, Dr. Langs, have called a framework deviation cure?

Langs: Yes, in a sense it is. Your comments bring me back to the known adaptive context for this session; who can identify it? (Pause.) Well, it's the therapist's intervention in the previous hour, which was an attempt to link the patient's manifest guilt about earning a great deal of money to his parents' attitudes. Now, we don't really know what the correct intervention would have been in that prior hour, but based on the standards we have developed to this point in the course, we do have reason to believe that the intervention was erroneous, that it avoided some unknown but crucial issue in the therapeutic interaction, and that it wasn't validated.

So, in the adaptive context of an essentially erroneous intervention, the patient's wish for a framework deviation cure becomes understandable. He needs a means of obliterating the disturbing contents within his mind, and, along the me/not-me interface, in the therapist's communications and mind as well. So he wishes for a framework deviation cure through the use of medication, and we will soon see the unconscious implications of that request.

Now, let's get this into perspective. This frame is altered in the following ways: he is being seen in the clinic, so there are records and the likelihood of supervision, and there is an absence of total confidentiality. Do you have a supervisor for this case?

Therapist: Yes.

Langs: So there is a supervisor, a third party, and in addition the boundaries are tenuous because the patient is a student at this center, and the therapist works here—is himself a trainee.

Therapist: In addition, he doesn't pay for his therapy.

Discussant: And we seem to be formulating that the interventions have not exactly been neutral, and that while the therapist has attempted to respond interpretively of late, you are suggesting that there are important countertransference factors involved, and defensive needs.

Langs: Yes, and if we continue to take this material along the me/not-me interface as a commentary on the state of the framework, what is the patient saying about these particular deviations—a subject that we now have considerable reason to introduce since the patient has asked for Librium.

Discussant: They are not conducive to treatment.

Langs: Yes, and what more?

Discussant: They are disorganizing.

Langs: Yes, you can't get yourself together under these conditions. You have to resort to artificial devices such as getting rid of radios and sounds, and taking drugs, as a means of obliterating the inner disturbance—it can't be insightfully modified under these conditions.

Now, we must touch upon some of the more unpleasant communications in this material as well. As is almost always the case, they can be identified only if we apply the "not-me" part of the me/not-me interface. Perhaps someone can be sensitive enough to do it for us.

Therapist: Well, allow me. If I monitor this material as applying to myself, the patient is saying that he believes that my interventions are more obliterating than helpful, more disturbing than calming, and that he suspects that I am quite confused myself.

Langs: There, that wasn't all that bad was it? These are hard truths that therapists must be capable of receiving quite consciously, culling them from the patient's derivative communications and then attempting to determine the extent to which they have validity, and allowing room for what is distorted.

Now, for us, we will emphasize that these are the patient's unconscious perceptions and introjects based in part on your mismanagement of the framework. Clearly there may well be other sources, especially those related to the erroneous contents of your interventions. And we will be prepared to identify still other factors, but for the moment we will concentrate on how this material helps us understand the patient's unconscious perceptions and introjections of a therapist who modifies the framework. Most clearly, this is a commentary on your early use of medication, and in derivative form the patient tells us that it was based on your anxiety and confusion, and your need to create a blank state in your patient—and probably in yourself and in the therapy. And this is quite characteristic of how patients unconsciously experience the offer of medication, despite their conscious request for it and direct words of appreciation. Here again, we are observing the typical split when it comes to alterations in the framework: conscious acceptance, and unconscious criticism; conscious appreciation and unconscious attack; a conscious view of a helpful therapist, and an unconscious view of a therapist who is quite disturbed and confused.

Therapist: I begin to wonder now why it is that this patient has, in general, been getting along well in his courses, managing to pass and all that, and even doing some decent research. Certainly there have been some periods of crisis, but he does seem to be getting along.

Langs: Well, can anyone offer an hypothesis to account for these periods of symptom alleviation, based on this material? (Pause.) Well, I think that he is telling us that his periods of relief have come through the use of Type C barriers, reinforced by the deviations in the framework—including the use of medication. This is reflected too in the material, which is rather ruminative and lacks a clear-cut adaptive context for the moment. He is suggesting too that the therapy has enabled him to erect impenetrable barriers against his disturbing inner world, but notice that he is now indicating that the barriers are weakening. Because of that, he turns to you for reinforcement of the barriers rather than for insight. The model of cure is not that of understanding and adaptive inner change; instead it is obliteration, falsifications, and Type C barriers.

I'm sorry that sounds so rough, but that's the nature of this material. A therapist must be prepared for the painful truths in respect to the manner in which patients receive some modicum of symptom relief. This can only be ascertained through the associations of the patient at such times. Granted, at this point he is alluding to a remission; but at the same time, he is indicating his unconscious sense of the basis for his "cure"—an interactional amalgam with inputs from both himself and the therapist. This patient is suggesting that he believes that that is all that the therapist can offer him; he does not, as yet, seek truth therapy. It may well be that he will shift as he continues to associate, but then again he may not. Let's see what happens.

Therapist: So he's starting to hear the music again coming into his head. And he said, Lately it's been a particular song, at least for two or three days before the session. The same song. And the lines that keep going through his head are, You can't change time, but time may change you.

Langs: I must tell you something that I was experiencing as I was listening. I was going to stop you as soon as I heard about the repetitive song and make a prediction. I didn't do it because I am well aware of my teaching style and the extent to which I keep interrupting to make comments and predictions. I do more of that in this seminar than I would under other conditions, because I also have a larger audience in mind—the people in the field who will be reading the book that will be based on the transcriptions of these presentations. I happen to prefer a predictive approach, because I think we need as many opportunities for validation as possible.

In any case, I was about to introduce one more adaptive context for us to keep an eye on. Can anyone anticipate what it will be?

Therapist: The time limit of therapy? The forced termination in the middle of this year?

Langs: Yes: the fact that this session takes place at the beginning of this year and that a forced termination is pending.

Discussant: Somehow that thought occurred to me when he asked for medication. I wondered if he was concerned about losing the therapist.

Langs: Yes, what you are describing there is how the patient's derivative communications shape our search for missing adaptive contexts. I had said earlier that I suspected the presence of an unmentioned context that was shaping this material around framework issues. And I soon began to suspect that it was the pending forced termination, though I also kept searching for another, more immediate frame issue as well.

So, I had made the silent hypothesis that this patient was concerned about a pending forced termination. And I now obtain a somewhat remote, though explicit, form of Type Two derivative validation; the song that is on the patient's mind has the lyrics, You can't change time, but time may change you. There is a sense of sadness and inevitability. For me, it was uncanny to hear these lyrics. And perhaps the best earlier clue is the patient's request for medication; not only does it bring us back to the beginning of this therapy, but also it serves as an attempt, in this particular adaptive context, to incorporate the therapist as a means of undoing the anticipated separation.

Notice how each specific frame issue provides a particular adaptive context for the organization of the patient's derivatives, which then affords these derivatives very specific unconscious meanings. Ultimately, this will be tied to genetic factors. Here, the patient sort of slipped in one genetic connection almost unnoticed: the fact that he had sent his radio and T.V. home to his parents, for safekeeping, so to speak. It was a means of maintaining his tie to them. So, now, unnoticed derivatives take on Type Two meaning around a specific adaptive context. The medication, which derives meaning from the therapist's somewhat inadequate interpretation, and from the presence of other deviations, now takes on additional meaning in terms of the pending separation—a typical theme for clinic patients at the beginning of a calendar year.

Therapist: So he paused and then he said, Sometimes I wonder if I'm going crazy or if things like that really are craziness, or what it represents. And he began to ruminate about whether or not he's really going crazy, whether this is really abnormal, whether normal people have this sort of symptom.

Langs: We are still generating and validating frame hypotheses. Which one do we have here?

Therapist: When the frame is modified, the patient goes crazy.

Langs: Yes, especially in the presence of a forced termination. The ego, the mind, thinking, everything falls apart. The patient begins to go crazy and to become disorganized. We've heard this before and when you modify the frame, you'll hear it again. Please go on.

Therapist: In a characteristic way, he's ruminating about whether he's crazy or not crazy. As he says it, he looks at me, and he goes back over it again: I don't know, maybe it's crazy. So I intervened, and I said, It sounds as though you're asking me whether I think you're going crazy or not, but are having trouble asking me directly.

Langs: An intervention calls for comment.

Discussant: I think that by now we are all familiar with this type of intervention: it lacks an adaptive context, and it addresses the manifest content.

Discussant: What strikes me is that he's asking the patient to force him to modify the frame by asking him a direct question.

Langs: I would put it this way: In every essentially erroneous intervention, there is a nucleus of truth. Here, it is in the fact that the therapist addresses the frame, and shapes his intervention around the patient's quest for a noninterpretive response. Beyond that, however, you are quite right: it makes no use of an adaptive context, addresses the manifest content, and presupposes a rather idiosyncratic implication— namely, that the patient's problem is in asking a direct question. I can see the thought behind this intervention, though I doubt its therapeutic efficacy. What *type* of intervention is it?

Discussant: A confrontation, and an effort at clarification.

Langs: And the unconscious communication involved?

Discussant: Let's talk about you and your theory of being crazy, and not about anything else that is going on here.

Langs: Yes, and I would add that it's focused entirely on the patient. What else?

Discussant: It does include the relationship though, because it addresses the idea that the patient wants something from the therapist.

Discussant: It makes no use of the me/not-me interface; it addresses the direct material, which involves the patient going crazy, and not the therapist.

Discussant: It avoids any consideration that the therapeutic situation is crazy.

Langs: Yes, it avoids the central area of chaos, focuses almost entirely on the patient, and denies not only the therapist's contribution but the possibility of unconscious perceptions related to the therapist: an introject of his fear of being or going crazy. And of course it totally neglects the adaptive contexts related to the framework. In this respect the frame may not be the major context for the moment, though prior to this intervention we were accumulating evidence that suggested that it is, at the very least, one of the more significant precipitants. But whatever the adaptive context, this intervention does not deal with it directly and in true interpretive fashion. And as you said, this is the type of therapeutic work that you have been taught, and it is rather representative of much of what is done today. Let's hope that *The Listening Process* (Langs 1978c) and the very book that these seminars will create will help to change that. For the moment, while the intervention manifestly attempts to approach the patient's problems, it will quite likely serve as a Type C barrier to the craziness, and possibly as a projective identification as well: the therapist is chastizing the patient for not being straightforward.

Discussant: The comment about the noise was to throw away the noise, the artificial noise, and create a Type C field. The fact that the patient brings it back to the craziness—isn't that his attempt to turn this into a Type A field and talk about that area?

Langs: It could be, but I don't think so. It seems to me that we have a Type C field for the moment, and that it is an interactional product based on the patient's own propensities and the type of intervention being offered by the therapist. As I hear the material to this point, the craziness comes up largely because of the anticipation of further modifications in the framework in the form of a forced termination, and perhaps because of other deviations as well. In addition, it would seem that the therapist's interventions have not generated understanding in the patient, nor supported his healthy defenses. Because of this, and because of other factors within the patient that haven't been communicated as yet, the patient's defenses, largely in the form of Type C barriers, seem to be weakening. There is, for the moment, a sense of chaos that reflects the patient's inner state, some dimension of the inner state of the therapist, and some of the primary qualities of the therapeutic situation and interaction.

We'll see now what happened. He may respond to this intervention, which I, of course, predict he will not validate, with either further defensiveness or a shift to derivative communication which will largely be an effort to respond to the adaptive context of this particular intervention and possibly to the current and anticipated deviations. The derivatives would largely constitute an unconscious working over of the therapist's disruptive inputs, and might even go so far as to reflect an unconscious attempt to cure the therapist. Right now it would be very difficult to identify additional sources within the patient for this disturbance.

Therapist: My broad adaptive context was that I had become more silent in the treatment, and he had been very vigorously working to get more and more from me. So my frame of mind in listening to the material was that he's bringing in an old symptom, he wants to go back to the way it used to be, he wants me to give him Librium like I used to, and he wants me to start telling him things directly. And when I made my comment, I thought I was addressing something about the relationship and that adaptive context.

Langs: It's clear that you are all appealing for clarification regarding the formulation and timing of interventions. Please be patient since we will get to that in the last part of this course. Nonetheless, I will respond here briefly.

First, if the adaptive context really is your relative silence, it must be represented in the material from the patient in some discernible form. Perhaps that will soon take place, but for the moment I cannot recall any clear-cut derivative of that context. You might suggest that in some way his hearing the lyrics of a song in his head is being used to represent the silence of the therapist, but that is a remote derivative at best.

The critical factor in evaluating silence as an adaptive context is the determination as to whether its use has been valid or invalid. Here, you are dealing with relative silence, which has been interrupted with sporadic, quite incomplete, and largely erroneous interventions. These comments will tend to overshadow the silence, though the patient will undoubtedly respond to your relative inactivity as well. Appropriate silence will have a positive influence, while inappropriate silence—that is, missed interventions—will elicit all types of indirect complaints and reactions.

In any case, you are approaching an issue related to the framework: your relative silence may be offering him a better hold, or it may be spoiled by your incorrect interventions. It may well be a factor here, though I do believe that other issues will loom even larger. In all, because of the way in which you are approaching this issue and because I do not hear it as a central concern of the patient, I do not expect validation. I think we have yet to allow the patient to provide us the selected fact that will shift our preconception regarding the need for an adaptive context to a conception that provides us the realization of a context that will give this rather disparate material integrated meaning. Please continue.

Therapist: Okay, so I make this comment. And he says, Well, yes, there have been several times I wanted to ask you something similar to that, but decided not to because I knew you probably wouldn't answer it anyway. After all, that's not your job, to answer that sort of a question.

Langs: So he tells you this directly. In the adaptive context of your intervention, you must recognize this as a commentary: your job is to intervene in a different way. In addition, this comment is a directive related toward rectification: modify your technique and secure the frame. That is his message.

Therapist: Then he started saying, But it's still something that bothers me; I think about it sometimes. At this point he began to put his finger in his ear and said that his ear has been itching him a lot lately. And then he shifted to talking about his mother, saying that his mother had really been getting on his nerves lately and has really been getting him very angry. She's been sort of hovering over him saying things like, Be careful when you go outside; you don't dress warm enough; it's cold out.

Langs: Well, in the absence of a clear-cut and dramatic modification in the framework, you can see how little new we learn about it. While deviations in the framework certainly constitute poor mothering, much of this last material is a commentary on the last intervention, and it takes the form I had predicted. It reflects an unconscious perception of the therapist as a provocative nag who makes use of clichés. Scratching his ear undoubtedly has some underlying meaning; we could speculate about it, but the cognitive material is hardly illuminating. I suggest we see where all of this goes.

Therapist: He went on: She said that the most important thing is having to take care of your health, because if you're not healthy you can't move ahead.

Langs: We are certainly hearing clichés—Type C barriers, with implications along the me/not-me interface for both patient and therapist. This is a Type C communicative style without an adaptive context and with material that is ruminative and distant. It's an interactional product, but again I see little relevance to the frame. I'm now open for a surprise—I hope it occurs.

Therapist: And then he pauses again and says, Ah, you know my mother's got all of that crazy magical thinking—which is something we've talked about before in the treatment: his superstitious mother, who's quite paranoid, in fact, in a lot of her thinking. And he said, You know, in some ways I may actually be quite like her in the way that I think sometimes.

Langs: What makes us all humble is monitoring this material along the me/not-me interface, and hearing this as a commentary on your interventions. It gives you a lot to think about, and slows you down a bit: it will help you to not pursue the mother, or even the patient, so quickly. It also gives you a lot of humility, something many therapists can really use. Okay.

Therapist: Here comes my intervention. I said, It sounds like you're really concerned about whether or not you're going to get into crazy thinking in the same way that your mother does now.

Langs: Brief comments?

Discussant: Isolated material, no adaptive context, use of manifest content with minimal inference.

Langs: Yes, avoiding the ''not-me'' part of the me/not-me interface, disregarding this material as a commentary on the last intervention and on the general therapeutic interaction, and offering now a comment that will serve as a Type C barrier—a psychoanalytic cliché. It's an excellent example of that kind of cliché, and its main function: to deny countertransference-based contributions from the therapist. But let's not elaborate and just hope that we can soon get to a frame issue. Still, watch what the patient says.

Therapist: He says, Yeh, maybe, she can really be ridiculous. (Laughter.)

Langs: Well, the material does take on quite a different meaning when you listen in the adaptive context of your interventions. Therapists are always talking about their patients' pathological mothers, and now it would seem that they often do so in order to avoid their own comparable behaviors and contributions. So we get no validation, but an honest comment. And it hurts a bit, but we can all learn from it.

Therapist: You know, you really don't realize what this is like until you actually present it here. Then it all seems so clear, you wonder how you could miss it before. I really don't mind this a bit; I'm learning more than I ever have before.

Discussant: I know just how you feel. I had the same experience when I presented. And once you get over the embarrassment and sense of hurt—the wondering about how you could have ever done anything like that—it really opens your eyes to a lot of important things.

Langs: Well, I appreciate the extent to which you have not only shown an increase in your ability to make good use of the concepts I have been teaching you, but have, along with that, a better perspective on this type of teaching—both its discomfort and its unique assets. Let's move on.

Therapist: So, Mother can really be ridiculous. Then he says, But you know, my father tends to be more understanding.

Langs: This is a typical split, and while it may reflect some pathology in the patient, for the moment it mainly reflects his unconscious perception of you: you are making efforts to understand him, but you can really be ridiculous. Please go on.

Therapist: So, Father is more understanding. He pauses a little bit and he says, I don't know, all this trouble that I'm having. I want so much to be a good researcher.

Langs: Now he returns to the wish for a good therapist. This is the introject that he's searching for; it expresses his longings. And of course, along the me/not-me interface, it can also express your own wish to be a good therapist.

Therapist: He said, My father would be so proud of me if I got through all of this. He then went on talking about his father, mentioning how miserable he is in his job. His father is working in a super-market and really hates it. He's getting paid very poorly, it's a miserable situation.

Langs: So the tone shifts again and the misery of the situation is emphasized—though with sympathy.

Therapist: Then he talks about how he doesn't want to be preoccu-pied with money in his work, especially when he goes into industry; he doesn't want to make that a preoccupation, and he went on with that a lit-tle. He said, I don't want to wind up making up for lost time and for all that I missed out on in graduate school by becoming one of those industry types who just has to have all the luxuries. And then he mentions again the Mercedes, etcetera, etcetera; he goes on with that sort of description.

Discussant: Isn't that a metaphor for the kind of treatment the therapist was describing? It's a way of giving him things, gifts—drugs, his phone number, and the like.

Langs: Yes, you might offer a Type One derivative of that kind, and relate it to the secondary context of the patient's request for medication. I am, for the moment, more struck by the image of lost time, a metaphor of the Type C field. If I were to derive a single implication regarding deviations in the framework from this material, it would be to the effect that the altered frame creates a communicative field in which Type C barriers are quite prevalent. The material builds a bit, even organizes as Type One derivatives around the therapist's superficial and erroneous interventions, only to become diffuse and scattered again. The deviations contribute to a fragmentation of the patient's communications, to the point where the material becomes quite empty.

And many therapists would simply continue to make interventions to this patient based on the manifest content and perhaps a few Type One derivatives, would engage in little effort to apply the validating process, would fail to recognize the absence of validation, and would not become aware that this material is flat and without an adaptive context through which it can be organized. The message to me is that rectification is essential for a Type A and symbolic communication, and for the possibility that the therapist might be in a position to develop an interpretive intervention. It doesn't seem feasible under these conditions.

Therapist: I intervened at this point. (Laughter.)

Langs: Well, we certainly have gotten our act together: the timing was perfect. And what did you say?

Therapist: I said, The song you've been preoccupied with seems to relate to what's going to happen to you with time, when you become a researcher and industrialist, and how you may change in certain ways.

Langs: Brief comment?

Discussant: It sounds clichéd, and there certainly is no adaptive context, no use of derivatives, and no reference to the framework.

Langs: Yes, you can see how these interventions direct the patient away from not only the frame, but also from the entire therapeutic relationship. They serve as a major Type C barrier to every critical underlying truth in the therapeutic interaction—whether related to the framework or not. As you can see, modifications in the framework that involve the more changeable aspects of the ground rules, such as the therapist's use of neutral interventions geared toward interpretation, can serve to obliterate rather than evoke meaning. Let's see how he responds.

Therapist: He said, Maybe, maybe I'm feeling guilty about becoming a rich executive. He said, It's not really what I want. All I want to do is be a good researcher. And then—this was the end of the session—as he was getting up to leave, he said, Oh, by the way, What about the Librium? And I just said, Why don't we take it up next session?

Langs: All right; enough said. Let's hear more and get to the frame.

Therapist: Okay. He came into the next session—the shorter one—looking terrible. He was unshaven, bedraggled, his hair all unkempt, and he started off by saying that he was really climbing the walls; he was so anxious. He's having tremendous difficulty preparing for his exams. He's very concerned that he's going to fail, just like last year. And he goes on and on with this sort of thing. He's really behind in his work. He can't concentrate. He's so anxious. And he just goes on for quite some time talking about how anxious and upset he is.

Discussant: I would have predicted that from the last session.

Langs: I wish you had. Why would you have predicted it?

Discussant: Well, I felt—I wouldn't say it as strongly as you did—but I felt that the therapist's interventions were not particularly on target in that session. And the patient probably felt that the therapist was being oblique. And when the therapist said, We'll take it up next session, the message the patient had was: I'm going to have to be very direct with him if he's going to get my meaning. So that accounts for the disheveled appearance and the rest.

Langs: That's an interesting line of reasoning, but too much of it is on a manifest level, and based on Type One derivatives, rather than being organized around an adaptive context. A problem would arise if you felt that your explanation should lead to an intervention along the lines that you described, since you are suggesting that the adaptive context is the therapist's failure to offer the Librium, and perhaps the inadequacy of his interventions. There is some truth to the latter point, although I do not believe that maintaining the frame by not prescribing medication will lead to an acute regression.

The point is that for the moment the disheveled appearance and anxiety constitute a therapeutic context, and the hope is that his continued associations, by shifting to indirect communication, will explain the unconscious basis for the regression. It is too simplistic to suggest that the patient wants medication and is trying to force the therapist's hand. My point will be clearer once we have more material.

So, we can now listen with your silent hypothesis in mind and my suggestion that the associations, if they shift away from the Type C barrier of the patient's simply repeating something about how anxious he is, will in derivative form indicate another adaptive context with which we could understand what is happening. Incidentally, as you can see, the patient can attempt to maintain Type C barriers in the face of acute anxiety, and can convey painful affect without derivative communication. This tends to be his mode of defense, and it is, as I said before, an interactional product.

Discussant: I wonder if the patient wasn't attempting to generate a projective identification by placing his anxiety into the therapist and making him feel guilty.

Therapist: What I sensed was that he was sitting there, saying, Look at me, I'm in a miserable state; do something.

Langs: Yes, there may indeed be qualities of a disruptive pathological projective identification here. The point is well taken. But remember, we will want to validate that thesis in the cognitive material. This type of anxiety could evoke a variety of responses in the therapist, and may be designed also to create a number of role responses and images, such as further modifications in the framework, so-called direct support, feelings of guilt, badness, and fright, and more. Go on.

Therapist: Then he started talking about feeling very sad because there's a girl, another student, that lives in the next apartment, and he felt very bad about having to go to her and talk about how anxious he felt.

Langs: Now, let's generate a silent hypothesis as to the unconscious basis for his anxiety. If you listen to this material as derivatives, where does it direct you?

Therapist: That he felt bad that he had to go next door to the apartment to talk to another graduate student, a woman, to start telling her how anxious he felt.

Langs: You are on a manifest level.

Therapist: It means that he has to go to somebody else.

Discussant: It's a representation of the therapist.

Discussant: He doesn't like going to the therapist, telling him these things.

Discussant: Well, he's just disguising his sexual feelings toward the therapist, in terms of making it into a heterosexual relationship.

Discussant: Disguising it, and in actuality, defending against it.

Discussant: But he talks to someone else—a third party.

Langs: Yes, you can now put it all together: the patient introduces a female third party as a protection against unconscious homosexual perceptions of the therapist, as well as unconscious homosexual fantasies. That, however, is a Type One derivative formulation and we now must—as a silent hypothesis—attempt to link it to some adaptive context. Any suggestions?

Discussant: Could that woman be a substitute for the therapist, and all of this a defense against his feelings about the anticipated forced termination?

Langs: Yes, those derivatives do suggest the adaptive context of the forced termination, but in addition they suggest a response to the presence of third parties to treatment. We can take that as another silent hypothesis. But if we take this as a commentary on the alterations in the framework, we could say that the patient unconsciously perceives the therapist's deviations as a defense against the therapist's unconscious homosexual countertransference. I would view that as a transversal communication with probable distorted and valid elements. We are touching here upon the instinctual-drive and countertransference aspects of unneeded deviations and the unconscious fantasies they communicate. These are, of course, all rather tentative silent hypotheses, but we'll soon have an opportunity to validate them.

Therapist: I know you're going to think I'm shifting it away from me, but where would you place the part from the last session, in terms of this as his way of going to somebody like mother, a woman who's going to mother him, tell him what to do, and hover over him?

Langs: Unfortunately, this is not the time to discuss the issues raised by your comment in any detail. You are conceptualizing without links to the therapeutic relationship, and working with simple, linear displacements. You thereby generate Type One derivatives, based on rather evident inferences from the manifest material. And certainly, much therapeutic work is done on that basis. And that is why the adaptive context concept—which is totally lacking in your formulation—opens up the possibility for far more complex formulations which, as I have said before, are much more pertinent to the dynamics of neurosis and which, quite empirically, lead us consistently to the therapeutic relationship. I can only hope that something in this material will help us to recognize the inadequacy of your formulation, and the pertinence of mine. Let's try to remain open enough to see which receives Type Two derivative validation.

Discussant: Along the me/not-me interface, couldn't this be an allusion to the therapist and his supervisor?

Langs: Of course, but we still lack an immediate adaptive context, something that would give specific and unique meaning to this material. Please continue.

Therapist: He said, After all, what right do I have to go to her apartment and spill my guts to her? He went on a little bit with that type of stuff.

Discussant: Is that sexual or ejaculatory?

Discussant: To me it sounds a bit like bodily disintegration. He's afraid of the consequences of therapy.

Langs: Well, it is fine to respond freely and imaginatively to this material, but remember that there is also another step: integrating all of this around an adaptive context, and for us at this point, around a context related to the frame. Continue.

Therapist: He said that he felt very angry with himself for having to speak with her, but it's just that he's so nervous he doesn't know what to do.

Langs: For us, this confused state must be related to the modifications in the framework, but I now suspect, since this is an intense Type C field, that we will have little opportunity to validate silent hypotheses related to the ground rules. Perhaps it is now time to comment on the unequal sessions and to suggest that there is, embedded in this material, a commentary on that arrangement in its confusing, inadequate, sexual, protective qualities. All of that has to be stated quite tentatively, since there is no immediate frame issue to serve as a strong organizer of this material, and we are left with a rather general monitoring process.

Therapist: So he pauses. And then he starts to wonder about the fact that he's very dependent on other people. For example, that he was asking in the last session for Librium, and the idea of having to depend on a pill was something that he had thought about, although for his last several exams he had decided not to take any. He thought it would be better to deal with it himself rather than to have to rely on a pill.

Langs: So, embedded in this material is a conscious comment related to maintaining and rectifying the frame: have faith in the ego functioning of your patients and help them to develop not only a belief in their adaptive capacities, but also the specific tools with which to deal with their anxieties and the sources of their difficulties—internal and external. It would be nice if we understood which additional framework issues the patient was alluding to in derivative form here, because I strongly suspect that this refers not only to your prescribing medication—which we now see that he took for some time—but also to other alterations in the ground rules, past and present. The patient's request for Librium is a therapeutic context, and a secondary adaptive context, not a primary one, which by definition would come from the therapist.

Discussant: I noticed in *The Listening Process* (Langs 1978c) that at times you suggested that things like a request for medication, the patient missing a session or being late, and the patient's wish to prematurely terminate treatment could be treated as adaptive contexts.

Langs: Yes, it was only after completing that book and turning my attention to the next step, the formulation and timing of interventions, that I realized I had been confused in that respect. The type of event that you just described is clearly an indicator for an intervention, and what I have termed a *therapeutic context,* a second-order organizer for listening, and an expression by the patient of a need for an intervention. At times these serve as what I now call *secondary adaptive contexts*— actualities generated by the patient to which he then responds. It is critical, however, to recognize that in therapy such contexts must ultimately be traced out to a primary, external context which, virtually without exception, will pertain to the interventions of the therapist. When we discuss intervening, we'll see that these distinctions are critical. If you were to attempt an intervention organized entirely around the patient's request for Librium, you would totally neglect the actual prevailing primary adaptive contexts derived from the therapist— which, in this instance could include the fact that the therapist had prescribed the drug earlier.

Therapist: Well, fortunately for me, this is past history, but I intervened again at this point. (Laughter.) I'm afraid to even look; I'm sure I delivered another psychoanalytic cliché. In any case, I said, The idea of taking the Librium obviously has a lot of dependency meanings

for you. And your anxiety over having to be dependent on somebody
was also evident in the last session, in that you waited till the very end
to find out about the prescription—remember that he mentioned it
again only on his way out the door.

He says, Yes, it's probably very complicated. After all, I can't
come in here and say to you, Give me some Librium. After all, you're
the doctor. It's your decision, and besides I still would rather not have
to depend on a pill. Because there would always be the question of
whether I would eventually be able to control it or whether I would just
keep having to take pills. He said, Maybe it has to do with my being
concerned about not being able to control the feelings that I have. And
I commented; I said, Well, the concern about being dependent on a pill
is really a way of talking about your feelings about being dependent on
me. And he says, I'd rather not be dependent, but I get so anxious.

And then he goes back to a year ago in the treatment. He said,
Remember when we first started, you brought up the idea about giving
me some Librium. I remember you said something like, This may be
helpful to you. And he said, Maybe I think what really was helpful to
me about it was the fact that you said it would help me—more than any
pharmacological properties of the pill. So then I made some comment
like, Was there an implication in my offering you the pill to the effect
that it meant that I didn't think you could handle things on your own?
And he said, Well, I don't know; it's all very complicated. It's hard to
know what I was feeling then. It had a lot of meaning.

Langs: We could simply hear this out, or we could comment briefly
here.

Discussant: Somehow, all of this seems pretty obvious to me. It's
rather flat and dull.

Discussant: The patient seems to be saying that the therapist had
the need to introduce the Librium, not he.

Langs: Well, this is what happens when an intervention is offered
around a therapeutic context, rather than a primary adaptive context.
There is, as yet, no immediate adaptive context, only the context from
some time back related to the therapist's decision to prescribe medication for the patient. We have here a Type C patient with a Type

C therapist, and therefore, of course, a Type C field. And I don't mean this as a personal criticism of the therapist, because I think that this type of work is rather typical of many therapists and supervisors. Taking a pill is a kind of dependency, and is something distressing for many individuals. That is indeed a psychoanalytic cliché, the type of statement that can be made of anyone at any time—it is entirely lacking in specificity or dynamic import. And it especially lacks any quality of unconscious fantasy or perception, of meaningful content. It is flat and empty, and let's try to learn that this type of intervention constitutes the offer, as the patient amply confirms, of an obsessive, ruminative Type C barrier, which, for the moment, is quite impenetrable. In a way, the patient also seems to keep calling for a search for meaning, though even as he does so indirectly, he continues to ruminate with the therapist.

There are a few things here that we can learn. First, the use of medication is often a substitute for a sound interpretive intervention, an effort to offer a framework deviation cure. It is, on the surface, a form of forced dependency, but the derivative material here indicates that it is, in addition, a significant means of creating a Type C field in which unconscious derivatives and meanings can be almost excluded. It seems likely then that psychotropic medication functions primarily as a Type C barrier and that that is perhaps the prime psychological basis through which it offers temporary symptom relief.

In terms of the adaptive context of your suggestion some time ago that he take medication, this material organizes as relatively general derivatives along the me/not-me interface. Unconsciously, he perceives your suggestion as a reflection of your inability to control or manage his inner state, and you own as well. Perhaps most important is his returning to your decision to prescribe the drug, and his emphasis on your need to introduce the medication and his own preference to function on his own. Here, as I said before, is a directive toward rectification, and it suggests that, unconsciously, a primary reason for his own request for medication toward the end of the last session was his wish to afford you an opportunity of that kind.

Technically, while you still lack a specific adaptive context, you could play back these superficial derivatives and identify his conscious and unconscious directive. You could thereby point out that the patient is indicating that whatever has prompted his current request for medication, he is clearly indicating that prescribing drugs undermines his own capacity to deal with his anxiety and emotional problems, and expresses a wish on his part—reinforced by your own earlier prescription of the drug—for some undue tie to yourself. Perhaps then we might get around to more derivative communication and to a clearer representation of the adaptive context—quite possibly his anticipation of a forced termination at midyear.

That's about all that I can do with this material for the moment. Let's see what happens.

Therapist: He said, But I do get very dependent whenever I get very anxious. But I remember that I used to get very annoyed with my mother whenever she would accept clothes from her aunt and uncle as hand-me-downs for her kids. She would protest about accepting the clothing from somebody else, but then would go ahead and take it. And then, her relatives who would give the clothes always had this attitude that they were better than we were.

Langs: How might this be a derivative related to the frame?

Discussant: Getting something for nothing.

Langs: Yes, treatment without a fee. How else?

Discussant: This must be some kind of image related to the therapist's insistence—at least as the patient perceived it—that he take medication. There is also a reference to third parties which sounds a bit like an allusion to a supervisor.

Langs: Yes. Perhaps because the therapist has not immediately prescribed medication—and this implies the possibility of rectification— we now hear a few derivatives. And, in the adaptive contexts of the earlier prescription, the absence of a fee, and the likelihood of supervision, the patient is indicating on one level that he feels demeaned and that this places the therapist in a holier-than-thou position. It cheapens therapy, in more ways than one, and makes the patient into the poor relation—an implicit reference to the positions of patient and therapist vis à vis one another at this center generally, and of course, within this particular treatment situation. The inequalities inherent to therapy need not have this kind of demeaning effect and would not have them were it not for the modified frame. On another level, along the me/not-me interface, the material also seems to touch upon the therapist's position as a trainee with a supervisor.

Now, the patient is also talking about saying one thing and doing another. The inconsistency is especially painful, and words mean little when contradicted by actual behavior. This is a sound commentary on a therapeutic situation in which the therapist speaks of inappropriate dependency yet creates conditions which include infantilizing modifications in the framework. And you can be sure that the therapist can verbally encourage a position of independence with endless comments, and the patient's dependency will remain. In fact, the therapist's own dependency on the use of medication will further reinforce these needs.

So once again we come to a moment of realizing that the framework is an actuality whose management by the therapist is filled with unconscious meanings that take precedence over his verbal interventions. I simply cannot stress that point enough: the unconscious implications of the therapist's actual behaviors, including the management of the framework, take precedence, as does the unconscious implications of his efforts as compared to those that are direct and conscious. The therapist who says one thing and does another is a Type C therapist—and in a striking sense, a lie therapist—who is utilizing deceptions which then influence the patient's perceptions of him and of everything he says. So it is the management of the framework that comes first, and further, because this management deals with actualities, rectification must precede or accompany interpretation.

Discussant: I'd like to make two comments. First, it seems to me that you're saying if you don't really ever want to get loaded material from the patient, all you need do is modify the framework, especially through the use of drugs. The second is this: Once you begin to get in touch with these issues, you have to rectify them, which is very hard to do within the confines of the clinic.

Langs: Yes, you are quite right: a major function of the use of medication is to provide both patient and therapist with impenetrable barriers against the derivatives of their unconscious fantasies, memories, and introjects. Now, such barriers may collapse, but nonetheless that is certainly the intention and this material illustrates it quite clearly. And further, rather paradoxically, these deviations, which are designed to help the patient manage his neurosis, actually confirm that neurosis and reinforce it by virtue of the unconscious communications they contain. Whatever that material about dependency ultimately refers to, that is certainly the case here: the deviations are reinforcing certain kinds of unconscious pathological needs and defenses that are critical to the patient's neurosis and which cannot be modified insightfully under these conditions.

As for your second point, as therapists become aware of the nature and the functions of the framework, and of the extensive implications of their management, it should become possible to design a clinic in which deviations are kept to an absolute minimum. But you are quite right: interpretation without rectification is a compromised effort. Ideally, in the presence of a modified framework the therapist becomes engaged in both rectification and interpretation, and he does so entirely on the basis of the conscious and unconscious communications and directives from the patient. Rectification without interpretation will prove helpful sometimes, as we saw to some extent when we studied that first session, but ultimately rectification must be backed up with interpretive interventions. Interpretations without rectification are virtually useless, since their main implications are those described by this patient: they will be taken as false statements and deceptions offered by someone involved in behaviors that contradict his words.

Discussant: What type of intervention would you be preparing here?

Langs: Well, the patient has represented the absence of a fee in a well-disguised and derivative way. I would be waiting for a clearer representation, and I would be planning to point out that being prescribed drugs and receiving therapy without a fee is seen by the patient as demeaning and destructive, and as strongly contradictory to his goals in treatment. He is saying that such arrangements very much remind him of the demeaning position that his mother put herself and him in, and of the contradictions between her words and her behavior. He is also pointing out that taking full responsibility for himself cannot take place under these conditions, so it seems evident that there should be no prescription for drugs and that a small fee should be set for the therapy.

Notice how I interpreted the genetics: the modifications in the framework are actual repetitions on some level of a past pathogenic interaction which contributed to the patient's psychopathology—in ways that are not entirely clear, though I have little doubt that this is the case. I did not propose to the patient that he was misperceiving the implications of medication and no-fee therapy by distorting the situation in terms of his earlier experiences with his mother. That would be a transference interpretation. I approached this first through non-transference because my own reading of the unconscious implications of these deviations have validated the patient's perceptions, as has the coalescence of his material. Transference elements could then emerge more clearly and be interpreted.

Please understand, too, that I would not intervene regarding the absence of a fee at this time unless the patient brought up the issue in some unmistakable form. However, even without a clear-cut primary adaptive context, in the therapeutic context of the request for medication and the presence of an old adaptive context, I would make this type of intervention focusing on the request for medication. I would do so in a way that leaves open the search for—or hints at—an unmentioned primary context.

Well, let's see where it all goes.

Therapist: So then he said, And my father, when they bought the house, there was that uncle who gave us, loaned us money to help us pay for the house. He said, You know, the guy that was living with us, I had mentioned him I think a long time ago. From Germany. And here, I mentioned the guy's name. The patient had spent a lot of time with him; they would go to ball games together and other places.

Langs: So we come now to a boarder, a third party and money provider, and the sort of figure who is often the source of homosexual stimulation. In this communicative field, we consistently obtain uncoalesced derivatives that hint at possible meaning, rather than being saturated with it. Incidentally, while relatively minor, your recollection of the boarder's name is a type of self-revelation—another slight alteration in the framework.

Therapist: Actually, he responded by being very surprised when I mentioned the name, that I still remembered it.

Langs: In this context it could be a seductive adaptive context with homosexual implications.

Therapist: Yes. To complete this session: he says, Father really had to depend on this guy. He couldn't do it himself. And I at the end of the session say, So really you're saying that you don't want to be dependent on other people like your parents were; you want to get by on your own strength. And then he says, Yes, but I still have that feeling that I did last year when I failed my exams, and he goes on a little bit about how he had failed and been upset.

Langs: So you see the commentary on your intervention: it's failing him as you have in the past. Everything remains quite linear, without a specific adaptive context. And you intervene without a consistent connection to the therapeutic relationship, and in terms of isolated contents—the patient and his parents. It's all straightforward and not neurotic in the least: his parents were overly dependent, and he would prefer not to be. Perhaps that might be a sufficient message to you to secure a therapeutic situation that no longer fosters undue dependency, but there are no mediating unconscious fantasies and the like, no sense of convoluted and neurotic communication; the Type C field prevails.

Therapist: Well, what I've been leading up to is this: he called me during the week after this session.

Langs: I would take that as an indication that you had failed interpretively, and as a directive to review the transactions of the previous session. So, the patient next further modifies the frame, and that should create a rather strong therapeutic context for the next hour. Since our time is up, we will stop for today in a moment. I just want to add one final thought: The Type C field is not only dead and nonfunctional for the patient and therapist, but is the field that is least evocative for supervisors and for anyone who wishes to learn about the therapeutic experience. It destroys meaning for all who are a part of it, or who wish to consider it. Still, we thank you for presenting to us, and will look forward to hearing more next week.

Chapter Ten

INTERVENING IN THE FACE OF DEVIATIONS

Langs: Today, we begin again without desire, memory, or understanding. We will just pick up this case at the point where you left off, and see what unfolds.

Therapist: After the last session we discussed, the next day, in the afternoon, I received a phone call from the patient, saying that it was very important that he speak with me right away. But they had buzzed into my office when I was with another patient, and I told him I couldn't speak with him but that if it was important I would get back to him. He said he would be in his apartment between four and five, and I told him I would call him then.

I called him later and he said he was extremely anxious. He was having a tremendous amount of anxiety, and for the last day or so had been unable to get any studying done for one of these exams that he was going to have. He was going to have one the next day, and one the day after. He had developed a marked anxiety and a fear that he was going to fail because he couldn't study. He said he was having palpitations and felt extremely anxious. And he went on for a couple of minutes relaying all of this and saying how anxious he was.

So I made a few comments. I said, We'll have a chance to discuss this more next session. But in a sense, he couldn't keep it together at all. He kept coming back to his being so anxious. And I said to him, Look, whether you pass or fail the examinations, it's not the end of the world.

Discussant: That's easy for you to say. (Laughter.) You passed yours.

Therapist: I said something to the effect that all he can do is the best he can, and to get as much studying done as he feels he can do and take the examinations—which were before his next session. Whatever happens, happens. And he went on a little bit, for a few more minutes, relating all the particulars of the difficulties he was having. Again, I just made some comment to him: try not to be so preoccupied with the consequences of passing and failing, just study as best you can, and see what happens.

Discussant: How do you usually handle telephone conversations, like when someone calls?

Langs: You really think it's possible that I get such telephone calls? (Laughter.)

Discussant: I mean, I'd just like a general approach.

Therapist: Hypothetically speaking.

Langs: Well, there is little doubt that such telephone calls can happen to any therapist, but the point of my little joke is that to the extent that you maintain a secure frame they will be far less frequent. Remember that I treat the symptoms within the patient in psychotherapy as interactional, as products of the bipersonal field, an approach that leads me to consider contributions from both participants. In this situation we must consider the therapist's alterations in the framework as well as the patient's psychopathology. Still, just to clarify and offer a silent hypothesis, what is the most likely adaptive context for this interlude?

Discussant: Do you mean the therapist's rather inadequate interventions in the previous hour?

Langs: Yes, just that: his flat, rather clichéd interventions and, I would add, his implicit decision not to prescribe medication for the patient. We'll soon sort out the effects of each.

Now, as for some general principles, I would call back in a situation like this, since there is the possibility of an emergency. But I would make the conversation as brief as possible. I would certainly not adopt a so-called supportive or directive attitude, nor offer direct reassurance. If the patient's comments permitted a quick interpretation, I would offer it, but short of that I would empathize with the patient's concern and leave the rest to the next hour.

Another major consideration arises when the patient is suicidal or homicidal; it then becomes important to determine whether there is any serious danger. Certainly, under those conditions an almost immediate session would be indicated. However, though under such circumstances we are justified in taking this life-saving measure, we must expect that in addition to its positive effects it will also have negative consequences. At such times, we should also carefully examine ourselves for countertransference-based contributions to the crisis.

Discussant: Are you saying that panic states of this kind do not occur when the frame is secured and the patient receives reasonably good interpretive interventions?

Langs: I'm saying that they will be far less frequent under those conditions, yes. That relates to the inherently ego-supportive aspects of a well-managed framework.

We now have a major therapeutic context for the session we are about to hear, an effort by the patient to further modify the frame. And while we still lack an understanding of the adaptive context which set off this sequence of events, we do have an immediate precipitant. Who can identify it?

Discussant: The therapist's nonneutral interventions on the telephone.

Langs: Yes.

Discussant: It's taken me two years, but I've learned how to handle this kind of call sympathetically, and without becoming either maternal or paternal.

Discussant: For me, I find that much of it depends on the counter-transference I have toward the patient, though obviously I realize that should not be the basis on which to develop sound principles of technique.

Discussant: I must say that when I have been able to follow your principles it has worked out quite well—exactly the way you say it will.

Therapist: Well, I experienced this patient as holding on quite tightly on the telephone. That's why I tried in some sort of nonspecific way to offer him an alternative to feeling that he absolutely must pass the examination. That's why I told him that the consequences wouldn't be life and death, and tried to suggest that we should discuss it further next session.

Langs: But what are the unconscious communications here?

Discussant: This could be an invitation to the patient to fail the examination or to be less concerned about passing.

Discussant: I see these comments as infantilizing the patient.

Langs: Yes, and they unconsciously promote the patient's clinging tendencies. In addition, it is the therapist who introduces the theme of life and death, which may well come across as a means of conveying his own anxiety and concerns. The point is to recognize that so-called supportive interventions are filled with unconscious implications, and that in addition they modify rather than secure the framework. Overall, there is little doubt that they prove more disorganizing than not, and more destructive than supportive. And we will soon have an opportunity here to test that hypothesis again. You seem also to be attempting to obliterate the unconscious implications of the patient's telephone call, and are once again offering him a Type C barrier in the form of a cliché—though here I suspect that the cliché will prove less serviceable because of the anxiety contained within it. You are attempting to offer a kind of desperate, defensive denial.

Therapist: But I was also attempting to deal with one level of reality. After all, it really *isn't* a matter of life or death. It seems to me that it depends on whether you are talking about external reality or unconscious implications.

Langs: Your comment assumes that this is a matter simply of your opinion or mine, while my remarks presuppose the position of the patient, which consistently demonstrates a great sensitivity to unconscious implications and communications. On that basis, I propose that we now let the patient speak for me—or for you, if that proves to be the case.

Therapist: Okay. He came a few minutes late for the session, which is not especially unusual for him.

Langs: So, the first communication is the patient's lateness. How would you characterize it?

Discussant: It is a nonverbal communication.

Langs: Related to what realm?

Discussant: To the frame.

Langs: Yes. This is another alteration of the framework on the part of the patient. As a first communication, it suggests a sense of being poorly held rather than an image of security. Please continue.

Therapist: Okay. He sits down. He says that he is very, very depressed. He's feeling very low. He feels that there's a good probability that he failed his physiology exam, and then he goes on with some of the details about why he feels he failed and how he feels about it.

Langs: Well, let's do what we can with this material. Any comments?

Discussant: The patient doesn't feel he's been helped. He speaks of failing, and—in the adaptive context of the therapist's interventions on the telephone—we would have to take that as the patient's commentary on the therapist's efforts.

Langs: Yes, in the adaptive context of the therapist's nonneutral interventions and the extratherapeutic contact on the telephone, we hear of continued symptomatic disturbance and a sense of failure. Here I am reminded of an issue related to validation, though I don't believe we have discussed it yet. There are many therapists who consider symptom alleviation a validation of their interventions. I do not accept this as so, and for several reasons. First, it is well known that symptom alleviation can occur on bases other than the securing of the framework and the imparting of a valid interpretation or reconstruction. I have identified a number of forms of misalliance cure and have found that it is essential to investigate the behaviors and associations of both patient and therapist (as well as their unconscious communicative interaction) in order to determine the underlying basis for symptom relief or intensification. Thus, variation in symptoms is not in itself an especially valuable means of validation or nonvalidation. At best symptom relief suggests the possibility that sound therapeutic work has been done, while symptomatic exacerbation suggests—though with certain exceptions, such as momentarily and immediately after the framework has been secured—that something is amiss. On that basis I would take the patient's allusions to his continued symptoms as a likely indication of the inadequacy of the therapist's interventions both in the previous session and on the telephone. Please continue.

Therapist: He went into considerable detail. He had reviewed the answers to the exam with the professor in class, and he didn't think he had enough points to pass. And he goes on and on about what's needed to pass the exam, and so forth. Then he said that he's also upset about the fact that he can't decide whether or not he wants to see a girl that he has gone out with a couple of times, and established a relationship of sorts with, a girl who is in Chicago, in graduate school in economics. She is evidently going to be in town over the weekend. And he was saying that he can't decide whether or not he should go out with her, whether he should see her, because the problem is that he has a final exam coming up on Tuesday in electron microscopy, and he doesn't know whether to study or to take off one day on the weekend and spend it with her.

Langs: Well, we're still in a predominantly Type C field, but let's make of it what we can. How could we tie this to the frame?

Discussant: He seems to be debating his duty: should he study and remain in a structured situation, or should he deviate and goof off or see a girl—perhaps there's something sexual to that.

Langs: And as a framework statement, how would you put it?

Discussant: That the patient's response to a deviation in the frame is to be unsure about whether there's going to be studying and exploring in this session, or something more sexual.

Langs: Yes, we are back to a statement regarding a lack of clarity of the nature of the transactions between patient and therapist when the frame has been altered.

Discussant: There may be some implied theme of seduction here as well.

Langs: Yes, that type of uncertainty also exists in any altered therapeutic environment. At the very least, the recent deviations have created a state of uncertainty within the patient. And this probably applies to both himself and the therapist: Shall it be the pursuit of insight and understanding, or some type of sexual contact or seduction? Will it be a Type A field or a Type B, with sexual pressures and projective identification? With so many alterations in the framework, the Type C barriers seem to be weakening. The patient's turning to a woman could well be a defense against the homosexual implications of the therapist's deviations, especially the exchanges on the telephone, as well as a manic-like defense against the therapist's introduction of life and death, and anxiety. I must say that I experience some degree of uneasiness in proposing these silent hypotheses based on this material. This is so predominantly a Type C field that it generates few really clear-cut formulations. A broken frame, as we have seen, produces uncertainty in both the therapy and its supervision. So let's not add more but instead hear some additional material.

Therapist: He said that if he winds up failing this exam, or failing the next one, he doesn't know what will happen to him. And he pauses; he says he's quite sure that he won't drop out. In other words, he won't be so upset that he would drop out of graduate school. But he said, I may wind up in the hospital, maybe with an ulcer or something like that.

Langs: Well, we've heard something like this before. What does this tell us about the functions of the frame?

Discussant: If there's a deviation in the frame, he'll get sick.

Discussant: Without a secure hold, he might have a psychosomatic illness.

Langs: Yes, an adequate and secure frame promotes symbolic communication, while an altered framework promotes expression through somatic channels, as well as through uncontrolled behavior and projective identifications. The hold is impaired and the sense of containment as well. We had a commentary of this kind from an earlier patient, as you may recall. And if the therapist can't help him contain and manage the psychopathology, the fantasy is that a hospital setting might be able to.

Therapist: I'll mention something in reference to his statement that maybe he'll wind up with an ulcer, something that I knew at this point and that had come up before. During a period in his life that he considered important, when he was nineteen, he had some tarry stools. He was worked up by a local doctor who never made a definite diagnosis, but the patient thought he might have had a duodenal ulcer. That is an important landmark, at least in his thinking, because it was after that illness that his parents, his mother in particular, became extremely protective and hovered over him; they became preoccupied over his health and his ability to do his schoolwork—he lived at home while in college.

Langs: So this is his model of an internal catastrophe—another commentary on the recent alterations in the framework. While this derives in part from his own sense of anxiety, it is also a derivative of your allusion to matters of life and death. That nonneutral intervention now appears to be serving as a pathological projective identification which the patient represents cognitively through the image of the ulcer—here, as pure speculation, it may signify the introjection of destructive pathological contents which will erode his insides.

Now that we are treating this material as Type Two derivatives around some of the specific deviations and the unconscious communications from the therapist that they contain, we can also turn to the me/not-me interface. This would lead me to suggest the patient's unconscious perception of the therapist is that he too is feeling poorly held, by both the patient and this therapeutic situation, but that he is determined to stick things out, though he too dreads some catastrophe. To the extent that this is an introject based on these deviations, you have an opportunity to observe the manner in which alterations in the framework can be disruptive to the patient's ego functioning, self-image, and capacities to hold and contain himself, and how they evoke specific unconscious perceptions and fantasies.

As you can see, there are two critical factors in respect to the ground rules. First, that they entail a set of relatively fixed constants which serve to implicitly hold and support the patient, and, second, that they are an especially important avenue of unconscious communication between the patient and the therapist. The first area has to do mainly with the establishment of the framework, while the second most often has to do with its maintenance—especially at times when the patient attempts to alter the frame. Together, these two qualities—the holding and the expressions of meaning—help to create the communicative properties of the bipersonal field and other important aspects of the treatment situation. Please continue.

Therapist: He wonders why it is that he's not able to cope like the other students, especially since he's now in graduate school and even has a certain guarantee to his future. He wonders if there really isn't something wrong with him.

Discussant: I hear some degree of validation in Type Two derivative form of the formulations that you have been making, Dr. Langs. Also, this material readily organizes along the me/not-me interface in terms of the unconscious perceptions of the therapist based on his responses to the patient on the telephone, and probably in the last session as well—as you had mentioned.

Langs: Yes, in my paper on the framework (Langs 1975c) I specifically stated that the manner in which the therapist manages the framework is a reflection of his own intrapsychic balances and his capacity to manage his own inner world—his ability to cope. And rather uniformly, deviations are perceived and introjected by patients as an inability to cope; it is from them that I learned this principle.

This patient seems to be working over these deviations a bit more explicitly now. Perhaps we will now hear a dramatic derivative that will help convince the skeptics that this material does indeed allude to the therapist's modifications in the framework.

Discussant: It would also be nice to see whether the therapist's reactions on the telephone are more important to this patient than the interventions in the prior session, which, it seemed to me, did not especially serve the countertransference needs of the therapist as much as they reflected the poor qualities of his supervision.

Langs: Well, I would always want to include both factors when the therapist makes an erroneous intervention. He will apply the poor principles that he has been taught, but will do so along lines determined by his own countertransference-based needs. After all, his interventions in the previous hour were designed as a barrier to the therapeutic relationship and the sense of chaos in this treatment situation. Nonetheless, his technical errors entailed a minimum of alteration in the framework, and did not modify the fixed frame. We would therefore expect them to have less of an influence than the telephone contact and the therapist's distinctly nonneutral interventions at that time. And I think the material to this point bears that out.

What seems most characteristic of this therapeutic work is its Type C qualities; the interventions during the sessions are far more the offer of Type C barriers than of disruptive projective identifications. However, the main comment that the therapist made on the telephone had more of a Type B, projective identificatory quality, and I think that this is the reason we have been able to organize this material mainly as Type Two derivatives around the therapist's reference to matters of life and death.

We can identify here the three types of alterations in the frame which I mentioned earlier. The fixed frame was modified by the telephone contact; the therapist's neutrality was altered by his comments on the telephone—he presented the patient with directives; and the other aspect of the more human and changeable part of the frame, as reflected in the qualities of the therapist's interpretive efforts, was also infringed upon by his essentially defensive, countertransference-based comments in the last session. We'll soon see which deviation has the greatest effect upon the patient. Please continue.

Therapist: So he's wondering if there isn't something really wrong with him. One of the other guys that he knows in his group went to college with him. And he says, This guy is getting by, doing well, he's not having any special problems. And he tells me how easily the guy is getting through, and then he mentions that this guy's father is a neurophysiologist. He talked a little bit more about the guy and how he's doing. And I asked, Why did you mention that the guy's father was a neurophysiologist? He said that it came in sort of out of context; he just threw it in. But I had something in mind. One of the major themes in the treatment, and something in one session, maybe four or five sessions back, has to do with his preoccupation that he was going to help his father financially; he would imagine him in a senior citizens' home, unhappy and unsuccessful. And one of the things that had cropped up was that he was very much aware of what other people's fathers did. And I was viewing this in the context of a number of his conflicts in terms of his own success and his father's failure.

Langs: Any comments?

Discussant: Well, it's a nonneutral intervention, though the therapist does have something in mind.

Discussant: It certainly doesn't deal with the frame.

Langs: Yes, it's another attempt to intervene without an adaptive context, and in terms of manifest content and readily available Type One derivative inferences. It moves again toward another common psychoanalytic cliché: the patient's father is a failure, and because of this he is conflicted about being successful. It's simplistic, attractive, and, perhaps above all, it leaves out the therapist. It would be far more disturbing to turn to the adaptive context of the therapist's recent interventions, including the alterations in the framework, and to derive our formulation from there. On that basis we would hypothesize that the patient unconsciously perceives the therapist's efforts as a repetition of his father's failure, and that because of this a number of unconscious fantasies, memories, and introjects, related in some way to his psycho-pathology, are now being worked over.

In fact, despite the intense Type C qualities of this field—we can see now how the therapist's interventions continue uniformly to function as the offer of Type C barriers—we have at least now learned something of the dynamics of this patient's symptoms. Can anyone state it for me? (Pause.) Well, allow me to do it with this preface: there must be many factors in this patient's uncontrolled anxiety and tendency to fail examinations. What is remarkable to me is that only one aspect emerges clearly in this material as Type Two derivatives, although other supposed determinants have appeared in far more simplistic fashion—such as the influence of his father's inadequacies. The more convoluted material leads to the insight that the patient's unconscious perception and introjection of the therapist is that of a person who is unable to manage his own inner state, is concerned with losing control and with catastrophe, and who has failed in his role as a therapist.

Now of course I regret that this happens to be the Type Two derivative communication from this patient, but it is my responsibility to state consciously what the patient has presented in derivative form. And we should not pause too long to regret that this is his painful message, since these are communications that every therapist will hear and must recognize if he is to clearly understand his patient and the source of his symptoms, and thereby undertake proper therapeutic work. Truth in psychotherapy is painful for both patient and therapist, and that is why there are so few truth therapists and so few patients really interested in truth therapy. The truth is painful, threatening, and disorganizing, but we must not forget that it also provides us lasting adaptive resources unavailable to us on any other basis.

Therapist: Well, I certainly did not have the telephone call as my therapeutic context, nor did I see the two comments that I made to him on the telephone as the adaptive context. I was still waiting to come back to the basic question of why the patient was so anxious. I also thought that he was approaching my role as a father, my helping him, and his view of me as a successful doctor. I really hadn't thought of myself as failing him and as unsuccessful, though your comments now are quite convincing in that respect. It's really a very sobering lesson, but I do think that it more clearly explains what happened to this patient than do my own formulations or those of my supervisor.

Langs: I appreciate your comment, but at the very least add this qualification: that you will accept what I have said if the patient validates it through Type Two derivatives. Your image of yourself as the successful one can serve as an alternative hypothesis to my formulation. Never accept the formulations of any supervisor without Type Two derivative validation from the patient, and secondarily from your own newly generated understanding of the case.

Therapist: Yes, I understand how important that is. I wish that we had been taught this a lot earlier, because I can see now that I accepted many fancy formulations that were never really validated in any way. As you can imagine, we were never taught very much about the validating process, or the listening process either, for that matter. I had been leading up to connecting this other student's father—who is quite successful and serves as a consultant at this center—connecting him in some way to me. He's a man of considerable influence and has done a great deal for his son.

Langs: So, there is an allusion to a rather strong and helpful figure.

Therapist: Yes, but someone who also uses his influence to get what he wants.

Langs: So he is at best a mixed figure, good and bad. Perhaps that best characterizes your interventions. You're trying to be a good therapist, but having difficulty discovering the means to accomplish that. Consciously, you are well meaning; your unconscious communications, however, do not serve the therapeutic needs of the patient.

Therapist: In a way, this guy's father is able to exert a lot of influence. You might say he has the power to deviate from the usual channels when it serves his own interests. He was able to do this in ways that have been quite helpful to the patient's friend, his son.

Langs: In the adaptive context of these deviations, I think that these derivatives express the best that he can hope for from you: powerful deviations that will somehow protect and cure him.

Therapist: Yes, going around the way it really has to be done, deviating from the usual channels, the usual frame.

Langs: Yes, and with a touch of dishonesty and unfairness. These are the qualities of alterations in the framework, and of the bipersonal field that they create.

Discussant: Are you terminating with him at midyear?

Therapist: Yes.

Langs: Something brings you back to the pending forced termination—another anticipated alteration in the framework. What prompted your question?

Discussant: I'm not sure. Perhaps it was the idea of failing and going through this entire therapy and not being able to resolve his problems. It might also have been the connection to the father, someone who is tied to this center.

Langs: Yes, they may well be Type Two derivatives around that possible adaptive context. We'll have to see if something comes up that more clearly validates that thesis. Please continue.

Therapist: He goes on to say that this guy wasn't such a great student, that when they were in college he once saw this other guy's transcript.

Langs: We continue to get fragments, such as this particular embedded derivative. What did you hear?

Discussant: A violation of confidentiality.

Langs: Yes, and a reference to records that are kept and violated—a modification in the framework. In this Type C field we are accumulating fragments that begin to afford us some evidence that the framework is indeed on this patient's mind, even though there's nothing dramatic. This particular reference to seeing another student's transcript can be taken as Type Two derivative validation of some of our postulates regarding the modifications in this framework—and the extent to which they are viewed by the patient as corrupt, dishonest, and perhaps even manipulative. As a general statement related to the characteristic qualities of an alteration in the framework, this patient is suggesting that it does in fact have these rather dishonest qualities. And please notice that this is not stated here as a moral commentary. It is descriptive and a reflection of the patient's associations. Deviations contribute to Type C fields, and to its dishonest and deceptive attributes. Okay.

Therapist: He just finishes up his comments about this fellow student by saying that his grades were not all that good, and that the only graduate school that he was accepted into was connected with this center.

Langs: In the adaptive context of these deviations, and along the me/not-me interface, what is the patient saying here about the therapist—and on some level, about himself? Can anyone state this in a way that could possibly tie all of this to the patient's own modifications in the framework, including his request for medication?

Discussant: Well, there's an inference of dishonesty and the use of pull.

Discussant: He's saying something about accomplishing a goal through dishonest means.

Discussant: Isn't there some type of defense against homosexuality involved here?

Langs: Yes, this material quite nicely conveys in derivative form an effort at a dishonest type of misalliance cure—achieving goals through inappropriate influence. And this of course is not only a general commentary on modifications in the framework and their misuse to achieve a framework deviation cure, but also a clue to the unconscious meaning of the patient's request for medication. If the therapist were to prescribe the drug, he would be joining the patient in this type of unconscious collusion.

On another level, along the me/not-me interface, this is a commentary on the actual deviations that the therapist has made use of in the past or is involved in at present. Similarly, the patient's own corruption and wish for a framework deviation and misalliance cure is alluded to as well, though it could not be interpreted unless the therapist himself maintained the frame, thereby bringing into bold relief the patient's relevant psychopathology.

And we do have some tentative evidence that much of this is designed as a form of secret unconscious gratification of the homosexual needs of both patient and therapist, and as a major defense against their more open expression and realization. Notice the references here to actual corrupt practices; they are our clue to the extent to which the patient, under conditions of a modified framework, feels endangered and uncertain as to whether some type of seduction may not occur in reality. In a sense, the deviations constitute such a reality in relatively disguised and derivative form; there is no certainty that the situation will not become even more blatant. Some of this was undoubtedly gratified during the telephone call. Perhaps now it becomes clearer as to the type of unconscious gratification and the kinds of anxieties that can be evoked when the therapist intervenes noninterpretively, and deliberately or actively attempts to assume something like a fatherly role. On the surface it's all quite well-meaning, while unconsciously the situation is filled with defenses and pathological gratifications. Please continue.

Therapist: At this point, he takes on an angry tone, and he says, These damn professors, they don't realize how they can really be helpful to students.

Langs: In the context of the deviation, while in derivative form, this is rather straightforward: The alteration in the frame is not the way to be helpful. We've certainly heard that before.

Therapist: They get you to the point, he says, where grades become the all-important issue. I wind up thinking more about my grades and how I'm going to do on the exam than I do about learning, about being interested in learning the material.

Langs: Well, we'll have to continue to take this in bits and pieces. What is he saying here about the framework?

Discussant: It sounds like he's saying that how you perform is more important than how you do the therapy. What I mean is that he may feel that the therapist is more interested in himself than in the patient.

Langs: Yes, in the adaptive context of the recent deviations, in Type Two derivative form—in part now, as silent validation—the patient is indicating to the therapist that psychotherapy should be practiced not through direct reassurance and other deviations, but through maintenance of the framework and the interpretation of unconscious processes and contents. And further, in the ideal therapeutic situation, the therapeutic needs of the patient should be the overriding focus, and the needs of the therapist should be minor and secondary. Certainly, they should not involve supervision and concern with his own performance. The goal, as he almost states it himself, should be the understanding of the patient, and only secondarily of the therapist. So, in the context of alterations in the framework, we hear what are now becoming rather familiar comments involving the theme of, This is not how it should be done. Patients want to be understood rather than manipulated. All right, let's hear where it goes.

Therapist: Then he said, These professors don't seem to know that occasionally what you need is a pat on the back.

Langs: And what is this?

Discussant: The latent homosexuality.

Langs: Yes, and in the adaptive context of the altered framework this now alludes to the unconscious homosexual gratification that deviations provide for both patient and therapist. We must also consider the alternate hypothesis here: that the patient is saying that deviations "cure." The material should continue to help us sort this out.

Therapist: He said, They wind up making you so nervous before exams. Then he went on to describe how he had been so nervous, and had had so much anxiety that he couldn't study at all.

Discussant: In our context, the patient seems to be saying in derivative form that deviations increase rather than lessen anxiety.

Langs: Yes, by implication he is alluding to the negative effects of the deviations. It would appear that they reflect an impaired hold and an incapacity to contain the patient's anxiety and its underlying basis. Much of this seems to be a response to the therapist's anxious, non-neutral comments on the telephone. It would certainly be more convincing if the patient were to come back again to still another frame issue, but in any case I hope that the repetitiveness of this type of indirect communication in the context of alterations in the framework is generating a relatively convincing message.

Therapist: He was so nervous that he couldn't study, and he says, Well, you know that from the phone call.

Langs: Thank you. This is, after all, a Type C field with fragments of Type A communication. As a result we hear relatively isolated derivatives related to the recent alterations in the framework, to which the patient clearly returns from time to time. The reference to the phone call can therefore serve as a Type Two derivative validation of the inferences we have been making from this material as it relates to the implications of an altered frame. We needed that.

At this point, one could prepare an intervention—a silent intervention—which, if it receives further support, could be made to the patient. I make this suggestion because the patient has now provided us a reference to the adaptive context on a rather manifest level, as well as a direct link to the therapist. Who wants to formulate a tentative intervention for us?

Discussant: Perhaps you could point out to the patient that he seems to be responding to the phone call by feeling more anxious rather than less so, and that he somehow saw the call as an effort at manipulation—something like the way in which his friend got into graduate school.

Langs: Yes, you are beginning to shape a reasonable intervention, though it needs to be stated much more in terms of the adaptive context of the therapist's actual responses to the telephone call, rather than primarily along the lines of the patient's own contributions to the situation. In this respect you can see that the patient has referred to the telephone call in a general way, without detailing the therapist's supposedly supportive but probably anxiety-provoking comments; for that reason, we would certainly wait a bit longer to see if the patient now provides a clearer derivative related to those remarks, or even a direct reference to them.

Still, in terms of preparation, you could be thinking that your efforts at being supportive and fatherly on the telephone, and your comment that it's not a matter of life and death if he failed, have led the patient to perceive you—here, with some validity—as not understanding his needs, as responding in a way that increased his anxiety, as failing to help him contain the situation and therefore creating a dread of somatization, and as participating in an inappropriate, seemingly corrupt effort at manipulation. You could plan to add that in some ways this was seen as a pat on the back and is even connected to his thoughts about whether to go out on a date with the girl from Chicago or not—sexual implications that may have been a factor in his coming late to the hour. Genetic ties to his father could also be made—though in the sense of how the deviations serve to actually repeat past pathogenic interactions with him and to produce on some level similarities in the patient's perceptions of his father and the therapist.

For the moment, the only sense of rectification would stem from the fact that you are preparing to offer an interpretive intervention, rather than something that is manipulative, or a further modification in the framework. However, you could also include some comment to the effect that the patient strongly feels that this is not the proper approach to his therapy, and that he has indicated that he would prefer efforts at understanding. You might also allude to the derivatives related to the lack of confidentiality and his view that these deviant measures are in some way self-serving for the therapist and corrupt, though for the moment they do not coalesce as nicely as the remainder of the derivative network. I very much expect that there would be full opportunity for definitive rectification and for the interpretation of the implications of the whole series of deviations once the therapist begins to turn his interpretive efforts in this direction.

Therapist: I was waiting for a point to intervene. But also, knowing him, I was waiting for more material; I was just going to see where he went. But I must say that in this session I was listening to this material in a way diametrically opposite to what you are saying. Some of my thinking was based on what follows here. To continue a bit, he made reference to the phone call and then said, I did feel somewhat better after the call. I was able to study a little bit after that. I thought that maybe what I actually should have done was ask you for the Librium last time, ask you for the prescription in the previous session. Maybe that would have been helpful to me also. These remarks of his led me to believe that he had found some relief through my comments on the telephone and hadn't been thinking of possible detrimental consequences.

Langs: Well, he does have a mixed reaction, and some of his conscious response is related to the idea of a degree of relief, while his unconscious and indirect reactions emphasize the increase in anxiety, the sense of not being understood, and the theme of manipulation and even corruption. This is the typical split in a patient's response to deviations.

In intervening, we first consider the indicator—which here is rather powerful since it involves an alteration in the framework in which you both participated. Next, we review the communicative network—here the adaptive context is your noninterpretive interventions and several background deviations, and they are represented in somewhat disguised form, although the link to you is present. We then evaluate the degree to which the derivatives coalesce—here we have a coalescing network of derivatives—and the presence of a bridge back to therapy which is, of course, readily available here. Overall, then, we have a strong indication to intervene and an interpretable communicative network. And with a patient prone to Type C communication, I would intervene earlier than later, because it is quite likely that if you fail to make an interpretive intervention, he will soon erect new Type C barriers to the meaningful aspects of this material and your opportunity to comment will be lost. We should consider the patient's usual communicative style in our timing of interventions.

So I would probably intervene at this point, along the lines I have already suggested. In addition, I would indicate that his request for medication is a further effort of his own, based on my earlier prescription of medication, to find relief through a drug that might help obliterate whatever is stirring within him, rather than through efforts at understanding. It would be important to acknowledge that this request is an interactional product, and not to place the entire responsibility for it on the patient. I think, however, that he now needs a sense from you that you are beginning to understand the implications of what has happened, and are prepared to rectify the framework and interpret his responses to these transactions. Here, failure to intervene would encourage the restoration of Type C barriers.

Therapist: He then says, I've also been thinking of other ways that may help me reduce my anxiety, things like transcendental meditation, exercise programs, and he goes on with several possibilities.

Langs: What do you hear?

Discussant: It sounds like he wants lie therapy, cure through Type C barriers, the denial of what's going on within himself and this therapy, and even two forms of simultaneous treatment.

Langs: Yes, in the face of your continued silence he now imagines all sorts of deviant therapies which entail a variety of alterations in the standard framework. This would provide him a framework deviation cure, a misalliance cure, and cure through the erection of shared Type C barriers—a set of interrelated efforts at symptom alleviation without insight. It is my hypothesis that this arises not only because of your own use of deviations, but also because of your continued failure to intervene interpretively in the face of a meaningful communicative network and a strong therapeutic context.

Therapist: He pauses now, then he mentions that one of his brothers had fallen somewhere, and had fractured his arm. His parents were going to sue because of the circumstances under which the injury took place.

Langs: More derivatives; who can formulate them?

Discussant: He feels damaged under these conditions, and he would like to sue the therapist.

Langs: Yes, the patient is getting rather nasty, and alludes to thoughts of suing the therapist for malpractice. In terms of the functions of the frame, the patient is indicating that deviations injure the patient; there's a loss of the hold, and the patient becomes endangered, falls, and is injured. The failure to intervene is similarly destructive to the patient.

Along the me/not-me interface, the patient is presenting as well an unconscious image of the therapist as damaged and unable to function fully—either interpretively or in terms of rectifying the framework. As you can see, the patient has become quite angry over the therapist's failure to intervene properly by now.

Therapist: He said that he had sent his brother to an orthopedic surgeon to have it taken care of. And when his brother went to the surgeon, he spoke to him about science and the like. His brother is having a little bit of a rough time in high school with science courses. And the surgeon sort of told him, Look, I remember when I was going to high school and college, it can be rough; it's very difficult, but look, you'll make it through. The patient goes on and on with this type of thing. Then I intervene.

Langs: Yes, the material is indeed getting quite thin again, much as I had anticipated.

Therapist: I said to him, It seems you would like me to deal with you in a way similar to the way the surgeon dealt with your brother.

Discussant: May I say this: Isn't the therapist approaching this material in terms of the patient's wishes, rather than through an approach that begins with his unconscious perceptions of the implications of the deviations?

Langs: Well, we'll have to hear the entire intervention before evaluating it, but the therapist does begin with the premise that he is dealing primarily with the patient's fantasies and wishes, and not with the implications of what he has actually done. He is certainly not approaching this by first identifying the adaptive context in terms of the meanings of his own interventions, though he may yet do so.

Discussant: But even this may not be completely off the mark, because even though the therapist did contaminate the field in that way, the patient might in fact, and probably does at least in some part, have a wish for the therapist to gratify him through the sort of fatherly comments made by the surgeon.

Therapist: As I see it, what I gave him, relative to what he wants, is very little.

Langs: But be careful; we are now shifting to the level of manifest content, even though we offered several formulations of what he wants based on an understanding of the unconscious implications of his derivatives. The issue for the moment is not whether your noninterpretive gratifications correspond to a wish or fail to entirely fulfill it, but whether you will use the allusion to the patient's wishes as a means of denying the actual implications of your interventions. For example, on the telephone you did behave in a fatherly way. And if you were to suggest that this perception or experience is entirely or primarily based on the patient's wishes and distortions, and is not—initially at the very least—a valid implication derived from your intervention, it would be very detrimental to this patient's ego functioning, reality testing, and unconscious perceptions and introjections of yourself.

But let's now hear what you said to the patient before we offer further discussion.

Therapist: I said, what you would really like is for me to be like the surgeon who spoke with your brother, giving you a lot of support, giving you Librium. You'd also like me to be with you like you are with your brother—he has a certain type of fatherly relationship with his brother. I went on: it frustrates you that I don't give you the pat on the back that you want. And in your phone call to me, you got outside of the session what you couldn't get from me in the session.

Langs: Comments?

Discussant: The therapist is stressing what he did not give the patient, while you have been emphasizing the inappropriate gratifications the therapist did provide.

Therapist: I felt that he got more from me on the telephone than he usually got from me in the sessions. I certainly had been more active and directly supportive than I had been in some while. And I felt that he had alluded to how his professors don't give him the pat on the back that he needs, and that this referred to the deprivation that he was experiencing in the session.

Langs: Well, for you, then, the main adaptive context is the deprivations the patient is experiencing in his sessions, and not the alterations in the framework, including your noninterpretive interventions on the telephone. And you are indeed suggesting that the patient has what would be termed an unconscious transference fantasy, a wish for you to behave in a fatherly manner with him, based on aspects of his early relationship with his father. In itself, this is a rather linear formulation—and intervention—without any use of a specific adaptive context, without reference to convoluted derivatives, and with no effort to use the me/not-me interface or to begin with possible valid unconscious perceptions. It presupposes that patients will be dissatisfied with a well-run interpretive therapy, and that runs counter to my own clinical experience. In any case, there are some who might feel that you were attempting to interpret the patient's efforts to have you modify the framework and some of its unconscious implications. And it is certainly true that on one level his efforts to have you deviate is a search for inappropriate and pathological gratification, undoubtedly related to unconscious homosexual fantasies and possibly to introjects derived from the patient's relationship with both his father and his brother.

This is a rather common type of formulation, and it does have a certain appeal. But nonetheless I believe that it contains some basic flaws, and that it will not be validated by the material from the patient through unique Type Two derivative responses.

First, it denies the actuality of your behavior and your actual effort to express yourself in a fatherly manner. It also denies that you had ever given him Librium and that you are contributing to that wish at this time, and it sets aside the fact that you responded to his wishes on the telephone by gratifying them. It treats this material as reflecting the patient's fantasies and wishes, rather than as responses to specific adaptive contexts, in which you had, in actuality, repeated on some level certain behaviors of his father which then, possibly, intensified the patient's wishes for further inappropriate gratification of that type. Your intervention sets the therapeutic interaction aside; in particular, the unconscious implications of your behaviors are rendered nonexistent.

By contrast, my own formulation begins with those very behaviors—the adaptive context—and traces out the patient's responses from there. Your intervention is relatively isolated and entirely intrapsychically focused, while mine begins interactionally, takes into account your contributions to the patient's response, and then carefully examines the valid and distorted elements in his reactions. It is an intervention aimed at both the interactional and the intrapsychic realms. And you can see that there are also quite practical differences between your intervention and mine. You stress the patient's sense of frustration, while I emphasize the extent to which he feels inappropriately gratified and, in addition, threatened. You hold him responsible for wanting deviations, while I hold both of you responsible, and the differences in our approach will have considerable meaning for the patient. We both would deal with framework issues, but you would stress your maintenance of the frame, while I would emphasize the deviations. It seems to me that the material rather extensively supports my thesis, while I have heard little in derivative form about anyone who is able to maintain boundaries and a secure framework and hold. Your approach is relatively manifest, while mine is more convoluted.

Well, that's my evaluation. Let's now permit the patient to have his say.

Therapist: He says, Yes, that could be. You must know, because you've been through all of this in the course of your going to medical school. I did notice that there was a little difference in the way that you responded to me on the telephone. You said more, you addressed yourself more directly to my feelings than you usually do in the session. It was really more of what you had done last year, when you were more directly supportive. At this point I asked him whether he could talk a little bit more about how he actually felt about the telephone conversation.

Langs: Any comments?

Discussant: There are few derivatives here. He seems to be saying that on the surface he realized that the therapist had shifted to a more gratifying approach on the telephone.

Langs: Yes, he is aware that the therapist has returned to a more noninterpretive stance. But that is relatively manifest. On the other hand, in the adaptive context of this intervention, the patient first refers to some personal aspect of the therapist's life, and then stresses the sense of actual gratification. Perhaps he's trying to convey how real this is to him. In any case, for the moment there is no sense of Type Two derivative validation of this intervention. In addition, you now address the manifest content and ask the patient to restrict the range of his associations. You are steering him away from derivative communication, but perhaps he will nonetheless offer one more telling comment.

Therapist: He said, I felt better after the phone call, even though I already knew what you were saying. I felt better hearing it from you. Somehow it carries more weight when it comes from you. He says, I guess I sort of put you in a position of authority, as knowing, being both a psychiatrist and a doctor. He said, It's as though what you say must be right. And then he pauses, and he says, I'm not sure why I feel that way. He says, For example, if you had given me the Librium, then it would have been helpful. Because you would know what would be helpful for me.

Langs: Any comment?

Discussant: It sounds rather empty to me.

Langs: Yes, at the therapist's invitation, we're hearing clichés. The material appears to be a facade now, and there's a sense of emptiness. On a deeper level, I believe that in the adaptive context of your intervention this material must be seen as a commentary and mirror of the quality of your comments: the patient has experienced them unconsciously as an invitation to develop Type C barriers, to ruminate and make use of clichés. In this context, he seems to be saying that a framework deviation cure through the use of Librium is his only hope.

Therapist: Then he says, Maybe I will need the Librium, actually need it at some point. And I just made the comment again: You're still looking for a pat on the back to help you along. He responded by taking issue with that and disagreeing with my reference to the Librium and the pat on the back. He says, I don't know about that. Really, the Librium would also have to do with my anxiety, my nervousness, and my muscle tension.

Langs: There is less and less meaning here. It is important to learn not to intervene a second time using the same silent hypothesis, when you have not obtained Type Two derivative validation. The patient is becoming repetitious, and now you are repeating yourself as well. He begins to get a bit annoyed and wants to maintain his claim for the Librium. He had begun to approach some doubts about your intervention when he said something to the effect that you must always be right. You should have allowed him to continue to associate and should have made some effort to reformulate in the face of nonvalidation. At the same time, you could apply the me/not-me interface to this material, and wonder if he's not talking about his introjection of some sense of anxiety and tension from you. The muscle tension may hint again at underlying homosexuality, but at this point the Type C barriers are so strong there is little to discern. Please continue.

Therapist: That's about it. He said, If you didn't give me the Librium, I have to trust you and whatever reasons you have not to give it to me. And then he says, The bad thing about taking the Librium is that it would be like I have no control over my feelings or my anxiety. He then says in reference to the intaking unit adjacent to my office, I don't know; sometimes I wonder if there's really anything that separates me from these really sick ones I see over there, anything between them and myself. (Laughter.)

Discussant: Only a wall—a Type C barrier.

Discussant: This seems to call for the use of the me/not-me interface. As a commentary on the therapist's intervention, the patient seems to experience it as an expression of the therapist's sickness rather than as anything more constructive.

Langs: Yes, both patient and therapist are now avoiding the more anxiety-provoking material, and clearly the patient saw the therapist's intervention as an invitation to develop Type C barriers and a Type C field. The patient now implies that both he and the therapist are somewhat alike, and really sick, indicating that true understanding and a positive introject are not feasible under these conditions. The patient is also concerned that neither he nor his therapist can manage his anxiety through holding, containing, and proper intervening.

Therapist: He pauses and then he says, I sometimes want to ask you if you think I've made any progress in therapy. There's a pause again, and he looks up at me. He says, I really can't expect you to answer. I guess it's my evaluation to make. Not that I would ever just leave therapy. He says, I really don't want to stop, but sometimes I wonder about how much progress I've made. And then at the very end of the session, he starts obsessing again about this girl from Chicago and whether he should go out with her on the weekend or stay in and study, and so forth. That was the end of the session. I said we'll have to stop now, and he very hesitatingly got up to leave.

Langs: Okay, let's hear the beginning of the next session. I was going to say that the next session may well begin with the unconscious homosexual stuff, but he gets back to it a bit toward the end of this hour. Just note here one repetitive theme that we've often seen after unanalyzed and unrectified deviations: Are you helping me? What do you think? should I stop therapy?

Therapist: He comes into the next session, which is a shorter session, and he still looks quite depressed. He feels that he probably passed his last exam, but he still fears failure on the first one. And he goes on and on about his exams. He has no energy or drive left. He's extremely angry at Anne, another student, and the other students who don't give a damn about anyone else except themselves. They're preoccupied about doing well in school, even at the other guy's expense.

Langs: Since time is short, I will offer a few brief comments. We have heard before that in situations where the therapist has not intervened adequately, especially in the presence of alterations in the framework, the patient raises major questions about the quality of treatment and the lack of progress. Then, in this session, we learn something of the sense of depression that often occurs under these conditions, and we hear a repetition of the theme of those who try to get by at someone else's expense—another allusion to the therapist who deviates because of his own inappropriate needs, and who is making use of a patient in order to learn how to do therapy.

Therapist: He brings up again this whole issue of having been preoccupied with whether to go out with the girl from Chicago or not,

Therapist: He brings up again this whole issue of having been preoccupied with whether to go out with the girl from Chicago or not, and says it was all academic and the end result was that it didn't matter anyway. They were supposed to see each other, but she called him and said she couldn't make it because something came up with a cousin of hers who was sick. So it wouldn't have mattered anyway, because he spent all of the next day worrying about not being able to work. And then he said, I really sometimes think my mother is right. You can't trust other people. They do things at your expense. For example, the other students show off how much they know at your expense—like when you present part of your research to the group. My mother always used to say, You see, you can't trust people; they turn around and hurt you, or stab you in the back. Again, he's feeling very much without a sense of confidence and he goes on a little bit about that. He's preoccupied with taking final examinations. He's thinking maybe he should go away for the weekend to get away from everything—maybe he should visit a girl he knows in Philadelphia, but he's not sure. If he failed his exam, he doesn't know if he could enjoy himself anyway. Two days later he called to cancel his next session.

Langs: Well, our time is just about up. It is somehow fitting that this presentation should end with an unexplained modification in the framework. There is much in this bipersonal field that remains unresolved, and little new can be learned from this material. We see in this last hour a strong Type C field, an interactional amalgam that validates my hypothesis that your main intervention in the previous session was essentially in error, and would serve as a Type C barrier to the underlying chaos that begins with the actualities of your deviant interventions. There is a sense of depression, of hopelessness, a feeling that nothing matters or will work out. And there is a strong sense, now, of mistrust and of being used and exposed—additional common themes that arise when the therapist is involved in altering the framework. There is no sense of confidence in the therapist or the therapeutic situation, nor within the patient himself. There are thoughts of escape, a step that the patient then actually takes. There is a sense of failure, and a reminder that in the presence of Type C barriers there can be no understanding or growth.

Deviations in the framework can function as powerful Type C barriers and shift the bipersonal communicative field to a Type C field. And just as the patient and therapist cannot grow under these conditions, there is little growth afforded to us as observers of this situation. Still, we are in the most fortunate position in that we do learn some rather sad lessons from this presentation, and these emerge in part because of the obvious sincerity of the therapist and his dedicated effort to understand the patient and even to secure the frame to some extent. Nonetheless, the patient is stating that too much has been missed, and there is a sense of continued deviation that frightens him and makes him mistrustful—probably of both his own and the therapist's unconscious homosexual fantasies and needs. It is sad to end this excellent presentation on such a note, but so it often goes with psychotherapy— it is a difficult taskmaster at the very least. Thank you again for presenting this material to us.

Chapter Eleven

MOTIVES FOR ALTERING
THE GROUND RULES

Langs: Who will be presenting today?

Therapist: I have a session in which some frame issues came up. Before I offer a preliminary hour, let me say that this is a thirty-two-year-old graduate student in biochemistry, who had made several suicide attempts prior to coming into therapy, and who is quite depressed. She hasn't worked on her thesis in two years, and has been kicked out of the program for now. She has been in therapy for about a year. She had begun her graduate work in another center and had transferred here around the time she began her therapy.

A great deal was going on prior to the sessions I will present. Two things I should say are, first, about four weeks prior to these sessions I had started the patient on antidepressant medication, which of course is an alteration in the frame.

Langs: Before you get to the second point, do you have your notes of the sessions before and after you put her on medication? Even if they are briefly summarized, they could be quite informative.

Therapist: Yes, I do have some material. Well, to begin with a session from the period before I put her on medication, she came in and told me (there's a lot of withholding—all of the contents are sort of explosive, but there's a lot of withholding), she told me that she had been taking Elavil covertly for months. This is the drug that she had used to make a suicide attempt. And she had gotten it prescribed by a friend who was a physician. She had gotten prescriptions for fifty at a time, and she was taking several at night, as needed to fall asleep.

Langs: With friends like that, you don't need enemies. Talk about deviationists.

Therapist: And I mentioned that I recalled that she had taken a bottle of Elavils all at once, as a suicide attempt. (It wasn't a lethal dose, but it wouldn't do her any good to take them again.)

Langs: I hope that everyone here is experiencing a sense of confusion. Without the prior sessions, it is impossible to organize this material around a specific adaptive context, or to identify Type Two derivatives. For the moment, perhaps our major insight is that medication is offered quite often when a therapist fails to work with adaptive contexts and derivative communication, and tends to address the manifest content of the patient's associations. It also seems characteristic of such therapists to introduce material that the patient has not presented in the given session, and to be somewhat confronting.

Therapist: She responded by saying, Yes, I took a whole batch at once.

Langs: Let's think of this material along different lines, related again to the framework. What framework issue has emerged here?

Discussant: Well, the patient has modified the frame by obtaining medication on her own.

Langs: Yes, this is a unilateral modification in the framework on the part of the patient. We would like, at this point in the course, to begin to concentrate on the principles of technique that should prevail in the presence of framework issues. How would we think of approaching this particular modification in the frame?

Discussant: Well, first I would plan to listen and hear more before relating it to a previous suicide attempt, because that already is pointing the direction in a certain way. You just wait and listen.

Langs: Yes, that's the point. The first step is to apply the listening process in this session, and to permit the patient to free associate. Often, an initial communication of this kind will evoke strong recollections of the prior session or two, an experience that will help you to review the prior hour and to search for the adaptive context for this communication. She has been taking the medication for some time, and this suggests a need to investigate the therapeutic relationship and your own interventions over a long period. But since this is a modification in the framework, it directs you in particular to explore your own management of the therapeutic environment.

At the same time, the patient now has chosen this particular session to announce her use of medication. This should shape your search for the adaptive context, since you wish to understand why this revelation occurs at this particular time. So you are attempting now to recall the previous session, to investigate the status of the framework and whether you made interventions in that area in recent sessions, and you explore your own subjective feelings, thoughts, and fantasies about the patient as well. You investigate your unconscious countertransferences to the extent that you can detect inner derivatives.

In the meantime you allow her to free associate, in the hope and expectation that she will express herself in derivative form and reveal the unconscious meanings and functions of the medication, especially in regard to its implications for the therapeutic interaction. It is important to remain relatively calm when you learn of a disastrous symptom of this type, and not to intervene prematurely. To do so runs the risk of cutting off derivative communication from the patient and thereby any opportunity for you to learn the adaptive context of this behavior. As a result the suicide risk may well increase rather than decrease, especially since you have yourself responded impulsively. There is simply no substitute for a full application of the listening and validating processes, and for a sound interpretation—and rectification of the framework if needed—under these conditions. On this basis we can briefly look at this intervention. What is its nature?

Discussant: A confrontation.

Discussant: It is also a self-revelation, in that the therapist shows the patient that he remembers something that she had done.

Langs: Yes, it is his own personal association to this announcement, and an immediate confrontation of the dangers involved in the drug taking. This is, of course, well-meaning, but how do you think the patient will experience it?

Discussant: It communicates some degree of anxiety in the therapist and some incapacity on his part to contain this information and to understand it. In addition, his introducing an association related to the patient's suicide attempt may carry some hostile implication.

Langs: Yes, it reflects an impaired ability to hold and contain the patient, her associations and her behaviors. If you think of Bion's *reverie* (1970), this type of comment certainly does not appear to reflect such a state. And since we know that the therapist soon elected to put the patient on medication, you can see how the offer of a drug may serve as a type of falsified effort at holding but is actually an unconscious confession of failures to hold, contain, and interpret. Often, the introduction of medication is based on the therapist's anxieties far more than the therapeutic needs of the patient. All of this can be stated as silent hypotheses and even predictions of the derivative material that we will soon be hearing from this patient.

Therapist: I would like to make a couple of comments. The first is that I had broached the use of medication in the past because I felt that her depression was so intensive and of such long standing that it could not readily be treated by psychotherapy alone.

Langs: We can certainly understand your thinking in this situation, even though we need not agree with it. Very often therapists feel quite helpless to deal analytically with depressed patients, and are quite fearful of their suicidal potential. I will leave it to the patient to let us know whether securing the frame and offering sound interventions would serve her far better than introducing medication, though you already know my anticipations in that regard.

Often, the offer of medication comes from a therapist who is unable to organize and understand either the material from the patient or the nature of the therapeutic interaction, including his own inputs. Unfortunately, this is reflected here, in that the patient communicates some rather potentially meaningful derivatives, something that is quite alive and filled with hope despite its destructive implications. And yet you immediately respond noninterpretively, with a confrontation and a certain degree of self-revelation which can serve as a pathological projective identification into the patient of your own sense of disturbance, inability to manage, and hostility. By modifying the frame you deaden the material and lessen the possibility of Type A communication from the patient. This deprives you of opportunities for interpretation. In addition, your own failures to hold and contain will make it more difficult for the patient to carry out such functions on her own, thereby promoting a pathological regression that will only further complicate the entire therapeutic situation and add to the risk of impulsive suicidal acting out.

Therapist: Well, I was well aware that I was angry, and I can see now that my confrontation reflected my hostility.

Langs: Yes, and that is typical of confrontations, which is why I have advocated that therapists not use such interventions (Langs 1978b). It is appropriate enough to feel threatened and angry upon learning of something like this, but it is quite another matter to allow these feelings to spill over to a direct verbal attack on the patient. The sense of anger should be managed and contained, and used to understand both yourself and the patient—to answer such questions as why she is being so self-destructive and provocative at just this time. You must ask yourself what the adaptive context is. Your response is a failure to metabolize her pathological projective identification to a point of understanding and interpretation.

Discussant: On this basis, the patient might view the therapist's own prescription of medication as an act of hostility or a punishment for her behavior, in addition to seeing it as a reflection of his difficulty in containing and understanding what she imparts to him.

Langs: Yes, these are typical qualities of alterations in the framework, and specifically, of the unconscious implications of the use of medication. For the moment, they are stated as silent hypotheses in need of validation.

Therapist: In this context, I must mention the difference in attitude on your part, Dr. Langs, and on the part of my supervisor for this case. With his encouragement I made a number of deliberate modifications of the frame throughout this treatment because I was having a great deal of trouble getting through to her. She had been quite withdrawn, she is still depressed, and she is somewhat flat—there is a flattening of affect, and it was very difficult to reach her. As a result, my supervisor and I agreed that I should be quite active with her, in a way that I would ordinarily not be with a patient.

Langs: We are now in a realm without clinical data, so I will be brief. You must make a distinction between more active intervention via interpretation to a withdrawn and depressed patient, and active intervention through deliberate modifications in the framework. The former can be undertaken as a response to the patient's therapeutic needs, and will have a salutary effect as long as you adhere to sound principles of technique. The latter, as we have seen, will tend either to disturb the patient through pathological projective identifications or to render her more inaccessible by promoting Type C barriers and the lack of any feeling of safety within the therapeutic relationship.

I do not use the words *inaccessible* and *noncommunicative* as often as most therapists do, or in the same way. For the moment I see no evidence that this patient is either, but of course my evaluation is made specifically in terms of how the patient responds to adaptive contexts, how clearly they are represented, and the extent to which the patient responds with meaningful derivative material. We will soon see if this is in fact a Type C patient, or whether the problem lies rather in your capacity to listen and understand.

Finally, be careful about attempting to justify active interventions that may serve countertransference-based needs within yourself to manipulate the patient. This is especially treacherous when you obtain sanctions from a supervisor who may well have similar tendencies. It is here that you must apply the validating process yourself, and not simply accept what a supervisor tells you only to discover some time later—if at all—that you are involved in a supervisory misalliance (Langs 1979). I state this as a matter of principle and not as a definitive comment regarding your actual supervision, of which I know very little.

Discussant: Isn't the very act of becoming more active with a depressed patient a modification in the frame?

Langs: No, not as I have defined it for you. It is the response to the patient's material and to the nature of his psychopathology, and it takes into account the strong indicators which are conveyed by these patients as an expression of their great need for interventions by the therapist. As long as the communicative network permits intervening, I would attempt to comment sooner rather than later with a patient who is profoundly depressed and suicidal.

The frequency of your interventions is an interactional product derived from the patient's therapeutic needs, his capacity to communicate, and your own ability to understand and respond to those needs. The rate of intervening will vary from patient to patient, and even with the same patient it will be different from time to time. However, all such work can be carried out within the standard framework defined in this course, though there is, of course, the possibility of an acute suicidal crisis that might evoke a temporary alteration of the framework on your part despite all efforts at sound intervention.

Let's recognize that we are defining here the therapist's flexibility within the standard framework, and how these principles can be applied with sensitivity and in keeping with the therapeutic needs of the patient. On the other hand, a deliberate approach planned in advance cannot be responsive to the immediate needs of the patient, which unfold on their own terms in each session. Such a blueprint is likely to involve countertransference-based reactions to the difficulties the therapist is having in working with a particular patient. Remember that the patient is unconsciously and exquisitely sensitive to the unconscious implications of your interventions, and on that level will be able to distinguish efforts in keeping with her therapeutic needs from those which are not. Let's hear more material.

Therapist: So, she had said, Yes, I took a whole batch that time. But don't worry. I'm not suicidal now. I'm just lethargic and out of it. I then said that I was struck by the fact that she used the pills without talking about them.

Langs: Any brief comments?

Discussant: The patient is trying to reassure the therapist.

Discussant: The intervention is another confrontation, and a criticism of the patient.

Langs: Yes, the patient is attempting to reassure the worried therapist. But, in addition, her reference to being lethargic and out of it, monitored along the me/not-me interface as a Type Two derivative in the adaptive context of the therapist's intervention, suggests her view that the therapist has been quite insensitive to her needs—he's out of it. It shows too that the therapist's nonneutral intervention served as an invitation to create a Type C barrier, designed evidently as an effort at false reassurance.

The therapist, for his part, continues his use of hostile confrontations, undertaken with good intentions and yet unconsciously communicating a failure to hold the patient, to contain her productions, or to manage his own sense of threat and anger. We begin to realize that the therapist has had significant difficulties in maintaining the framework as regards his ongoing interventions—the more changeable aspect of the frame—and in respect to his related capacities to hold and contain. On that basis we might now suspect that the patient's self-medication and her keeping this a secret from the therapist are interactional symptoms, alterations in the framework with contributions from both members of this therapeutic dyad.

The therapist is responding here to being poorly held and contained by the patient, and you can see how threatened and angry he is. I trust that you can all experience this patient's poor hold of the therapist; it is strongly reflected in her taking the medication on her own and in her keeping it a secret. The patient withholds, in part because the therapist has not provided sound interventions, and her conscious lie suggests the presence of a Type C field with intense falsifications designed as barriers to the chaotic truth—which here, undoubtedly, lies within the therapeutic interaction, both the therapist and his patient.

When you know a patient has made use of a lie, you must go beyond attempting to understand it solely in terms of individual psychopathology. View it also as a commentary on your therapeutic work and as a clue to the presence of a Type C field in which meaning and relatedness are being destroyed. There is strong evidence here that this is just such a field. And, for the moment, the therapist's interventions are designed to focus the entire problem within the patient, an effort that serves also as a barrier to the truth of his own contributions and, in that sense, as an unintentional lie. It may well be that the patient's confession of her own lie is an attempt to modify precisely these qualities of the therapeutic relationship. In any case, there may well be certain constructive intentions involved, and realizing this might lessen your sense of anger and betrayal.

Self-medication should also lead you to question your technique, in regard both to interpretations and to management of the framework. As long as you take it as an interactional product and try to identify your own contributions, you may discover that you have been modifying the framework in various ways that have been destructive to the treatment situation and the patient, and that you have been failing to help her understand her unconscious perceptions and fantasies, her intrapsychic and interactional pathology. These efforts must be viewed as an attempt at self-cure, and must lead to consideration of your own possible failings. Remember: therapist before patient. Once you have ferreted out your own contributions to such a behavior, you would then be in a position to identify and analyze those that stem from the patient's own pathology.

So. We have here the use of noninterpretive and nonneutral interventions—specific alterations in the fluid framework. Remember, we are viewing this material as an effort to understand the conditions under which a therapist prescribes medication and, in addition, those under which patients take medication on their own, an all too common occurrence these days.

Discussant: If the patient feels scolded for what she does, she is also likely to keep secrets.

Langs: Yes, and what is important for the moment is that you recognize this as an interactional symptom and are prepared to investigate contributions from both therapist and patient. We sense here a poor therapeutic environment, with impaired holding and containing on both sides, and significant difficulties in interpreting—witness the use of nonneutral interventions. This appears to be the climate in which the use of medication unfolded with this patient.

Therapist: She said, I had the pills. I was using them at the beginning of therapy too, you know—or maybe you don't know. They're renewable the first of every month. Anyway, I know that you were concerned about my depression, about my dysfunction, and you wouldn't have given me the pills. In any case, I am so dysfunctional I thought I needed to at least have a good night's sleep. Here I intervened. I said, Just how impaired are you in your work?

Langs: Any comments?

Discussant: The patient seems to be indicating that the therapist might well have noticed her self-medication had he only been more attentive.

Discussant: Along the me/not-me interface, and in the adaptive context of the last intervention, the patient seems to be saying that the therapist is very much out of touch and dysfunctional. As a result, she turns to the drugs as a means of finding symptomatic relief.

Discussant: The therapist has again intervened on a manifest content level, and I would suspect some lack of neutrality since he chose to inquire in only one of several possible areas.

Langs: Yes, thank you. That's all quite perceptive. You see here again the typical split that arises when there is an issue related to the framework: consciously, the patient acknowledges the therapist's concern about her depression, and this includes some appreciation of the positive nucleus to his essentially erroneous interventions. On the other hand, when we view the derivatives—organized, as you said, around the adaptive context of his recent interventions and as Type Two derivatives along the me/not-me interface—we learn that the patient unconsciously views his nonneutral interventions as a reflection of a dysfunction, as being out of touch.

By now we can see that these are typical commentaries to therapists who deviate, and that they are almost always offered in derivative form, often through self-references meant to reflect introjections of the therapist far more than the immediate psychopathology of the patient. Clearly they reflect both, but remember: therapist before patient, valid introject before distorted fantasy.

We may restate a general observation at this point: many modifications in the framework, especially the use of medication, appear in
therapeutic situations in which other modifications have already
occurred, and in which a sound interpretive approach is lacking. They
arise too where nonneutral interventions are frequent, and in situations
where the therapist tends to work on a manifest level rather than with
derivative communication and unconscious meaning.

Therapist: She said, I'm very lethargic; I'm not doing any of my
work. I'm sitting in my room in the lab leafing through pages of a
book. It's work that I actually let go and pass on to the people I work
with. Some of this talking that we've done here has relieved matters,
but I just really can't get going. So I said, I am surprised, given the
situation that you describe, that you remain so opposed to the use of
antidepressant medication. This was a subject I had broached before.

Langs: So at this point you introduced medication.

Therapist: Yes, but I had suggested it before.

Langs: Would anyone care to comment?

Discussant: This is all taken on a manifest level; there is no effort
made to understand the underlying meanings of this material.

Discussant: The intervention regarding medication is manipulative. It even seems like an attempt to exploit the patient: she is doing
so badly, how could she possibly oppose the use of antidepressants?

Langs: Yes, work on a manifest level that disregards derivative
communication, especially listening in terms of an adaptive context
that reveals unconscious perceptions as well as fantasies, seems almost
invariably to be accompanied by the use of nonneutral interventions
and alterations of the framework, including the use of medication. I
would put it this way: if the therapist has the capacity to contain the
patient's projective identifications and the unconscious implications of
her cognitive associations, and to metabolize them toward an interpretation, he has no need for medication. Here, the drug is being

utilized as a nonhuman holding and containing device, in the presence of a relative incapacity within the therapist to maintain these functions vis-à-vis the patient.

In addition, as part of a Type C barrier, the medication is used as as means of denying the patient's unconscious perceptions of your own incapacities, which, paradoxically, are confirmed to her by your shift to another confrontation with overtones of scolding and the proposal that she accept medication. This is a form of lie therapy—and the patient's lie certainly suggested this—in which the surface seems well-meaning, innocuous, and even sort of innocent, while the unconscious communications are rather devastating and pathological on both sides of the relationship. In derivative form, the patient again states that you have passed on to her the responsibility for the work of therapy, and this too is a factor in her self-medication and poor job performance.

Discussant: But don't you feel that if a therapist is incapable of understanding his patient, and of offering her interpretations, that he has no alternative and so must give her medication? After all, she is quite depressed and potentially suicidal.

Langs: Well, that in itself is a rather depressing conclusion, one that would certainly further depress this patient. And you may be quite right, though I would suggest that an alternative does in fact exist: the therapist can learn how to listen, how to manage the framework properly, and how to interpret. Let's now hear the patient's response to this intervention, a response which is, as we know, a proposal to modify the framework.

Therapist: She said, Funny, but I don't want to rely on medication. But this is the third time that this depression has happened. It has happened three times: once with you and once with the psychiatrist I saw where I used to go to school. And once a couple of years earlier. (Interestingly enough, talking about hidden agendas, she had left therapy with another therapist-in-training elsewhere, over the introduction of medication, a couple of years before this.)

Discussant: The therapist wanted her to have medication, and she wouldn't take it?

Therapist: Yes, and I spoke to this therapist and found out that he was in analytic training too. He claimed that he couldn't get her to talk either. He gave up; he couldn't induce her to talk, he felt frustrated, and he attempted to give her medication. I begin to wonder if these things can actually be worked out.

Langs: Well, until now you have had no concept of rectifying the frame, and little concept of how to listen and interpret. The hope is that with these tools a great deal of this *can* be worked out.

You have, however, touched again upon a question for which I have no definitive answer: can a framework as greatly modified as this be rectified to the point that the patient will accept a secured therapeutic situation, along with an interpretive therapeutic approach, and be able to change from a negative therapist introject to a positive introject? Experience will show you that once you have deviated in significant ways, patients will continue to expect further alterations in the framework, and will attempt to manipulate them from you consciously and unconsciously. They maintain a sense of uncertainty about your position and remain conflicted about their own wishes. On the one hand they want a secure frame in order to do proper therapy, but on the other they have been so pathologically gratified through deviations, and have had so many pathological defenses reinforced, that they are reluctant to do the other type of work—truth therapy. And these problems will arise whether you continue as her therapist or whether she goes to another therapist, one capable of maintaining the framework and carrying out an interpretive treatment. These experiences leave their marks, and it remains to be seen to what extent they can, with good therapeutic work and rectification, be erased, or at least modified. Now what about this material?

Discussant: Well, she attempts to refuse the medication and is reminded of another therapist who apparently did not understand her and who attempted to offer drugs. It is interesting that he discussed his work with this patient with the present therapist, which is another modification in the framework. But, in addition, he too indicated that he offered this patient drugs at a point where he felt angry and frustrated with her. The patient is almost saying that she is depressed by how poorly she is understood and how angry her therapists get at her.

Langs: Yes, the present attempt to modify the framework by this therapist reminds her of a previous similar situation. Consciously, the patient wishes not to be forced to rely on medication; along the me/not-me interface, in the adaptive context of this last intervention—the offer of medication—she is expressing her wish that the therapist too would not have to rely on medication. She responds to all this with depression, and wonders unconsciously whether the therapist too is not depressed. She is reminded of a previous therapist where something similar happened, and certainly a repetition of this kind can be quite devastating to the patient, especially to her image of herself and of therapists. Please continue.

Therapist: You have given me your phone number, she said, at which I could reach you. And I know that I am more difficult than most of your patients, but I don't know at all whether these things can be worked out.

Langs: Any comment?

Discussant: The telephone number implies, I take it, the therapist's home telephone number.

Therapist: Yes, I gave it to her because of the suicidal threat here.

Discussant: Well, that's another deviation.

Discussant: She does feel that she's an especially difficult patient, and now she is depressed and discouraged.

Langs: Yes, she has clearly introjected the therapist's inability to help her interpretively and to offer a secure framework. She has introjected his sense of depression and hopelessness, which he has expressed manifestly to us in this seminar. And she realizes that he tends to resort to modifications in the framework as substitutes for adequate therapeutic work. Her commentary is unmistakable: under these conditions, nothing can be worked out. And she is quite right; here there can be no inner resolution of her problems, no understanding, and no growth. All that is left is the hope for a framework deviation cure, some sense of symptom alleviation through Type C barriers. However, the patient is not optimistic and in fact anticipates that such efforts are bound to fail.

Now, in light of your belief that this patient is noncommunicative, it is well for us to recognize that she is here expressing herself in a Type A mode in response to your noninterpretive interventions and efforts to modify the framework; she is communicating through Type Two derivative responses filled with unconscious perceptions and some degree of fantasy. And however painful this may be, it would seem fairer to say that it is you who have been noncommunicative. You have not attempted to understand her symbolically at all, and have shifted to an area of nonmeaning and framework deviation—drug use. Still, your responses are filled with unconscious communications that the patient detects and works over. There is a dynamic quality to her associations here, much of it in the form of unconscious perceptions. We can now sense that you are offering yourself to the patient, via the medication, to be taken inside of her, just as you offered her your telephone number. You promised her a positive introject that will protect her from her depression, but she experiences all that you offer as a negative and destructive introject, which only reinforces her sense of depression. Strachey (1934) said this many years ago: if you attempt to deliberately behave as a good object, the patient will introject a bad one.

There is another point here. At moments when you are not attempting to modify the framework, this patient might become noncommunicative. But we can appreciate why this is so. You have not permitted Type A, symbolic communication to be the medium of cure. You have failed to understand her and to work with her derivative responses, and as a result she has become discouraged, depressed, and feels a pressure to join you in Type C barriers or in exchanges of pathological projective identifications. One senses in so many ways the depressive qualities of this therapeutic situation and the hopelessness of it all. Perhaps this is a strong reminder that without a capacity to secure the framework and to offer interpretations there is little else constructive that the therapist can offer. It is a difficult and painful lesson to learn, but it can motivate us all to be better therapists. Please continue.

Therapist: So I gave her a little speech. I said something to the effect that I felt that she had made some progress, and that we have made some progress in understanding some of the things that set off these depressions. I specifically mentioned a couple of episodes where she had been rejected and hadn't acknowledged it. And I said that I feel that we can work some of these things out. However, I said, I wouldn't foist it on you. I feel that antidepressants can be helpful in relieving some of the pressure that you feel you're under. And she said, No, I don't want medication now, but I do feel some hope that I can work things out with you. That's surprising since I came in really mistrusting you, thinking you were worse than even the previous trainee who treated me. (Laughter.) She said, But you've gotten better over the course of the last couple of months. And with that the session ended.

Langs: You can see why we cannot rely on the patient's conscious comments. Her derivative communications directly contradict her last remark.

Therapist: I felt that she was trying to make me feel better, and I would have to say that she did.

Discussant: We must account for the hope that the patient expressed in this session. Perhaps the therapist had reached her, after all.

Discussant: Or it could be a false hope, especially in light of the therapist's remark that he and the patient had understood some things, when throughout this session he made no effort at understanding.

Langs: Yes, in the adaptive context of the therapist's interventions we see something of a very deceptive, falsifying Type C field. The therapist pretends that insight has occurred, but his examples are quite linear and simplistic. In addition, of course, no effort at understanding had been manifested in this hour. And on this basis I would agree that this is an offer of a false hope, and that the patient has joined you in a sector of misalliance, a bastion, and a Type C barrier in which you both pretend that understanding is possible in this bipersonal field, and that there is hope, when deep down probably both of you feel quite discouraged and hopeless. The patient expresses this when she refers to her earlier mistrust of you—a displacement that represents her present feeling as well.

Your comment that you and she had made some progress is a non-neutral intervention, a self-revelation, and it may well be a falsification, conscious or unconscious. I would view it here as the equivalent of your offer of medication: the drug too is offered as a false sense of hope and promise, and as a denial of a sense of inadequacy and hopelessness. Perhaps the most positive aspect of your interventions toward the end of this session is your acknowledgment that you would not force the patient to take medication. This provides her with some relief, since she is evidently under considerable pressure from you, based on your interventions and proposals. That may be the kernel of hope that she is trying to develop in her own mind, but I do not expect it to prevail.

We now need to hear the next session, especially her first communication, as a means of seeing whether you have offered her something resilient and valid, or something false and unserviceable. But before we get to that, one final comment: in the midst of a number of alterations in the framework that are inherent to this clinic therapy, and the specific effort by the therapist to further modify the frame through the use of medication, we once again hear an allusion to not trusting the therapist. The therapist who modifies the frame cannot be trusted, there is no knowing how far he will go. She is saying that deviations generate mistrust and uncertainty. It is well to note how repetitive this response is under conditions such as these. Now let's hear what happens.

Therapist: Well, as I said, she ended the last session by refusing the medication. She then began the next hour by saying, There's nothing to discuss today. I'm not doing any work; I'm not doing anything of consequence and of course Gene—Gene is this boyfriend she's breaking up with—is still a thing; that thing with Gene is still a merry-go-round.

This is remarkable: I don't even need your comments anymore. (Laughter.)

Langs: Of course not; you have hers—the patient as unconscious supervisor.

Therapist: She said, We come close, then we get distant, etcetera, etcetera. And she said, Work is going slowly, if at all. I have a project to test the impairment of cognition and learning capacities. (Laughter.) It's with patients exposed to household toxins like lead.

Langs: Your laughter attests to the transparency of this material, as long as it is heard in the adaptive context of the therapist's interventions—primarily his offer of medication. The patient is, indeed, unconsciously functioning as supervisor to the therapist.

Therapist: What is so remarkable is that my supervisor and I didn't pick any of this up, and he is a senior analyst. In fact, he expressed his interest in that particular project. (Laughter.) We gave no thought to this material as a commentary on my offer of medication, even though, as I say, it all seems pretty obvious now.

Langs: Would someone please state it for us?

Discussant: Well, it seems to me that the patient is now using a Type A communicative style around the adaptive context of the therapist's offer of medication. Her first words were very striking: there is nothing to discuss. To me this means that the medication is, as you said, an alternative to insight therapy, to work in the cognitive sphere. And who could miss her reference to impairments in learning and cognitive abilities, and its connection to household toxins—chemicals, drugs?

Discussant: It would seem that the motivation for this patient's research lies in her unconscious perceptions of the therapist.

Langs: Yes, when the adaptive context is so clear-cut, the listening process is simplified a bit. We can readily organize this material as Type Two derivatives and recognize the prevalence of unconscious perceptions: the therapist does not wish to work with the patient's free associations; he is attempting to create a situation where nothing of consequence will be done; he is suffering from an impairment of cognitive and learning abilities; he wishes to impair her cognitive abilities and growth by providing her medication—a poison, no less.

And the patient takes it even further: she links this up to a merry-go-round relationship with a boyfriend, a relationship where there is closeness and then distance in never-ending alternations. Here the unconscious perception of the therapist—and the interpretation to him—is that the patient believes that much of his difficulty lies in the sphere of erotic countertransference. If that were rectified, it seems quite likely that the patient's own erotic transference fantasies would then emerge. For the moment, she can unconsciously view the therapist's pressured efforts to give her medication as a form of seduction, and can hide her problem within his.

And all of this is, on another level, a commentary on any alteration in the framework: it impairs the communicative properties of the bipersonal field; it creates Type C barriers so that nothing of consequence is done; it is seductive and confusing, and the boundaries are unclear; it is a reflection of poor cognitive functioning and a learning disability; and it is ultimately toxic or poisonous, endangering the patient and, on another level, the therapist. Let's not tire of cataloguing these effects, at least until we are all convinced that they exist. Please continue.

Therapist: She then explained the project. If the results don't come out, she said, it is meaningless. I have one experiment that can be repeated with both positive and negative variables. Then she said, Even though my supervisor feels it will work out okay and he cares about his graduate students, what does he have to lose?

Discussant: Since this patient works at this center, I would take her reference to her supervisor as a displaced comment on the therapist's supervisor.

Discussant: If we look at this material in terms of the deviations, it seems to me that the patient is saying that nothing definitive can take place under these conditions, and that the therapist protects himself by modifying the therapeutic relationship.

Discussant: Isn't she also saying that meaning is destroyed?

Langs: Yes, it seems to me that the main derivative thrust of this material relates to the manner in which deviations such as medication generate Type C barriers and Type C bipersonal fields in which personal investment, meaning, and risk are destroyed. Notice too how the patient senses a lack of support from her supervisor: he is concerned, but he gets them involved in a situation where he can't be hurt. The therapist's deviations are similarly self-protective and self-serving, and not at all in the therapeutic interests of the patient.

I would agree that the patient is also attempting to alert your supervisor to the lack of accomplishment in this treatment situation.

Rather typically, she appreciates the sense of care and concern that exists within the therapist and his supervisor, but she wants them both to know that nothing is being accomplished. Concern is not enough.

Therapist: Okay. She says, A friend of mine came to the lab. She told me that people are beginning to say that I'm not very thoughtful about my work. Said that the initial work I did in the laboratory was quite capable, but that my last couple of months here I've worked in a half-assed way. The patient then said, I don't know what to say to this or to my supervisor; but I'm not making any headway. He must be wondering what the hell I'm doing.

Langs: Any comments?

Discussant: It seems to me that the patient had some positive impressions of the therapist at the beginning of treatment, but clearly, at this time, based partly on his offer of medication, and I guess also on his repeated failure to intervene interpretively, she sees him as doing distinctly half-assed work. Also, she keeps mentioning her supervisor— I agree that there must be a message to the therapist's supervisor here.

Langs: Yes, the patient gives you a model of third-party information—the girlfriend who tells her how people are viewing her work. And clearly this is a derivative related to another modification in the framework of this therapy: the presence of a supervisor. The patient feels she cannot reach the therapist and is making thinly disguised appeals to his supervisor.

Now, as I stated in my recent book on supervision (Langs 1979), most supervisors never see themselves in the material from the patients whose therapy they supervise. If they do any sort of supervisory work that approaches the type of listening I have been developing with you, they may well hear certain unconscious commentaries on the supervisee's work, and they might even identify some unconscious perceptions—though, I must add, most supervisors seldom think of unconscious perceptions, and formulate almost without exception in terms of unconscious fantasies and distortions. Even the more sophisticated seem not to recognize that the patient unconsciously monitors not only the work of the therapist, but the efforts of his supervisor as well. Often a supervisory intervention will be introjected and worked over by the supervisee, and then passed on to the patient, who will in turn work over the introject-amalgam and respond with unconscious perceptions, commentaries, and even interpretations relating to the supervisor's inputs. A supervisor must be prepared to validate his interventions in the subsequent material from the patient, and to hear the patient's critique of his supervisory efforts.

Discussant: Would you have made an intervention at this point?

Langs: I would have remained silent, fully aware of the richness of this derivative complex, waiting for her to get around to bridges to therapy, to closer derivatives, and to some clear-cut representation of the adaptive context. Once the adaptive context is represented, either directly or in readily detectable form, I would be prepared to intervene interpretively, largely in terms of the patient's unconscious perceptions of the implications of my offer of medication. I would find a way of working in the necessary rectification: since drugs, like toxins, are destructive, they should not be utilized; it is clear, then, that I should withdraw my offer of a prescription.

Discussant: I take it that you wouldn't give her the phone number of your supervisor? (Laughter.)

Langs: No, that's for the deviationist, not for me. Let's hear more.

Therapist: She said, I don't even have many alternatives. I would tell him that I am depressed, but what am I going to do, tell him that every six months I go into a depression where I'm not functional? How can he recommend my returning to school and advancing when my psychological integrity is so frail?

Discussant: I hear the patient saying something about not being able to talk in confidence, and fearing betrayal or third parties. Perhaps this also alludes to the supervisor—to that particular modification of the frame.

Langs: Yes, revelations in a modified bipersonal field can actually be damaging to the patient, where ideally material should be utilized for understanding and positive inner adaptation.

Discussant: I think it may also refer to her working at this center.

Discussant: As an extension of the patient's introjection of the therapist, I hear her suggesting that his offer of medication evokes a view of him as nonfunctional, as not deserving to advance.

Langs: Yes, and also as attempting to cure his own sense of depression, despite his manifest intention to help the patient with hers. Perhaps most impressive is the depressing and negative tone of this material as it serves as a commentary on the therapist's actual and proposed alterations in the framework.

Therapist: She said, I thought about talking to him, but I don't think it would go anywhere. I'm also bothered by Gene. Sex is not joyless with him, but he's sarcastic with me and is constantly toying with me. Yet I'm still very bothered by his absences; he left now for the four hundredth time. Here I mentioned to her that it seems to me that in all the discussions of Gene she seems to be more concerned about his absence than actually about seeing him. I added that she seems to feel no real sense of absence in his presence. She just doesn't like it when he's away. And she says, I know.

Langs: Any brief comments?

Discussant: In the adaptive context of the offer of medication, I hear the patient saying again, Why bother to speak or to attempt to communicate? It's pointless. I also hear the patient commenting on the therapist's noninterpretive interventions, which she experiences as sarcastic and as toying with her. I guess she is also saying that she experiences it as some kind of desertion.

Discussant: The therapist's intervention is a confrontation, and again I think I detect a hostile tone. It also addresses the manifest content, without an adaptive context—unless the boyfriend's leaving her is being used as a context. In any case, that's external to the therapeutic relationship at a time when I think the patient is really working over a number of derivatives involving her relationship with the therapist.

Langs: Yes, for the moment, we must stress the nonneutral qualities of this intervention, and its many limitations. It is an invitation to form a bastion in respect to the therapeutic relationship, and to deal with outside relationships on the surface, when the relationship with the therapist and the unconscious communicative interaction is what clearly concerns the patient. She is reacting especially to the therapist's proposal for medication and his noninterpretive interventions—his deviations—and the therapist offers a rather confusing, clichéd intervention clearly designed as a barrier to these more disturbing truths.

Unconsciously, the patient has again suggested that there is a sexual element in the therapist's deviations, and perhaps in her evoked fantasies as well. But in the main she is pointing out that alterations in the framework are experienced as manipulations, as a toying with her, and as an abandonment; she no longer feels that the therapist is holding her in any therapeutic sense.

I hope you can all see that the therapist's offer of medication serves to intensify the patient's depression rather than lessen it. She is attempting through indirect, derivative communication to convey much of this to the therapist, and I very much suspect that this intervention, with its denial of the patient's unconscious communications, and its failure to contain these meanings and to metabolize them toward interpretive understanding, will greatly intensify the patient's depression. Eventually, if the therapist maintains this approach, the patient will either give up or become acutely suicidal.

At this point, I would put together these derivatives and suggest that her main unconscious interpretation is that you have an enormous need to distance yourself from her because of your unmanaged and unconscious erotic countertransference. And this is why she sees sexual implications in your offer of medication; it can be seen as both an unconscious gratification of, and a defense against, your unconscious or even conscious—though this is not the place to determine that— erotic fantasies or even perceptions of the patient. This is reinforced when you suggest that you and she talk about Gene, and avoid each other. For the moment, the Type C barriers are mainly an effort to obliterate your erotic countertransference, and the patient's own erotic responses to it.

Therapist: Well, she says, I know. We discussed this before. It seems to be ridiculous: what can I do, tell people that I am moody and withdrawn, perhaps even suicidal? Then people will reject me. She said, It's a flimsy sort of construction.

Langs: This is her commentary; it's a flimsy formulation and its ridiculous. She alludes to her suicidal feelings, and perhaps we can all learn the somewhat sad lesson that noninterpretive responses do not provide patients with successful defenses against suicidal impulses and fantasies, and that they in fact heighten the risk of such behaviors.

If you will forgive the sense of concreteness and the pun involved, her comment that it's a flimsy sort of construction alludes on one level to the altered framework, both the offer of the medication and the therapist's nonneutral interventions.

Discussant: Are you planning to terminate with her at midyear when you go into private practice?

Therapist: I don't know if it is for her good, but I am taking her with me.

Discussant: Does the patient know about this?

Therapist: Oh no, at this point in therapy, that had not been worked out; it came up a couple of months later.

Discussant: Well, I asked, because there are references to being rejected, and I wonder if this patient doesn't know that this is the therapist's last year at this center, and that he will be leaving. That's an alteration in the framework that may well be in the background of all this.

Langs: Yes, I thought of that when the patient referred to having so few alternatives. We'll keep it in mind, and see if additional material appears that provides us Type Two derivative validation of that thesis.

Therapist: So she says, What are we going to keep doing? Are we going to sit here month after month, and slog through all this mess to work it out? That was that session.

Langs: So the session ends on a note of discouragement; the therapeutic field is a mess. Let's go on to the next session.

Therapist: Well, she missed the next session. She called and said that she would skip it because she had to rest for a job interview. She said she doesn't think she's going to get it; it's being offered to her as a formality, but she will see me next session.

Langs: Comments?

Discussant: The patient modifies the framework here, perhaps as a reflection of her hopelessness about treatment.

Langs: Well, she makes it clear that this is a form of living or acting out, in that there is no essential reason for this absence. This is an important therapeutic context, and the material in the next session will further clarify her absence. On the other hand, the absence itself, as a commentary on the therapist's interventions, suggests something of how poorly held the patient feels, how discouraged she feels about treatment, and how poorly she wishes, in turn, to hold the therapist.

I had sensed that something of this kind might happen, since I experienced the patient in the previous session as involved in an unconscious curative effort directed toward the therapist. His single intervention showed a total failure to appreciate the patient's unconscious therapeutic endeavors, and the missed session represents a giving up on both the therapist and herself. It is hard to know what will follow; she'll either be flat and empty, or renew her therapeutic efforts now that she has missed an hour.

When patients miss sessions, the event should be taken as a signal to review your interventions in the prior hour. Absences are characteristically a negative commentary on your therapeutic work, and in addition suggest the presence of a damaged framework. A missed session may serve to alert you to the need to rectify and interpret framework issues. Here it could have brought your proposal to medicate the patient to mind and led you to review this material in terms of the therapeutic relationship. Let's see what happened next.

Therapist: Okay. She came in next time and said, I got the job. I thought I wasn't going to get it, but I got it. They interviewed me. It was a complete farce. They just ask you the questions and you have to give them the right answers. For example, the woman asked me, Do you feel that students who go to junior colleges (this is where she was interviewed for the job) are inferior? (Laughter.) And of course I said no, they're not inferior; they need special help. And there were other questions on how work with communication blocks should be incorporated into the program. I answered wrong on that one, incidentally. But it's all a game; it's all a game. The woman says she felt there should be special classes for remedial work. And I was supposed to say no, there shouldn't be special classes; remedial work should be incorporated into the regular course work. When I mark science papers, for example, I should also correct for spelling.

She went on: It feels good to get a job. I didn't tell you, but last week I was getting suicidal again. I was thinking that there were no stars on the horizon. But don't worry, I'm not suicidal now. The job did give me a boost. I was beginning to lose some of my professional identity. The problem now is that I've let this thesis drag on for such a long time and I've lost some sense of what it would actually be like to have some palpable sense of identity. I was thinking about it the other day. I was also thinking about the guy who supervises me, an internist here. He's an M.D., but nevertheless is known for some substantial research. He supervises five or six people but manages to maintain a sense of enthusiasm, even with all those people to supervise. And he just met with me, incidentally, about my work. And I just said something like, Oh. (Literally just something like Oh, because she had said that she wasn't going to meet with him.) She said, Well I told him that my work has not been up to par lately. I told him that I do get these depressions that interfere with my functioning. He was very skeptical. He asked, Who are you seeing that tells you you're depressed? (Laughter.)

Discussant: Despite the fact that there is indirect communication—perhaps—about the relationship and the therapy, would you call this a Type C field?

Langs: Well, I would put it this way: since we know the adaptive context, this material can be organized as Type Two derivatives around the therapist's erroneous and noninterpretive interventions, and his effort to alter the framework by offering the patient medication. I must also add that the patient seems acutely aware of the lack of confidentiality and the presence of a third party—the therapist's supervisor—to treatment; that is clearly a background adaptive context.

And we can certainly identify the patient's responses to these contexts: the therapist is functioning quite inadequately, is inferior, and has need of special help which he is not getting from his supervisor. In an effort to protect herself from becoming overwhelmingly depressed and suicidal, the patient attempts to invoke a Type C barrier by destroying the meaning of the relationship and trying to experience everything as unreal again. As she introjects the therapist's inadequacies, and his own failure to establish his professional identity, she experiences a sense of loss of identity herself, and this serves to heighten her depression still more.

Now, there is a considerable degree of repetition, and there are definite Type C communicative qualities to all of this, much of it at the therapist's prompting, though a good deal of it stems from within the patient. However, at the point at which you interrupted, the patient was moving closer to an allusion to the therapist, and if she does get around to him specifically, and to any definitive adaptive context, then I would have to think of this as a mixed communicative style, Type C and Type A, though, as we have now seen repeatedly, the symbolic and meaningful communication relates entirely to framework issues.

It seems to me that getting the job provided the patient a momentary manic defense because of the gratification involved. But in the main she is rather cautiously attempting to let the therapist know her unconscious perceptions and introjections based on his various erroneous interventions, both interpretations and mismanagement of the framework. So there is again an attempt to be curative or to direct the therapist toward finding some means of functioning more adequately through educational measures taken up on his own.

We will have to see where she goes. She may continue on this level until the therapist finally makes a meaningful intervention; she may soon give up and become quite depressed; or she may get back to a working over of the unconscious sexual countertransference, and secondarily of the transference and nontransference, trying to let him know again that it is issues of this kind that underlie this disturbance.

Therapist: She said, So he asked me who I was seeing, and I told him I saw you, and I also saw Dr. _____, who screens employees and such. He was pretty skeptical about this whole psychiatry business, but he won't press me. He's loyal.

Langs: Any comments?

Discussant: In the adaptive contexts we have identified, she is expressing her skepticism about treatment.

Langs: Yes, but what about that last comment: "He's loyal?"

Discussant: She would like the therapist to be loyal to her, and she herself continues in treatment, so she is loyal to him.

Langs: If you listen to this material around the adaptive context of the actual and proposed alterations in the framework, and especially in respect to the modifications in the confidentiality of this treatment, her comment can be taken as an unconscious directive to rectify the frame: be loyal to her, don't betray her confidences by presenting to a supervisor who, as far as the patient is concerned—and she may be quite right here—is not proving helpful at all. This, of course, may be due to the nature of his supervision or to learning blocks in the therapist. In any case, the message is be loyal to her and don't modify confidentiality.

And I must say this: I have serious doubts about the feasibility of treating patients who are students at this center or who work here, especially since you are all in training and work in the same place. If it is to be attempted at all, every effort must be made to avoid modifications in confidentiality. A bipersonal field should be established which is quite private, and not open to supervision. Save that for work with patients not connected with the center. In this situation I would discontinue supervision, thereby placing the supervisee in a position where he can approach material such as this in the knowledge that it is fantasy and distortion—though not at all surprising or necessarily reflective of major psychopathology—rather than a valid inference or perception. Interpretations could then be made that would imply that her treatment is in fact totally confidential. This would get the message across to this patient and would afford her a significant feeling of being well held and safe, at least as far as third parties are concerned. As a supervisor, then, I would take this directive regarding rectification quite seriously, and would propose that supervision be discontinued.

Therapist: Well, she went on: Anyway, we started talking about projects. He had ideas; I had ideas. We both really got worked up.

I went out; the feeling lasted about a half hour. I just couldn't get going, couldn't make a structured setting.

Langs: "Couldn't make a structured setting."

Therapist: Except for a structured setting like the job I just got, I can't do well. I do well in structured settings, but an ability to develop an internal sense of energy is really lacking within me.

Langs: Thank you. I trust it is quite clear: if she had a clearly structured setting, she could develop some inner strength of a kind presently unavailable to her. In derivative form, the patient states her need for a secure hold and its ego-integrating, ego-building qualities.

Therapist: Well, at this point I gave my pitch for antidepressant medication once again. I did it by bringing up the question of whether medication might not help her out of this trough.

Langs: Any comments?

Therapist: Well, let me say it. I certainly couldn't find any meaning in this material, and I thought that the medication might offer her a structured setting, which is pretty absurd now that I understand the implications of offering her a drug. I guess I felt that I couldn't offer her an interpretation or any understanding, so I offered her medication instead.

Langs: Yes, and look at the timing. The patient just got this job; she is feeling a bit better; and she is attempting to let you know how disturbed she is about your errors and alterations in the framework. And what is your response: unfortunately, you once again make no effort to understand her communications, and suddenly bring up the medication. It is indeed an expression of helplessness on your part, and the timing here, in the absence of acute distress in the patient, has to raise serious questions about your unconscious motives and counter-transferences.

I might mention in this context an article in the 1977 volume of the *International Journal of Psychoanalytic Psychotherapy*. It is by a therapist named Levy and is on the introduction of medication in the treatment of inpatients. He demonstrates repeatedly that the drug is typically introduced at a time when the therapist doesn't understand the patient and is under the influence of major countertransference difficulties. It is a study that is quite relevant to this interlude, and is well worth reading.

Discussant: Don't you think that the therapist was responding to the patient's anger? I think that she was attacking him pretty directly.

Discussant: But I think we can also sense the therapist's feeling of helplessness. She did mention hiding the fact that she had been suicidal again.

Discussant: She is feeling better, but you yourself said it was a manic defense.

Langs: It seems to me that we can put this all together and generate a tentative formulation. First, I want to address the patient's concealment of her suicidal feelings: withholding information is a function of the Type C field, and of needs and defenses within both patient and therapist. Alterations in the framework interfere with the conscious and unconscious communication between patient and therapist and often lead to dissembling and lying.

As for deriving from this material some thesis regarding the nature of the therapist's countertransference—a step necessary in order to understand the associations that will follow now, since this is what the patient will be working over—it does seem, on the surface, a direct reaction to the patient's derivative and then direct skepticism regarding the therapist's capabilities. We could therefore postulate that on this level the offer of medication served unconsciously as an attempt to fend off the patient's hostility and to placate her. And yet on another level the offer expresses the responsive hostility of the therapist.

Discussant: I also noticed that the patient named the therapist to her supervisor, thereby inviting specific criticism and also breaking the confidentiality of the treatment situation.

Langs: Yes, her behavior duplicates that of the therapist, as she either correctly imagines it or has actually been able to determine. It is a form not only of attacking the therapist but of holding him poorly as well, a way of paying him back for his poor hold of the patient. She threatens to expose him and to ruin his reputation as a therapist. And he responds not by attempting to incorporate this provocative projective identification, and to metabolize it toward understanding and interpretation, but with a pathological projective identification of his own: the renewed offer of the medication. On this level, not only is unresolved hostility an issue on both sides, but interactionally we now hear exchanges of pathological projective identifications between two individuals who both lack a capacity for reverie.

Interactionally, then, the patient placed into the therapist a sense of being poorly held, a sense of inadequacy, depression, anxiety, and uncertainty, that she had introjected from you based on your previous erroneous interventions. She found a way of reprojecting these qualities back into you, in a relatively unmetabolized form, and your response was to introduce the medication again—in itself, an unmetabolized reprojection of the patient's projective identification—a projective counteridentification.

In regard to the frame, then, alterations reflect and express the countertransferences of the therapist, his inability to interpret, and his own pathological need to projectively identify disturbing contents and functions into the patient. I think that this all must be stated quite specifically, so that we can then attend to the material that follows in an effort to validate these hypotheses beyond the fact that we are now discovering these meanings with great consistency in different clinical situations.

Therapist: Obviously, I didn't feel that I was attacking her, although I felt that I was a bit confused, rather upset with her having been suicidal without telling me, and quite perplexed as to what to do.

Langs: That your conscious intentions were good is more than evident. We are attempting here to formulate your unconscious intentions and your communications to the patient, since we have every reason to expect that she will react to those implications far more than to your manifest intentions.

Discussant: I see the situation as one in which there is a strong sense of competition. It's as if the patient is saying that her supervisor thinks treatment and medication are really unnecessary, as if she believes that the therapist's supervisor has decided that she should receive medication. And when a patient becomes competitive, the ultimate weapon in the arsenal of many psychiatrists is, Well you're sick, so you need medication.

Langs: Yes, I would agree that this is part of a destructive armamentarium. Your concept of competition may be valid, but for me it is a more superficial way of describing the exchanges here of pathological projective identifications. Competition misses the sense of another quality of this intervention: the patient will experience it as an attempt to disorganize her, to break the hold and drop her further, and to fragment her functioning—perhaps, as you are suggesting, to have her in a chaotic state quite similar to what the therapist himself is experiencing.

Discussant: I also see an attempt by the therapist to avoid a sense of separation.

Langs: That may be so, but there are also efforts to avoid sexual material and the impact of the patient's suicidal feelings. I think we now need to turn to the patient for some answers to these questions and for validation of our various hypotheses.

Discussant: I just wanted to say that I have seen this sort of thing happen quite often. I can think of patients whose attempts to get me to give them medication I was able to resist, but just up to the point where it seemed almost superfluous for me to give it to them. And then I give it to them after all. I later became aware that this is definitely based on my countertransferences, but I didn't understand why. I find that this discussion is helping me develop the tools and concepts with which I might return to some of those sessions to discover what I was reacting to. I knew there was something about each of these patients that was bothering me, but I just didn't know how to find out what it was all about.

Langs: Yes, the answers will lie within the therapeutic interaction— and then within related factors in yourself and the patient. Let's now look for answers in this particular situation.

Therapist: Okay, she said, I won't take drugs. If it makes you feel better, I do intend to read a new book in the library on depression freedom capsules. (Laughter.)

Discussant: You can sense the competition between the patient and the therapist.

Discussant: But the therapist is failing her; she has to turn somewhere else.

Therapist: She said, I intend to read the book so that I may make an informed response. That's the end of that session.

Langs: So she will now modify the frame through reading, and as an effort to deal with your pressures—the book will be her means of coping with you. Notice too that she is indicating her wish to make you feel better—a Type Two derivative validation of my formulations in that regard.

Discussant: I wonder if the patient doesn't have some fantasy that the drugs could harm her or poison her.

Langs: Well, we heard earlier some allusion to toxins. But remember too that, on the first level, her refusal to take the medication is well founded. It would be important to discover whether the underlying basis is essentially pathological or nonpathological; it could be either or a mixture of both. It's another question that might be clarified as we continue. Let's hear the beginning of the next hour.

Therapist: Well, two things had happened before the next session. (I am trying to reconstruct the sequence.) What happened was that I had cancelled the sessions of the next two weeks because of several legal holidays, and she was also leaving the area.

Langs: Well, we have heard this type of communication before: Oh by the way, we then missed four sessions. And you will notice, of course, that that's entirely omitted from the presentation up to this point. There was a major separation pending, and we didn't even know it was an adaptive context. You can see how this particular information serves as a selected fact: we could now return to the sessions presented to this point and meaningfully organize them using this as an adaptive context. And you may remember that the patient had referred to her boyfriend leaving her, to needing third parties, and to a sense of loss—though she spoke of it in terms of her professional identity. Some of us had sensed something of this kind and wondered about a pending forced termination. There are other threads, but let's for the moment focus on the implications of this information on the framework.

Without knowing it, we have actually been listening to a sequence of sessions that preceded a nonpathological break in the frame—the therapist's vacation. As an adaptive context to be added to those that we have already identified and discussed, we can see that the patient's suicidal feelings and her decision to cancel a session were also responses to the pending separation. But the main point is that the therapist, rather than understanding this material in that particular context, truly obliterated its implications and attempted to utilize the medication as a means of avoiding the entire issue—in short, as a Type C barrier. In addition, of course, it constituted the therapist's attempt to deal, however pathologically, with both their separation anxieties. Yes, the discussant who suspected that there was a separation issue in the air is to be congratulated; his formulation is quite dramatically validated.

Therapist: Well, as I recall, she called me, and was quite agitated. She said that she wanted to see me, and I arranged to see her the next afternoon. This was during the two weeks that we were not to meet. (I was working on and off.) Actually, that particular session had been cancelled because she was not planning to be in the area. Otherwise I would have seen her.

Langs: Well, we have now learned that a major motive in altering the framework is that of separation anxieties within the therapist. This has a bearing on the frequency with which therapists modify the frame in the termination phase of therapy, making use of all sorts of rationalization which, I would propose, are never validated in the material from the patient. Such deviations are efforts at framework deviation cure for both therapist and patient, and at times serve the former more than the latter.

And, as an interactional product, we see the patient taking her cue from you: you could not tolerate the separation and offered a framework deviation cure; she, also unable to tolerate the separation, resorts to a comparable effort at symptom alleviation. There is, of course, the unfinished business of her cancelling sessions during a period when you were at least partially available. But overall, I trust that you can sense that there is no sense of structure or hold; instead, there is chaos, and this derives significantly from both participants. Under these conditions, the patient regresses and becomes agitated, much as we had predicted, even though we did not know of this added dimension. Well, let's hear what happened in that session.

Therapist: She began by saying, I am very agitated, and I feel alone. And I just can't stand being in the room anymore. I'm now willing to take medication. So I started her on Tofranil. She was very agitated, and said she felt that she needed Librium as well. I started her on both. And then she refused to talk for the rest of the session.

Langs: This is dramatic Type Two derivative validation of one of my earlier hypotheses: medication is an alternative to insightful cure. I am well aware that the drug houses and many therapists have attempted to state the matter otherwise: that medication will facilitate communication between patient and therapist. I let this material speak for itself: the therapist prescribes two drugs, and the patient stops talking. Alterations in the framework do more than simply modify the communicative properties of the bipersonal field—they can destroy them. And we can speculate: is it that she fears speaking, feels unsafe, or no longer has a need to do so? Is there no point; is she suddenly quite suspicious of the therapist; does she need distance? Something about the boundaries—perhaps that they have been fragmented and must be restored through silence. Is there something too about the additional session? All of these questions have to be framed as silent hypotheses to be borne out when the patient—I say this hopefully—begins to talk again.

Therapist: Well at that point, we made an appointment for about ten days later. However, she called me again for another emergency appointment which I can only summarize briefly. In it she spoke at length about how depressed she is, how she just can't stand it anymore, and how she doesn't know if she will ever get better. And she said, If you hospitalize me, don't hospitalize me here. And I don't remember how I responded, but I mainly emphasized that she had just started to take the medication, and that she should give it a chance to work.

Langs: Any comment?

Discussant: Well, with the frame fragmented, the patient regresses further. It's as if she is now proposing yet another deviation: hospitalization.

Discussant: But she adds some sense of rectification: don't hospitalize me here.

Langs: Yes, in the adaptive context of two major deviations—the offer of an additional session and the prescription of medication—the patient regresses and wishes for further modifications in the framework, now in the form of hospitalization. Once committed to framework deviation cures, there seems no turning back. Unfortunately, very much as we had predicted, she seems to be disintegrating under the influence of the therapist's noninterpretive interventions.

Discussant: It seems to me that we could propose an alternative adaptive context, namely, a new job, and see this as an increase in anxiety and depression based on fears of getting into a new situation.

Langs: Well, it is important to propose alternative hypotheses, especially the possibility of adaptive contexts outside the therapeutic relationship. But it seems to me that for the moment it would not be feasible to organize this material as derivatives related to the context you have suggested; by contrast, considered as Type Two derivatives around the adaptive context of the various alterations in the framework, the material takes on a great deal of meaning. Let your proposal stand as an alternative silent hypothesis, and we'll see how the material in the next session relates to it: will the material be linear and unrelated, or actually convoluted to the point that we are convinced that the patient's new job situation has evoked pathological unconscious responses? We would then have, at the very least, an additional adaptive context, but not necessarily one that would replace those related to the therapeutic interaction.

Discussant: Another adaptive context, since this is taking place at the turn of the year, could be the patient's anticipation of a forced termination at midyear.

Langs: Yes, we will be testing out that hypothesis in the material to come.

Discussant: I suggested that as a context because the patient had said she felt very alone, and was emphasizing a sense of separation.

Therapist: Okay, I'm going to breeze through this session. (Laughter.) This is now her regular session and it is in January. She walks in and is very calm, and says that she is feeling much happier and much more motivated. She says, I don't want to switch off drugs; I'm very pleased with them. You seem to know what you are doing.

Langs: I must say that I anticipate no need to revise my hypothesis regarding the therapist's use of medication. Can anyone state what I do anticipate?

Discussant: Well, you've described again and again what you call a typical split in regard to deviations in the framework: conscious appreciation, and unconscious questioning and chaos.

Langs: Yes, this is her manifest response; we will soon see her derivative reaction.

Therapist: I think that they are a little sedating, she says, But I suspect that I'll become habituated to the sedative effect.

Langs: There are some qualifications; we'll soon hear more.

Therapist: Then she told me that she had raised the dose of Tofranil by herself. (Laughter.) She described how she had increased the dose of the medication though I had specifically cautioned her against doing so. And later in this session, when I said that the increased dosage might be a little too much, that it may make her lethargic during the day, she said, No, I don't want to switch. I feel very good on this dosage. She was cool.

Langs: Here again is a bit of pathological projective identification and reprojection. The first unconscious communication here is that the medication might prove toxic or even lethal, and this evokes an anxious response on your part with a direct effort to have her desist. Again you respond noninterpretively, and she responds as if she has decided to work all of this out on this interactional level—much as you had suggested. There are strong qualities of a Type B communicative field here, and this too is a product of the deviation—the use of medication.

Therapist: She said, I read the chapters in the book on drugs and on depression. I know now that I am quite depressed.

Discussant: For me, it seems that she is taking over her own cure. She had suggested the second drug and had even increased her dosage, and perhaps that's what she needed.

Langs: Yes, the patient is now creating her own framework and making her own efforts at self-cure, probably because she has given up her unconscious efforts to cure the therapist, though these no doubt will recur. She is to be admired for these efforts, especially since we have seen that the therapist has, in reality, proven incapable of meaningfully helping her.

Now that's all quite sad to state, but I do so because many therapists would view all of this as major resistances deriving from the psychopathology of the patient—her competitiveness, her need to demean the therapist, and the like. And while these behaviors combine resistance with revelation, the resistance component would have to be understood as an *interactional resistance,* with significant contributions from both participants. It is important to recognize the nonresistant aspect of these efforts, which involves recognition of any actual failings on the therapist's part. Given the painful qualities of such recognitions, you can readily imagine how few therapists allow themselves a true perspective on these transactions.

Therapist: She said, I'm not sure whether I have a neurotic or a psychotic depression, but I tend to think that I sort of hit in the middle. Maybe I'm more on the psychotic side, but I really sort of sit in the middle (which in fact she does).

Langs: Well, I thought you would be more cautious with such remarks after hearing what I just said. So for you this has nothing to do with the prevailing adaptive context, and nothing to do with the me/not-me interface. She was only looking up her own diagnosis, not yours. How easy it is to be defensive. It hurts to state directly what she is saying indirectly: here, that based on the quality of your work with her, she has stated your diagnosis. It's a pretty awful statement, but that is how she experiences it, and I must say that I can see little fair basis on which to dispute her impression. If you wish not to take this personally, let it be a diagnosis of your therapeutic work, but let her contention reach you and lead you to reconsider what you are doing, and to take a fresh look at yourself. It's pretty rough, but that's the nature of psychotherapy, and we must get to know the truths that the patient speaks, even when they pertain to ourselves and may cause us pain. Then, once we have established the meaning of this for ourselves, we can turn to the patient and understand the implications there.

Therapist: Well, she said, of course, as you may know, this sort of depression doesn't have a good outcome. (Laughter.) So I asked her, Why do you say that?

Discussant: She may know something you don't know.

Langs: Yes, it's easy to step outside of this and hear the patient's grave pronouncements about the therapist, and perhaps even about herself. But remember there is something of each of us in this therapist, and something about the deviations in the framework and their implications that each of you have made and must own up to—and I as well, though mainly in the past.

Therapist: She said, As we've discussed, there are no precipitants to my depression, at least not any good ones that we have been able to identify.

Discussant: She is saying that there is no material, no precipitants; it all has nothing to do with the things we could talk about.

Langs: But you have reverted to listening on a manifest level without an adaptive context.

Therapist: Is it that she is feeling hopeless about my prognosis?

Discussant: It seems to me that this is a commentary on the therapist's intervention. She perceives that the therapist is unwilling to listen to the derivatives and precipitants of her illness.

Langs: And what are they?

Discussant: They are to be found in the therapy, particularly in the therapist's interventions.

Langs: Yes, this is her commentary on the therapist's noninterpretive interventions and alterations in the framework. She's saying that this is a hopeless situation, and she goes on in derivative form to make a telling comment on the listening process: if you do not work with an adaptive context—and it is remarkable to me that she utilizes that very concept in the form of her allusion to precipitants—there is no hope. That is a truth that could be stated about every therapeutic situation: hope comes through listening to adaptive sequences. And if they are ignored, and if bastions are created in respect to the therapeutic relationship, there can be no understanding and the prognosis is quite poor. Shifting now to a consideration of the alternate hypothesis presented earlier, I must say at this point that I see nothing in this material that could be related to the patient's new job.

Discussant: Yes, I would agree with that. I do hear her working over unconsciously the nature of the therapist's work, but I don't hear anything that validates my hypothesis in that respect.

Langs: On the other hand, behind all of this may lurk the pending forced termination and the recent separation: we'll have to see what emerges next. But in any case, I want you all to hear how this patient has, if I may put it this way, directed the therapist to read *The Listening Process* (Langs 1978c).

Therapist: So she said, I know that we have discussed these episodes of rejection and loss, but they really don't add up. If you want to construct a one-to-one relationship between my depressions and these events, she said, You would be hard pressed to. Then she sort of changed her tone; she said, You know—and this was always of great concern to her—are these sessions confidential?

Langs: This is a Type Two derivative validation at its best. The patient is concerned with a whole series of alterations in the framework, including the medication, and with the dangers they pose; now she brings up a related issue that reflects some degree of displacement and disguise, but at a minimal level. I hope that this convinces all of you that the central issue here is indeed the modifications in the framework and the need for rectification. This is a rather direct model of rectification, but it must be taken to apply to all of the deviations in this frame.

Therapist: Well, this was at the very end of the session, and I said, I know that you have had doubts about the confidentiality of the sessions all along.

Discussant: This implies that it's the patient's problem, and it has nothing to do with the reality of the situation.

Discussant: It seems to me that her question must have made the therapist anxious. It's as if he's implying that she doesn't trust him, rather than tacitly admitting that the patient might have some reason not to.

Therapist: She then said, I know that in general you operate in private with me, but do you have a preceptor? And since this was at the end of the session I said yes.

Langs: This is what happens when you deal with material on a manifest level, when you lack a capacity to understand derivatives and to interpret. You modify the framework and the patient seeks further deviations—responding to them with chaotic periods of pathological regression which alternate with sudden moments of relief, in a manner that almost defies understanding. But there is some gratification in framework deviation cures, however dangerous they are—a point that the patient has already made.

And now she asks for another deviation, a self-revelation. She also asks to have confirmed the absence of total confidentiality and privacy in this treatment. It may well be that she feels quite unsafe being alone with this therapist, and would actually welcome a third party to treatment. It may also be that this would help her understand some of the chaos of this therapy and thereby give her some small sense of relief. But this could also have rather catastrophic consequences. The presence of a supervisor to a psychotherapy should be implicit, not explicitly stated. This is not a matter of concealing information from the patient, but a matter of creating the best possible frame under disruptive conditions.

The therapist who deviates once will tend to deviate again. And patients who obtain deviant gratification and defenses will attempt to seek them again as well. I would predict a rather intense response to this revelation, and a strong unconscious commentary from the patient.

Therapist: Well, she next asked, what are his credentials? (Laughter.)

Langs: You give more; she wants more.

Therapist: I said, He is an analyst. She then asked me if he was a senior analyst, and I said yes. She said, sarcastically, Oh, wow! And that was the end of the session.

Discussant: She keeps wanting more, and he keeps giving her more. This no longer resembles psychotherapy as I think of it, but something of a question and answer session with more revelations from the therapist than from the patient.

Langs: Yes, it has become the therapy of the therapist, and a form of lie therapy as well, despite the therapist's determination to tell the truth. There will be a strong response to all of this, but for the moment it is serving as both an indicator of, and a barrier to, the chaos of this treatment situation.

Therapist: Oh, there is a bit more to this session: she said, I think I know what it is that made me depressed for the first time. It was a couple of years ago, and I exposed myself. It was just before that first episode of depression that I made a couple of pornographic movies over a period of time. I let myself be used.

Langs: I must say that if time had permitted, I really would have paused to make some specific predictions. There have been only a few occasions I have observed in which the therapist revealed the presence of a supervisor to the patient. And each time the response was remarkably similar. And we will have to pause now, because there are some important lessons here. I see a copy of *The Technique of Psychoanalytic Psychotherapy,* and I would like to read you a passage that you can compare with what we just heard (Langs 1973b, pp. 191–193). I will excerpt the material:

Mr. E. I. had been in therapy for two months for characterological and narcissistic disturbances. He was divorced, not working, and using drugs. He was fifteen minutes late for a session and ruminated about his inaction and plight. The therapist pointed out that Mr. E. I. had been repeating himself in recent sessions and that he had not done anything different in his outside life either. The patient agreed, became self-critical, spoke of feeling annoyed, and ended the session by saying that something has to happen or he'll get kicked out of his apartment on his ass.

He missed the next session without calling, and began the following hour by saying that he had stayed away because he had nothing important to say. He spoke of taking drugs and of not functioning constructively, then of his father's laziness and how one of his brothers was living off a prostitute—an arrangement he would like. He thought of having his sessions taped and resented the therapist's occasional note-taking, which he felt reflected a lack of interest in him. The therapist then informed him that he was a supervised case, and that the notes were made to be clear about the content of the sessions. The patient nodded and said that he had to go out and find work.

In the next session, Mr. E. I. described how he would not allow his drug-addict, prostitute-dependent brother to stay with him—He's a leech who just wants to suck off me, he stated. He recalled that when he was about five, a doctor humiliated him by telling his mother that his penis was very small. Next he remembered that a friend had called him last night and had offered his wife for sexual relations to the patient, who had refused the offer. He then spoke of wanting a job, but said that he wouldn't return to his previous career as a dancer because there were too many homosexuals around.

So that vignette came immediately to mind. There are striking parallels between this material from Mr. E. I. and the material we've just heard. Mr. E. I. saw the therapist as a helpless leech, as a doctor who would expose his frailties to others, as someone who is unconsciously making sexual and homosexual misuse of his patient, and as a therapist who had created a ménage-à-trois. Now it may well be that there are pathological tendencies, in both of these patients, toward an inappropriate sexualization of relationships and experiences. But I think that you will find, in addition, that there are universal unconscious sexual implications to making use of a patient for supervision. As a rule these meanings remain quite unconscious and peripheral, but in therapists who have a need to reveal this fact to their patients the underlying erotic countertransferences take on major significance. The patient then has every reason to believe that the self-revelation has unconscious sexual implications, and the patient's own sexual pathology is thereby concealed within the pathology of the therapist. Perhaps it is the revelation, far more than the actual presence of a supervisor, that gives the situation its definitive unconscious sexual meaning. These implications may also serve to defend against underlying depressive and aggressive trends—sexualization is often used as a manic defense against such tendencies, in all human beings, patients and therapists alike.

In this instance the sequence is remarkable. In the adaptive context of the therapist's revelation about himself and his supervisor, the patient recalls various experiences that created her depression. And we discover that this has to do with exposing herself and allowing herself to be used sexually—with her having acted in pornographic movies. What could be clearer? The alteration of the framework that introduces a third party to treatment constitutes a sexualized exposure of both patient and therapist, and creates a situation in which both are exploited, especially the patient. The patient permits herself to be mis-used, and suffers a narcissistic mortification that lowers her self-esteem and evokes an intense depressive response.

And it is here that an important point can be demonstrated: alterations in the framework generate conditions and introjects that replicate on some level the very conditions that created the patient's psychopathology. These are therefore conditions under which this pathology cannot possibly be insightfully modified, because no matter how extensive the verbal efforts are under these circumstances, the behavioral reinforcements will preclude any adaptive inner structural change for the patient. And though for the moment we do not have the genetic figure or figures that relate to this repetition, you can be certain that they involve the patient's interaction with one or both of her parents. The pathological past is repeated when the frame is modified, and its influence cannot be insightfully modified so long as such conditions prevail.

This is really quite dramatic. I can well imagine that a therapist who is not listening to this material in terms of the spiraling communicative interaction, and who would not use his own interventions as the adaptive context for the patient's material, might immediately think: Great, I've made a breakthrough. I now know something of why the patient became depressed. I must be doing something right. And this would be terribly self-deceptive, and it would not be validated in the subsequent material from this patient, who, I suspect, will soon become quite depressed and perhaps even suicidal again. But this is what I mean by the *functional capacity* of the material from the patient: material cannot be traced in isolation but must be understood in the context of the ongoing therapeutic interaction. Viewed this way the unfortunate unconscious meanings of this communication are all too clear.

Now, technically, how should this have been handled?

Discussant: By saying nothing and allowing the patient to continue to free associate, in the hope of understanding the material and making an interpretation.

Langs: He eventually must respond, not only with an interpretation, but also with rectifications of the frame. The patient implies that she regrets having allowed herself to be used to make pornographic films, and she implies too that the conditions under which her depression can be insightfully cured must include, first and foremost, the establishment of a sound and stable framework for this therapy—a noncorrupt setting. I think there can no longer be any doubt that my earlier recommendation, that this patient's case no longer be supervised, must be carried out, along with many changes in the nature of the therapist's verbal interventions.

In principle, then, and not because I say so but because patients say so, the therapist should not modify the framework through self-revelations of any kind. The question about the supervisor must be understood in terms of its latent implications regarding the adaptive contexts of earlier deviations. Understanding derivative communication provides you the means of properly handling situations of this kind, and in fact allows you to prevent their unfortunate occurrence. Beyond that, the therapist should respond with interventions and interpretations that implicitly accept the truth of the patient's valid perceptions, and should explore their meaning for her, both transference and nontransference.

Self-revelations and even most direct acknowledgments of errors do not serve the therapeutic needs of the patient. Certainly, if a blatant mistake is allowed to occur, such as coming to a session a half an hour late, you have to acknowledge that to the patient; but with more subtle errors, you can accept the patient's perceptions as valid through qualities implicit in your intervention and by not treating such reactions as distorted. That is all the patient requires: implicit validation of her correct perceptions, and interpretations of her responses to technical errors in terms of their nontransference and transference, valid and distorted, components.

Discussant: I have seen patients, and some of them have worked at this center, with whom the issue of supervision seemed to wreck the therapy. At the time, neither I nor my supervisors knew how to deal with it, and maybe I also missed some important interventions, but I do think that your proposal to actually terminate this supervision provides a resolution that would be essential to the possibility of any constructive work under these conditions.

Therapist: So now I guess I'll have to go to my supervisor and say, Langs told me to get rid of you.

Langs: No, no! The patient did it! (Laughter.)

Therapist: This guy's not too fond of me anyway. (Laughter.) And by the way, he supported the idea of medication all the way.

Discussant: In fairness I must say that many of the personnel who come into treatment at this clinic are told by the screening staff member that they will be seen by a resident who will have a supervisor. It is presented as a condition of therapy.

Langs: Well, I hope that you have now learned something about the consequences of such conditions.

Therapist: You know, this is actually a remarkable moment in her therapy. She had told me from the beginning that there was a secret that she wouldn't mention to me. And I had wondered about it. And I had thought that this was actually a very important moment in the therapy because she had revealed it to me. In the past, she said she couldn't tell me the secret because she didn't trust me. And now I thought, Maybe she does trust me. But I must say, I no longer believe that. It's pretty rough to discover that there are ways to get secrets out of patients other than creating a safe setting. I guess it's a matter of going to the other extreme, of so destroying the sense of safety that the patient feels that she is once again in a setting where she's being used and exploited. Your formulation is pretty convincing, and it sure as hell is a remarkable discovery for me.

Langs: Well, since our time is up, let's conclude on that note. Next week we will continue with this patient, after which I have arranged for an outside therapist to present to us for two additional weeks. Thank you. It has really been a very informative presentation.

Therapist: I will be away for two weeks; may I finish up upon my return—I'd like to.

Langs: Yes, of course; we will look forward to it.

Chapter Twelve

SOME UNCONSCIOUS
IMPLICATIONS OF DEVIATIONS

Langs: Despite the three-week break, we'll begin once again without desire, memory, or understanding. Let's get right to it.

Therapist: I was in the middle of a session.

Discussant: I wasn't here last time. Could I just hear a summary of the session to this point?

Langs: Well, we needn't be purists. The rest of us have heard the material to this point; what do you recall?

Discussant: I think that she had just said that she had been in several pornographic movies.

Discussant: I remember that there was something about the therapist being prostituted to the clinic, or seeming to have that role.

Discussant: That's interesting, because I remember something about the patient's reacting to a vacation that the therapist had taken. And there was something about either payment or termination.

Langs: Well, this is turning out to be an interesting exercise in memory and recall. Anyone else?

Discussant: I'm trying to remember why the patient spoke about prostituting herself.

Discussant: Oh, I remember now. She had said something about her job here and a supervisor she had told about the treatment.

Langs: When we complete this exercise, I think you will all have experienced firsthand something of what we mean when we talk about derivative communication. In actual fact, we had broken off at a point where there had been a series of specific communications, which we can eventually identify. These recollections, to the extent that they differ from—or are an incomplete version of—what actually transpired, are derivatives of those transactions. And we're seeing here a progression of derivatives, fortunately with a gradual diminution of defensiveness. Who can take this further?

Discussant: Somehow this was more related to the therapist's supervision.

Langs: Yes; this is remarkable. You are getting closer still.

Discussant: I remember something about the therapist giving the patient medication, and the patient saying that she was feeling well and had gotten a job. And then there was something about the therapist giving her an antidepressant or some other medication, and our wondering why the therapist had done so at a time when the patient seemed to be saying that things were going well. But I don't remember whether she reacted to that in the session, or if that's where we stopped.

Langs: What do we see in that formulation?

Discussant: It sounds like a Type C barrier or the use of repression.

Langs: The two differ: in the latter underlying meaning shows through, but not in the former. Even though we do not know as yet the exact nature of the reality we are seeking to recall, we have enough information to suggest that in this situation we are observing the presence of rather massive repressive barriers—the underlying truths are conveyed in derivative form. And interestingly enough, we're still lacking the crucial adaptive context—and we'll soon see where that lies. To refine my comment a bit: actually, the earlier responses, which contain in derivative form more of the actuality we are trying to recall, had Type A qualities, while these last comments were more barrier than revelation.

Discussant: Yes, I had a feeling that I was drawing on unimportant details, but I'm still not sure where we left off.

Discussant: Was the immediate precipitant for the patient's revelation something about the taping of the sessions, and the presence of the other supervisor?

Discussant: Is this the patient the therapist was taping sessions with, and she had wanted to know if he was in supervision—was there some issue involved of that kind?

Therapist: That's another patient I taped.

Langs: Okay, so we're hearing derivatives and condensations, now in a form that represents but still disguises the truth—the adaptive context.

Discussant: I think we've almost got it now: the patient had asked the therapist whether he had a supervisor, and the therapist had told her that he had supervision with an analyst, a senior analyst, I think.

Therapist: Yes, that's where we left off.

Langs: Well, you can all review your responses now as derivatives of that incident. And not only can you identify the presence of defenses; you can also see that most of them were directed against the specific adaptive context of the therapist's self-revelation regarding the presence of a supervisor. And this is quite typical: therapists attempt to defend against the awareness of their own personal and shared countertransferences, including the ways in which they contribute to unneeded modifications in the framework.

Discussant: Are we therefore concluding that the therapist's break in confidentiality and his self-revelation indicated to the patient that he's exposing her sexually and prostituting the therapy?

Langs: Yes, it is seen as a corruption of treatment, as are all deviations to some degree. This is a transversal communication filled with meaning: truth and distortion, self and not-self, fantasy and perception, pathology and nonpathology. It is an immediate and exquisite commentary on the implications, the functional meaning, of what the therapist just revealed; it is a communication that can only be understood in terms of its own functional meaning in the adaptive context of the self-revelation and its nature.

Therapist: Can I just bring up two points that have troubled me since this happened and our last discussion of it? I'm still not clear about how you would have intervened in response to these questions. When I went over this material with my preceptor, he felt that something had changed in this patient, and that she had used her secrets as a way of provoking me early in the therapy. And he felt that at this point she's really getting to trust me; that was his interpretation of the material.

Langs: Well, I said last time that many therapists would view this material in that way, and pointed out that in order to do so, it would be necessary to deny that the adaptive context for the patient's revelation was your own self-revelation and the modifications of the framework. Instead of reviewing my earlier comments, which are no longer fresh in my mind, I will allow the patient to help us decide which of the two hypotheses are validated: that this self-revelation reflects an increased trust in the therapist, or that it reflects a lessened trust and a desperate attempt to show the therapist that she is now, once again, in the very kind of situation that had evoked and reinforced her pathology and depression in the past.

Therapist: Then, when she asked me so directly about the supervisor, how would you have dealt with it in order to correct the frame and to handle her question? Because the question she was asking was not just a fantasy, an internal production on her part; it was related to the actualities of treatment.

Langs: Yes, I'm glad that you appreciate that this involves the actualities of the conditions of treatment. But don't make the mistake of assuming that such actualities do not evoke fantasies, which they certainly do. In addition, recognize that the reference to this actuality in itself served as a derivative communication, a point that you missed in the session because you heard only the manifest content. As I recall, I saw her question as a derivative response to your previous alterations in the framework, and especially your use of medication. And all I can say for the moment in regard to technique—in the session we are about to hear, I will perhaps be able to be more explicit—is that I would be attempting to understand this material as Type Two derivatives in the adaptive context of my recent deviations, and I would be preparing, first, to rectify the frame and, second, to interpret the patient's unconscious perceptions and fantasies as stimulated by my deviation.

Therapist: If I may, then, because several people weren't present, I would like to start with the beginning of this session.

Langs: Go ahead.

Therapist: She came in and said that she feels okay. She doesn't feel happier or more motivated, but she does feel calmer. She doesn't want to switch off the medication. She said: You seem to know what you're doing. I think I'll become habituated to the sedative effect of these drugs. (Remember, this is the session after I had put her on Tofranil and Librium.) Here I mentioned something to the effect that if the sedative effects were significant we could shift to another antidepressant. She said, No, I'd rather not switch. (I realize very well now that I was simply addressing the manifest content. I was offering her a Type C barrier.)

She said that she had been reading a book on psychiatry, and that this seems to be the appropriate treatment for what's bothering her. She said, I still don't know exactly what's wrong with me. (By the way, I must say that most of my supervisors listen just as I do, mostly on a manifest level, and occasionally in terms of Type One derivatives. It may be that I have missed some other message from them, but this is certainly how my supervisor heard this particular material.)

So, I asked her what her impression was of the nature of her problem. (I know, I'm asking her to talk manifestly about her diagnosis;

and along the me/not-me interface, especially in the light of the way I'm intervening here, she's going to really tell me something of her impressions of me as a therapist.)

Discussant: I find it disquieting to hear this material again. The errors seem so obvious. But I must say that I share with the therapist an experience of having been taught to address the manifest content, to be naively supportive, to be what's called flexible with the framework, and that I've never been given any understanding of the nature and the functions of the frame.

Therapist: I can see the extent to which I was trying to keep this patient on the surface, and away from unconscious communication.

Discussant: As I understand you, all of this means that medication is an alteration of the framework and should not be used in insight psychotherapy.

Langs: Yes, I think that this patient is making that unmistakably clear.

Discussant: Do you think that there are some patients who need medication?

Langs: I can't possibly answer a question of that kind; I can only say that Searles (1965) and others treat schizophrenic patients without medication, and there are analysts who treat manic-depressive and psychotically depressed patients without medication as well. I can't answer that question for populations of patients with which I am not especially familiar, though I certainly can immediately support a treatment modality for schizophrenics without the use of drugs. It is my main purpose here to provide you with the tools to answer that question with any particular patient, and to do so in the light of a broad understanding of the nature and functions of the frame. In general, with psychotherapy medication is seldom if ever indicated.

Therapist: Well, I saw this patient as a fragile, borderline patient, but I must say that she's well enough integrated now to pursue a graduate degree. My initial inclination was not to put her on medication, and it was my supervisor who initially suggested that I consider the use of antidepressant medication.

Discussant: Do you find that the framework functions in the same way with inpatients as with outpatients—with schizophrenics and the like?

Langs: We are moving now too far away from clinical data. I have supervised cases of patients on inpatient services, and the findings are quite comparable. Please leave it at that, with enough tension to prompt you to investigate these issues by making full use of the listening process that I hope you have now learned quite well.

Therapist: To continue: She said, I'm not sure. It's hard to tell from the book. I don't think I'm one of those psychotic depressives, what do you think? And I said that I agreed with her that she falls more into the realm of neurotic rather than psychotic depression.

Langs: I'm not sure if you mentioned this last time, but I'm certainly impressed at this point with the multiplicity of deviations and self-revelations to which this patient was subjected. And we can see again how one deviation begot another, all as part of a rather confused, circular interaction. The situation is chaotic and, as you already know, it became even more so quite soon.

Therapist: She then said, But it has a bad outcome, this illness I have. And I said, Why did you say that? Why do you feel that way? She said, Well, there were no precipitants to my depression. Sometimes I feel that I have to be sacrificed to science.

So I said that we had discussed the various losses which she would never acknowledge and how they had precipitated the other depressions that she had had. I mentioned that there had been a loss prior to this one when she broke up with her boyfriend, and when she had to leave her roommates and move to her own apartment.

Discussant: If I may say so, this is all very confronting, and the therapist is introducing many of his own associations; he's not allowing the patient to lead the way.

Langs: Yes, there are many kinds of noninterpretive, nonneutral interventions: the use of questions directing the patient toward the surface, aggressive confrontations, and so-called supportive interventions which are clearly filled with unconscious destructiveness. Much of this continues to be quite self-revealing. Please continue.

Therapist: She said something to the effect that that may be so, but she said, If you went about to prove there was a one-to-one relationship between these events and my depression, I think you would be hard pressed to prove it. And I said, Well, there are a complex of factors which feed into these things, and other things may have contributed as well.

Langs: A statement of a psychoanalytic cliché, serving as as Type C barrier.

Therapist: As an aside, I'll tell you something. It's interesting to me because in a way this is an insight case. But I've never been sure about how to treat her. Because you know I feel she's fragile, and I'm reluctant to be too withholding. But then I make these interventions which don't bear fruit. So it's been complicated.

Langs: Yes, I can appreciate how you feel. These are the rationalizations for so-called supportive therapy, which includes many of the noninterpretive interventions that you actually made to this patient. And as you can see, not only are they never validated in her associations; they are also responded to in terms of their unconscious destructive implications. Patients seem never to tire of responding on the surface with appreciation and of then reacting to the underlying devastation in extremely disturbing ways. All you need do is adopt the use of adaptational sequences and listen to the material in terms of each adaptive context as determined by your interventions; you will then learn from your patients all you need to know about this so-called supportive approach. It's anything but that, as we have already seen with this patient.

Therapist: Well, it was at this point she said, Is this therapy confidential? So I said something to the effect, Well, we discussed that you had doubts about the confidentiality of the therapy all along, and I'm curious why you bring this up now.

Discussant: If I may be permitted, I just now have the fantasy that maybe she's asking this question in order to protect the therapist, or to expose him. I'm not sure, but I sense that she either hopes that he's not revealing this kind of work to his supervisor or, on the other hand, that he will and that he'll either be reprimanded or corrected.

Langs: Yes, you can pose that as a silent hypothesis open to validation. It seems likely that she's concerned about everyone: herself, the therapist, and his supervisor.

Therapist: She said, I know that you operate in private here, but does anyone else know about this? And she says, specifically, Do you have a preceptor? So I said, with a little bit of my normal nonchalance, Yes. So she said something asking for elaboration: What are his credentials? So I said something to the effect that he was an analyst, and then to the effect that he was more than an analyst—he was a senior analyst. (Laughter.) So she said, sarcastically, Oh, wow! And then she said—no, I said, something to the effect—well, I pointed out that she was being sarcastic, that I knew the issue of confidentiality concerned her, and that she may therefore have been inhibited in discussing things that brought out into the open might have lifted her depression.

Discussant: There's a strange message there: there is no confidentiality, and maybe it's inhibiting her—almost implying that it shouldn't.

Therapist: She said, Well, I was in a couple of pornographic movies for a couple months, a few years back, when I had my first depression. She said, I just got into it on a lark. She said, I was tight for money, I was moving and I didn't know what to do. My mother was reluctant to give me money; she couldn't afford it because my father had died some years back and had left her very little. And a friend of mine said, I've been into porno films, would you like me to give them your number? And I said, Fine. And she went on to elaborate about being in the films, feeling used and like a prostitute, and making some money, and even getting involved with the director. She said, I ended up making some money, but I had nothing but contempt for them.

Langs: Any comments? We are now hearing new material.

Discussant: It's really very bleak: she had nothing but contempt for them. This must refer to the therapist and his supervisor, and I guess to herself as well. There are no boundaries, and she's exposed and used.

Discussant: She mentions how a friend got her into all of this, an allusion to a third party.

Langs: And what else? There's an important embedded derivative there.

Discussant: Her mother didn't help her by giving her money. Maybe that's related to the therapist, and something about his not helping her in the right way, and making her depressed again, and somehow pressuring her toward getting back into something illicit.

Langs: Yes, that's quite important. I can now remember that at the time we first heard this material I spoke of how the patient was indicating that the present situation with the therapist replicated an earlier situation that contributed to her depression and, I would now add, her degradation and desperate behavior. And I said that we would expect this ultimately to link to a genetic figure and set of experiences, with one or both of her parents.

As you can see, the patient now provides us an initial genetic link. In the adaptive context of these repeated, so-called supportive but clearly degrading, self-revealing, and noninterpretive interventions, this patient is responding with extremely meaningful Type Two derivatives, filled with unconscious perceptions, probably some fantasies, and, now, important genetic links. She is working over the alterations in this framework in terms of their unconscious meanings for the therapist, and for herself, including genetic implications that would really apply unconsciously to both of them. This is a coalescing network of derivatives, and if the therapist were suddenly capable of recognizing the adaptive context for this material, he could make an extremely meaningful intervention and could quite readily proceed to rectify this framework.

Discussant: Would you tell us how you would intervene?

Langs: Would anyone else like to try?

Discussant: Well, I guess you could say something like, You began the session by saying you were feeling fine with the medication, but now you're getting into references to situations in which people are not helpful, but seem to abuse and demean you. In some way, then, you must see my use of medication as demeaning and abusive.

Langs: Well, that's really just a beginning. At this point, there's not only the medication to deal with, but also the series of self-revelations, especially the one related to the supervisor. I would begin with the adaptive contexts you have mentioned, but would be more inclusive: You began the session by saying the medication had helped you to feel better, but not entirely so, and that you had increased the dosage as well. You then went on to ask me a number of questions about this treatment regarding the presence of a supervisor, and the lack of total confidentiality. And I responded by answering your questions, and your reaction has been very striking. You have gone on to talk of how you became so deeply depressed when your mother didn't provide you the funds you needed that you allowed yourself to be used in pornographic movies. This must be your perception of the treatment situation and my using you for supervision, a situation in which you see the supervisor as something of a sexual voyeur. And you're saying that you get something out of it, but that it's quite demeaning and that you have nothing but contempt for the others who are involved in it. In fact, you are indicating that all of this is really quite a destructive way to handle your problems, and it seems clear now that while you are helped on some level by the medication, and you view the supervisor as possibly being helpful, to some extent both the drugs and the supervision are creating extremely destructive conditions to your therapy.

Here you'll notice that I took the matter of rectification only as far as her material permitted. I can assure you that you would obtain Type Two derivative validation in response to an intervention of that kind, and that it would include clear directives toward rectification, which I would then pick up and play back to the patient, clearly implying that the necessary measures would be taken—and eventually doing just that, at her behest. The discontinuation of medication would quickly let the patient know that you are indeed rectifying the frame, and your statement about the need to exclude the supervisor would have to be made in a way that would clearly assure the patient that you were going to eliminate him from the situation.

Discussant: I have the impression that the boundaries, holding, and containing in situations where pornographic films are made are quite poor and quite destructive. I would take all of that as a characterization of the therapeutic situation at this time.

Langs: Yes, it's a form of destructive and bad mothering. And what about the issue of trust; how does this material resolve the differences in the two silent hypotheses: one, that this revelation emerged in the context of an increased trust of the therapist, and, two, that it was a reflection of mistrust and an effort unconsciously to convey to the therapist the seductive and destructive implications of his intervention?

Therapist: I don't think there's any question; the material is filled with a sense of mistrust and abuse.

Langs: Yes, that is the patient's answer. All you had to do was listen to the patient and understand these derivatives in the relevant adaptive context. To risk a generalization that we will attempt to validate in the next two sections of this course: meaningful therapeutic work is always centered on the current therapeutic interaction and its implications—to which all else is appended.

Therapist: I can see the business with the friend now as her way of saying that people who are supposed to help you and be your friends wind up in the end doing something that's very destructive and demeaning.

Langs: Yes, they make prostitutes of you. And notice too, both she and the friend were in these films; they were two of a kind. The therapist who deviates replicates in some form the patient's own psychopathology, and that of the destructive mother who helped create that pathology. And all of this is in the derivatives from this patient; it's all there for the listening.

Therapist: I'm amazed at how differently I hear this material now as compared to how I heard it when working with my preceptor.

Langs: Well, I must say this much: there could have been no effort at validation on your part, or that of your supervisor. Learn to validate, and don't accept anything from a supervisor without validation from the patient.

Therapist: So she said she has nothing but contempt for those people, even though the director would often give her gifts.

Discussant: That must be a reference to the medication.

Langs: Exactly: something for nothing; this is once again seen as a form of seduction.

Discussant: I can hear the patient saying that the therapist is attempting to seduce and exploit her, again in the adaptive context of the deviation.

Langs: Yes, and what's the overall message?

Discussant: The patient feels she's being screwed and sexually exposed by the therapist.

Langs: Yes, and in instinctual drive language, this is a valid unconscious perception. As I have said before, in a bipersonal field whose frame is modified, it is impossible to determine how much of this is perceptive, and how much distorted.

Therapist: She said, And those guys in the film, they all asked afterwards, Was I the best? was I different from everybody else? And I would say to them, Oh, there was no one else like you. But they didn't realize what I was actually saying—I was saying that they're the scum of the earth; there's no one as bad as you are. But they never realized it.

Langs: Comments?

Discussant: I hear something related to the split that you referred to and the patient's response to deviations: she says they're fine, but underneath she feels they're awful, and that this nice therapist is really the scum of the earth.

Langs: Speaking the truth about the therapeutic interaction can really be awful, can't it? If any of you were skeptical about the issue of trust or mistrust, you can hear the continuing derivatives: she is falsifying; there is need to lie. In truth, she feels that what the therapist is doing is screwing her, and screwing her badly. He is no different from the rest. There's no one more degraded.

And how else shall we understand it? Is this the patient's self-image? It certainly is. But where does it come from? It comes from a circular interaction with someone who was degraded, and with whom she identified and created an introject, which then influenced her self-image, which then influenced her unconscious perceptions of the therapist, which were themselves influenced by the actual nature of his behaviors, and their valid unconscious implications. This is what I mean by the spiraling unconscious interaction, and the role of unconscious set as well as of actual external unconscious communication. It's what Strachey (1934) and Racker (1957) called a neurotic vicious circle; and it is degrading as well as vicious, and reinforces the patient's pathology and expectations, confirms the worst part of her own inner mental life, and forms a terrible soil which cannot sustain growth, and which will ultimately evoke depression and suicidal thoughts and impulses.

Discussant: I hear also a metaphor of the Type C field: there's a reference again to a lie, a falsification.

Langs: Yes, that's quite true. Remember, this patient has been attempting to communicate symbolically to a therapist who keeps shifting her to the surface, and to a form of lies, barriers, and falsifications. And perhaps soon now, she will give up, will use the barriers the therapist has unconsciously offered her. For the moment, she very clearly characterizes the Type C field, in which empty questions and lies prevail, and we can see the destruction and uncontrolled sexuality concealed beneath these barriers. And you can see too that a person who is prone to a Type C communicative style can engage in all sorts of behaviors, and cover over their implications with a type of dissociation and falsification.

Perhaps the most painful falsification involves the implications of the deviation: the therapist pretending to do therapy, and to be helpful, when in actuality he is being quite seductive and destructive. This is the patient's way of characterizing the lie therapy that exists here, with the use of medication, supervision, self-revelations, and the rest; these are some of the characteristics of lie therapy.

Therapist: You were talking a moment ago about validation, so you'll really be pleased to hear what she goes on to next.

Langs: I'm glad you want to continue. (Laughter.) No, I'm really quite pleased to see how you are taking all of this, and how well you are handling the realizations of the patient's actual unconscious messages to you, especially of her image of you. In all seriousness, as you very well know by now, this is the only way to learn psychotherapy. Not because I say so, but because in actuality this is what your patient is trying to tell you.

Therapist: She said, I must tell you that one of the directors of this center and one of his cronies invested in one of the films. They even tried to get involved in the sex. I wouldn't allow it.

Langs: I'm sure someone wants to comment on this material.

Discussant: It sort of puts a limit to the extent to which she will allow the supervisor to become fully a part of this transference/countertransference interaction. She's making clear how she sees the supervisor's and the therapist's participation with her; in light of the material that you read from your technique book last time (Langs 1973b), she's describing another ménage-à-trois.

Langs: Yes, and in addition, what is this a model of? (Pause.) It is a model of rectification: threesomes of this kind should not be permitted—especially not in front of the others. Therapy should be private and not public, even if it is sexualized, and we can only hope that under those conditions this sexual aspect can be resolved.

Isn't it remarkable, in light of your diagnosis of this patient, and of the evidence of poor controls, of enormous sexual and pregenital conflicts, and of the extent of her depression and suicidal tendencies, that on an unconscious level she is so remarkably perceptive and conveys so much that is meaningful? She even directs the restoration of the framework of her treatment. You can sense here what a great difference it makes whether such abilities and insights are available consciously in terms of both cognition and behavior, or remain as an inaccessible unconscious potential.

And isn't it remarkable too, how many of our initial silent hypotheses are now validated? None of this now seems based on any sense of trust. Instead the patient is attempting, as clearly as any derivative communication could express it, to let the therapist know just how corrupt and inappropriate his use of the supervisor, the self-revelations, and his offer of medication are. She brings it right to the doorstep of this center.

In general, alterations in the framework are self-revelations with strong sexual implications. They promote the sexualization of the bipersonal field, and that is one specific factor in the disruption of its communicative properties. They constitute powerful sexual pathological projective identifications, which have a destructive influence on the patient and reflect the countertransferences of the therapist.

Oddly enough, there is a sense here of the patient's efforts to hold the therapist, and to engage in rather extensive unconscious curative efforts. There are unconscious interpretations here, efforts at rectification, and efforts to alert the therapist to the nature of his difficulties. The patient is attempting to obtain a more secure hold from the therapist, and is also offering such a hold to him. In this context it is well to remember that the therapist's hold of the patient is an interactional product influenced by the needs and behaviors of the patient. Some patients make it quite easy to hold and support them implicitly, while others make it quite difficult.

Well, we are certainly seeing some dramatic examples of Type Two derivative validation. It would have been a far more pleasant experience if the therapist had understood some of this, and had been able to rectify the framework and make a sound interpretation to the patient.

Discussant: And would you have intervened at this point?

Langs: Yes, now that I have a clear directive for rectification, I certainly would have intervened. As you can see, in order to carry out this work you would have to have understood the adaptive context for this material, and its unconscious implications.

Discussant: What might you have said?

Langs: I have already outlined my intervention for you, but will state it again since you have had so little opportunity to clarify the specific methods of intervening in the presence of a modified frame. In brief, I would now focus on the presence of the supervisor. And I would say something like this: You are talking now about a situation in which there is no sense of limits or boundaries, and one that is filled with corruption and inappropriate sexuality. And you are relating it to personnel at this hospital, and talking about it in terms of threesomes, two men who wanted to use you sexually. And all of this follows your having asked me if there is a supervisor on your case, and my having acknowledged that there is. Quite clearly, then, you see the presence of a supervisor as creating a situation in which you are exposed and misused sexually. And your comment on that is quite clear: it's inappropriate, corrupt, and demeaning. It involves people you consider the scum of the earth, and it shouldn't be done. And you are certainly making it very clear that the presence of a supervisor and my participation in supervision is creating conditions quite similar to those under which you became profoundly depressed. Your comment that it shouldn't be this way reflects your wish to have a private therapeutic relationship within which it should become feasible for you to resolve your depression and your suicidal thinking. And based on what you have said, it seems very clear that there must no longer be a supervisor involved in your treatment.

From there, based on her further associations, I would find some way of linking this up to the medication, and would rectify that deviation as well. And once you have stated to the patient that you will no longer present her case to a supervisor, you must be sure to keep your word. To do otherwise would be absolutely disastrous.

Discussant: Would you actually say to the patient what you just told us?

Langs: Yes, under these conditions, that's exactly what I would say. It would be an implicit acknowledgment of the errors that I have made, an acceptance of the validity of her unconscious perceptions, and a transversal intervention that would leave room for her distortions of the situation as well—pathological contributions which I would analyze as we moved on. And this would have to include a direct effort at rectification.

Therapist: You don't seem to think that an intervention of that kind, since I operated on a different level for such a long time, would have gone right by her.

Langs: Oh no; quite to the contrary. You have already heard from this patient a type of validation that could in one stroke have convinced you of everything I have said here about the listening process and the nature and functions of the framework. And you would also hear derivatives of a positive introject of a kind that unfortunately has not been present here. It seems odd to me that you would expect the patient to not appreciate a truly valid intervention. Of course, that reflects something of your own skepticism, but I can assure you that your patient will not show it.

As I will soon explain in detail, you have here a situation with a therapeutic context or indicator as urgent and clear-cut as can be imagined. The patient is in a state of extreme therapeutic need, and the intervention that I outlined would legitimately and therapeutically meet those needs and provide her the beginnings of a safe framework and hold, as well as cognitive insight and a much-needed implicit positive introject. Well, time is passing quickly. Let's hear this session out.

Therapist: Then she said something to the effect that her experience in pornographic films ended one crazy week when some director got her to do an orgy scene in a place not far from here.

Langs: She is still commenting on the altered framework: chaos and psychosis break loose; boundaries are destroyed; you are in the midst of an uncontrolled sexual situation, and in the presence of a supervisor; it's an orgy. The bipersonal field becomes a crazy space filled with pathological projective identifications, and filled with danger. There is clearly no sense of trust here. In fact, these are conditions under which no one can be trusted.

And I must add this: I very much hope that the fact that the derivatives have now moved directly into this neighborhood, and include personnel high in the echelon of this center, will convince everyone that these derivatives pertain unconsciously to the therapeutic situation and interaction. The level of fit and Type Two derivative validation is so striking. I guess a few skeptics would still say that she's anticipating a new job and talking about the old one. But that would be something of a farce: the old job was totally corrupt, while the new job is quite honest and untainted. The connections are thin and flat, and virtually meaningless. Organized around the adaptive context of the therapist's interventions, the material is not only convoluted, but also remarkably filled with coalescing derivatives that constitute an extended lecture on the implications of alterations in the framework.

Therapist: She said, People never learn, and she sarcastically offered to give me the address where the orgy scene took place, implying that they had a lot of orgies there. She was being quite sarcastic.

Langs: Yes, but recognize the implications for our understanding of the framework. As I said before, once you modify the frame, the patient no longer knows where the boundaries are to be drawn. You had promised her sound psychotherapy, but unfortunately the reality has turned out to be rather different. Any expectations she might have had that you would be a therapist, and nothing more or less, are now quite disappointed. You are willing to medicate her, expose her to a supervisor, and to reveal yourself. How is she to know how far you will go? Clearly, she wants to find out. She has every reason to wonder whether you are ready to go to bed with her, or to participate in other orgies. She can't be sure that this will all not lead to direct sexual acting out; and she must discover where the limits will be drawn.

Some of this, of course, comes from her own difficulties in establishing boundaries and her own unresolved, pathological wishes and conflicts, but much of it comes also from your problems in this area. And boundaries, limits, and controls are a serious part of her problem. A therapeutic situation in which none of these are secure greatly increases the risk of actual suicide in a patient of this kind.

So she might accept a sexual liaison with you; she may well be the type of patient who would permit her therapist to actually seduce her. On the other hand, there are many indications that she would also like to rectify this situation and that she is trying to give you the opportunity to do so. As you can see from this material, an actual seduction would be devastating and could easily precipitate a suicide attempt. The rectification of the frame would offer her the new beginning she so desperately needs.

Therapist: Well, she said that she had started to get so involved with the orgy that she lost contact with the outside world. She stayed in this place a long time and really felt that something disturbing was happening to her. And she just cut it all off after that weekend.

Discussant: There's some message here about getting ready to terminate her treatment, as a means of saving her sanity.

Langs: Yes, as a desperate or perhaps necessary framework deviation cure. The therapist's deviations are unconsciously experienced as an attempt to drive the patient crazy, an important theme that Searles (1959) has so nicely illuminated. And I must say that we are remarkably fortunate to have this patient as a final presentation of the consequences of modifying the frame; there are so many alterations here, and she is so remarkably perceptive and expressive in response to them. One can sense that she was exposed to experiences of this kind quite early in life, and probably throughout her childhood. They relate to the etiology of her illness, and she vividly, though indirectly, describes how this therapeutic situation, rather than offering her a chance for adaptive change and cure, has become a chaotic and psychotic repetition of the earlier traumas. Of course we have almost no genetic data with which to validate that point, but under these conditions little genetic material would be available. Once the frame has been stabilized and rectified, all of that will likely emerge.

She's also telling you something about Type C barriers in the form of psychoanalytic clichés. You tried to tell her earlier that she had her depression because of some kind of separation anxiety, and we now learn that the suicidal depression actually was an effort to deal with a panic-like, regressive, psychotic state. We learned too that it is the result of the deterioration of her capacity to maintain contact with reality, and that it took place under conditions of utter chaos and lack of boundaries, and in the presence of demeaning, abusive people. And she concludes this description with another allusion to rectification: let's stop the whole mess. And yes, she might well leave therapy if you don't soon get the message. And you can see that you don't have to introduce anything on your own. She gives you all of the unconscious meanings and functions that you need, and the directive for rectification as well.

Discussant: I got the image of her being overwhelmed, and sensed the dread of overdosage.

Langs: Yes, but that too is a way of describing these deviant interventions: they're overloading the patient; they have created a disorganized and psychotic—in its loose sense—therapeutic situation. It tells you something of how alterations in the framework can lead to psychotic episodes, and it makes clear that it would not occur in a secure therapeutic situation.

Therapist: She said, Well, that's really all I have to say about it. And she meant it, because she then fell silent. This led to my last intervention, in which I pointed out to her the blandness with which she related the episode.

Langs: I'm sorry to say it, but that's really tragic. She will be so hurt, so crushed, and so disillusioned. Not only are you critical, but you show a remarkable incapacity to understand any of the unconscious implications of this material—and it's so rich in meaning and perceptiveness, and so much more. I must also say that I see your intervention as a projection—it is you who are bland, far more than her.

Therapist: Well, now that I appreciate the implications of what she has said, I must agree with you: there's something really empty about that comment.

Discussant: I hear it too as a refusal to contain the intense meaning in this material. I for one experienced nothing bland about what the patient had said.

Therapist: I just felt that there was a lack of appropriate affect.

Langs: That may be, but there was nevertheless a great deal in what she had to say.

Therapist: She said, Well, I talked with my roommate about it and she said that I shouldn't be depressed about it. So I'm not going to. I thought that I should tell you about it, but I'm not going to get all upset about it.

Langs: Now she becomes bland and defensive. She accepts the Type C barrier and I suspect she will soon feel quite desperate. I don't see how she'll be able to contain her reactions to this session. Let's hear just the beginning of the next hour.

Therapist: She came in, and she was furious. She didn't want to talk to me. So I asked her what she was thinking.

Langs: Well, you can see her response. She's in a rage and there's no sense talking. Unfortunately, I see that our time is up.

Therapist: I'll just say that she did express a tremendous amount of rage in the next hour, and I realized now that much of it was directed at me. I'm sorry there isn't time to go into it in more detail, but as I look it over I can tell you that a lot of your formulations in this session were validated.

Langs: Well, I think at this point it would only verify the formulations that we have already made, and while I'm sure it would be quite interesting and, I suspect, quite convincing, I believe that we have learned a great deal from both this patient and yourself, and I can only express again my appreciation for the attitude with which you have presented this very difficult material. Unfortunately, given our schedule, we will not be able to continue with this presentation next week. Instead we will be hearing from a guest presenter. It will be his intention to offer some clinical material in which rectification of the frame was a factor. Thank you once again.

Chapter Thirteen

RECTIFYING THE FRAME

Langs: For our two last meetings on the framework, we have a guest who plans to present patients being seen in private psychotherapy with whom some effort was made to rectify the framework. This will give us an opportunity to study the influence of such technical measures and to review other aspects of technique related to the establishment and management of the ground rules. Since I have already introduced our guest, I'll ask him to start right in.

Therapist: Thank you. It's a pleasure to be here and I am anticipating a most stimulating response from all of you, including Dr. Langs. I will begin by presenting some material from a patient I will call Sidney, whom I have been seeing in once-weekly psychotherapy for a little over a year. I must mention as background, however, that some years back I saw Sidney, his brother, his two sisters, and his parents in family therapy on and off over an extended period of time, and that one of his sisters was in once-weekly psychotherapy with me a few years ago for about a year.

In the past few months, much of it under the influence of my work with Dr. Langs, I have been attempting to clarify the ground rules and secure the framework, as best I can. In this connection I should mention that my office is in a large hospital complex, situated in a psychiatric outpatient department where I am the director. In recent months I have been able to stop all interruptions, such as people knocking at my door or telephone calls. In the past, I would briefly respond to these people while in session with patients in therapy—something I now see as having created considerable chaos with my patients.

In any case, with Sidney there had been in addition a number of other opportunities to secure the frame. For example, I had been accepting telephone calls from his parents, who would contact me from time to time to complain about one or another of his symptoms and to ask about his treatment. Basing myself on a good deal of material from the patient, I was able to interpret some of his feelings about these contacts and indicated that I would no longer accept such calls, that all communications with me had to be funneled through Sidney alone. At other times there were hints that one or another of his siblings might want to see me in therapy, and I was able—again based almost entirely on material from the patient—to make clear that I would not at any time ever again see any other family member in therapy; I was to be Sidney's therapist only, as far as this family was concerned.

I must say that, in general, while he at first denied any concern about these arrangements as they had existed when I first started to tighten things up, his indirect communications revealed to me that unconsciously they had many meanings for him that I had never realized. I very much suspect that he had not communicated many of these derivatives under the conditions that had prevailed, and that only as he recognized that I clearly meant to secure the treatment situation did he begin to trust me enough to tell me some of these things—most of them in derivative form. In addition, he began to function both socially and on his job in ways that he had been incapable of in the past. It was really quite a remarkable experience for me, since I really had done very little in the way of interpreting, and yet his response was so strong.

The situation had been quite complicated, and far more messy than I had realized. As I had begun to actively work these areas over, rectifying and interpreting as I could, his associations led him to another young man, a year or two older than himself, whom I had also seen in therapy and with whom the patient had had homosexual experiences. It became clear that, quite unconsciously, Sidney felt I was attempting to protect myself from homosexual feelings and fantasies toward him through the presence of other people at the clinic, and by maintaining at least telephone contact with his parents. All of this was quite surprising to me, since, as I have said, there had never been any material of this kind until I had begun to undertake these clarifying and rectifying measures.

Discussant: If I may ask a question, how do you find having your office in a hospital influences the framework?

Langs: Good question. Though I knew of your clinic office, I must say I didn't know it was not entirely separate and private.

Therapist: Well, I must say that I have discussed this particular matter with Dr. Langs many times. I find that it keeps cropping up in the material from my patients, almost always indirectly, and that I have a difficult time in interpreting the patient's unconscious perceptions and fantasies in response to those arrangements. In all honesty, now that I have seen some of the ramifications of these arrangements, I would prefer to have a private office all my own in a professional building. It becomes a matter of finances, but I can assure you that I'm working toward that goal.

Langs: Any good question should receive some type of answer from a presentation that is relevant to the issue raised. Perhaps, then, it will be possible to listen to the material that will be presented to us for the patient's commentaries on this particular office arrangement. Hopefully, it will provide you a definitive answer, though much will depend on whether something in the therapeutic interaction has brought this issue to the fore. Modifications in the framework in which the therapist has a personal investment tend to evoke highly disguised reactions from patients, except when a relevant issue is stirring. So, we'll keep this question in mind as we proceed.

Therapist: To briefly summarize the sessions prior to the one on which I will focus, the patient began this hour by saying he hated to talk about his sister (the one I had treated individually), since he felt it was a waste of time. However, she had threatened suicide because her fiancé had criticized her and she felt no one could help her. Her mother had said that his sister was fine and the patient had then seen her. She told him a dream in which her leg is injured and bleeding; she turns to her mother, who walks away. The patient felt depressed, and later, when his parents fought with each other, he felt quite helpless. He recalled times when his father would not allow him to help in the business that he ran.

Here I intervened and suggested that the patient had been counseling his sister. In the dream, someone is not being helped. I mentioned that his sister had been in treatment with me and suggested that the dream must have some implications regarding his own therapy. The image of someone not getting help could relate to treatment. In addition, after the patient had talked to his sister, I noted that he had become depressed. He also said something about being unable to help his mother and father, and recalled his father not allowing him to help him. Similarly, with his sister he had also been in a helping situation and ended up feeling inadequate and helpless.

The patient agreed with me that he had been counseling his sister, and he said that he thought he deserved a handsome fee. He remembered a time at supper when he started to wheeze at the dinner table and left for a moment. When he returned, his sister had been given the steak that he wanted, and his parents ignored his protests—they thought he had finished dinner. In the next session . . .

Langs: Well, since this material is familiar to me, I won't comment, though I would welcome brief comments from the group.

Discussant: Well, if I try to listen to this material in terms of previous modifications in the framework, the one point that strikes me most is the fact that this therapist treated this patient's family, his sister in particular, before treating the patient individually. I'm not entirely clear, but it seems to me that the patient is working over some implications of this arrangement. I hear something that relates to a denial that it can create difficulties, and the main theme seems to be that it interferes with the therapist's ability to help the patient and, I might add, with the patient's ability to help the therapist. The patient seems to reverse it in that way, and maybe he's saying that within an altered frame the patient's unconscious therapeutic efforts are also destroyed.

Langs: That's an interesting point. When you apply the me/not-me interface to this material in the adaptive context of the initial lack of a one-to-one relationship—as well as of impairments in the therapist's neutrality, anonymity, and total confidentiality—this material has a powerfully depressing and negative tone. The patient is saying that under these conditions treatment could end in disaster; there is an absence of any helping, holding figure. In genetic terms, the patient experiences the therapist as relatively unavailable and insensitive, much as his mother had been in his childhood—and his father as well.

But your point about how the patient's unconscious curative efforts toward the therapist are also damaged when the frame is modified is well taken. Of course, we do not know the specific adaptive context for this session, and it may well be that the therapist had failed to heed some unconscious curative effort on the part of the patient in the last hour. Still, it is quite legitimate to offer, as a silent hypothesis, the suggestion that this material contains derivatives related both to modifications in the framework and to the need for rectification. Your point is, of course, a variation on the observation that an altered frame creates a poor hold for patient and therapist, and disturbs the communicative properties of the bipersonal field. It follows that curative efforts by either, whether conscious or unconscious, will be significantly impaired.

Discussant: I found the intervention a bit diffuse, if I may say so.

Therapist: Please be candid. If nothing else, I have been working for some time with Dr. Langs—I assure you I can take it. (Laughter.)

Discussant: Well, I felt that you were trying to say something about how your having seen his sister was interfering with his treatment, but somehow it didn't get defined.

Therapist: Yes, you remind me that in the previous session I had made a rather ineffectual intervention, which I think caused the patient to doubt—on some level—whether his unconscious therapeutic efforts on my behalf were being at all helpful.

Discussant: Perhaps we could view this along the me/not-me inter-face. Since the sister involved the patient in order to handle her own depression and suicidal feelings, could the patient not also be saying that he wonders if the presence of family members doesn't serve the therapist as a defense against some type of depressive constellation? And it perhaps serves the patient similarly.

Langs: Yes, alterations in the framework are often designed as an unconscious attempt at framework deviation cure of depressive symptoms. Anything else? (Pause.) Well, I'll add this: that last segment may well refer to some belief that in seeing the sister first the therapist favored her and gave her the good things that he—the patient—feels deprived of in his own individual therapy. It seems rather clear too that the specific deviation of modifying the one-to-one relationship creates a variety of images of competitiveness, rivalry, family competition, and the like, much of which has a realistic unconscious basis that would preclude interpretation without prior rectification. We could offer further comments on this session, but let's move on instead.

Therapist: He began this hour by saying that he had little on his mind, although he was glad to be at the session. He had begun to think about women sexually (and I must point out that this was new for him); also, he was masturbating less often. He wondered if he was responding to his mother's pressures since she kept insisting that he was doing much better of late—and this was true. On his job, he had a long talk with a young man who was working as his assistant teacher. He then described some homosexual fantasies about this man, such as being in bed with him and embracing him, but not having an orgasm. In his fantasy, this student needed help and the patient helped him sexually. However, he cut off the fantasy because he was afraid that he might imagine actual sexual contact.

He next described being with a friend who had also been a patient of mine. He reviewed in some detail the development of an overt homosexual relationship between the two of them when they were teenagers. The friend had been the aggressor at first, and the patient had eventually broken off the relationship, though he did reinitiate the sexual contact some time later. He recalled incidents where the friend had wanted him to hide his penis and resisted stimulation to the point of orgasm, but the patient had pressured him and they had performed mutual fellatio.

The patient felt relieved over having told all of this to me, and described how he would like now to go out with a woman. I intervened and pointed to the patient's daydream about the assistant teacher.

I noted that it did not reach closure and that the patient had prevented himself from imagining having an orgasm. I then pointed out that he went on to talk about women, fears of exposure, fears of being inadequate, and needing to cover up. I also commented that his friend—the one he had the homosexual experience with—had refused to look at his penis and had denied having an orgasm, emphasizing that here too there were qualities of hiding and secretiveness.

The patient said that the image of secrets stirred him up, and he then recalled a striking series of childhood secrets: finding his father's pictures of nude women and having an erection; not being able to undress in the locker room in high school in front of the other guys; having nocturnal emissions that his mother would tease him about and talk about in a way that humiliated him; being bathed by his mother well into his childhood; and experiencing intense fears of damaging himself when he first began to masturbate.

That ended the session, and I would suggest that you comment rather briefly on this session, because I see that I have one more introductory session before I get into the hour that I want to present.

Langs: Okay, let's try to focus on the framework. Will anyone comment?

Discussant: I was rather struck by the fact that the therapist had treated someone the patient had had homosexual experiences with. This may well imply that when the frame is altered, there is a sense of sexual seduction, and that in addition there is no telling how far matters will go. That is now a rather familiar theme when the frame is modified.

Langs: Yes, it seems to me that perhaps the most important lesson to derive from this material is that even in a situation where a patient is being seen in private therapy, associations emerge quite similar to those we saw in clinic patients. We must remember, of course, that this private patient is being seen on clinic premises, and must recognize that that could have its effect. But I can assure each of you that should you set up a private office in a professional building, and should you then significantly modify the framework in ways comparable to the deviations we heard with this patient, you too would hear similar material with similar functional capacities.

Discussant: It seems to me now that the therapist's recognition that his treating the patient's sister had in some way created problems for the patient's therapy, even though it wasn't spelled out, may have reassured the patient that his privacy would be respected, at least at the present time. As a result there is a sense of rectification here, even though it is not clearly defined, and I see several trends that follow. For one, the patient himself seems less homosexually involved with the therapist, and seems to have been more involved in this way previously, when the framework was poorly defined and open. That seems to be the basis for his interest in women, at least as far as I can tell. On the other hand, he's still having homosexual fantasies about the assistant teacher, so we have a mixed picture.

But the second trend I noticed is that the patient can now talk about his homosexual relationship involving someone his therapist had treated. He seems to feel a greater sense of trust and the communicative properties of the bipersonal field appear greatly improved, perhaps mainly because of the implied rectification I just referred to.

Discussant: There's this whole business of not reaching orgasm which keeps appearing. To my mind, this could be a reference to the clinic-office arrangement, and perhaps a commentary by the patient that under such conditions the therapeutic work cannot be brought to total fruition.

Langs: Yes, I entertained a similar silent hypothesis, but we must both remember that it is in need of validation. It's quite legitimate to take the office arrangement as a background adaptive context for this material and to recognize that the patient may be making some derivative comments about it. To complete the silent hypothesis, I could suggest that it creates a mixed therapeutic setting: on the one hand, the remainder of the frame is secure, and this provides an opportunity for conflict resolution and, for this patient, heterosexuality; on the other hand, it creates a situation in which total fulfillment is not possible, mainly because of the presence of clinic personnel who are seen unconsciously as serving as a deviation-based defense against the underlying homosexual conflicts and fantasies of both patient and therapist. There is also something about the arrangement that gratifies the unconscious homosexuality of both participants and that disturbs the field a bit even at a point when its communicative properties are considerably improved.

Perhaps the clearest derivative related to the clinic arrangement is the patient's fear of exposure and his need to cover up—as I understand it, the patient waits for the therapist in a waiting room shared by other private patients and clinic patients as well.

Therapist: Yes, I have thought of doing something about that, but have not been able to effect any change in that respect.

Langs: So, in some derivative way, the patient does represent the office arrangement, and this lends some Type Two derivative support to the silent hypothesis that this material is a commentary on the therapist's location—though in a way that would not for the moment lend itself to intervening, since the link to the therapeutic situation has been obliterated. Notice too that most of his childhood secrets center on exhibitionism and voyeurism, on fears of being humiliated, and concerns about being damaged—additional commentaries regarding the patient's feelings about the exposure in the clinic waiting room. In addition, looked at along the me/not-me interface, these associations constitute an unconscious interpretation of some of the anxieties and fantasies that the patient sees as prompting the therapist to maintain an office under such conditions. It would be essential to treat this material from his early childhood in terms of the prevailing adaptive contexts, and as containing both unconscious perceptions and fantasies related to those contexts; it would be an error to attempt isolated reconstructions on this basis, and to ignore the current functional capacity of this material in light of the ongoing therapeutic interaction.

In all, then, this material is a commentary on the therapist's efforts to secure the framework, on those aspects that remain as yet unfinished business, and on the implications unconsciously for both patient and therapist. I would propose that it is the rectification of the frame that offers the patient the possibility of becoming heterosexual, and of having an openly communicative bipersonal field in which he can analyze his own homosexual constellation, without having the opportunity to conceal it within the homosexual problems of the therapist. The patient distinctly welcomes these developments, though he also showed some anxiety, as might be expected. Still, the sense of rectification has created a field in which the psychopathology of the patient seems considerably more focused, and that of the therapist less so. The patient seems to feel less seduced by the therapist, though that sense still exists to some degree because of the office location, and he seems to be increasingly aware of his own seductive tendencies and the related conflicts.

This material displays many of the same dramatic qualities we have seen with clinic patients when major alterations in the framework have occurred. The difference, it seems to me, lies in the nature of the adaptive context and the functional capacity of the derivative network. With the patients presented from the clinic, with whom no rectification was attempted, the adaptive context consistently entailed deviations in the frame, and the material organized around unconscious perceptions and introjections of the implications of the altered frame. There was a sense of regression and disorganization, what I have termed a *non-therapeutic regression,* that alternated with manic-like efforts to create Type C barriers and defensive flights.

Here, I trust, you sense the difference in the quality of this material and its functional capacity. Unfortunately, we do not have a totally secured framework; we do, however, have one that has been rectified to a significant degree. The instinctual drive derivatives reflect this transversal and mixed quality, and you can sense that its functional capacity involves that aspect of the framework that remains unrectified, along with the initiation of expressions of the patient's own intrapsychic conflicts and pathological fantasies, memories, and introjects. There is a sense of improvement that lacks the brittle, empty, manic-like qualities that we saw with clinic patients, and the material is rich in analyzable derivatives that pertain to the patient's inner problems, as well as to the unresolved frame issues. We are seeing, then, a *therapeutic regression,* and it should prove quite analyzable.

In all, it is not a matter of material per se, but its implication around the specific prevailing adaptive context, its functional capacities, and the manner in which it serves as a commentary on the ongoing therapeutic interaction. Incidentally, to establish the term, I would call the symptom relief derived from establishing, securing or rectifying the frame a *framework rectification cure*—it is far more constructive than the momentary relief seen with framework deviation cures.

Therapist: I must say that in many ways the framework is now quite secure compared to how it was even three months earlier. Then there were many interruptions and leaks to the parents, and my efforts at interpretation were far more inadequate than those that I have just described. I am well aware, however, that even my present efforts are not as clear and definitive as they might be. Still, I think it's important for the group to appreciate the extent to which this frame has been rectified, both implicitly and explicitly. There followed a striking improvement in this patient, which had emerged slowly over a number of weeks, and which now began to take on fairly stable qualities.

To continue: In the next session, the patient began by describing his discomfort in the waiting room; he felt that there were too many sick people around. He had felt better after the previous session and described how well he was doing at work, where he was receiving positive feedback and anticipated a promotion. He was now worried about leaving his job and going through a farewell party, during which he might break down emotionally. Even the principal of the school had praised him, but he had then had some homosexual thoughts about him. He spoke in some detail about whether he should leave the school and seek a more advanced position elsewhere, or should remain and await a promotion.

I intervened here and pointed out that the patient had said he felt strange and uptight in the waiting room and that this was connected to some ambivalence regarding change and to his concern about public exposure. I told him too that there seemed to be various meanings to the themes he was talking about. The patient responded that he had no thought of leaving treatment, if that's what I meant. He then spoke again in some detail about leaving his job, and about becoming too tearful and upset at a farewell party. He remembered that his mother once attended the funeral of a near stranger; she had made a fool of herself by carrying on. He spoke about his sister's depression and described how sometimes he still gets a bit upset when he has to speak in front of his class. There's no place where he can cry—not at home, not with friends, and not in treatment.

Here, I pointed out how the patient had now brought up his mother and sister, and that they somehow were connected to his facing a problem in changing jobs, speaking in public, and speaking freely. I said he seemed to feel similar problems here in therapy, where he's unable to cry. At this point he said that therapy had actually changed considerably. At first, he hated it and felt betrayed, but now it was working out well. The old way, I was a member of the family, but now he felt safer and could talk and feel secure—as just a moment ago, when I had not answered the telephone when it rang. He still felt afraid of revealing himself, but wondered if I had induced that and he had then taken it outside. I commented that there could be a kernel of truth in his last thought, and he went on to talk more about the differences that he had picked up in my work. He then detailed several ways in which he felt considerably better. When he's anxious, his hand shakes, but he controls this now with strangers; still, he feels it's keeping up a facade. He's two people living in a shell: one part is a stranger, but competent and liked, and now top dog and interested in women, and doing well; while the other part is a little boy under the covers, masturbating and afraid of exposure.

Here I pointed out that he had referred to my involvement with his family, and had then mentioned exposure and having two parts to himself: one strong and the other immature. I told him that I felt he was referring to therapy, and that he was now feeling better and safer and revealing more because of the strong side, and that the immature side was related to my previous involvement with his family, especially his sister, which had been quite inappropriate. He responded by saying that he had stopped going to pornographic movies of late, and no longer frequented the back rooms of pornographic shops where he used to masturbate. He no longer needed them because he now had a sense of privacy in treatment. That's the end of that session.

Langs: Well, there's a great deal there; what more can we say about the framework in the light of this material?

Discussant: As I have been listening, I have been trying to find models of rectification. I haven't seen them too clearly. In the first session, there was a weak reference to not taking away his meal—his appropriate therapy. In the second session, there was the patient's struggle against homosexuality, in which he seemed to indicate fairly clearly that the homosexual relationship should be brought under control and stopped. I had wondered if this was a representation of the therapist, who was seeing other family members and, unconsciously, as the patient sees it, was involved in some type of unconscious sexuality.

Langs: Yes, I too have been listening for a clear-cut directive toward rectification. I think those you have mentioned are well stated, and I might add in this context the patient's control of his own homosexual fantasies and impulses. These might have been offered as a model to the therapist, and might well relate to rectifying the frame. I would agree, however, that for the moment the models of rectification here are quite weak and inferential. And I think that is partly because many aspects of the framework have already been rectified and the patient is mainly working over the aftereffects of the previous arrangements. In addition, the unrectified aspect of the framework is one in which, as I have noted, the therapist has a vested interest, possibly even a blind spot. In any case, as is typical with vested interest deviations, the patient seems to be working it over through well-disguised derivatives. However, it is here, in his representations of the fact that the therapist's office is in a public clinic, that he tended to imply the need for rectification: a father should not possess pictures of nude women or at least should not keep them in a place where his young son could find them; his nocturnal emissions should not be the subject of humiliating comments from his mother; and he should not have been bathed by his mother well into latency. Still, these are less dramatic derivatives of the patient's unconscious awareness of the need for rectification than we saw earlier, in presentations where the frame had constantly been altered and the patient was working over multiple existing modifications of many aspects of the framework.

Disregarding, for the moment, the single issue relating to the fixed frame—the patient's use of the clinic waiting room—we can see that the more fluid framework qualities of the therapist's interventions have involved him in efforts at interpreting; he is no longer making use of noninterpretive interventions. As I said earlier in this course, we should think of three levels and types of alterations in the framework: (1) *interpretive errors*; (2) *noninterpretive interventions unrelated to the fixed frame*; and (3) *interventions which modify the fixed aspects of the framework*. As you may remember, I suggested that the patient will have the most powerful responses to the last group of deviations, and that under those circumstances they will most clearly represent the adaptive context and communicate coalescing derivatives.

In the first situation, which characterizes much of this therapist's present work, the adaptive context will tend to be poorly represented, and though the derivatives may well coalesce they will be somewhat more difficult to decipher as compared to situations in which fixed frame alterations are involved. In situations in which the therapist intervenes noninterpretively, with so-called supportive measures, directives, self-revelations, and the like—interventions which as a rule significantly modify his neutrality and anonymity—you will find an intermediate response: a tendency to represent the adaptive context, though not as clearly as when the fixed frame is altered, and the likelihood that the patient will produce a meaningful coalescing derivative network—though again it generally will not be as clear as when the stable aspects of the framework have been modified.

Certainly this material supports my way of classifying alterations. Understanding the principles involved will enable you to anticipate the material from the patient, and should facilitate your capacity to intervene. In this respect, when you have intervened interpretively but erroneously, in the main there will be two courses you can follow, though with notable exceptions. First, you can play back selected derivatives around the unmentioned adaptive context, hoping that the patient will then work it over more specifically; second, you can let the error pass if the adaptive context is represented in highly disguised fashion and if, in addition, the derivative network does not seem to coalesce. Here the most therapeutic measure is an understanding of the patient's unconscious perceptions of, and interpretations about, your erroneous intervention, and an *implicit* demonstration of your capacity to benefit from these efforts by making your next intervention—whatever it may be—a correct one based on the patient's subsequent associations.

In the presence of nonneutral or noninterpretive interventions there is a greater need to specifically work over and work through, and to interpret the patient's unconscious responses. We should be more inclined to intervene, even if only by playing back selected derivatives around an unmentioned adaptive context. Certainly, in those situations in which the context is clearly represented with a link to the therapist, you would offer the best possible interpretation available from the material—first in terms of unconscious perceptions, and only then of unconscious fantasies.

Finally, when you have modified the fixed aspects of the framework, the patient will experience a powerful need for an intervention, and one should be made if at all possible in the subsequent session. Often the adaptive context—the deviation—will be represented directly or with relatively little disguise, and with the link to the therapist intact. Under these conditions an interpretation is feasible, and as a rule it can be based on a meaningful, coalescing derivative network of unconscious perceptions and responsive fantasies. When no clear-cut representation of the adaptive context is available, there are usually very powerful derivatives that can be played back to the patient to help him recognize the central adaptive context and carry out further working through.

Discussant: In this last session I heard a clearer communication related to the need to rectify the frame. I feel it came up because the patient had, in the terms you just gave us, represented the adaptive context, which is the deviation related to the location of the therapist's office, quite directly—the patient described his discomfort in the waiting room. To me this meant that the patient was now working over this deviation rather intensely, largely because of the work that had been done to rectify and interpret around the framework in the previous two sessions. What I am referring to came up at the end of the session, when the patient said that he had stopped going to pornographic movies and shops because he now had privacy in treatment. To the extent that the relatively public waiting room unnecessarily exposes this patient and detracts from his sense of privacy in therapy, he seems to be saying quite clearly that this is an inappropriate arrangement and that he should be given a therapeutic setting in which total privacy can prevail.

Discussant: It seems to me that this lack of privacy was, according to the patient, interfering with his having a therapy situation in which he could freely communicate and express himself.

Langs: Yes, I don't think we heard from any of the clinic patients as intense a plea for a Type A field as we hear from this patient—his wish for a protected play space in which illusion, symbolic language, and feelings can be communicated. This is crystallized in his longing for a place to cry. And I think that the contrast exists because clinic patients know that their therapeutic bipersonal fields will forever be compromised, while a private patient has some hope that the therapist might recognize the consequences of even the smallest alteration in the framework, and can rectify the situation by moving to a private setting.

Therapist: The patient began this last hour by describing his discomfort in the waiting room. Would you take that as what you term Type Two derivative validation of your formulations, based on the previous hour, that this was, indeed, something that was disturbing him and that he was working over?

Langs: Yes, especially because it appears at the beginning of the session. It rather directly validates my silent hypothesis and serves admirably as a means of organizing the subsequent material in this particular session.

Since we would like to hear the main session that our guest therapist wishes to present, allow me to close off this part of our discussion by making a few additional comments on this last segment. In the adaptive context of the office arrangement and of the recent rectifications of the framework—actualized when the therapist did not answer his telephone—we see a distinct mixture of positive and negative communications. I would link the positive side to the rectified frame, and the negative side to the remaining deviation.

And as you can see, the therapist's efforts to interpret the patient's unconscious perceptions and fantasies about the waiting room evoked a distinctly mixed response. The reference to the funeral may allude to the deadness of the therapeutic space under these conditions, and the allusion to his sister's depression and his anxiety when he has to speak in front of the class can also be easily related to the office arrangements. The patient is implying something about his own sadness and anxiety under these conditions, as well as the therapist's need to defend himself against separation, loss, depression, and anxiety by maintaining his office in the clinic setting. The patient concludes that this deprives him of a truly therapeutic field or space, something that is quite to the point since this aspect of the framework has not been rectified. This shows us that interpretations have a limited effect in the absence of rectification, and that they do not resolve a disturbed therapeutic situation—findings you would readily anticipate given the principles we have developed.

Matters seem quite different when the patient and the therapist deal with the therapist's previous contacts with the family and the sister. Here, rectification had been effected, and the patient was able to communicate some of his conscious impressions about the earlier and the later circumstances. He then quite perceptively portrays his unconscious perception of the therapist—and, I would add, of himself, though secondarily under these conditions—as divided: doing well on one level, still afraid of exposure and overstimulated sexually on the other. This refers first of all to the two images of the therapist: one based on his earlier contacts with the patient's family—unconsciously gratifying sexually, a situation of exposure for all concerned—and another based on his recent treatment of the patient in a relatively secured framework—a sign of confidence and of resolution of underlying homosexual problems. Secondly, it is a reflection of a divided image of the therapist who secures the framework in many areas, but fails to do so completely.

Still, the material to this point indicates that there can be many positive and therapeutic consequences to a therapeutic situation in which the frame is almost fully secured, to the point where the patient at the very least has some sense of confidentiality and privacy, and is no longer exposed to additional alterations in the fixed framework and to noninterpretive interventions. Along the me/not-me interface, the patient is telling us that this represents the therapist's capacity to control his unconscious sexual conflicts and fantasies, to better manage his own inner state, and to better hold the patient in a noninstinctualized manner—all that about the therapist. In addition, it provides the patient a setting in which he feels more secure, far better able to manage himself, and has far less need to live out his unconscious perceptions of the therapist as elaborated by his own unconscious fantasies and pathological needs—his attendance at pornographic movies and shops, and his masturbatory practices.

This material is really quite rich, which is another tribute to the importance of the framework and the even greater importance of its rectification as this effects the communicative properties of the bipersonal field. We have had a series of sessions with rich and coalescing derivatives, filled with unconscious meaning in terms of the current therapeutic interaction and the relevant aspects of the patient's genetic experiences—especially as these pertain to his psychopathology. Recognize that in this material the patient was saying that the therapist, at a time when he saw the family and the sister, and when he saw the patient while maintaining contact with other family members, was inappropriately exposing the patient and using him for self-gratification—much of it unconsciously sexualized—in a manner similar on some level to the misuse of this patient by both his parents. We hear of his father having nude pictures, and of his mother bathing him, and humiliating him for having nocturnal emissions.

The image of the therapist in light of his alterations in the framework was, for this patient, quite identical to these aspects of his parents' behaviors. And so, the very soil upon which the patient's psychopathology developed was being repeated in the treatment situation, a primarily nontransference-countertransference interaction in which the pathogenic past was being repeated in actuality, rather than introduced through major distortions and displacements by the patient. On the other hand, with the frame largely rectified, the interface of the bipersonal field shifts more toward the patient's pathology and transference expressions—a thesis we should try to validate with the material of the next hour. Let's hear some fresh material.

Therapist: He began this session by talking about his difficulties in school, and how he has been procrastinating recently, unable to get into the schoolwork—he's taking graduate courses. He feels nonetheless that he's very work-oriented when he is with the seminar group members, and that's where he does all his work and thinking. Next, he thought about how his fantasies were shifting from having homosexual fantasies about strange men in pictures, men he doesn't know, to people now whom he does know. He can only embrace them if he has fantasies about them, and a lot of it still revolves around men, but from time to time he's beginning to have fantasies about women.

Then he gets into a long story about work, about looking for a job. And how, when he went for an appointment, it was just so great. He felt so in charge of things. And he goes on about how in the past he would have been nervous and worried about it, but not this time. And then he tells me about one job in Englewood. And he talks for a while about the two or three interviews he's gone to, all where he felt in charge. And he says that trains don't frighten him any more, and he feels really great.

He then says, You know, I'm a little troubled by something. I really was disappointed: the Englewood job didn't come through. They took a guy with a lot more experience than me. He says, You know that's the fellow I told you about a while ago. (This was a fellow he met right at the end of his student teaching, with whom he was very friendly. He was Sidney's last supervisor, and had then taken a job in Atlanta.) And he says, You know, I had some homosexual thoughts about him. He was a very nice guy. Well, he called me about a month ago, and said, You know, I'm coming back to the city; I want to live in the city, and I hear the Englewood job is open. But I understand that you work there. (He works there one day a week.) And are you trying for it? So Sidney said, Yes. And he said, All right, I'll look for another job, and hung up.

So later Sidney found out that the fellow got the job. The fellow is older and has a lot more experience than Sidney. So Sidney says, I can understand why he got the job, but it doesn't feel right. You know, it's like I've been betrayed. I spoke to a friend of mine and he said, Look, Sidney, don't get upset. It wasn't nice, but that is the best job around and it's a lot of money, and this guy is married—maybe he couldn't get anything else.

He kind of ruminated for a moment or two and said, All right, so anyway I don't have to leave. Now I don't have to leave the area; I have many friends, so it's not so terrible. And then he says, You know, there was a job available in my old neighborhood. I went for it and had a great interview, and met some people I had known. Then he shifts and says, Before the session I spoke to my father and he was very helpful. We went over money and Father is a good businessman; he talked to me about the kind of salary I should ask for. But then when I got home after the interview, my father didn't even greet me; he wasn't even interested. He asked only about the money and then ignored me. Sometimes he's on and sometimes he's off.

When I told my mother about the job in Englewood, she put me down and said I wasn't good enough for it. In a way, she was right. I haven't done much at work in the last month or so, especially now that I'm looking for another job. Still, I wonder why she had to say it. I have to rely on her more than on my father, because he's just not around. I've always been closer to her, whatever that has to do with the homosexuality. My sisters both say that my mother has a big mouth. Even if I got the job in Englewood or a big raise, she'd just tell me that I'm eating too much.

He says, When I got home and discussed money with my father, he asked about your bills. For two or three months now, he said, the man hasn't billed you. And I told him, Look father, I've been paying myself. Sidney went on: I really feel the cord's been broken. Wow! This is really some session. We got into a lot last week, and I never thought we'd get into all that stuff, and now this is an important session too, and it's remarkable: the difference between a year ago and now. I'm getting into a lot more stuff and it's fantastic.

I'm troubled by something, though, he went on. I feel so much is going on here, and yet I don't get into it during the week. I don't think about the session. I used to plan to tell you things, but now I just come in and lean back and it comes out, and that's really great.

He says, You know, when I was in graduate school, I had a friend who was in treatment. And he liked it and felt he was getting better, and I asked him how he knew that things were going well. And his answer was that things just happen, you can't go over it intellectually. Things happen and suddenly you feel better. And that's like what I feel here.

And that's how the session ended. I hadn't intervened.

Langs: Any comments?

Discussant: I found a lot of this session rather boring, and began to wonder if we were observing a Type C field.

Langs: Could you identify any factor in that development?

Discussant: I thought about the unrectified part of the frame, but that silent hypothesis didn't hold up because the patient got around to describing another part of the frame that was rectified—he's taken over responsibility for paying for his sessions.

Langs: Yes, where does that take you? (Pause.) Well, it would follow that this session is, in the main, a response to the further securing of the framework.

Therapist: At the time, I felt that he had become defensive in response to the revelation of the sexual material related to his friend whom I had had in treatment. I had really missed the reference to his having taken over payment for the session; it was the first that I had heard of it. He has either paid me in cash or with his own check drawn against funds that his father gave him, so I had no way of knowing.

Langs: Yes, I am glad once again to hear an alternative hypothesis. Many therapists would think of this almost entirely on an intrapsychic basis, without any thought of the framework: the patient had gotten into material heavily laden with instinctual drives and conflict, and now becomes defensive. And undoubtedly, there is some truth to that and it will be a factor in creating a Type C field from time to time. But in my experience it is seldom the sole factor, and there are usually either some interactional factors or, as here, something related to the framework; otherwise we would have a Type A field with ultimately analyzable resistances.

Discussant: Would you take his looking for a new and better job an expression of his wish for a better therapeutic situation?

Langs: Yes, and a reflection as well of his unconscious and even conscious awareness of the improvement of the actual conditions of his therapy. Under these circumstances, his own homosexual pathology begins to emerge more clearly; it is no longer concealed within the therapist's own unconscious homosexual countertransferences.

It is here that the two silent hypotheses would come together: The field has been further secured, and material is now emerging that centers around the patient's psychopathology, rather than that of the therapist. As I said, there has been a shift in the interface of the bipersonal field. This is the development of what I have termed a *therapeutic regression* (Langs 1976a, c), an approach to the underlying psychopathology of the patient and, especially, to the psychotic part of his personality. And while the patient will welcome it on the one hand, he is understandably quite fearful of it on the other—which accounts for the defensive rumination and the anxiety over betrayal and harm.

Remember, once a previously modified framework is secured, or if you offer a steady frame from the outset, the patient will have a mixed reaction: unconsciously, he will welcome the opportunity for an insightful resolution of his emotional problems; but in addition, since that will entail the exposure of the most disturbed parts of his inner world, he will react too with considerable dread and show a need for defensiveness. Quite early in this course I indicated that the secure hold from a therapist must be distinguished from the maternal hold. And it is in the area I am now discussing that this difference is most striking. The maternal hold is protective and directly growth-promoting; by contrast, the therapeutic hold, while protective, must promote growth circuitously, by creating conditions under which the patient will regress and expose the sources of his psychopathology. It's a mixed blessing and will evoke a mixed response. You can see that in this session: defensiveness, fleeting allusions to homosexual difficulties, a specific reference to a rectification in the framework, gratification because the pathological symbiotic tie has been broken and hopefully resolved, and many positive feelings and anticipations.

Discussant: Isn't his decision to pay for his own treatment a model of rectification?

Langs: Yes, it is rectification itself. But remember, it is an interactional product: it stems not only from an increase in strength within the patient, but also from a therapist who has proven himself capable of rectifying the frame, thereby serving as a positive introject. The patient has broken his pathological tie to his parents, but this happened only because the therapist himself had proven capable of a comparable resolution. It all began when he gave up his contact with the patient's family. And just think about it: All of this tells you about some of the unconscious functions of family treatment and of contact between a therapist and the parents of a patient. Whatever the rationalization, this patient is stating that, unconsciously, such contact serves to protect the therapist—and the patient—against sexual conflicts and fantasies, as well as to gratify his pathological oral-dependent, symbiotic needs. And the patient is showing you that under such conditions true independence and conflict resolution is impossible; true freedom cannot be achieved. Rectify those conditions and it all becomes possible.

Discussant: Doesn't the sense of betrayal refer as well to the therapist's failure to completely secure this framework?

Langs: Yes, it certainly does. As long as the flaw remains, the patient will react to it. Nonetheless, his predominant response appears to be a reaction to having had the frame almost entirely secured, and it is that major thread that I have tried to trace out for the moment.

Now let's clarify a few more points. What is the adaptive context for this session?

Discussant: The therapist's interventions in the previous session?

Langs: Could you be more specific?

Discussant: Well, there were several attempts at interpretation which were somewhat successful, but also somewhat diffuse.

Discussant: There was also further rectification of the frame-work;the therapist implied that he would no longer see the patient's family and he did not answer the telephone when it rang in that hour.

Therapist: I thought of the adaptive context as the revelation of the sexual material about his former boyfriend who had been a patient of mine, but I now realize that that might have been a therapeutic context, and not an adaptive context.

Langs: In the broadest sense of the term, an adaptive context can arise from within the patient; I now term them *secondary contexts*. The primary context will stem from the therapist's interventions. Still, these are contrasting silent hypotheses, and it would be important to see how well each formulation fits with the material in this session. Any further thoughts?

Discussant: Well, he continues to get into the homosexual material at the beginning of the session, but then he shifts to heterosexuality and soon becomes quite defensive.

Langs: How would you formulate what's going on?

Discussant: I guess he's frightened of his homosexual fantasies and erects some Type C barriers.

Langs: Anything else?

Discussant: I think that we would want to tie this to the securing of the framework, and maybe to the part that remains altered, but I'm not sure how to do it.

Langs: Yes, let's do it both ways. First, in terms of the continued modification of the frame: the patient persists in unconsciously viewing it as a reflection of some type of unconscious homosexual counter-transference, and as both a defense against the underlying needs and a gratification of them. Exposure implies homosexuality to this patient, and we should view that as a transversal communication along the me/not-me interface. It alludes to both patient and therapist, and has valid components in addition to the distorted elements stemming from the patient.

In any case, the continued alteration in the framework does not entirely account for this material, particularly not for the emerging change in the nature of the patient's conscious sexual fantasies. I think that here we have to work around the adaptive context of the further securing of the framework, a context represented in the patient's revelation that he is now paying for treatment on his own.

So in light of the stabilization of the framework, the patient describes both his need for defensiveness and the safety he feels in the presence of a group. Having his family available to him, while fraught with destructive implications, also provided him a type of protection. But, with the frame relatively secure, we now learn quite clearly what the patient was attempting to defend against. It entailed his own psychopathology, his homosexual fantasies and conflicts, and his heterosexual conflicts and problems. Once again we see that with the frame relatively secured the interface of the bipersonal field shifts toward the pathology of the patient, and away from the counter-transferences of the therapist. We see here a therapeutic regression in which the patient is gaining access to his own psychopathology and is moving toward the psychotic part of his personality, the most disturbing aspects of his inner world. And while this will afford him an opportunity to explore, work through, and insightfully resolve the nature and sources of his homosexual problems, it may well be momentarily disorganizing and terribly anxiety provoking for him; and this can prompt a subsequent shift to Type C communication.

Therapist: Well, this is where I stand with Sidney for the moment. If there is time I would like to present a session with another patient.

Langs: Yes, we do have sufficient time. Any final comments about this first presentation? (Pause.) Well, I think we've learned a great deal from it, and I hope that it has given all of you a sense of the material from patients in a therapeutic situation in which the frame has been rectified, although, unfortunately, not completely secured. Let's hear about your other patient.

Therapist: Briefly, this is another young man I've been seeing in once-weekly psychotherapy, for about eight months now. He entered

treatment with fears that he might be crazy and with intense homosexual fantasies and anxieties. He had also been impotent with women.
This is a patient with whom I've had a great deal of difficulty. He
creates a lot of interactional pressure on me, and generates powerfully
disruptive projective identifications that I have had many problems in
handling—metabolizing.

For most of this treatment I did not realize that his parents were
paying for his treatment. One day approximately four months ago, I
looked at the check and he mentioned at that moment, probably out of
some self-consciousness, that his parents were paying for therapy. In
the next two or three weeks, he responded to some pressure on my part—
I wanted him to pay for his own treatment—by becoming extremely
antagonistic, and the therapeutic alliance really broke down during this
time. I backed off and the issue did not come up again until the session
preceding the one I will describe here, when he brought in the fact that
his mother had become very angry at him that he had spent fifty dollars
on veterinary fees for his new kitten when she was paying for treatment. I used that to again rather bluntly pressure him into paying for
his therapy with his own funds. As a result, during this session he
decided that his parents had been using their payment of his fee
throughout therapy to demean him and to demean the therapy, and he
made a decision that he would pay for his own treatment.

So next session he comes in and brings up the money issue right
away. His speech is pressured and he talks very quickly. He says, I'm
paying tonight and I really feel responsible. I had a dream. It has to do
with cats. (He has a cat and a dog at home.) In the dream I have these
cats, and a kitten is giving them trouble and I get rid of it. (He had
picked up a stray kitten, and it created a lot of trouble with the cat and
dog at home, and he was thinking of getting rid of it.) In the dream, he
buys a big cat. And his mother says to him, You got rid of the cat. He
says: She put it as if I were wrong and irresponsible. (Much of this was
quite vague.)

And he said, I got up, and when I was emerging from the dream, I
had this thought: I wished that when I went home for dinner and told
my mother that I got rid of the kitten, she would just say: See, you're
wrong, you're wrong, and I would then say to her, But I bought this
other cat and you're wrong. (That is, he would attack his mother
because she had made a statement that he was irresponsible, and this
didn't apply to him.)

And then he says, I've had this fantasy a long time about being a big brother. (He's single, and has often thought about being a father or an uncle.) And I always wondered how I would do it. Would I lose my temper? Then he describes how he's dating a girl who works as a teacher and how he went with her mother and one of her younger brothers to a baseball game, and felt like a big brother. And he describes what a great day he had, and how appreciative the boy was. Then he says, But this kid is surrounded by women and is growing up very effeminately. He needs a man and I think I'll take him out again. The mother said I was saving the boy's life and I hope that my girl-friend hears it because, you know me, I need approval.

Next he talks about work and says he's been doing a nice job at work lately. He works with plastics and has invented something that he plans to show his boss. It will improve production. He's made a couple of suggestions lately, and they've been picked up and have been very successful. He says, A lot more is getting done at the plant. But the boss doesn't smile at me and I'd like him to do that. He didn't say a word, and I like approval. I'll tell him about the invention and see what happens.

Then he begins to talk about a fellow at work that he's had some problems with. The boss was away and this guy was fucking off. And the patient says, I got very angry and was going to tell him off, but when I went over to him he offered me a Coke and I relaxed. I forgot about it. You know, I need more money. I'm paying more here and I got a raise last year, but it's not enough. I deserve a raise and I'm going to ask for it. Sometimes they offer you some merchandise rather than money, and I don't want that. Other guys have gotten raises and that upsets me because they keep it a secret.

I asked for a raise recently and the boss hasn't answered. I think I'll pressure him until I get an answer. I'm not going to be passive like my father. I'm doing so well, I should be one of the bosses there. They're all making a lot of money from my ideas, and I just work my balls off. I should have a piece of the business, but he'll never give it to me when I let myself be used like that. They get big vacations, and I keep working.

Here I made a comment. I said, There are a lot of images here about men fighting, and about money. He cut me off and said, Sure there's a lot about money; it's on my mind. I say, Images about fighting and men struggling, and money. And he cuts me right off again. He says, I know. I'm paying, and it's on my mind. It goes back to, like, I'm responsible. And then he kind of mumbles, And you're responsible to me. And he goes into that for a moment too. Then there's a long silence. So he's looking at me and I'm looking at him, and I didn't say a word. Then he said to me, Why aren't you talking? Why the heck, why the fuck are you so quiet? Say something! I've been talking all session and you don't say a word. You're just looking at me. He goes over that for a moment or two. And I said to him, It's interesting: you bring up the fact that this is the first session you're paying for, and this is the first time you've ever asked me a direct question.

Langs: Well, there's a good deal of material here, and since you intervened at this point let's pause for some discussion. Any comments?

Discussant: Well, the adaptive context appears to be the therapist's attempt to rectify the frame in the prior session. I wonder if you could tell us anything more about that session?

Therapist: Yes, as I presented this hour, I could recall considerably more. Briefly, he had described in the previous session how his mother kind of brought up the whole business of their paying for treatment, asking him how he can buy things and spend money when she and his father were paying for therapy. And it was in that session that he mentioned his dog and his cat, and several stray kittens, and getting rid of one of the kittens which he had been hitting, and somehow blaming his mother for his anger. He had taken that kitten for shots and everything, and his mother had resented the money he had spent on the kitten because they were paying for therapy. That really wiped him out, and in this context I had brought up the criticism of how he's spending his money; fairly directly, I suggested that he should be taking full responsibility for his sessions. I don't remember much of his response, except that he said that he knew he had to give it some thought, and then he said something about his having gotten his big cat in order to catch the mice in his apartment. That's about it.

Langs: Any comments?

Discussant: Well, in this preliminary session, his mother offers a model of rectification: she brings up the idea that he should be paying for his therapy, and not depending upon them.

Therapist: Yes, I realized after the session that I had missed that and that I had been rather abrupt. Instead, I could have done it all from the patient's associations.

Langs: Yes, that principle of technique still holds: The patient will offer you in direct or derivative form all you will need to rectify the frame. Here the derivatives were hardly disguised at all, and I would suspect that they emerge in this form because of other efforts on your part to secure the frame.

Therapist: Yes, I had been doing this with all my patients. While I was still having difficulty offering him good interpretations, I had stopped answering the telephone and interrupting his sessions, changing hours whenever he or I needed to, making noninterpretive interventions, and things like that.

Discussant: I'm not sure how it all ties together, but it seems clear that the material in that preliminary session included the day residue for the dream. For that reason the dream must have something to do with rectifying the frame. Maybe the message is that he's trading in a kitten for a grown cat, and that with the frame rectified he becomes a responsible man instead of a child dependent upon his parents and the therapist.

Therapist: Yes, I think you are right. This patient tends to express himself in a confusing way, but in the dream the kitten was replaced with a bigger cat. There was an image of greater effectiveness as well.

Discussant: I can see the theme of standing up for himself and being more effective running through all of this material; it comes up rather clearly in the work situation.

Langs: Yes. How would you view it as a commentary on the therapist's effort to rectify the frame?

Discussant: It offered the patient a chance to be a man.

Langs: Yes, though I would state it a little differently: The therapist's ability to secure the frame is introjected by the patient as reflecting a capacity to be strong and mature—to be an adult. The patient accepts the introject, and immediately feels a sense of strength himself—*a framework rectification cure.* In addition, the securing of the frame in and of itself provides the patient the secure hold that previously had been lacking, which in turn gives him the strength to stand up and go after the things he is entitled to—including, specifically, money. We must remember, however, that this frame remains somewhat modified since, as I understand it, the patient is being seen in the therapist's office in the clinic. How is that reflected in this material?

Therapist: Yes, I do see him in my office at the clinic.

Discussant: Well, I was wondering about that. The patient brings up an image of his mother as being very provocative and wrong. At first, I thought that had to do with the abrupt way that the therapist presented the rectification of the framework, and I still think there is some reflection of his approach in that material. But then it also may have to do with what the therapist is still doing wrong. I'm not clear, since the therapist also tells us that he has not been able to intervene correctly with this patient.

Langs: Yes, we have a limited amount of data, and these are all viable silent hypotheses that would have to be validated in subsequent sessions.

Discussant: I was impressed with the positive qualities of this material. With the clinic patients we have heard here, and in my own experience with these patients, I have seldom heard such positive images, especially on a sustained basis. When I hear something positive, it often sounds defensive and has a strong quality of denial. It also is rather restricted and thin, and doesn't get represented in the rich variety evident here.

Langs: Yes, while this frame is still not entirely secured, it is now appreciably more defined than it had been at any other time in treatment. And while the therapist did, indeed, approach the rectification of the framework in a rather abrupt and destructive manner, it nonetheless led the patient to take the necessary steps to become fully responsible for the cost of his therapy.

Now, the abruptness undoubtedly was on some level a repetition of the patient's mother's behavior, her harshness and destructiveness—an unconscious perception that is essentially in the realm of nontransference. On the other hand, notice that it was the mother who encouraged the patient to rectify the frame. On that basis the therapist's positive intervention was a different kind of repetition. It repeated in some form the constructive aspects of the mother's relationship with the patient. The positive unconscious perception and introject therefore iterated an earlier constructive experience between the patient and his mother—a positive aspect of a nontransference response.

And even though we are not studying the total therapeutic relationship at this time, I would like to stress that last point since we have seldom seen a positive introject and traced out its genetic elements. And such introjects have been rare not only because you are all in the process of learning how to intervene properly, but also because you are all working within significantly modified frameworks. Here is further evidence that securing the frame leads to strongly positive introjects with many meaningful and constructive behavioral consequences.

Now, intrapsychically, the rectification has also had a positive influence. Did anyone pick it up? (Pause.) Well, the patient says that boys who are surrounded by women become effeminate—have significant homosexual problems. And we know that he entered therapy with such difficulties himself and that his mother's involvement in paying for his treatment is represented in this segment of the material. We can therefore conclude that the modified framework would contribute to and perpetuate his homosexual difficulties, while the secure framework creates the conditions under which it can be analytically resolved. This is the spirit of the patient's comments about wanting to be a big brother: the therapist has been a big brother, and again, through a positive introjection and identification, the patient becomes stronger and more of a man. Certainly this would be only a preliminary step to the full exploration of the derivatives of his unconscious homosexual conflicts, but it is a crucial step that would give him the strength to undertake that analytic work. And remember, that strength is coming from the ability of both of these participants to tighten up the framework.

Now while we really haven't had an opportunity to observe a good example of the combination of rectification of the framework and interpretation of the patient's unconscious fantasies and perceptions of both the deviant frame and the secured frame, we have had an opportunity to validate an earlier hypothesis. I refer here to our thesis that rectification of the framework must take precedence over interpretation of the relevant issues, and that rectification in itself can have a considerable salutary effect on a patient. However, to sustain such gains, the appropriate interpretations must be forthcoming from the therapist.

I see that our time is getting short and we do want to hear the balance of this session. I only want to point out that in response to the major adaptive context of securing a piece of the frame, the patient speaks of his daydreams coming true and of creating a work situation that is far more productive and fair to the patient than before. These are characterizations of the communicative properties and therapeutic opportunities of a bipersonal field whose frame has been rectified. In the patient's language, anything else leads to "fucking off"—to not working and to not being rewarded.

In addition, there is even more genetic material here: you'll find in general that genetic connections emerge quite meaningfully within a secured framework. The patient says that the therapist's intervention is distinctly different from his father's passivity and his own. In a way, he seems to be experiencing the therapist's wish to be paid directly by his patient as ascertaining his right to what is fair and due him.

Finally, we must come now to the therapist's intervention. Any quick comments?

Discussant: I wasn't clear where the therapist was heading with his first intervention about money and men fighting. The patient seems to respond to it by emphasizing how constructive he felt his taking responsibility for therapy is.

Discussant: In the second intervention, there's something of a confrontation. There's a framework issue, but all that the therapist is saying is that the patient seems to have become demanding because he's now paying for therapy.

Therapist: Well, with the first intervention, I was trying to get at his view that I had behaved something like his mother and put him down with the way I had approached his paying for treatment. With the second intervention, I was really feeling under interactional pressure and was attempting to link his question to the rectification of the frame.

Langs: I think you had difficulty sorting out his positive responses from hints related to his anxiety that with the frame secure he would soon be confronted with his own homosexual psychopathology and the primitive parts of his inner world. Much of this must stem from his father's passivity and his mother's hostility, themes that are now emerging in a context that will soon render this material quite interpretable. After all, he makes it clear that involving his mother in the payment for therapy placed him in a vulnerable position, open to her attack, something like a helpless kitten. But once you stand up to him—and her—by rectifying the frame, he stands up to her himself and feels a sense of hope that he can prevent her from destroying his life. Rectification becomes a lifesaving measure. But remember, lest we see only the destructive part of this mother, that she too wanted him to be a man and on his own. There are mixed messages here from the mother, from yourself, and from the patient.

So the altered frame allowed his mother to invade the therapy and, in a sense, his mind. It created incestuous sexual anxieties that intensified his homosexual needs and fantasies, and made him experience himself—and you—as a helpless child, animal, kitten, and such. With the rectification, he becomes a man, stands up for himself, becomes a big brother who can now rescue others suffering from his plight, and becomes inventive. That last image is a rather beautiful allusion to the symbolic and creative qualities of the secured bipersonal field. It typifies the kind of theme that did not emerge with this type of functional capacity with the clinic patients; when it did appear there, it was clearly a wish and longing, not an actualization.

For this patient, as long as he wasn't paying you himself, you and what you were giving him were not worth anything. Now, through your rectifying the frame, you indicate your own sense of value, and he supports you there. In that way he too becomes worthy; he can now cope better with his mother and soon, I would expect, with himself. Here I would like to stress that the framework is not simply a matter of managing a set of rules; rather, it is in fact deeply embedded in the unconscious communicative interaction for both patient and therapist.

And I think that here it's a technical error to attempt to stress the destructive part of what you had done, without acknowledging the patient's unconscious perceptions of its positive implications. I think that's why the patient almost shouted you down with your first intervention, and this may also account for his becoming silent and challenging you. Some of that may also stem from the anxieties that begin to develop within the secured frame—a fear of the necessary therapeutic regression. Had I chosen to intervene, I would have begun with my pressures toward having him take financial responsibility and his enormously positive response to it. From there I might have gone on to mention that he had perceived the abruptness of my efforts as somewhat attacking, much as his mother had been. In general, I would not be inclined to interpret the patient's positive responses to the rectification of the framework unless there were additional derivatives of his anxiety and fear of the secured frame. If that emerged, I would point out the nature of his fears, and I would counterbalance that side of things with a delineation of the patient's unconscious positive perceptions of the rectification.

One last point: his taking on financial responsibility, as he so clearly states it, means not only that he will be responsible to you, but that you are now responsible to him. In the face of such derivatives, it is really quite inadequate to simply attempt to confront the patient without tracing out the adaptive context for his questioning you. As I said, I believe that these pressures stem from your last intervention and his deep concern that you yourself don't appreciate the many positive elements to what had transpired. Now let's hear how this hour ended.

Therapist: If I may just say this first: There are other therapists at the center at which I work who involve their secretaries with their patients, by having them make appointments and even, sometimes, collect the fee. I'd like to make it clear that, while I do make use of the clinic waiting room, there are no third parties to this therapy in any direct way. Oh, I must qualify that: phone calls do come to me through my secretary, but she does not involve herself with patients. With few exceptions, I collect my own fees and make my own appointments. So there is near total privacy, and I do maintain total confidentiality. I'm beginning to see that small compromises do creep in, but to a large extent I have secured the setting with my patients.

Langs: Yes, all of that is important. If the alterations in the framework are relatively blatant, the reactions will be gross and extensive. If they are subtle, relatively minor, and isolated, the response will still be there, but it will be more manageable—though there is, as yet, no way of telling the extent to which they can undermine the treatment experience and outcome. Certainly the safest bet is to have as totally secure a framework as humanly possible, without obvious compromises, especially in respect to the fixed ground rules. Let's hear more now.

Therapist: So he says, Well, I am asking for things. You know, I have a girl that calls me up all the time, and she likes to talk to me over the phone. But she's got a boyfriend. And I know she's got a lot of nice attractive girlfriends, and I always think I should ask. So damn it, she called me up again, and she's bullshitting about her boyfriend. And I said to her, Anne, will you shut up? I don't have a girl, and how about setting me up with some of those beautiful young girlfriends of yours? She says, Of course, all you had to do is ask. So now I have a date for this weekend. And then he smiled, and that's how the hour ended.

Langs: Any comments?

Discussant: Well, that certainly sounds like another very positive image. It's remarkable to me how much he is standing up to everyone in a very legitimate way, and how many constructive things he's doing for himself and others, just on the basis of the rectification of the framework.

Langs: Yes, let that be a lesson to all of us as to its power and implications.

Discussant: It's like he's saying that he missed an opportunity for constructive therapy for a long time, and now he has it. And once he has just that, he feels entitled to a lot more for himself. He even becomes actively heterosexual.

Langs: Yes, no more bullshitting; now the search for heterosexuality begins. This is really an excellent example of a framework rectification cure, and we can see how extensive its influence can be. It is important, however, not to believe that this is the end of his therapy, and that he has resolved his conscious and unconscious homosexual conflicts and the rest of his pathology. This is what Balint (1968) aptly termed "a new beginning." This positive phase might well last for a while, but you can be sure that sooner or later the therapeutic regression will take place, critical derivatives will begin to emerge, and the therapist's capacity to manage the framework and interpret the material will be tested.

In this context, I come back to your last intervention. In a way I can see now that in an ambiguous way you were alluding quite noninterpretively to the positive influence of the rectification of the framework. And I think that's why he settled back again, and brought forth another derivative of his positive introject of you. Which leads me to another point: the interplay of your hold of the patient and his hold of you. With the first patient, we saw a good deal of evidence that once you had further secured the framework and your hold of that patient, he responded by holding you fairly well. He did that by accepting the newly defined framework and by offering you meaningful material for interpretation. It seems clear now that the patient's hold of the therapist has a number of elements: his acceptance of the framework; his rectification of a frame that the therapist has altered; his producing interpretable material; and his offering unconscious curative communications within the particulars of that material.

In general there is a rather direct and reciprocal relationship between the therapist's hold of the patient and the patient's hold of the therapist. Disruptions from either will adversely influence the holding responses of the other, while a secure hold by either will almost always elicit a like response. In psychotherapy it remains the therapist's responsibility to experience disruptions in his patient's hold of himself without enacting holding disturbances of his own.

We see similar trends in this second patient: as the therapist endeavored to further secure his hold of the patient, the patient himself responded by stabilizing the framework and better holding the therapist. He decided to pay for his own treatment, accepted the balance of the framework as it stands, and offered the therapist considerable material for understanding and interpreting.

With both patients there were minor disturbances in their hold of the therapist. With the first patient this occurred around the office-clinic arrangement, a precipitating flaw in the therapist's hold of the patient. With the second patient, it came up when the therapist failed to understand and appreciate the patient's positive response to the rectification of the framework, though it may also have had something to do with the office-clinic residual. Still, the predominant picture is clear in both cases: securing the hold of the patient leads the patient to better hold the therapist. Notice too that a secure hold entails both a secure frame and valid interpretations—the latter have powerful holding and containing capacities.

Well, I see that our time is up. On behalf of the entire group I want to express our sincere appreciation to our guest for having worked with us today. He promises us a lively final seminar next week; his topic will be insurance coverage and the therapeutic environment, a loaded subject if ever there was one. Thank you.

Chapter Fourteen

INSURANCE COVERAGE AND THE THERAPEUTIC ENVIRONMENT

Langs: Today's seminar will be the last in which our central focus is on the therapeutic environment. To give us as much time as possible for a final clinical discussion, I will ask our guest to begin immediately with his presentation.

Therapist: There has been so much controversy regarding the influence of third-party payers, such as insurance companies, on the therapeutic situation, I thought that we could all learn a great deal from a presentation in which that issue seems to play a major role. It involves a patient I have just begun to see in psychotherapy, and frankly I could use some help.

I will begin with a brief condensation of the first session. Actually, the patient's first contact was with my secretary rather than myself, largely because he would be paying his fee to her on behalf of the clinic—after which it was to be turned over to me. He had discussed with her the fact that he had insurance coverage, and in a preliminary way, on her own, she had cleared his coverage for treatment. In the first hour he spoke initially of having had extreme anxiety attacks over the past seven years. They are so painful that he sometimes takes off from work. They began while he was in Los Angeles—he had moved there from New York, soon after his wife had given birth to their second child, who was now seven. They had moved to California because most of his family, including his parents, were living there at the time. He is an insurance adjuster.

He went on to recall that his first anxiety attack was actually toward the end of his wife's pregnancy; he was afraid it might be his heart. He moved back to this area and experienced some improvement, only to have another episode about six months ago. He saw a psychiatrist in the city, but stopped because the fee was too high. At that time he refused an offer of medication.

Next he said that while in California his wife was very unhappy. Oddly enough, a man he knew from his former neighborhood had also moved to Los Angeles, and he spent so much time with him that his wife became furious and asked him to choose between her and him. Restricting his time with this friend was quite upsetting for the patient.

He said that it was his wife who persuaded him to return to this area, where most of her friends and family live. His thoughts then turned to his mother, whom he described as nice and slightly overprotective. His father was quiet, his childhood uneventful.

I said very little in this session since the patient spoke quite spontaneously. About ten minutes before the session was to end, I said that it certainly seemed that he needed treatment. The anxiety attacks, though lessening, were still very much present. He seemed very unclear as to why or how these attacks originated, and coming in and talking about them seemed to offer some hope. I told him that I wanted to establish some ground rules, and he said that he knew them from his first treatment and from his conversation with the secretary. Nonetheless, I told him that he would be responsible for his time, and he said that he knew that. I suggested that he say whatever comes to his mind and added that I would try to comment when I have enough material. He then asked me what's involved in psychotherapy, mentioning that he had taken some psych courses in college. I said that the therapy is cognitive as well as emotional, and that it would unfold between the two of us. I stated the fee but said nothing about insurance; nor did he. After the session was over, the secretary handed me an insurance form.

Langs: Any comments?

Discussant: In terms of the frame, it is evident that the secretary had served as a third party to treatment, and that this gave the patient an opportunity to kind of split off the business about the insurance and to present the form to her. It seems to me that in a way the patient and the therapist have created a bastion in this area.

Langs: Yes, I am now in the process of collecting clinical data on this subject. It is a complicated topic. For now, I will confine myself to ideas suggested by the material. This initial bastion leads me to point out that there are two kinds of issues that arise in regard to the therapist's completion of an insurance form: first, the implications of his completing the form itself; second, the remarkable number of additional deviations in the standard framework and in basic technique that arise in the context of insurance. It is rather easy to comment upon this second group of deviations since, despite their remarkable prevelance— and I say this based on a study of the literature, a large number of presentations made to me, and discussions with colleagues—it is readily evident that they constitute self-serving, antitherapeutic, and downright destructive modifications in the basic therapeutic environment. I refer here to such practices—all of which have actually been reported to me—as a therapist's increasing his fee when insurance is involved, either beyond his usual charge per session or beyond what he would ask of a particular patient; signing the form and permitting the patient to complete it; utilizing a nondescript diagnosis, often telling the patient that it has no meaning; reporting more sessions or higher fees than actually exist; and falsifying the date on which treatment began so the patient may obtain coverage. I have also heard of situations where a patient has double insurance coverage and may actually earn money for each session that takes place. Each of these practices is clearly a form of dishonesty and corruption that would insure the development of lie therapy, with all the destructive consequences we have seen in response to unneeded deviations, here with a fierce intensity because of the mutual corruption involved.

In this situation, a third party was permitted to accept the insurance form—and the fee as well, which I will set aside for the moment—and the patient and therapist immediately formed a bastion in this area. This variation includes the introduction of a third party, which of course is an unneeded modification, though it lacks the sense of gross corruption I referred to earlier. Nonetheless, it demonstrates the strong tendency in both patients and therapists to seal off the presence and unconscious implications of the insurance within the therapeutic bipersonal field, thereby severely compromising its communicative properties. Beyond that, it remains for us to discover whether completion of the insurance form itself, and the deviations so derived, further compromise the communicative properties of the field.

Discussant: With all that you say about the power of completing an insurance form and its ability to disrupt the treatment, why is it that most therapists accept insurance forms and seem to have no awareness of detrimental consequences? In my discussions of insurance with supervisors, most of what I have heard involves the suggestion that the implications of insurance should be analyzed, though the forms should certainly be completed.

Langs: Can anyone help me answer this in theory, before we hear the next session?

Discussant: Well, you have repeatedly alluded to the typical split in patients—and I guess in therapists as well—in response to deviations in the framework: conscious acceptance on the one hand, unconscious objections and detrimental responses on the other.

Discussant: I suspect that most therapists, if not all, have approached this issue without making use of the insurance as an adaptive context.

Langs: Yes, you are both quite right, and the second point is especially critical. As long as the therapist waits for conscious references to the insurance, and as long as he is unable to distinguish therapeutic work with Type One derivatives from that with Type Two derivatives, he can delude himself into believing that the insurance is having little influence on the treatment situation and that the patient has set the matter entirely aside—or has worked it over quite well so that it becomes a peripheral concern. In fact, some of you may have had that impression from this initial session. On the surface we heard nothing at all about insurance. But suppose, on the other hand, we take the patient's anticipation that the insurance form would be completed by the therapist as our adaptive context, who can offer us some Type Two derivative responses in this material?

Therapist: I must say that the patient did expect me to complete the form, since the secretary had accepted that as part of the conditions for treatment. Somehow, I knew that this was an important issue, but I really blocked when listening to this material. I had a good deal of anxiety, I realized afterwards, about getting into the insurance issue because I was afraid that I might lose the patient.

Langs: Yes, insurance is a unique deviation in that it entails a conscious desire on the part of the therapist to cooperate in a way that will guarantee continuation of treatment. And since this directly involves the therapist's finances—is a vested interest deviation—it has an enormous potential for creating countertransference-based blind spots and further deviant practices. These are on the surface gratifying for both participants, while—and you may take this as a prediction—they are actually quite destructive. But let's not move too far ahead of the material; who can help us with some Type Two derivatives?

Discussant: I heard something about his quitting the first therapist because the fee was too high. However, the best I can do with that as a Type Two derivative around the adaptive context of the insurance is to suggest that in some way the fee situation—here, the use of insurance— will mean the end of therapy.

Discussant: He also refused medication. That could be a model of rectification.

Langs: Yes, as long as we take these as tentative hypotheses open to validation, they make a great deal of sense. There is also another derivative here. Can anyone identify it? (Pause.) He introduced a third party into his marriage in an effort to deal with his anxiety attacks while in Los Angeles, and there is some indication of a certain palliative effect. Notice that particular point, because it hints at the possibility of the insurance serving as a framework deviation cure in the present therapeutic situation, an experience which would quickly preclude analytic exploration and resolution. As for rectification, notice that his wife told the patient that he must make a choice between his wife and family and the tie to his friend. Here in derivative form is posed a choice the patient must make: he must choose between the framework deviation cure of the insurance, with all its inappropriate gratifications and pathological defenses, and the adaptive, insightful symptom resolution that can take place only within a secure therapeutic environment and through the holding and interpreting of the therapist.

Now all of this is stated as a silent and tentative hypothesis, but one I believe will be validated. If on the one hand you wait for direct references to the insurance, you may hear little or nothing about it for long periods of time; on the other hand, if you maintain it as your adaptive context—and in principle, this is quite justified since it is a modification of the fixed frame—you will quickly discover meaningful Type Two derivatives that begin to reveal its unconscious implications. Here I must add two points: First, as long as the therapist completes the insurance forms or maintains an agreement to do so, the derivatives from the patient will tend to be rather weak and well concealed. This happens because the therapist has a vested interest in the deviation and because the communicative properties of the bipersonal field have been significantly modified. However, as soon as you begin to initiate rectification—for example, by asking the patient to hold onto the insurance form until its implications can be more fully analyzed—you'll begin to obtain a whole new set of derivatives that had previously been repressed.

Second, we must approach this subject by recognizing that the completion of an insurance form is an actuality with extensive unconscious implications. Direct discussion, even verbal interpretation of its apparent or derivative implications, is hollow and meaningless as long as the therapist continues to complete the forms. His actions belie his words and lend the therapy a pervasive aura of falsification and evasion that may well undermine any hope of adaptive structural change.

Now, since there are certain self-evident qualities to this deviation, let's identify them at the outset so that we may see whether our formulation has any predictive force. What ground rules are modified when the therapist completes an insurance form?

Discussant: Well, it certainly modifies the total confidentiality of the treatment situation, and to some extent privacy and the one-to-one relationship.

Discussant: It has a certain exhibitionistic quality; it exposes the patient.

Discussant: It also involves the fee, but I'm not sure how I would state it.

Langs: Perhaps your difficulty arises from the peculiar fact that in a way the therapist becomes responsible for part of the patient's fee, and the patient's total responsibility for payment is thereby altered.

Discussant: Are you implying that the patient must make a sacrifice of his own? This idea often arises when the fee is discussed.

Langs: As I said at the beginning of the course, each ground rule has extensive ramifications, and we have by no means traced out all of them in this course. Full responsibility for the fee certainly implies a commitment by the patient, a cost and to some extent a sacrifice. It entails as well the patient's direct compensation to the therapist, whereby the latter is afforded an appropriate form of gratification for which he provides his services as a therapist.

Can anyone identify another ground rule that is modified when the therapist completes an insurance form? (Pause.) When a therapist reveals the patient's diagnosis, as he must on these forms, he is involved in a noninterpretive intervention and a self-revelation; in that way his anonymity is modified. Some forms ask for responses to additional questions, all of which would further modify the standard frame. Even the request for the therapist's social security number has comparable implications. In addition, it is quite evident that there is an alteration in the rule of abstinence—the patient receives considerable extra-therapeutic gratification, as does the therapist who might not have the patient at all were it not for the insurance.

As you can see, then, the completion of an insurance form modifies major dimensions of the fixed and variable framework. We have already observed a wide range of implications of such deviations, and if we maintain as our adaptive context the patient's expectation that this therapist or his secretary will complete his insurance form, we will soon have the patient's commentary on the nature and implications of the alterations in the framework.

Incidentally, touching on another matter, I do believe that it is quite appropriate to establish the patient's need for therapy and to indicate your belief that you can be of help. However, I think it is is well to forgo any characterization of the treatment experience beyond establishing the fundamental rule of free association for the patient and indicating that the therapeutic work will unfold from there. Beyond that, your comments are likely to be nonneutral and self-revealing. Let's continue now.

Therapist: Well, as I said, I was somewhat surprised when the secretary came in and handed me his insurance form. What I usually do is give it to my secretary at the end of the month. She completes it, stamps in my name, and forwards it either to the patient or directly to the insurance company.

Langs: Any comment?

Discussant: There certainly seems to be something inappropriate in the therapist's not completing the form himself, and certainly in his not signing it.

Langs: Yes, this is what I meant when I spoke of the many extra deviations that occur in this context. And you can see that I was by no means attempting to introduce a moral tone, that I was being quite descriptive when I stated that they often involved obviously corrupt or dishonest practices. What else is involved here? (Pause.) Well, as it has been described to us, the therapist is releasing information about the patient without his written permission. Am I correct about that?

Therapist: Yes; I hadn't realized it. There are many therapists who work at the hospital where I have my office, and as a rule they simply accept the form with the patient's name and address on it, and take it from there.

Langs: So in addition to having his form completed, this patient is anticipating a violation of his confidentiality without his written permission.

Discussant: As I understand it, many therapists discuss the implications of filling out insurance forms with the patient, and then complete it in his presence, explaining everything that is put down. It is their belief that this clears the air and enables them to complete the form with full knowledge of the patient.

Langs: Yes, but as you no doubt realize, you are describing a manifest interaction without any data regarding the unconscious communicative interaction that precedes and follows what you have described.

Therapist: I must say that I sense a major blind spot here. Whenever we are asked to release any other kind of information, we get the patient's full permission. I have no idea how we came to overlook that with the insurance form, but somehow I sense that our own need for the patient and a fee is a factor.

Langs: Please continue.

Therapist: He begins his second session by saying he's feeling better and has had no anxiety attacks. He's had only one attack in the past year, but now he feels he's almost all better.

Discussant: That could be the framework deviation cure.

Langs: Yes, we almost predicted that. Let's see what follows.

Therapist: He says, Boy, was I nervous coming here. What the heck am I going to talk about? Everything's fine, nothing's new, my wife is fine and we're talking, the kids are well, and work's going okay. Well, I can talk about my parents, maybe you want to hear about them. They're old now, but my mother was nervous and overprotective when I was younger. She'd watch me closely and impress me with the dangers of the world: accidents, getting hurt, stuff like that. She'd tell me to be careful around people and watch what I'm doing. She was very nervous, and often took to bed, out of commission. She was on tranquilizers.

He becomes silent and says, I have nothing else to talk about. I'd like some feedback from you. What do you think about what I've said? And he presses me to tell him, and when I'm quiet he becomes extremely anxious. He says, Wow, you're not going to answer me. I can't take it. He gets anxious and begins to shake. At that point, I thought I'd better say something. I said, You know, you're becoming very apprehensive and you're pressuring me to respond, hoping that in some way that will ease your anxieties. And it appears that all of the tension is very much related to your being here, becuase you keep talking about your mother telling you about very dangerous places, about being hurt. You seem to be saying that this is your perception of what's happening here or what you're anticipating might happen.

Langs: Any comment?

Therapist: If I may say so, I was implying that the adaptive context was his beginning treatment, and his anxieties about it.

Discussant: Nonetheless, I get the feeling that much of this is being handled on a manifest level, although I did see that the therapist attempted to use the derivatives about the mother.

Langs: How so?

Discussant: Well, as I understand it, it was as if the therapist was telling the patient that he was afraid of being hurt and of some danger in therapy based on some type of displacement and distortion derived from his relationship with his mother.

Langs: Yes, and what would you term that?

Discussant: Well, we haven't been able to use the term correctly in this course as yet, but I think what we have here is a transference interpretation.

Langs: Yes, it is an attempt to interpret a transference distortion derived in the manner you described. Can anyone specify what the therapist is attempting to help the patient to understand?

Discussant: Well, the therapist may be trying to deal with the patient's symptom, but the patient seems to be clamming up. I would call that the development of a resistance.

Langs: Yes, we will be discussing resistances when we discuss the therapeutic relationship and intervening. But a brief comment will be necessary here.

Therapist: Yes, I saw this as a major resistance, and felt hard pressed to intervene. I had never seen a patient become so manifestly anxious during a session, and I intervened for both reasons: the symptom and a sense of resistance.

Langs: It may help if I tell you that I now classify resistances on two levels: first, *gross behavioral* blocks in associating or other major behaviors which interfere with the therapeutic work. These include acting out, leaving treatment, and the like. The second level of resistance is *communicative*: the patient either fails to represent the adaptive context or the derivative network is fragmented and does not coalesce. Without going into detail, you have here an evident gross behavioral resistance: the patient has little or nothing to say, and he begins to pressure you to speak, long before you feel you have adequate material for intervening. On a communicative level, matters may be different. Who can help us here?

Discussant: Well, the therapist used the adaptive context of the patient's entering therapy. But in our discussion, we decided to use the context related to the anticipation that the insurance form will be completed. It seems to me that both contexts are valid.

Langs: Yes, that is quite true. There are several adaptive contexts, among which the two you mentioned are extremely important. However, remember that in principle an alteration in the standard framework will take precedence within the patient over any other context. And I think that you will find that thesis validated here, since I would expect that any effort to deal with this material in terms of the anxieties about entering therapy will find far less Type Two derivative validation than an attempt to interpret or play back derivatives around the unmentioned insurance issue.

Discussant: I would have to agree with you. I can sense that the patient is afraid of revealing himself, and that he does see treatment as dangerous. But I keep thinking about the insurance form: could the expectation that the therapist will fill it out be a factor in that sense of danger? There really is no way of knowing how he would react to treatment within a secure frame, but to some extent we could certainly anticipate that therapy under conditions of a modified framework would be experienced by this patient as quite dangerous.

Discussant: There is some support for the notion the patient is concerned with the framework in his reference to his mother's taking tranquilizers and going to bed and being out of commission.

Langs: Yes, that's all quite excellent. Based on indirect agreement with the earlier presentations that we have heard, we can accept this material as offering us secondary validation of the thesis that alterations in the fixed frame create unsafe and dangerous bipersonal fields, in which patients can be badly damaged. Further, the deviation is seen as infantilizing and immobilizing, and the patient fears that he might become nonfunctional. Most important, in the adaptive context of the insurance—let's call it that for short—we once again hear a response in which the anticipation of danger and damage are prevalent and in which the patient is also reluctant to communicate meaningfully.

Notice that in addition the patient refers to his mother as inappropriately overprotective. Completing the insurance form will be overprotective, overgratifying, and will repeat in some way the pathogenic interaction with his mother. And along the me/not-me interface, the allusions to his mother's nervousness and need for tranquilizers has considerable importance: it is the patient's way of indicating in derivative form that the therapist's decision to complete the insurance form is based on unresolved anxieties and on his own needs for a framework deviation cure—in a few words, on his own weaknesses and incapacities. This is in keeping with our observations that deviations are consistently experienced by the patient as a failure on the part of the therapist to manage his own inner world and, further, as a failure in his holding and containing capacities. In derivative form, this is exactly what this patient is now communicating.

On the basis of this formulation I must make several additional points. First, we could postulate that the anxiety attack took place because of the therapist's failures in holding and containing, and because of the dangers created by the modifications in the framework involved in filling out the insurance form. We have seen here, I believe, a nontherapeutic regression (Langs 1976c) which will indeed prove difficult to interpret and modify through insight. This, then, is what I have termed an *interactional symptom,* one with contributions from both therapist and patient.

The same thinking applies to the resistances: they are inter-actional resistances rather than essentially intrapsychic. We must remember that an evaluation that the patient is in a state of resistance is a subjective one open to countertransference-based influence—a point we will discuss later on. In addition, it is important to realize that the therapist's deviations have contributed significantly to the patient's reluctance to talk and to reveal himself. And when I state that devia-tions modify the communicative properties of the bipersonal field, one of the implications is to the effect that it invites and reinforces the patient's resistances. This is by no means the only consequence, but it is an important and prominent one.

Finally, you can see how these formulations, built around the adaptive context of the insurance, lead us largely into the sphere of nontransference. We conceptualize this particular interlude as one in which the therapist is in actuality repeating a past pathogenic inter-action which the patient experienced in his childhood, and that in addi-tion the therapist's behavior and unconscious communications to the patient resemble those he experienced from his mother. We can extend that line of thought by indicating that the patient has undoubtedly introjected aspects of his mother's pathology, and that for the moment the therapist is not only confirming these pathological introjects but is behaving in a manner that reinforces those introjects. This leads the patient to believe that both he and the therapist are very much alike, thereby occasioning the loss of certain important differences on which both positive introjects and sound interpretive work are founded.

I must add this: there is for the moment not a single direct refer-ence to the insurance. The allusion to the tranquilizers is the closest the patient comes to representing that adaptive context, doing so through an allusion to another modification in the standard frame. Any therapist who would ignore the adaptive context of the insurance and not use it as a key organizer would therefore see this material as totally divorced from that factor. He would then tend to see the material in terms of the patient's intrapsychic pathology and distortions, and would intervene in a manner not very different from that of our therapist today. We'll soon see how the patient responded to this intervention. But I can assure you that it would be quite easy for such a patient and therapist to establish a Type C narrative field, or even a Type C barrier field, and feel that they are doing therapeutic work, vir-tually all of which would allude to manifest contents while lacking Type

Two derivative validation. There would be a significant bastion and sector of misalliance under these conditions, and from time to time the patient would unconsciously attempt to modify the situation. For the moment it is quite evident that the patient has a very mixed response to the anticipated deviation: on the one hand it is terrifying him and creating a sense of endangerment, while on the other it is offering him noninsightful symptom relief and an opportunity to avoid approaching the most disturbing elements of his inner mental world.

Therapist: I somehow sensed that there was a frame issue when he began to question me and ask me directly for feedback. I experienced that as an impingement upon the frame and as some type of projective identification—subjectively, I experienced interactional pressures. The material in his associations, however, did not enable me to validate that impression, and I really did not know how to formulate it any more clearly.

Langs: Yes, we have seen in a number of presentations that when the framework is modified, the patient will directly pressure the therapist to respond noninterpretively. Deviations are critical unconscious communications. In general, an altered frame creates interactional pressures on the patient, placing into him a variety of anxieties and unconscious fantasies which he has difficulty metabolizing. We should listen to what follows with this formulation in mind.

Discussant: Medication is a framework deviation cure, at least when it works.

Discussant: It seemed to me that the therapist's intervention was rather linear, and that he simply made use of a single displacement rather than a convoluted network of derivatives.

Langs: Yes, the intervention is manifest and linear, while the playback of derivatives around the adaptive context of the insurance would be far more convoluted. And since the patient does not directly or readily represent that particular context, a playback is for the moment all we can avail ourselves of here.

By the way, we should not fail to identify, as a background adaptive context, the presence of this therapist's office in a clinic. Since we traced out the effects of this particular office arrangement at our last meeting, we will not attempt to do so here. I simply want to suggest that each of you could review the material of this session with that context in mind and see how it adds to the patient's sense of anxiety and to his unconscious perceptions and introjections of the therapist. It would be important for us to establish from the material that follows that the insurance is, indeed, the major context for this particular hour.

Therapist: I can say this much already: the intensity of this patient's reactions, and the clarity of the derivatives now that you have organized them for me, is quite unusual in my experience. This type of anxiety reaction does not occur when I have a frame that is secured except for the location of my office. On that basis I very much believe that your point is valid.

Langs: Well, as you know, that is not Type Two derivative validation; while I appreciate what you are contributing, the ultimate validation must rest with the patient.

Discussant: Dr. Langs, what sort of intervention would you be preparing?

Langs: Well, I have already outlined it. If his pressure and anxiety build further, I would actually intervene. I would make use of a playback of derivatives around the unmentioned adaptive context of the insurance. I would point out to the patient that he seems concerned about my silence and the way I am structuring and managing his treatment. There's something frightening about it even though he felt quite well during the week. It seems to have to do with his having little or nothing to say here, and to connect with his mother's view of the world as dangerous and with a need to retreat to bed for safety. There seems to be some concern about the process of cure, since he has mentioned that his mother took tranquilizers. And whatever is disturbing him about the structure of treatment is prompting him to feel quite anxious.

In this way I have played back a set of coalescing derivatives around the unmentioned adaptive context, and have attempted to link it to the therapeutic context or indicators—the patient's resistances and symptoms. And I have intervened in a transversal manner that leaves room for him to identify contributions from both of us, and for both valid and distorted elements in his response. By contrast, the intervention that the therapist made is essentially the offer of a Type C barrier, and while it may provide the patient momentary relief, the actualities the patient is perceiving unconsciously have been neither modified nor interpreted, and additional regression is likely to follow.

Notice too how this patient responds according to another principle we have identified: once gratified and protected by a deviation, the patient will want additional alterations in the framework. In fact, the use of deviations is for the moment an essential part of the therapeutic contract, and he will continuously press the therapist to further fulfill his part of that particular bargain.

Discussant: How much of the danger do you think is coming from some sense within the patient that the form is being filled out without his permission?

Langs: It is difficult to know, but it will be a significant factor. In addition, the patient's own propensity to experience anxiety will play a role. Based on the material to this point, it would seem that among the unconscious factors in his symptom is the experience of a poor hold, a sense of being in a dangerous place where he can be harmed, and a deep sense of mistrust of the other person involved. There is a claustrophobic quality here, but it is based in part on the dangerous enclosure that the therapist has created, and only in part on this patient's unconscious fantasies and memories. As I said before, symptoms develop on a dual basis: from unconscious perceptions and introjects on the one hand, and, on the other, from primary and secondary (reactive) unconscious fantasies and the resultant pathological distortions.

Discussant: I begin to wonder what would happen if therapists refused to accept insurance forms from their patients.

Langs: Yes, that is an important consideration. The enormous need for therapy among patients with relatively insufficient funds, not to mention the need among therapists for fee-paying patients, creates tremendous pressures not only to simply accept insurance as a part of the therapeutic situation, but also to fail to examine analytically its meanings and functions. These attitudes are reinforced by the tendency of many therapists and analysts to think of the treatment situation as a world of fantasy in which actualities, not to mention the actual disruptive unconscious communications of the therapist's deviations, play little or no role. It is beyond the province of this seminar to discuss the socioeconomic implications of the clinical findings we are developing. It should be our goal to determine the truth about the influence of insurance on the psychotherapeutic situation and to establish our conclusions through the use of psychoanalytic validation. It can then be left to others—or to ourselves later on—to work out the extended implications of our findings. Please continue.

Therapist: He responds by telling me that he's suddenly feeling very upset and by agreeing that this is a very dangerous place. That's what his parents always talked about. Then he's silent and begins to cry. He cries for the balance of the session while he's talking, and seems to be falling apart. He was raised to be sensitive about hurting people and is very apologetic. As a result, others exploit him and do things to him, and he really can't defend himself. His parents said: Don't hurt anyone; they'll be angry at you. Some of his friends snipe at his wife and say things to her that they shouldn't, and so do his parents. He goes on: My wife looks to me for help and I can't help her. I get annoyed, and would like to stand up and say something, but I can't. I'm a pacifist; I stop fights. I feel so threatened by others, I compromise. I feel vulnerable and I'm frail.

At this point, he began to sob and say how ashamed he feels, and how humiliated. I told him that he somehow feels very threatened here. He used the words *vulnerable* and *frail,* and seems to be hinting that he feels that in some way he's going to be not only humiliated here, but also very hurt. And he seems to perceive treatment as a situation in which he's going to be embarrassed, humiliated, and possibly even physically hurt.

Langs: Any comment?

Discussant: Before I began this course, I believed in flexibility with the ground rules and thought it cruel to maintain the frame. And my view of something like insurance was that it could be discussed with the patient and even analyzed, and though with selected patients it might have detrimental effects, with most patients it would fade into the background. But I have learned that the truth is rather different:

flexibility now seems to me a cover for a therapist's destructiveness. And insurance is an actuality—as you put it—with pervasive unconscious implications. And I could listen to this material in that adaptive context and hear the patient saying that there is something hurtful about filling out the insurance form, something exploitative against which the patient feels utterly defenseless and helpless. The tone of his associations and their implications are really quite remarkable.

Discussant: I noticed something else: there is a reference to third parties who snipe at his wife, and the patient describes himself as responding with rage and yet unable to express himself. He then goes on to talk about being a pacifist and a compromiser, but ascribes it to his frailty and vulnerability. In the adaptive context of the insurance, this material seems to fit along the me/not-me interface as an unconscious perception or perhaps even an unconscious introjection of the therapist's own compromised position, and the patient seems to believe that it reflects a form of frailty and vulnerability.

Langs: That's excellent. You both have stated the implications of this material quite well. And after all, these are now familiar themes. When the therapist has a need to modify the standard framework, the patient experiences it as a reflection of unconscious hostility and the therapist's inability to manage not only his own inner state—his frailty and vulnerability—but the treatment situation as well. And all this is, indeed, introjected here, partly—as the patient states in derivative form—because of his fear of expressing himself directly in a manner that would hurt the therapist and be experienced by him as hostile or offensive.

It seems that therapists in general have considerable difficulty in coming to terms with the finding that flexibility in respect to the ground rules is in no way an act of kindness or a means of creating a sound therapeutic space for the patient. Forgive the repetition, but therapeutic kindness, or what could appropriately be termed therapist love, takes a distinctive form. I trust that this material brings that point home quite clearly.

Now, once again, the therapist intervened with the adaptive context of the patient's initiating therapy in mind. There is a nucleus of truth in what he has said: the patient does anticipate being humiliated and hurt, and even wonders about being physically harmed; but he has reason for this because of the implications of the insurance. As we have learned in this course, once a therapist deviates the patient becomes quite fearful. He just does not know how far the therapist will go. Let's hear more.

Therapist: He says, as he cries and is silent from time to time, I didn't expect this. I'm upset that I'm crying, but I can't control myself. I didn't think I needed treatment that much, and I kept postponing it; I thought I could handle things myself. Only crazy people come. And I saw some psychiatrists and they told me what to do, they answered my questions, and it was all intellectual; and I thought you'd tell me something and I'd feel better. But you're seeing how I am and the pain I have. This is what happens when I have an anxiety attack. You said treatment would be an emotional experience. You were fair to me. This is what it is; I can't deny my problem any more. I can't handle it by myself. I haven't told anyone I'm coming here; only my wife knows. And I told her father because he's been in therapy. I try to hide it from everyone; I try to keep this terrible fear and anxiety a secret.

The time was almost up and I mentioned that he had given the receptionist an insurance form last week. And I asked him if he had any questions about it. And then he said, No, I was told that the secretary would fill it out from month to month, and that's all right. I also told him that I would be away two weeks hence, and as he left, he reached out and grabbed my hand, and shook it.

Langs: Who will comment?

Discussant: I wondered if this patient was having a homosexual panic, but I really didn't hear any homosexual material.

Therapist: Yes, I wondered about that, especially when he shook my hand. When he mentioned that only crazy people come here, I sensed a tremendous fear of being psychotic.

Discussant: I think we're losing sight of the insurance and the framework issues. His other therapists answered his questions and created an intellectual atmosphere, probably some form of Type C barrier. But what is most striking to me is his reference to secrets and the model of rectification he offers: he doesn't tell anyone about his sickness; he maintains almost total confidentiality.

Langs: Yes, these are very telling derivatives. They arise in the adaptive context of the therapist's last intervention, which in part offered the patient a bastion in regard to the insurance. On a manifest level the patient accepts the sector of misalliance, while on a latent level it seems quite evident that he continues to work over the issue. Along the me/not-me interface, he is concerned about the exposure of his own craziness and views a therapist who will complete an insurance form as also being crazy. He makes an appeal for confidentiality and it would seem that the therapist, perhaps quite unconsciously, finally picked up the message at the end of the session.

We must recognize, however, that his intervention was quite a mixed one: while he finally alluded to the insurance form, he did so with a noninterpretive intervention—a question regarding the patient's manifest thoughts and feelings about the form. And while the announcement of his coming vacation provides us with what we have seen as the inevitable complication, it will be quite wise of us to take the therapist's reference to the insurance form as the adaptive context of the session that follows. While nothing was stated definitively, the therapist implied that he would be working with the receptionist toward the completion of the form.

In all, then, there is a striking split on the part of both patient and therapist: both appear to have readily identifiable reactions to the implications of the insurance, reactions they express in derivative form though consciously they treat it as a matter of routine. Ultimately, the therapist must heal this breach so that he can respond interpretively and pick up the patient's derivative directives toward rectification. Ultimately he should be able to indicate that the patient has expressed an awareness that completion of the insurance form is a crazy and destructive act that would inappropriately expose his craziness and make the treatment situation extremely dangerous.

The therapist's decision to mention the insurance at the very end of the hour, when the patient could barely respond directly and would certainly have no opportunity for indirect and derivative communication, is representative of prevailing practices in this area. The effort is made to treat the insurance as a casual reality, and the unconscious countertransference-based defenses are such that, without realizing it, therapists make extensive efforts to preclude derivative communication around this topic. So it goes beyond the simple fact that many therapists have not learned to apply the full listening process to the insurance issue.

Discussant: How would you have handled the insurance form?

Langs: Well, for one thing, I have no secretary or receptionist, so the patient would have to present it to me directly. If he were to mention it in the first hour, I would respond in two ways. First I would scrutinize the material to that point for the patient's unconscious appreciation of the implication of introducing the insurance, and would interpret the material in terms of this valid perceptiveness. Second, I would offer the patient an essentially secure therapeutic situation, with total confidentiality and privacy, and with a fee that he can afford entirely on his own. And I would indicate that any wish on his part to modify any of these conditions should be subjected to full exploration, and that on the basis of whatever unfolds in that work a decision could be made in regard to the proposed deviations. As I have said many times before, I have never seen a clinical situation in which the patient did not then communicate an extensive series of coalescing Type Two derivatives around this particular adaptive context. He will produce a communicative network which reveals his unconscious awareness of the destructive consequences of this modification in the frame, and will include his unconscious directive to maintain a secure therapeutic environment.

The problem is not whether the patient will express himself in this way, but how he will respond to my interpretation and his own realization of the implications of what he has expressed. As a rule there is a critical moment at which the patient realizes the meaning of the secure frame you are offering; in particular, he senses that you will expose him to the psychotic part of his personality and the most disruptive elements of his inner world. If he can believe in the possibility of adaptive resolution of that terrible inner pathology, if he wants it, he will accept the secure therapeutic environment and become an analyzable patient. If he is in utter terror of these inner contents and in dread of losing control and going crazy, if he lacks—often for good reason—faith and trust in the therapist's ability to help him manage and understand, and if his propensities are toward Type B communication through action-discharge, he will find some way of repudiating the secure therapeutic space and will probably flee the treatment situation. He will seek out a therapist—he will not have to look very hard—who will without a second thought complete the insurance form and who will protect him from himself through some form of lie or barrier therapy.

There are so many relevant issues here that we can touch only briefly upon a few of them. Some of them will be clearer once we have studied the therapeutic relationship and have a better understanding of interventions. In practice, if a patient simply presents an insurance form, I suggest that he hold onto it and permit us an opportunity to explore his responsive associations. From there, the techniques are pretty much as I have already outlined them. The very fact that I do not immediately participate in the deviation maintains the security of the therapeutic space so that relevant material can emerge—as in my experience it does without fail. Let's now hear the next session.

Therapist: He comes in and says, I'm very apprehensive, tense. I kept thinking about the session and how upset I was about my outburst last week. I let loose and felt embarrassed. I started to plan today's session; I like to be in control. Then I decided it would be better to just let it happen, even though it's very difficult.

I then commented briefly on his need to plan out the session, and he agreed that he was trying to control the situation. He went on: Let me tell you about my first anxiety attack when I was a child. I was in fifth grade and president of the class, and I had to make a presentation. I had done this before very well, but this time, even though I had it all on paper, I froze. I couldn't talk and I don't remember if I finally did; it was a very frightening experience. From then on, I was always nervous and had to plan out what I would say in class, which affected my school performance and limited what I would say in the presence of others. It had a detrimental effect, but I lived with the anxiety and somehow managed. I would be cautious and watch what I said, but then I found that when I joined the choir and there were fifty or sixty people in it I could sing well and not feel frightened—as long as I avoided solo presentations. I was okay as long as I was one of sixty bodies.

I didn't do as well as I should have in college, but I studied business. I would study and study, but wouldn't do so well on my tests. The anxiety prevented it. I always thought I was much smarter than the marks indicated. I was disappointed with my college record.

I never went out with girls. I was shy. I had two brothers, and the three of us shared a bedroom. My parents slept in the living room and there was no privacy. I was uncomfortable and couldn't bring women home. There was no privacy at all.

At college, I joined a fraternity but felt uncomfortable at the parties. The girls were frivolous, but not my wife; she was very serious. I should have married someone who was more frivolous, but my wife and I shared the same goals and I felt comfortable with her. The only problem was with her mother, who would be nice one minute, bitchy and angry the next. Maybe she's schizophrenic. She manipulated my wife. I always felt that they had secrets and were doing things that I didn't know about. My wife is still too close to her.

The engagement was stormy—and here he went into some detail: My mother-in-law opposed the marriage and my parents had to arrange the wedding. Her parents would never get involved, and would always be off by themselves, hiding in the corner. Everyone else had to make a fuss about them. At family gatherings they would leave abruptly and my future wife would go with them. They were strange and inappropriate, and my mother would become angry. She kept asking me what in the world I was getting into. My parents and my in-laws never had a relationship. My mother tried but they didn't, and my mother opposed the marriage. Maybe it would have been better if she had kept quiet because she caused a lot of trouble with everything she said.

Oh, I forgot to mention that when he came in I had the insurance form on the desk. He had responded immediately by saying, That's my insurance form, the one I gave the secretary last week.

Langs: As you can see, the insurance remained an afterthought and a disturbance for the therapist. He now tells us that the form was there at the beginning of the session, and that the hour began with the patient's acknowledgment of its presence. There is a great deal of material here, but let's attempt to restrict ourselves to the adaptive context of that form. Who will comment?

Discussant: On one level, the material is overorganized, ruminative, and something of a Type C barrier. I think now of your comment about the implications of the therapist's reference to the form at the end of the hour and its focus on the surface—an intervention that invited a sector of misalliance and a Type C communicative response.

Nonetheless, from time to time we hear derivatives related to the implications of the insurance. We learned, for example, that the patient's anxiety attacks first developed when he had to present some material to a group. For me, that was Type Two derivative validation of your formulation that the patient's anxiety attack in his last session had to do with the insurance and his dread of exposure. I must say that I was unconvinced until I heard these derivatives, but I will now accept your formulation.

Langs: I am quite pleased with your attitude. You should not accept any tentative supervisory formulation until it obtains Type Two derivative validation, and I am glad to see that you are now capable of identifying this critical form of confirmation. The symptoms occurred in uncontrolled fashion under conditions of exposure. This implies that the therapist's supposed act of kindness, the completion of the insurance form, will serve as a virtually unanalyzable stimulus for the patient's symptoms. However he conceives the dangers of public speaking, they now exist in the treatment situation—his therapy is open to the public. It is inconceivable that under these conditions he could communicate material related to the unconscious basis for this symptom in a manner that would permit its analytic resolution. The therapist is now part of the dangerous audience with whom he feels unsafe.

Discussant: He also said that he was able to manage his anxiety by writing things down. The insurance could then provide him reassurance in that way, although I recognize that along the me/not-me interface the patient may also be suggesting that the therapist would be quite frightened of the patient if the insurance was not there as a protective device.

Langs: Yes, on one important level, the completion of an insurance form is an unconscious effort to create a bastion against the disturbed inner parts of both patient and therapist. Treatment situations undertaken with insurance are characteristically flat and empty, and tend to follow the pattern we saw earlier, with one of the patients for whom psychotropic medication was prescribed (see chapter 9). You will obtain a few fragmented derivatives but little in the way of coalescence, and true therapeutic regression is precluded. In perhaps the only paper on the subject, Halpert (1972) described this very phenomenon. He concluded that, at least in situations where the insurance covers all of the therapist's fee, the realities are such that the patient's defenses are reinforced to the point where meaningful analytic work is precluded. I would advise you to read that paper as a follow-up to this discussion.

Your comment that the insurance would work at cross purposes, both intensifying and diminishing his anxiety, can be validated in still another way from this material. We have seen considerable evidence that the insurance places the patient in the very conditions under which his symptoms first began. If this were the only effect, we would expect the patient to take flight. But he does not do so. He remains because on another level he also feels quite protected and fairly certain that the underlying basis for his symptoms will not emerge or be subjected to analytic exploration. Did anyone hear how he expressed that very point? (Pause.)

Well, the patient said that if he is alone, in a situation without protective companions, he becomes uncontrollably anxious. On the other hand, in the midst of others, as he was in the choir, he feels safe and protected. Thus, while the presence of an observing insurance company might well intensify his anxiety, the third-party payer will also be experienced by the patient as present in the treatment situation and as protecting him against the therapist on one hand, and the sources of his anxiety on the other. In fact, he can face an audience as long as he is just one of many. In this way, for periods of time it seems likely that the insurance will provide the patient a framework deviation cure that would entirely preclude the emergence of the critical derivatives related to his symptoms.

For me, this is a very compelling representation of the inappropriate gratifications and defenses offered in actuality when the therapist completes an insurance form. As long as the patient is one of many, he will feel safe and his problems will not emerge. And such are the actual conditions of this therapy—the true implications of the insurance.

Discussant: This question of the actual influence of deviations has been a difficult one to clarify, but I do think that this material helps considerably. I also noticed that the patient referred to his lack of privacy at home, and to sharing a bedroom with his two brothers. That too seemed to relate to the presence of the insurance company in the treatment situation.

Discussant: Another derivative relates to the patient's recall of his then pending marriage. He states things like his having made the wrong decision; alternations in his view of his mother-in-law, who I believe represents the therapist here; the presence of secrets; and the destructive consequences when his mother spoke out. All of this can easily be organized around the adaptive context of the insurance. And the way his in-laws would hide would also tie in.

Langs: Yes, we have a very rich coalescing network of derivatives around the insurance form, much of it in response to the therapist's allusion to it at the end of the previous session and its physical presence at the beginning of this hour. Since the patient's anticipation is that the therapist will probably complete the form, and since interactional bastions have already been created in this area, we may well be deprived of closer derivatives related to this subject. I hope, however, that seeing that the insurance serves as a selected fact—a fact giving coherence and meaning to what otherwise would seem very scattered associations— helps convince those of you who are skeptical that this is indeed a major adaptive context for this material. Please continue.

Therapist: He spoke about his thoughts of postponing his marriage, but his wife pressured him because she wanted to get away from her own parents. Her pressure was too much, he said. I can't stand my mother-in-law. She's always there. I feel secrets, like I'm being manipulated and that they talk on the side by themselves. My wife seems more loyal to her than to me. A lot is going on behind my back. You just can't be involved in two homes; you can't be master in two places.

Here I intervened. I said that the insurance form is on the desk and there seems to be a number of references in the session to its possible implications. He's talking about his wife and mother-in-law, and things being said behind his back, secrets. There are other allusions to the sense of privacy and his need for it. He had also said that when his mother spoke out and said too much she got into a lot of trouble. I told him that I felt that these allusions had to do with the implications of the insurance form.

Langs: Any comments?

Discussant: The intervention attempts to deal with the adaptive context of the insurance, but it seems somewhat incomplete. The patient seems pressured by the therapist, even though it is he who has brought in the insurance form and created the pressure for the therapist. He also has a rather paranoid response to his anticipation that information about him will be released.

Langs: Yes, some time ago I termed this *iatrogenic paranoia* (Langs 1973b). And as we have seen before, deviations in the framework are one means through which the therapist can not only drive the patient crazy, but also make him appear quite paranoid.

Discussant: Somehow the patient's comment that you can't be master in two homes seems to tie in. It's as if he feels that the therapist either has to make his commitment to him, the patient, or to the insurance company—it can't be both.

Langs: Yes, that's an excellent point, and it is quite true. Here again this is not so much a matter of distortion, but a form of valid perceptiveness. On another level, it alludes to something I referred to earlier: the choice between truth therapy and lie therapy—a treatment situation in which meaningful derivatives will unfold as compared to one in which falsifications, barriers, and uninsightful symptomatic fluctuations will occur.

In any case, the therapist begins to approach the implications of the insurance. And he does so in a transversal manner, implying that the patient may be quite correctly perceiving some very detrimental consequences to his completing the form. His intervention also hints at the possibility of rectification—he might not complete the form if the patient's impressions are borne out.

Discussant: Is my impression correct that you had not as yet filled out the insurance form?

Therapist: That is correct; I hadn't completed the form. Incidentally, I now remember another derivative: the patient had spoken in some detail of how he tries to make telephone calls at home and has no sense of privacy. His wife, his mother-in-law, and the children keep intruding. There was a sense that he was implying that he really can't function under those conditions.

Langs: Well, in the adaptive context of the insurance, the implication is unmistakable and quite valid. Your recollection offers us a form of secondary validation that is not uncommon in supervision.

Two additional comments: this material could be organized around the additional adaptive context of your pending vacation and your interventions of the previous hour, but because of time limitations we will not pursue those formulations here. Secondly, in intervening it is always best to include the clearest representation of the central adaptive context; in regard to the insurance, what form did that take in this session?

Therapist: Actually, I had thought of the reference to the telephone situation as just that.

Discussant: But didn't the patient mention the insurance form at the beginning of the session, when he saw it on the therapist's desk?

Langs: Exactly, and by alluding to the patient's remark at the beginning of the hour, you could have offered your intervention in a manner that would have been even more convincing for the patient.

Discussant: There is another problem that comes up when you try to deal with the issue of insurance. Patients tend to rationalize by stating that they have paid for their insurance and are entitled to the money. This touches upon the split you described earlier. Now that I listen for derivatives around the adaptive context, I have begun to pick up the patient's unconscious awareness of the detrimental consequences of insurance. But the problem is that I have never seen a patient who has been able to state this directly, and I usually run into a great deal of denial when I begin to approach the implications of their indirect material.

Langs: Yes, while there are exceptional patients who almost immediately sense the destructive implications of insurance, most patients communicate in this area exactly as you described: they express conscious entitlement and even a casual attitude in regard to your completing the form, while their derivative associations are, as we have seen here, filled with perceptive contradictory meanings. Occasionally patients will worry about the information you will release to the insurance company, and some will decide to exclude insurance on that basis. It is only with extended analytic exploration that you can determine how much of this is based on pathological unconscious paranoid fantasies, and how much is based on the patient's valid concern about the release of such information. Too many therapists, however, simply assume such anxieties to be paranoid symptoms and therefore fail to recognize their essentially valid core.

In dealing with the split, it is important that the therapist intervene by addressing how divided the patient seems. You can indicate to him that while he seems nonchalant in his request that you complete the insurance form, indirectly he has said a great deal about the actual consequences of your compliance. He might have noticed that he had mentioned the presence of the form when he began the session, and while he dropped the subject consciously, much of what he went on to say organizes extremely meaningfully as indirect commentaries on the implications your completion of that form might have. And he also may have noticed what he said: how terrified he is when he feels unduly exposed, and how he is unable to function effectively when his privacy is invaded; how disturbing it was in his childhood when he had no privacy; how much trouble there can be when one says everything that comes to mind under certain conditions; how much he compromises when he feels under undue pressure; how concerned he is about secrets and about being manipulated; and how badly he feels in situations where there are divided loyalties and things are going on behind his back. You could say that all of this indicates his awareness on some level that completing the insurance form would betray him; would be disloyal; would disturb the privacy that he needs in order to function, to grow, and to resolve his symptoms constructively; would be a betrayal of his secrets; and would create conditions where his saying whatever comes to mind could, instead of being entirely helpful, actually prove damaging to him. And at that point you could add that it seems clear that on another level the patient would feel safe and protected in the presence of the insurance company because that was the way he resolved his anxiety attacks when he was younger. When he was one among many, he felt safer. But he also realizes that he is making a choice about the mode of treatment, and this is reflected in his comment that you cannot be master in two homes. One must make a choice: symptom alleviation through the introduction of third parties to the treatment situation—the insurance company—or the exclusion of the insurance company, the creation of conditions of total confidentiality and privacy, and the opportunity to resolve his symptoms in a safe setting, even though it may be one that will expose him to some of the most disturbing things within himself.

In this way, you will have begun your interpretive work by touching upon the patient's valid unconscious perceptions and realizations regarding the completion of the insurance form. Follow the principle of truth before distortion, as there will be plenty of time later on to deal with the distorted aspects of his response, aspects in which his psychopathology is reflected. Here you are making use of the patient's constructive unconscious functioning, an approach that he will appreciate, that will secure a truly sound therapeutic alliance and create the conditions under which he will be inclined to reveal in derivative form the most disturbing aspects of his inner world. You are also, by excluding the insurance company from treatment, approaching rectification and taking it just as far as the patient has directed you to this point.

And you can see here that the patient's split is not only that he is divided as to whether or not he wants the insurance form filled out; he is also split between a conscious wish for the insurance—he needs the money—and an unconscious wish to exclude it. He would like to deny that the insurance has any implications for treatment: consciously, so that he won't have to pay; unconsciously, so that he can secure the impenetrable Type C barriers it would create within him and within the bipersonal field. In addition he could obtain, consciously or unconsciously, directly or indirectly, various inappropriate gratifications—homosexual, perhaps, or possibly by those attendant on being provided a maternal-like protector. On that basis the insurance might well work a temporary framework deviation cure, though, as we have seen, the many immediate dangers in the insurance constellation tend to undermine that type of symptom relief.

But beneath all of this the patient seems to sense that no growth or true mastery is possible under the conditions of insurance. The Type C barriers do not permit understanding or adaptive working through, nor do they allow symptom resolution based on insight and implicit positive introjects. The therapist who completes an insurance form generates, without exception, a whole variety of destructive and negative introjects which undermine the therapeutic relationship and alliance. The communicative properties of the field become flawed and massive defensiveness prevails, with the full unconscious support of the therapist. He cannot be trusted and is dangerous, and a therapeutic alliance in the sense of the true search for insight is simply precluded. It is, as the patient says, one house or the other, truth therapy or lie therapy. The insurance is an actuality which influences the conditions of treatment and thereby the transactions between patient and therapist. It is a matter of choice and not one of intermixtures or gradations. It is an issue of the core quality of the therapy.

Let's now hear how he responded to your initial effort to intervene in regard to the insurance issue.

Therapist: He says, There is a whole story about the insurance. My wife wouldn't let me come here unless the insurance covered most of the fee, and she made the calls to check it all out. I was very upset because I have a sensitive job now, and I'm concerned that somebody else would be reading my diagnosis and other information about me. There are some who think that people who go to therapists are crazy. I work in insurance and I don't know what will happen. I hadn't even realized that my wife had called up the insurance company, and she wondered if other insurance companies could get hold of the information. They told her that they don't release such information, and I guess I have to believe that because I need treatment desperately. My wife insists that therapy be covered by insurance; all she's interested in is the money. She was very poor as a child and is terrified that we won't have money. She's crucifying me about this insurance thing. If it was up to me, I'd see your point, but I feel desperate. I need the money and I can't come without the insurance; my wife makes life miserable for me.

Here I intervened and said that he seemed to be very upset, that it was clear that the insurance was very important to him, and that it would be something that we would discuss further.

Langs: Well, this is very dramatic material. Who will comment?

Discussant: I must say that I have several very strong reactions to this material. First, I was amazed to hear that so much had gone on about the insurance that the therapist hadn't known about. It seems obvious to me that the patient went along with maintaining this sector of misalliance as long as the therapist wished to place the insurance in a bastion. But as soon as the therapist attempted to intervene with some understanding of the destructive implications of the insurance, and with some hint of the possibility of excluding it from therapy, the patient took his cue from that and revealed some extremely meaningful material, both direct and indirect. I see this as further evidence of just how divided the patient is on this issue: he will leave the matter alone and permit you to fill out the form if you say nothing about it interpretively, but if you bring up the issue in a meaningful way he has plenty to say about how destructive the insurance is and how terrified he is of it.

Langs: Yes, here you can experience, in a clinical way, one meaning of the term *splitting*. This is not a matter of repression, since much of this is quite on the surface, nor does it come across as deliberate suppression or concealment. It is all there, but it is split off until the therapist initiates a resolution of the Type C barriers and bastion—the sector of misalliance. The patient has a whole story to tell, as he puts it, but he will not tell it under conditions in which the form seems certain to be completed. The communicative properties of the field are marred, and certain avoidance mechanisms within the patient are intensified.

This also illustrates what I meant when I said that the actual material you will hear will depend very much on how you handle the question of the insurance form itself. Had the therapist already completed the form, I suspect we would have heard fewer and more highly disguised—more distant—derivatives initially. However, since the form has not been completed and is now on the desk before them, we hear a sequence of close derivatives, disguised but readily decipherable around the critical adaptive context. This permits the therapist to make an interpretive intervention and an approach toward rectification. And even though his intervention is somewhat incomplete, you can see that the patient offers not only Type Two derivative validation—in a form we will soon discuss—but also direct confirmation through unanticipated material giving new meaning to all that preceded it, and extensive support for our formulations of the implication of the insurance. And finally, if full rectification is effected we will hear an additional constellation of derivatives that will provide us further insight into the specific meanings of this deviation for the patient.

Discussant: This material validates many of the points you have made. In a very moving way, the patient touches upon the critical social problem regarding insurance. On the one hand, it is often necessary as a means of enabling a patient to remain in therapy when there are financial difficulties, while on the other it destroys the very treatment situation—it crucifies the patient, as he put it.

Langs: Yes, I'm glad you heard that derivative; it was quite a dramatic communication. And you are quite right: there is a split between financial need and the proper conditions of therapy. In an entirely different vein, the patient's own split regarding the insurance is represented here, interestingly enough, by his splitting off into his wife the part of him that wishes to have the insurance as part of the treatment situation, and keeping within himself the part that is opposed. And you can see his characterization of his wife and of the wish for the insurance company as a third party to treatment: it is approached in a suspicious and almost clandestine way; it is based on anxieties that may reflect undue suspiciousness or be quite well-founded—it is well known that insurance companies pool information—anxieties that are difficult to sort out; it involves a fear of being exposed as crazy that comes across once again in a form that is difficult to sort out in regard to valid and distorted elements; it is carried out irrationally and with intense and inappropriate emotions; and it is stated in the form of an ultimatum.

But notice too that it is also unclear as to whether this patient could not afford one session a week on his own, and whether his wife—and his own—fear of being destitute is rational or not. There is something about this material that suggests a significant distorted element based on early childhood deprivation, but my main point is that the financial need may, in reality, not be so great as to preclude once-a-week therapy.

Discussant: What is the fee here?

Therapist: Thirty dollars per session.

Discussant: Well, on that basis, while we don't know the details, I could see that it might be possible that the patient actually could afford therapy on his own.

Discussant: I was impressed with the Type Two derivative validation of Dr. Langs's formulation that the patient felt endangered and exposed by the completion of the insurance form. Along the me/not-me interface, he seems to be saying that he would be crazy to be in therapy with insurance, and that the therapist himself would be crazy to complete the form. I was also impressed with how important the patient felt the insurance to be, in that he did a great deal to check out its implications before ever coming to the therapist; that makes it all the more impressive that he said absolutely nothing about this subject until the therapist's last intervention.

Discussant: I was struck too how easily the patient saw the therapist's point about the destructive implications of the insurance. He seems to have validated the therapist's intervention on several different levels.

Therapist: Yes, I too felt that my intervention had been validated, but now I had a different problem. Would eliminating the insurance mean the end of therapy for this man?

Discussant: That really seems to be the issue. It seems quite clear that the patient himself is saying that the use of the insurance is crazy and would crucify him, but that his wife won't let him be in treatment without it. I thought that the way he put it, in terms of her anxieties based on her childhood experiences, at least allowed room for exploration and the possibility that the patient could continue treatment on his own. From what I have heard, I think he would be strongly inclined to stay with a therapist who was capable of understanding his realistic fears about insurance, and I guess of interpreting some of the more irrational responses that would emerge later—and who was capable of rectifying the frame.

Discussant: It seems to me that there can be no choice: I'm convinced that the insurance destroys all hope of a constructive therapeutic experience, while it might be possible for the patient to work out his financial situation so that he could come to therapy once a week.

Discussant: Would you reduce the fee, if necessary?

Therapist: My experience with reducing the fee is that it is a rather seductive deviation that also undermines the communicative properties of the field.

Langs: Yes, in principle it is best to state a single fee and to maintain it. A reduction in fee is bound to create significant complications, though it would be considerably better than filling out the insurance form, since it would not entail blatant violations of the patient's privacy and confidentiality. The influence of a reduced fee needs to be put to an empirical test through a full application of the listening and validating processes.

Technically, all you need do under these circumstances is show the patient what he is saying, directly and indirectly, about the consequences of your filling out the insurance form. State quite clearly that he is indicating that there really is no choice: if he is to have any sort of safe and viable treatment situation, it clearly must be without the insurance. He is indicating that the problem now becomes a question of whether and how he can afford the fee, paying entirely on his own.

Discussant: Would I be correct in formulating one aspect of this problem in this way—that he may well have persecutory anxieties and fantasies, and that with the insurance the therapist, while helping him out on one level, would on another be involved in an actual persecution of the patient? Stating it that way, I am able to see how the patient's persecutory fantasies and anxieties could never be resolved in the presence of the insurance.

Langs: Yes, that's excellent. There is a striking split in the implications of the insurance: it is a hoped-for protector, and a dreaded persecutor. And the insurance would indeed be an actuality with persecutory unconscious functions that would confirm both past persecutions and the persecutory introjects within the patient, reinforcing their presence and rendering them unanalyzable. To make a related point, completing the insurance form would place the therapist not only in collusion with the insurance company, but also with the patient's wife. It is striking that it was she who investigated the insurance, a fact that highlights the extent to which third parties become involved under these conditions—his wife on his side, and your secretary on yours.

I see that time is growing short, so let's now hear the next session.

Therapist: This is the session after my vacation. The patient came in and saw the form on my desk, and said, I see that the form is still there, unsigned. It's still not signed. Money is important in my family; it's a big problem. I'd like to talk today about my wife. She's very practical when she shops, she watches prices and analyzes every purchase. She looks for bargains because she feels we can't afford things, but she's really such a sour woman. And I worry about money too, but I'm not like her. I like to have fun sometimes.

My wife would like to buy a house, and we now have three children, and I'd like to save a little and buy a home, maybe take a vacation. She manages all the money and does a great job. Last Saturday it was raining and she was anxious. She was tight, upset, and walking around. Once I said let's go to her parents she was extremely happy. Their relationship puzzles me. They used to fight like cats and dogs, but once my wife was away from her mother she missed her. Now she sees her all the time. The two of them make all the decisions. I dislike my mother-in-law. I feel she is irresponsible, and she has never worked. She's just like my wife; she takes care of the money in her family. But she's irresponsible and owes money to everyone. Her house is a mess. My father-in-law makes a lot of money and they have nothing. My father-in-law once spent his weekly allowance and his wife wouldn't give him a penny more. They fight a lot and the house is chaotic. Their marriage is on the rocks and their other two children are pretty nutty.

He went on: My mother-in-law is too involved with my wife and my children. It's already making my children anxious. My wife and her mother are together all the time and I can't stand it. He went on in some detail about how his mother-in-law always intrudes on his relationship with his wife, and how furious he feels toward the both of them. He said, My wife should make new friends. They're always putting other people down. My wife is too withdrawn because of all of this.

At this point I said to the patient that he had commented on the insurance form and wondered whether it was signed or not. And in a way, we could take what he went on to say as a kind of commentary based on his concern about the insurance form and what it means to him. I said, You know, you talk about safety and protection, and how your wife handles the bills, and that initially this made you comfortable. But on the other hand your mother-in-law is quite irresponsible in handling money and uses it to humiliate and hurt, and even take revenge on, your father-in-law. In a way you're saying that although there is some protection in the way money is handled, there is also an element of irresponsibility. And the same applies to the insurance: you want the insurance money, but you're also saying that it would be irresponsible and could lead to destructive, angry things happening here and to destructive, angry feelings.

You've also talked about how overinvolved your wife and mother-in-law are, and how unimportant the things that they say are. This has implications for your feelings about the insurance form: you're saying that if I accede to signing it, I in some way become identified with your mother-in-law and wife as someone who on the surface provides you essential safety, but who would also be doing something inappropriate. I would be doing something to make treatment superficial and even meaningless. And your reaction is divided: on the one hand, you would like to stand up to your wife and mother-in-law, but on the other you feel somewhat safe with the way things are and so go along with it. The same is true with the insurance form: you feel safe going along with my signing it, but nonetheless you see it as irresponsible and as something that would make me destructive and instrusive like your mother-in-law.

Langs: Well, that is, of course, a rather long intervention. Any brief comments?

Discussant: It seems evident that the therapist made a rather lengthy and somewhat confusing attempt to indicate to the patient the destructive consequences that would follow from his signing the insurance form. However, the intervention became a bit diffuse and I think that it lost its sense of precision and definition.

Discussant: I was struck that the patient's comment was that the insurance form is sitting there still unsigned. There is a strong likelihood, I think, that the patient is alluding in derivative form to the fact that he did not give written permission to the therapist to complete the form. In addition, of course, it's almost as if he's directing the therapist not to sign the form, not to complete it.

Discussant: I get the feeling that the therapist should have been more selective. He might have picked out a communication which shows how split the patient is about the insurance situation. As I recall, the patient praised his wife for her economizing, but then saw this as a reflection of her being a shallow woman and objected that they should have fun sometimes. Then he said that allowing the wife, the woman, to take care of his money, gives him relief, but that such management can be either obsessive or irresponsible. In any case, he was quite clearly saying something about the detrimental consequences of allowing a third party to pay for therapy.

Langs: Yes, I too would have been quite selective in highlighting those derivatives that reveal the patient's unconscious realization of the destructiveness of completing the insurance form. And I certainly would have used his inital comment to show that the first indication of the patient's mixed feelings about the insurance lies in the fact that he did not give written permission for the release of information. From there it would have been easy to touch upon the split image of his wife in regard to her management of the money, and to mention the two women, one of whom manages very tightly and goes to an extreme of economizing, and the other, who is quite irresponsible.

The reference to the mother-in-law not giving her husband an extra penny, and to the large income that his father-in-law commands, hints very strongly at the likelihood that the patient himself realizes on some level that he could afford a once-weekly psychotherapy at the fee asked by the therapist and that he really does not need insurance coverage. Notice too the allusion to the chaotic house: under conditions of deviation, the treatment situation becomes quite unmanageable.

The patient also repeats the theme of the third-party intruder, and indicates how the use of a maternal figure for symbiotic needs is quite destructive to more mature relatedness. It is this highly gratifying function of the insurance that the patient rightly, though indirectly, describes as undermining the mature sectors of the therapeutic relationship. Insurance gratifies to the point of parasitism; it destroys the therapeutic field. His objections to the intrusion of his mother-in-law are unconscious directives toward rectification which could be readily utilized in your intervention to the patient. Recognize too that the patient ends his commentary by saying that his wife, because of her symbiotic-like tie to her mother, is withdrawn and has no friends. Her more mature relationship to her husband has been disrupted. These are but some of the consequences of the presence of insurance for the treatment relationship, and they could have been spelled out to the patient quite specifically.

Discussant: For me, the derivatives in this session were somewhat weaker than in the previous hour. Dr. Langs, do you have any thesis that could explain this shift?

Therapist: If I may, I might not have made clear in my description of the end of the previous hour that I couched my intervention, especially since I was responding to the patient's distress about not having insurance, in a way that I think suggested to him that I would sign the form. That was another implication of the patient's remark at the beginning of this session about my not having signed the form.

Langs: Yes, I believe that you have answered the question. The resistances intensify because of that likelihood, and we see again the influence of the actualities of the management of the framework on the patient's communicative resistances—the latter are clearly an interactional product. As a result, the derivatives become somewhat more distant, in contrast to the close derivatives we saw when you made your first intervention and included some hope of rectification.

Discussant: I had an additional impression. This is a session after the therapist had taken a vacation. And certainly the material related to a sense of fusion between the patient's wife and her mother must reflect certain longings within the patient for a comparable relationship with the therapist, especially in light of the early interruption in the sessions. But then it occurred to me that the completion of the insurance form would serve as a way of binding the therapist to the patient, of gratifying these symbiotic needs, and therefore of setting them apart from any possible analytic work and, at the same time, of infantilizing the patient. It would seem that completing the form would give the patient the very type of gratification he is objecting to.

Discussant: I had always thought of resistances as being equivalent to intrapsychic defenses as they are expressed in the therapeutic relationship—I won't say in terms of transference, because I now know that resistances can have both transference and nontransference underpinnings. What I realize now is that resistances can derive from the very way in which the patient and therapist create the treatment situation—the therapeutic environment, as we are terming it. It seems then that there can be many sources of resistance in psychotherapy—in the patient, in the therapist, and in the very conditions of treatment.

Langs: Yes, for that reason I will postpone an extensive discussion of resistances until the last part of this course, when we will deal primarily with interventions. Many analysts think of resistances in terms of transference resistances and consider them as primarily intrapsychic phenomena. Here we have established the importance of interactional resistances, with the very sources you just identified. And because of the complexities, despite its critical importance in the therapeutic interaction, we will have to wait until we have completed our examination of the relationship between patient and therapist before turning to that subject.

Discussant: To come back to this patient, it seems to me that he is also saying that in the presence of a third party conversation becomes something like meaningless chatter. I would see this as a reflection of the Type C communicative properties of the bipersonal field under such conditions. For me, the Type C barrier qualities are being emphasized in this session, far more than the manner in which deviations constitute expressions of the Type B communicative mode and projective identification.

Langs: I would agree. This may have arisen because the patient is himself in desperate need of some Type C barriers, especially if he is not to have the Type A communicative field and an opportunity for true insight. In addition, the therapist has not as yet specifically signed the insurance form, an act which would certainly constitute on one level a projective identification into the patient. It is there that you might experience the patient's fears of being crucified and his sense of assault, since that would certainly be one quality of the interactional projection under these conditions. On an object relational level, it seems to me that the patient is saying that the therapist who completes an insurance form is himself rather crazy and in a state of chaos, and that he is weak, exploitative, and destructive.

Discussant: On the subject of how the insurance form protects the patient from separation anxieties, the very fact that the therapist keeps a form provided him by the patient enables the patient to experience a piece of himself in the therapist's hands.

Langs: Yes, that is quite true; there are both pathological defenses and pathological gratifications for both patients and therapists under these conditions. Recognize that the therapist too may well find this a means of alleviating his separation anxieties vis-à-vis the patient. In a sense, then, through this deviation both patient and therapist offer each other an unpredictable and pathological hold fraught with danger and anxiety. The containing functions take on a pathological tone, and in addition the therapist expresses his refractoriness toward certain contents from the patient. By signing the insurance form he is indicating on some level that he wishes not to contain the sickest and most disturbed parts of the patient's inner world and their expression.

Finally, your comment gives me an opportunity to emphasize again that the therapist's possession of the insurance form, and even its ultimate completion, alludes not merely to a fantasy, but to an actuality filled with realistic and imaginary unconscious implications and meaning. On one level the therapist and patient truly become inseparable and fused. That level of experience is not some fantasied distortion or a projection; it is a reality that the patient has introjected, one that precludes interpretive work in this sphere for the very reason that we are not dealing with distorted fantasies but with the real implications of an actuality.

It is this concept that seems so difficult for many therapists to grasp. They see the therapeutic situation and the material from the patient as falling almost entirely into the realm of fantasy. They believe that anything can be analyzed and that that is enough, but they are mistaken. The unconscious implications of a reality cannot simply be analyzed; the reality itself must first be rectified. Only under the conditions of a new reality can the therapist deal primarily with distorted fantasies and undertake analytic work as usually conceived.

As we shall see in some detail later on, there are therefore two types of interpretation: the first is the classical interpretation of a distorted unconscious fantasy, memory, introject, or perception; the second, which must be accompanied by rectification, touches upon the unconscious implications of actualities within the therapeutic interaction, most of them deriving from the therapist's unconscious communications. I do not believe that this distinction has been made in the literature, and it is a crucial one. We will return to it when we discuss interventions.

Discussant: As I understand it, then, you would have given the insurance form back to the patient pending further exploration.

Langs: Exactly.

Therapist: I must say that I experienced a very deep split in respect to insurance. I feel like a real bastard when I do not sign an insurance form, even when the directives are quite clear from the patient. On the other hand, I have now come to feel like a real bastard when I do sign one, because I now realize how destructive my seeming act of kindness really is. It's a terrible dilemma.

Langs: So it is. This type of therapeutic work can only be undertaken with a full use of the listening and validating processes, and with a sound capacity for appropriate interventions. You are struggling here with something every therapist has difficulty with: the need to recognize that the development of a secure therapeutic space is founded on a capacity to reasonably and appropriately frustrate the patient, to effect a sensible version of the rule of abstinence. You need a quite deep understanding of the implications of a failure in that regard in order to give you the strength to maintain what is on every level a sound therapeutic attitude. I can only hope that each of you has been able to gather some of this strength from observing this particular clinical situation, and from seeing the extent to which our hypotheses regarding the implications of signing the insurance form have received Type Two derivative validation from this patient.

Discussant: I can see how easy it would be to completely miss the implications of the insurance if you lack a sensitivity to adaptive contexts and to the listening process as it has been developed in this course. Throughout this meeting I have been thinking about Medicaid patients who have one hundred percent insurance coverage, and for whom we are required to keep voluminous records. For some time I have experienced a sense of frustration in my work with these patients, and I have seen many therapeutic situations which I would now describe in terms of the Type C bipersonal field. Your remarks also have helped me understand why so many of these patients cancel their sessions, and why the therapeutic work is so very unpredictable.

Therapist: Yes, I too have seen an inordinately high percentage of cancellations with such patients.

Langs: Since time is short, let's hear how this session ended.

Therapist: As I spoke, the patient kept saying that I was right about his wife and mother-in-law, but once I had stopped he said he wasn't sure that he could buy everything I said about how all of that connected to the insurance. He could see how his mother and mother-in-law dominated him, and how he didn't feel safe, but he was not sure that he could buy all of that. He said, I've been feeling better, coming here. I feel like talking to you, but we need the money. My wife feels that there is no money and she's telling me how poor we are. She wouldn't let me come to treatment even though I had suffered for a long time. She kept saying the checkbook wouldn't allow me to go for treatment. There's no extra money. Finally, when I got this insurance, she said that I could go. If you don't sign that form, I'm afraid to go home to my wife. She will become irrational and go crazy. You don't realize what will happen at home.

I then concluded the hour by saying we will continue to explore the question of the insurance, and will come to a decision about it soon. That's where we are right now, so it won't be possible to give you the final word on this subject.

Langs: In brief, the patient alludes to the positive introject that he is deriving in the context of the therapist's hesitation about completing the form. While he does not entirely accept on a conscious level the therapist's intervention, he does so by implication and splits off onto his wife his own anxieties about a secure therapeutic field in which his craziness will appear. Largely because of his uncertainty about what you will do, we for the moment do not obtain additional Type Two derivative validation.

Well, there are many issues that we could discuss on the basis of this material. For me, the final note for the moment is the patient's dread of a therapeutic regression within an unaltered bipersonal field, an issue that would have to be handled interpretively in order to permit the continuation of this therapy.

The reality of time is now upon us, and we must stop for today. I want once again to thank our guest for his extremely illuminating presentations, and since we are completing another segment of this course I would also like to thank the group for their many perceptive comments. I can think of no more fitting way to end this part of the course than having confronted one of the major issues regarding the therapeutic environment in today's psychotherapeutic and analytic practices. We have worked over the data, drawn some conclusions, and each of you can now seek additional validation on your own. Thank you all.

POSTSCRIPT

I have been able to obtain a one-month follow-up on this last therapeutic situation. Between the last session presented to us and the following hour, the therapist completed and signed the insurance form. It was on his desk at the beginning of the next session, and the patient noticed that the therapist had signed it. The therapist acknowledged he had done so and reminded the patient that he must either sign the release on the form or provide him a separate letter giving him permission to release the information involved.

The patient agreed and then went on to talk about a few things, which I will briefly summarize. First, he had begun to realize that his wife attacks and destroys him, and ruins everything they have. She makes him feel helpless; she's such an angry person, and he feels weak in coping with her. He realized that his main problem is in his marriage and that his contribution stems from the fact that he never had a strong father to identify with—his father never stood up to his mother or to anyone, and the patient is the same. He resented too the way in which his mother infantilized him, and he kept repeating that he's unable to cope with his wife and mother-in-law.

At this point, the therapist intervened and pointed out that he had signed and completed the insurance form, and that the patient, rather than responding with a sense of gratitude or gratification since his direct needs had been met, went on instead to talk about weak men like his father, men who were unable to handle assertive women, and men who are helpless. This seemed to reflect how the patient saw the therapist once he had signed the insurance form. Now they had both of them given in to his wife. The patient responded with denial and with a statement that he was glad the insurance form had been signed, and with that the hour ended.

The patient was sick and missed the next hour, and in the following session he apologized for having been ill and then spoke at some length about how great the previous session had been. He had realized that his problem is with his wife and he had discussed a lot with her, and for the first time in his life he had taken responsibility for the finances and checkbook. He described in detail how his wife blames him and sees him at fault, and how she saw him as totally lost in fantasy, as introverted and as deserting her. She also felt that he was a hypochondriac and that he had done many destructive things in their relationship. The patient felt that the conversation had cleared the air and he was now ready to terminate the treatment. The therapist intervened by saying that it might be wise for him to wait a while before effecting that decision, and the patient agreed.

In the following session he continued to describe how well everything seemed to be going. After ruminating along those lines, he then revealed that he had twice experienced during that week a sense of dissociation in which his mind left his body, and he required a great burst of energy to bring them together. He ruminated about not being certain why all of that had emerged, and then spoke in some detail about how much better things were at home.

The therapist intervened here because the patient had failed to pay for the session he had missed, and he asked the patient what came to mind about that. The patient responded with an intense sense of outrage and denied that he had ever been told that he was responsible for missed sessions; he felt he was only responsible for the hours that he kept. The therapist clarified the ground rules and with that the hour ended.

To comment briefly, we can see that the therapist experienced himself under considerable countertransference pressure to sign the form, much of it masqueraded in terms of the pressures from the patient's wife. In discussing these sessions with me, he felt that he had acted inappropriately and impulsively, and he had been rather depressed by the patient's response. He had failed to allow the patient to express unconsciously, through derivatives, the directives and realistic implications of completing or not completing the insurance form. He did not allow the patient to lead the way, to put the interventions into him. The fact that he acted unilaterally without such material suggests that strong countertransference factors were at work.

In the first session after the form had been signed, we see the type of split discussed earlier: conscious gratitude and its unconscious opposite. In derivative communications the patient indicates that the therapist's decision to sign the form was, on some level of actuality, an act of destruction, an infantilization, and a moment of weakness in response to which the patient feels helpless. Through an exquisite derivative, the patient conveys his experience of a negative and destructive introjective identification of the therapist on this basis, one that is a repetition of introjects derived from his weak father. The genetic element here falls primarily into the nontransference realm since the therapist has now, in reality, repeated the traumatizing behaviors of the patient's father. The patient also states that he and the father are alike—that he and the therapist are now the same in respect to their psychopathology. The growth-promoting, insight-generating differential between therapist and patient no longer exists.

Why then the immediate repudiation of the therapist's intervention which approached some of these issues? It seems likely that the primary reason lies in the fact that the therapist has in reality signed the form, and that as a result his verbal interventions have lost their meaning and are seen as an empty facade. The therapist presents himself as split: behaviorally he signs the form, while verbally he speaks of its destructive implications without rectifying the situation. Here too the splitting of both patient and therapist are comparable, and insightful therapeutic work unfeasible.

The patient's illness the following week is a striking form of Type Two derivative validation of the thesis that the signing of the insurance form destroys the therapeutic environment and its holding and containing qualities to the point that somatization often takes place. This is followed in the next hour with a massive effort at denial and with thoughts of leaving treatment. A model of rectification appears, in that the patient has taken responsibility for the family finances. But when it is not picked up, the patient attempts to develop a type of manic-defensive denial which undoubtedly is strengthened by the manic-like qualities of the completion of the insurance form. In addition, through a series of introjects, he alludes to his feelings that the therapist is somehow in his own world and has deserted him.

Rather sadly, the thesis regarding the splits in both patient and therapist is validated in Type Two derivative form in the final hour described here, when the patient reveals two episodes of mind-body dissociation. With the communicative properties of the bipersonal field disrupted, the basis for this experience does not emerge in derivative form either in terms of the therapist's contribution or that of the patient. This is, in every sense, an interactional symptom.

That hour—and quite appropriately, this discussion—ends with the patient's own modification of the framework: his not paying for a missed session. As a Type Two derivative organized around the completion of the insurance form, we can once again observe the patient's intense rage regarding the conditions of the treatment, his sense of betrayal, and his expectation that there will be no semblance of security or structure to this treatment situation. The inappropriately and symbiotically gratifying aspects of the completed form—in a sense, free sessions—are also conveyed through this action-laden derivative. However sad this final note, perhaps it can be transformed into the hope that these transactions and their all-too-evident implications will help us all to recognize the need for a sound therapeutic environment and, more specifically, for a major reconsideration of the effects of insurance on the therapeutic situation.

A final note regarding this patient: The very next week he came in and told the therapist that he had decided quite definitely to terminate. He spent the entire hour detailing the extent to which his relationship with his wife had improved. He described feeling considerably better and felt that he no longer needed therapy. According to the therapist, the material was quite flat and empty. He attempted on several occasions to confront the patient with his apparent denial and flight, but to no avail. On that note the treatment ended.

Appendix A

THE STANDARD
THERAPEUTIC ENVIRONMENT

I. The basic components
  A. The stable ground rules or frame
    1. The spatiotemporal setting and fixed arrangements
        a. The use of a private office, with a soundproof consultation room, in a professional building
        b. A set fee with the patient fully responsible for all sessions
        c. A set time and length for all sessions
        d. Set positions for patient and therapist, either face-to-face in two chairs, or with the patient on the couch and the therapist behind him, out of sight
    2. The guaranteed constants
        a. Total confidentiality
        b. The one-to-one relationship with total privacy
  B. The fluid frame: the ground rules open to variation despite all efforts at consistency
    1. The therapist's relative anonymity and the absence of personal opinions and self-revelations
    2. The therapist's use of neutral interventions geared toward the securing of the therapeutic environment and toward interpretive-reconstructive responses

3. The therapist's physicianly concern and qualified offer to help the patient, and his full attention to the patient during sessions, including his use of free-floating attention
4. The therapist's commitment to work therapeutically with the patient until the point of symptom resolution
5. The rule of abstinence: the attempt to eliminate or minimize all inappropriate gratifications for both patient and therapist
6. The fundamental rule of free association
7. The agreement to analyze all major decisions before enactment

II. The functions of the therapeutic environment (as an actuality managed by the therapist, whose efforts are filled with unconscious implications)
   A. The establishment of a therapeutic space and open communicative field: the frame as the main background determinant of the unconscious implications of the transactions between patient and therapist, their meanings, purposes and functions
   B. Offering the patient a therapeutic hold and a container for his pathological projective identifications
   C. A means of providing the patient implicit ego strength and positive introjective identifications
   D. A basis for the development of a sound therapeutic alliance
   E. Creating the conditions for truth therapy (as opposed to lie therapy)
   F. A means of conveying a variety of fundamental and background communications from the therapist that pertain to the relatively fixed and stable elements in his relationship with the patient
      1. A reflection of the therapist's capacity to manage his own inner state, the patient's, and the therapeutic interaction
      2. Depending on how managed, a vehicle through which the therapist's noncountertransference- and/or countertransference-based unconscious constellations are expressed
   G. A way of providing secure and well-defined boundaries, psychological and physical, between patient and therapist
   H. The means through which the conditions for an analyzable therapeutic regression are created

III. The therapist's management of the therapeutic environment
   A. Establishing the therapeutic contract (usually in the first session)
   B. Maintaining that contract, and with it a communicatively open and growth-promoting therapeutic environment
   C. Managing the therapist's own propensities to inappropriately alter the framework
      1. The use of restraint and self-analysis
      2. The maintenance of a steady frame in the absence of conscious or unconscious directives to the contrary from the patient
   D. Managing and interpreting the patient's wishes or actual unilateral efforts to modify the frame
      1. The response to inappropriate pressures (e.g., a request to change a single hour, to forgo the responsibility for sessions, or to alter any of the other basic components of the therapeutic environment)
         a. The maintenance of a steady hold with maximum nonparticipation by the therapist
         b. Analyzing the implications of the proposed deviation in terms of its unconscious meanings and functions
         c. Rectifying the framework when the patient has modified it (restoring the basic environment)
      2. Responses to the rare expressions of an appropriate need for an alteration in the framework (e.g., a new hour based on a job change; and sometimes in response to a therapeutic emergency such as the threat of suicide or homicide or an acute regression)
         a. The necessity of maintaining the steady frame as the initial response that will permit full and open analysis
         b. The use of the patient's direct and especially derivative material as a guide
         c. A full analysis and interpretation of the implications of the deviation under consideration, with a full conception of its actual implications, as well as its distorted meanings for the patient (and the therapist)
         d. A private self-analytic investigation of inappropriate contributions to the proposed deviation derived from the therapist's countertransferences

        e. The basic value of maintaining the frame wherever possible rather than deviating

        f. Deviating only if absolutely necessary, with full subsequent analysis and rectification (if feasible) at the earliest possible juncture

    3. The critical role of maintaining the frame and rectifying it once a deviation has occurred, as a basis for open conscious and unconscious communications from the patient, and consistent and symbolically meaningful interpretations from the therapist

  E. The handling of inevitable agreed upon (in the basic contract) breaks in the therapeutic environment (e.g., a vacation by the therapist)

    1. Maintaining all such breaks as an adaptive context for listening to the material from the patient

    2. Maintaining the security of the other dimensions of the framework

    3. Rectifying and interpreting frame issues before all other types of therapeutic work

IV. Basic types of alterations in the therapeutic environment

  A. Changes in the fixed frame

    1. Those that take place within the basic therapeutic contract (e.g., the therapist's vacation)

    2. Those that extend beyond the fixed therapeutic contract—virtually all other alterations in the ground rules

  B. Nonneutral and noninterpretive interventions—directives, personal opinions, direct reassurance, and the like

  C. Erroneous interpretations, which maintain the fixed frame but express aspects of the therapist's countertransferences

  D. Inappropriate alterations in the therapeutic environment

  E. Failures to rectify the frame

V. Common unconscious communications that are realized and gratified through alterations in the framework

  A. Uninsightful *framework deviation cures* (in contrast to ego-building *framework rectification cures*, which occur when the framework is held steady)

  B. The creation of lie therapy and an avoidance of the most disturbed parts of the patient's—and therapist's—inner mental life (in contrast to truth therapy, which takes place within a secure frame)

C. The reinforcement of unmodifiable resistances supported by the actualities of the therapist's unconscious communications as reflected in the deviation

D. The development of pathological and disruptive holding and containing efforts, or failures in these areas of the therapist's functioning

E. The direct gratification of pathological instinctual drive wishes, defenses, and superego inputs

F. The infantilization of the patient—and the therapist

G. The dissolution of clear-cut boundaries through which the transactions accrue actual seductive and aggressive—sadistic and masochistic—implications

H. The gratification of a variety of unconscious fantasies and memories which render their contribution to the patient's psychopathology fixed and unanalyzable

I. The destruction of a sound therapeutic space and the sense of trust and safety

J. The creation of sectors of misalliance and bastions

K. The repetition of past pathogenic interactions which reinforce the patient's psychopathology and render it unanalyzable

L. The confirmation and reinforcement of aspects of the patient's own pathological inner mental world and pathological introjects

M. The gratification of a variety of merger and fusion fantasies that alleviate separation anxieties but preclude growth and eventual independence

N. The generation of negative role and image evocations, and pathological projective identifications

O. The development of impenetrable Type C barriers

P. The likelihood of nontherapeutic regressions

Q. The introduction of the countertransferences of the therapist into the bipersonal field

R. Additional functions and meanings that are actualized on the basis of the specific unconscious implications of a given ground rule and its alteration

Appendix B
GLOSSARY

Abstracting-Particularizing Process, the. That aspect of the listening process in which first-order, manifest themes are used to derive more general or abstract themes, from which second-order specific themes are generated. The latter are often monitored in terms of the therapeutic relationship and the me/not-me interface.

Adaptational-Interactional Viewpoint, the. A clinical-metapsychological approach to the patient and therapeutic interaction which takes into account both intrapsychic and interactional processes, conscious and unconscious in both spheres.

Adaptive Context, the. The specific reality stimulus that evokes an intrapsychic response. *Direct* or *nonneurotic* adaptive contexts are those stimuli which evoke linear intrapsychic reactions and nonneurotic communicative responses; in essence, they are unrelated to psychopathological reactions and mechanisms. *Indirect* or *neurotic* adaptive contexts are those precipitants that evoke convoluted, derivative intrapsychic responses that contain pathological unconscious fantasies, memories, and introjects; they are related to psychopathology and to neurosis. Often an adaptive context outside of the therapeutic relationship will have a direct context within its manifest content, and an indirect context in its latent content. The latter is, as a rule, a derivative of a significant adaptive context within the therapeutic situation itself, communicated in disguised form. On the whole, the major indirect and neurotic adaptive contexts derive from the therapeutic interaction. The term *primary adaptive task* is a synonym for adaptive context.

Adaptive Context, Form of Representation. The manner in which the patient portrays the manifest and latent contents of the adaptive context, and its links to the therapist, in the course of his behaviors and associations. A key factor in determining the possibility of interpretive and reconstructive interventions by the therapist, it is comparable to the mode of representation through which the manifest dream portrays latent dream contents and meanings.

Adaptive Context, Primary. A term used to specify the need to ultimately identify those adaptive stimuli which arise within the therapeutic interaction from the therapist and to which the patient responds, consciously and unconsciously. The word *primary* alludes here to the central and ultimately critical role of the interventions and behaviors of the therapist in the derivative responses of the patient. See also *Adaptive Context, Secondary*.

Adaptive Context, Secondary. A term reserved for adaptive stimuli generated by individuals other than the therapist and by the patient himself—within or outside of therapy—to which he responds in both conscious and unconscious form. The term is of importance in that it stresses the more peripheral nature of such contexts. It points to the need to ultimately link such a constellation of stimulus and response to a prior or additional adaptive context derived from the therapist. Secondary adaptive contexts may occur in the patient's outside life or within treatment, the latter illustrated by a patient's lateness, absence, or other notable segment of behavior to which the patient himself then responds.

Associational Matrix. See *Communicative Network*.

Bastion. A term first used by Baranger and Baranger (1966) to allude to a split-off part of the bipersonal field which is under interactional repression and denial, so that the contents involved are avoided by both patient and therapist or analyst.

Bipersonal Field, the. A term first used by Baranger and Baranger (1966) as a metaphor for the therapeutic situation. It stresses the interactional qualities of the field, and postulates that every experience and communication within the field receives vectors from both patient and therapist or analyst. The metaphor requires the concept of an *interface* along which communication occurs between the two members of the therapeutic dyad, and points to the need to conceptualize the presence, role, and function of a framework for the field.

Bridge to the Therapist. A manifest allusion to the therapist or therapy occurring in the patient's associations toward the latter part of a session. Its importance lies in facilitating both interpretive interventions and the playing back of selected derivatives that pertain to an unmentioned adaptive context related to the treatment situation.

Commentary. A term used to describe the patient's responses to interventions from the therapist (including managements of the framework). These associations and behaviors contain validating and non-validating communications, and they are to be viewed as a mixture of fantasy and reality, accurate perceptiveness and distortion. Often, commentaries take the form of *transversal communications;* unconsciously, they convey the patient's evaluation of the intervention.

Communication, Convoluted. An image used to describe the presence of derivatives and the indirect expression of pathological unconscious fantasies, memories, introjects, and interactional contents and mechanisms. It is one of the hallmarks of neurotic communication. See *Neurotic Communication.*

Communication, Linear. A sequence evoked by an adaptive context in which the intrapsychic response is relatively logical, readily apparent or easily inferred, directly responsive, and relatively undisguised. It is a form of reaction that characterizes the direct adaptive context and nonneurotic communication. See *Nonneurotic Communication.*

Communicative Field. The amalgam from patient and therapist that characterizes the dominant mode of communicative interaction in a given bipersonal field. See *Bipersonal Field, Type A Field, Type B Field, Type C Field.*

Communicative Interaction, Unconscious and Conscious, Spiraling. A term used to describe the central transactions between patient and therapist within the bipersonal field. It alludes to the conscious but, more especially, the unconscious exchanges between the two participants to therapy, as these exchanges take place as part of a to and fro interactional process.

Communicative Network. That aspect of the material from the patient which contains conscious and especially unconscious meaning. It comprises the adaptive context, the derivative complex, and the bridge back to the therapist or analyst. As a rule, analysis of the unconscious implications of the communicative network will reveal the implications of the therapeutic context or indicator. The term is synonymous with *associational matrix.*

Communicative Space. A metaphor for the interior of the bipersonal field and for the realm in which communication occurs between patient and therapist or analyst. The image suggests that there are a number of possible communicative spaces, each with a set of defining attributes. It allows, too, for the recognition that patient and therapist may be in separate communicative spaces, rather than sharing the same mode.

Communicative Style or Mode. The form of communicative expression that characterizes the interactional thrusts and form of relatedness of the patient and therapist or analyst. See *Type A Field and Mode, Type B Field and Mode, Type C Field and Mode.*

Conception. A term first used by Bion (1962) to describe the outcome when a preconception mates with appropriate sense impressions. More broadly, the term may be used to describe the saturation of a preconception through a realization that satisfies its inherent expectations.

Confirmation, Primary. A term used to describe the patient's initial response to an intervention, often in the form of direct affirmation or negation. In general, direct agreement has little bearing on the validity of the intervention, while negation often suggests nonvalidation, though, in exceptional circumstances, it will constitute a defensive response that emerges prior to secondary confirmation.

Confirmation, Secondary. The extended response to the therapist's interventions (including managements of the frame) which contain selected facts, uniquely original and previously unknown communications from the patient that extend the intervention, especially in the form of Type Two derivatives. Psychoanalytic confirmation of an intervention requires the presence of truly unexpected Type Two derivatives. In general, their absence constitutes nonconfirmation. A synonym is Type Two derivative validation.

Contained, the. A metaphor first used by Bion (1962) to allude to the contents and psychic mechanisms that are projectively identified by an infant into his mother, and by a patient into his analyst. More broadly, they allude to the contents and functions of a projective identification emanating from a subject toward an object.

Container, the. A metaphor first used by Bion (1962) for the recipient of a projective identification. The container may be open to containing such projective identifications, or may be refractory. The metaphor also implies the processing or metabolizing of the introjected contents and functions. An adequate container is seen as being in a state of *reverie.*

Containing and **Containing Function.** A metaphor used to describe the taking in and processing of projective identifications. An adequate containing function has been described by Bion (1962) as a state of *reverie* in the mother or analyst, and may also apply to the therapist or patient. Containing function alludes to the receptiveness to projective identifications, and to an ability to metabolize and detoxify pathological *interactional projections,* returning them to the subject in appropriately modified form. For the therapist or analyst, this process implies the metabolizing of a projective identification to conscious insight, imparted to the patient through a valid interpretation and through the maintenance of a secure framework and hold.

Countertransference. A term used in this volume to allude to all inappropriate and pathological responses of the therapist to his patient. These reactions are founded on pathological unconscious fantasies, memories, introjects, and interactional mechanisms (see Langs 1976c).

Day Residue. A term first used by Freud (1900) to allude to the reality stimulus for the dream. More broadly, it may be seen as the external stimulus, filled with latent and unconscious meaning, that evokes any intrapsychic response. In that sense, it is virtually synonymous with the *adaptive context*.

Denudation. A term used by Bion (1962) to metaphorically represent one type of effect that the contained may have on the container, and the reverse: the generation of a disruptive and destructive experience and set of affects, leading to some form of inner disturbance that often is characterized by the destruction of function and meaning.

Derivative Complex. A term used for the material from the patient as it is organized around a specific adaptive context in order to reveal unconscious implications, Type Two derivative meaning. This is one of the four elements involved in the basic formulation of each session.

Derivative Complex, Convoluted. See *Derivatives, Coalescing*.

Derivative Complex, Linear. A simplistic group of derivatives, related to a particular adaptive context, which tend to flatly repeat a single theme or function, without complexity or depth. See also *Communication, Linear*.

Derivatives. Manifest communications, verbal and nonverbal, which contain in some disguised form expressions of unconscious fantasies, memories, introjects, and perceptions. These are, then, the communicative expressions of neuroses, and the basis on which they are maintained. See *Type One Derivatives, Type Two Derivatives*.

Derivatives, Coalescing. A derivative complex which, when organized around a specific adaptive context, indirectly and quite unconsciously reveals a wide range of divergent, underlying meanings and functions in relationship to that context. Such a group of derivatives may include unconscious fantasies and unconscious perceptions, and reflect as well a variety of unconscious dynamics and genetics. They may also include the patient's unconscious interpretations and other speculations pertaining to both the therapist and himself. Together, they form a divergent but organizable entity which reveals a multiplicity of meanings pertaining to the relevant adaptive context. The term is a variation on the concept of convoluted communication. See also *Communication, Convoluted.*

Derivatives, Close. Associations from the patient which contain disguised representations of unconscious processes and contents in a form that is readily detectable, minimally defensive, and easily understood as a manifestation of the underlying qualities.

Derivatives, Distant. Those aspects of the patient's associations which represent unconscious processes and contents with considerable disguise, barely detectable meaning, and great defensiveness and resistance.

Derivatives, Embedded. A representation of an unconscious fantasy, memory, introject, or perception that is communicated as a seemingly irrelevant component of a sequence of manifest contents, in a form that seems peripheral to the main conscious intention and to the major first-order and general themes.

Derivatives, Playing Back. An intervention offered in the presence of a strong indicator and a meaningful derivative complex, but in the absence of any clear representation of the adaptive context with an evident link to the therapist. It is designed to create a state of tension and need—a preconception—which can be transformed into a condition of fulfillment—a conception—only through the direct recall and clear representation of the adaptive context—a step that is essential to further interpretive work.

Detoxification. A term used to describe the metabolism of a projective identification so that its relatively primitive and destructive qualities are altered through some appropriate means, usually through cognitive understanding directed toward insight. This process is an essential quality of *reverie*.

Empathy. A form of emotional knowing and noncognitive sharing in, and comprehending, the psychological and affective state of another person. Empathy involves both affect and cognition, and is based on a relatively nonconflicted interplay of introjective and projective mechanisms, and a variety of forms of unconscious sharing. It is a temporary form of immediate engagement and understanding, which must then be processed and validated along the lines designated for any subjective experience by the therapist or analyst—or patient.

Faith. A term used by Bion (1962) to describe a form of passive listening or intuiting by the therapist or analyst that is founded upon entering each session without desire, memory, or understanding. It implies a fundamental belief that the patient will put into the therapist or analyst in derivative form all that he needs for his own cure, and all that the latter requires for his interventions. It also implies an appreciation of the principle that each session should be its own creation, and that, unconsciously, the patient will provide the therapeutic situation with all that is necessary for his cure, except for the therapist's or analyst's interpretive interventions and management of the framework, which are themselves based on the ingredients provided by the patient.

First-Order Themes. See *Themes, First-Order.*

Frame. A metaphor for the implicit and explicit ground rules of psychotherapy or psychoanalysis. The image implies that the ground rules create a basic hold for the therapeutic interaction, and for both patient and therapist, and that they create a distinctive set of conditions within the frame that differentiate it in actuality and functionally from the conditions outside the frame. The metaphor requires, however, an appreciation of the human qualities of the frame and should not be used to develop an inanimate or overly rigid conception.

Frame, Fixed, Stable, or **Steady.** The relatively unchangeable or easily set ground rules such as the fee, time and length of sessions, the physical setting, and total confidentiality and privacy.

Frame, Variable or **Fluid.** Those aspects of the ground rules which will inevitably vary based on the presence of some degree of humanness and residual countertransference reflected in the ongoing work of the therapist. While the therapist strives to maintain these aspects of the framework at an optimal level, variations are bound to occur. Included here are the ground rules related to the therapist's relative anonymity and neutrality, the rule of abstinence, and, for the patient, the fundamental rule of free association and the need to analyze all major decisions.

Framework. A term used synonymously with *frame,* usually as a means of referring to the ground rules of the bipersonal field.

Framework Cures. The maladaptive alleviation of symptoms through an inappropriate modification in the frame.

Framework Deviation Cure. Previously termed *framework cure,* this concept covers the maladaptive alleviation of symptoms through inappropriate modification of the framework by either patient or therapist.

Framework Rectification Cure. The adaptive symptom alleviation that occurs through the establishment, securing, and maintenance of the ground rules of psychotherapy or psychoanalysis. Though unaccompanied by cognitive insight, such relief derive from unconscious positive introjects of the therapist, in terms of his constructive management of the framework, and from the inherently supportive holding and containing functions that are expressed when the framework is rectified and then maintained in a stable manner.

Functional Capacity or **Meaning.** A term used to indicate that associations never exist as isolated mental products, and that among their most essential dynamic implications are the unconscious communications contained within the material as they pertain to the therapeutic relationship and interaction. In essence, it is a concept that stresses that all associations have some dynamic relevance to the prevailing primary adaptive context.

Ground Rules. The implicit and explicit components of the analytic or therapeutic situation which establish the conditions for treatment and the means through which it shall be undertaken (for details, see Langs 1975c, 1976a, c).

Holding. A term used to describe the therapist's or analyst's establishment and maintenance of a secure and safe therapeutic situation. The result is a holding environment that is created through the implicit and explicit delineation of the ground rules, explicated through their maintenance, and significantly elaborated through valid interpretive efforts. The holding capacity of the therapist or analyst may be likened to his containing capacity, although the former is a more general concept, while the latter specifically refers to the taking in of interactional projections.

Identification. An intrapsychic process through which the self-representations and other aspects of the subject's internal mental world and defenses are unconsciously modified in keeping with a model derived from an external object.

Indicators. A clinical term that refers to all communications from the patient which point toward a need on his part for an intervention from the therapist. See *Therapeutic Context*.

Interactional Defenses. Intrapsychic protective mechanisms which are formed through vectors from both patient and therapist. This type of defense may exist in either participant to the therapeutic dyad, and has both intrapsychic and interactional (external) sources.

Interactional Projection. A synonym for projective identification (Langs 1976a).

Interactional Resistances. Any impediment to the progress of therapy that receives vectors, usually on an unconscious level, from both patient and therapist.

Interactional Symptoms. An emotional disturbance in either participant to the therapeutic dyad with significant sources from both participants (Langs 1976c).

Interactional Syndrome. Clusters of interactional symptoms (Langs 1976c).

Interface, Me/Not-Me. See *Me/Not-Me Interface.*

Interface of the Bipersonal Field. A metaphor used to describe a hypothetical line along which the communications between patient and therapist take place within the bipersonal field. It implies that vectors which determine this interface are derived from both patient and therapist, and that these may be contained in relatively fixed intermixtures or may vary considerably. Among the determinants of the qualities and location of the interface, pathological inputs from both patient and therapist are especially significant.

Interpretation. An attempt through verbal communication by the therapist to render unconscious meanings and functions conscious for the patient. Properly executed, this intervention alludes to an adaptive context, and to the relevant derivative complex in terms of unconscious perceptions and fantasies to which genetic implications are appended. Proper execution requires also that the intervention be stated in terms of the prevailing unconscious communicative interaction between the patient and the therapist, and its extension into the present and past from that nodal point, and that it illuminate the prevailing therapeutic contexts.

Intervention, Manifest. An intervention, usually verbal, offered by the therapist to the patient, designed to meet the therapeutic needs of the latter. The major interventions include silence, establishment and management of the framework, and comments designed to impart cognitive understanding, either through interpretation or reconstruction, or through the playing back of selected derivatives around an unmentioned adaptive context.

Intervention, Silent. A tentatively formulated intervention constructed as the therapist listens to the patient and subjected to silent validation before being presented.

Introject. An intrapsychic precipitate which stems from the process of introjective identification. Its specific qualities are determined by the extent to which it is transient or becomes structuralized, the degree to which it is incorporated into the self-image and self-representations or maintained as separate from them, the extent to which it is pathological or nonpathological, and the degree to which it is constructive or benign rather than destructive or malignant. In addition, these internal representations of conscious and unconscious traits and interactions have a variety of specific qualities in keeping with the nature of the object, the subject, their relationship, and the qualities of their separate and shared experiences. See *Unconscious Introject*.

Introjective Identification. The interactional process through which introjects are formed. As a rule, it is invoked by a projective identification from the object, although it may also entail active incorporative efforts by the subject. The process is influenced both by the nature of the object, the contents and processes that are being taken in, and the inner state of the subject.

Intuition. An immediate form of knowing, understanding, or learning developed without the conscious use of reasoning and knowledge.

Latent Content. The hidden dimension of the patient's associations contained in disguised form within the surface of that material. The term is usually used to refer to readily available inferences from the manifest content—disguised specific unconscious fantasies, memories, introjects, and perceptions.

Link to Therapist. A term used when investigating the manner in which the patient represents the adaptive context in the material of a given session. When this representation includes some allusion to the therapist or therapy, the link to the therapist is present. By contrast, when the adaptive context is represented through some outside relationship, the link to the therapist is absent. This distinction proves critical in that by and large the presence of the link fosters the use of interpretations, while its absence suggests a need to intervene through the playing back of selected derivatives around the unmentioned or poorly represented adaptive context.

Listening Process, the. A term used in the broadest possible psychoanalytic sense to refer to all conscious and unconscious intaking and organizing processes within both patient and therapist. For the therapist, the term includes all available cognitive and interactional sources of information about the patient, verbal and nonverbal, and his own use of sensory and nonsensory, conscious and unconscious, sensitivities. Included too are efforts at synthesizing and formulating cognitive material, the experience of role pressures and image evocations, and the metabolism of projective identifications. The process culminates in conscious understanding or insight, in proper holding and containing, and in the formulation of a valid intervention. Similar processes take place within the patient, although, as a rule, much of it on an unconscious level.

Manifest Content. The surface of the patient's associations and the therapist's interventions. The term refers to the direct and explicit meanings so contained.

Me/Not-Me Interface. An imaginary interface of the patient's communications so designed that every aspect refers on one level to the patient himself, while on another level to the therapist or analyst. The me/not-me is stated from the patient's vantage point and indicates that every communication contains allusions to both himself and the therapist or analyst.

Metabolism, or the **Metabolism of Projective Identifications.** A term first used by R. Fliess (1942) to describe the processing by the analyst of temporary trial identifications with the patient. The concept is used more broadly to refer to all efforts to work over sensory and nonsensory inputs from the patient, and in another specific sense to refer to the introjective identification and containing of a projective identification from the patient, ultimately processed toward cognitive understanding and insight. This last sense of the term may also be applied to the patient's efforts to introjectively identify and contain projective identifications from the therapist, so long as efforts are made toward understanding.

Misalliance. A quality of the basic relationship between patient and therapist, or of a sector of that relationship, which is consciously or unconsciously designed to bypass adaptive insight in favor of either some other maladaptive form of symptom alleviation or the destruction of effective therapeutic work (Langs 1975b)

Negative Projective Identification. A term used to describe an empty or voidlike interactional projection designed to destroy meanings within the bipersonal field and to disrupt the mental capacities of the object or recipient of the interactional projection.

Neuroses. A term used in a special sense to allude to all forms of psychopathology, ranging from symptomatic disturbances to character disorders, from neurotic disturbances to borderline syndromes and narcissistic disorders to psychoses, and from psychosomatic disorders to addictions, perversions, and other emotionally founded syndromes. In essence, then, the term refers to all types of syndromes based on intrapsychic and interactional emotional disturbances and dysfunctions.

Neurotic Communication. That form of behaving and conveying meanings that is related to the neuroses, and which is characterized by the use of derivative and convoluted sequences, related ultimately to pathological unconscious fantasies, memories, introjects, and perceptions.

Nonconfirmation. See *Nonvalidation.*

Noncountertransference. The essentially nonconflicted sphere of the therapist's or analyst's functioning expressed in his appropriate capacity to relate to the patient, listen, intervene, manage the framework, and the like.

Nonneurotic Communication. A means of conveying conscious and unconscious meaning that is essentially unrelated to neuroses. It is characterized by manifest messages, readily available inferences, and linear causal sequences.

Nontransference. The essentially nonconflicted areas of the patient's valid functioning within the therapeutic relationship. It is exemplified by validatable conscious and unconscious perceptions and reactions to the therapist, and by other spheres of adequate functioning and interacting.

Nonvalidation. A response to an intervention by the therapist or analyst (management of the framework or verbal) that is flat, lacking in unique contents or a selected fact, repetitious, linear, and without surprise. It is an indication that the intervention has been erroneous, and falls largely into the sphere of secondary confirmation—here constituting secondary nonconfirmation.

Parameter. A term coined by Eissler (1953) to refer to those alterations in standard psychoanalytic technique that are required quite specifically because of a patient's ego dysfunctions or impairments. The concept is based on the thesis that certain patients with severe psychopathology require a modified therapeutic situation. It properly includes the idea that these modifications should be kept to a minimum, should be rectified as quickly as possible, and that the entire experience—deviation and rectification—should be subjected to analysis. It was also noted that parameters can be utilized in the service of the therapist's countertransferences and as an inappropriate replacement for interpretive technique. In addition, the effects of parameters may not be resolvable through verbal analytic work, and may result in unanalyzable restrictions in therapeutic outcome. The thesis that parameters are necessary in the psychotherapy and psychoanalysis of severely disturbed patients has been questioned by a number of analysts (see Langs 1975c, 1976c).

Precipitant or **Reality Precipitant.** A synonym for *day residue,* and a term synonymous with *adaptive context* when used to refer to the evocation of an intrapsychic response.

Preconception. A term first used by Bion (1962) to represent a state of expectation and more broadly a state of need, a quality in need of fulfillment or closure—an unsaturated state which once saturated would generate a *conception.*

Predictive Clinical Methodology. A mode of psychoanalytically oriented therapy founded on the validating process, and especially on efforts at prediction so designed that validation takes the form of Type Two derivatives.

Primary Adaptive Task. A synonym for *adaptive context* (Langs 1973b).

Projective Counteridentification. A term coined by Grinberg (1962) to allude to all countertransference-based responses within the analyst to the patient's projective identifications. The term implies a failure to metabolize the relevant interactional projections and the reprojection into the patient of nondetoxified contents and mechanisms.

Projective Identification. An interactional effort by a subject to place into the object aspects of his own inner mental state, inner contents, and unconscious defenses. The term *identification* is used here in the sense of remaining identified with the externalized contents and wishing to evoke in the object an identification with the subject.

Proxy, Evocation of a. A form of projective identification described by Wangh (1962) which stresses an interactional effort to place into the object areas of malfunctioning and disturbance, largely as a means of evoking adequate responses which can then be introjected.

Psychoanalytically Oriented Psychotherapy, or Insight Psychotherapy. A form of psychotherapy which takes place within a well-defined bipersonal field and which is designed to provide the patient symptom relief based on cognitive insights and the inevitable positive introjective identifications that derive from the therapist's capacity to hold the patient, contain and metabolize his projective identifications, establish and manage the framework, and interpret the neurotic communications and expressions from the patient.

Psychoanalytic Cliché. An intervention based on psychoanalytic theory and on the material from the patient at a point at which it is communicated in a nonneurotic form. It is a statement of apparent psychoanalytic meaning or truth which is essentially and functionally false in light of the prevailing adaptive contexts—sources of inner anxiety and turmoil, conflict and disturbance within the patient and/or the therapist. It is therefore unconsciously designed to serve as a barrier to the underlying catastrophic truths and as a means of disrupting the meaningful relationship links between patient and therapist.

Reconstruction. An attempt by the therapist, through a verbal intervention, to indicate to the patient important events and fantasies from the past, most often in his childhood, of which he has no conscious recall. Such an intervention would begin with the adaptive context and the derivative complex, would be linked to a therapeutic context, and would on this basis derive implications in regard to past actualities; it would always be rooted in the current communicative interaction, and would extend into the past from there.

Regression, Nontherapeutic. A shift toward more primitive communication and expression of derivatives of unconscious fantasies, memories, introjects, and perceptions that takes place under conditions of unneeded modifications in the framework and in response to other errors in technique by the therapist or analyst. The impairments in the framework render such regressions difficult to analyze and resolve, and the restoration of the frame is essential to a shift from a nontherapeutic to a *therapeutic regression.*

Regression, Therapeutic. An adaptive form of regression that takes place within a secure bipersonal field and is a means of describing the constructive emergence of unconscious fantasies, memories, introjects, and perceptions related to the patient's neurosis as mobilized by the therapeutic interaction and based on earlier genetic experiences and traumas. This emergence of relatively primitive material occurs in a form and under conditions that render the neurotic components analyzable and modifiable through insight (Langs 1976a).

Resistance. A term used to describe any impediment within the patient to the work of therapy or analysis. It is a conception that is based on a subjective evaluation by the therapist or analyst. In its narrow clinical sense, these obstacles are founded on defenses against intrapsychic conflicts and anxieties, as they are expressed within the therapeutic relationship. See *Interactional Resistances.*

Resistances, Communicative. Obstacles to the work of therapy or analysis that are discovered through an analysis of the communicative network. Most common among these are the failure to represent the adaptive context with the link to the therapist, and the development of a fragmented or noncoalescing derivative complex. The evaluation of communicative resistances is subjective for the therapist and is open to countertransference-based influences. In addition, the presence of all such resistances may receive unconscious contributions from the inappropriate interventions of the therapist, including misinterventions and mismanagements of the framework. The analysis of all types of resistance requires the rectification of the therapist's contribution and interpretations in which both unconscious perceptions and/or introjections and distorted unconscious fantasies and/or projections are considered.

Resistances, Gross Behavioral. Impediments to the work of psychotherapy or psychoanalysis that appear in the direct behaviors and associations of the patient. While all such evaluations by the therapist are subjective and must be checked for possible countertransference contributions, these obstacles to therapeutic progress tend to be readily recognized. They include silences, gross disruptions of the session, thoughts about or efforts directed toward premature termination, absences, direct but inappropriate opposition to the therapist and repudiation of his interventions, and the like. As manifest phenomena their unconscious meanings and functions must be determined by an identification of the prevailing adaptive context and the relevant derivative complex—the associative network.

Reverie. A term used by Bion (1962) to describe the state of the mother, therapist, or analyst who is capable of receiving the projective identifications from the infant or patient, appropriately metabolizing them, and returning them to the subject in a relatively detoxified form. In a psychotherapeutic situation, this implies a correct interpretation and appropriate management of the framework.

Second-Order Themes. See *Themes, Second-Order*.

Selected Fact, the. A term used by Bion (1962), borrowed from Poincare, to describe a newly discovered formulation, finding, or fact that introduces order and new meaning into, and unites into a whole, previously disparate elements. It is the realization, then, that links together elements not previously seen to be connected.

Silent Hypothesis. A formulation derived from the various avenues of the intaking aspect of the listening process, developed, as a rule, around a specific adaptive context. Its development relies too on the abstracting-particularizing process, monitoring material around the therapeutic interaction, and utilizing the me/not-me interface, as well as all other means available to the therapist or analyst for generating dynamic, adaptive conceptions of the most pertinent unconscious meanings of the patient's material. In its most complete form, it will entail the identification of the most active unconscious fantasies, memories, introjects, and perceptions within the patient, and will include links to his psychopathology. While these hypotheses may be developed at any point in a session, they are especially common in the opening segments of each hour, and are maintained by the therapist without intervening. In principle, they should be subjected to *silent validation* before the therapist or analyst intervenes, doing so most often at a point when there is a relevant bridge between the silent hypothesis itself and the communications from the patient.

Silent Intervention. See *Intervention, Silent.*

Silent Question. An issue that arises within the mind of the therapist as he listens to the patient, leading him to raise it subjectively while not directing it to the patient. When pertinent, such queries will, as a rule, be answered in some derivative form by the patient's ongoing associations. In principle, silent questions are to be preferred to direct queries of the patient, which tend to serve a variety of defensive and countertransference needs within the therapist or analyst, and to impair the patient's use of indirect, derivative communication.

Silent Validation. An aspect of the evaluation of the material from the patient that follows the development of a silent hypothesis. When subsequent material further coalesces with the initial hypothesis, and supports it through the communication of Type Two derivatives, the silent hypothesis is seen as confirmed. See also *Validation.*

Supervisory Introject. A partly conscious, but primarily unconscious, incorporative precipitate within the supervisee based on his work with his supervisor. This introject derives from the conscious and unconscious communications of the supervisor, and may be positive or negative, constructive or destructive, in various intermixtures. The term *supervisory introject* implies the incorporation of mental processes within the supervisor and his transactions with the supervisee, while the related term *supervisor introject* woudl stres incorporation of dimensions of the supervisor himself—attitudes, mental contents, and the like.

Termination, Forced. The premature cessation of a therapeutic situation caused, as a rule, by some circumstance external to the direct therapeutic interaction. Among the most common causes are clinic policies, the move of therapist or patient, and a major change in life circumstance or health in either. A termination of this kind modifies the standard tenet that psychotherapy should be undertaken until the point of insightful symptom resolution within the patient.

Themes, First-Order. The general contents and specific subject matter that can be derived from an examination of the manifest content of the patient's material.

Themes, Second-Order. Derivative contents developed through the use of the abstracting-particularizing process. First-order manifest themes are identified and general thematic trends are then formulated; inferences derived on that basis are considered second-order themes. As a rule, such themes are developed in terms of the ongoing therapeutic relationship and interaction, and take on specific form and meaning when related to pertinent adaptive contexts within that relationship.

Therapeutic Context. A term synonymous with *indicator,* and a component of the listening process. It refers to any communication from the patient that suggests a need for understanding, resolution, and intervention from the therapist. Such communications serve as important second-order organizers of the patient's material. His associations and behaviors are first organized in terms of the communicative network—the adaptive context, its representation, the derivative complex, and the bridge back to the therapist—to provide Type Two derivative meaning in terms of unconscious processes, fantasies, perceptions, and introjects. Once these unconscious meanings and functions are identified, the material is then reorganized around the therapeutic context and the revealed derivative meanings as they pertain to the unconscious implications of the indicator. Therapeutic contexts may be divided into those involving life crises and symptoms within the patient (e.g., homicidal and suicidal concerns and impulses, acute regressions, acting out) and those involving disturbed aspects of the therapeutic interaction (e.g., alterations in the framework by therapist or patient, errors by the therapist, ruptures in the therapeutic alliance, and major and minor resistances).

Therapeutic Interaction. A term used to describe the conscious and unconscious communicative interplays between the patient and therapist or analyst.

Therapeutic Misalliance. An attempt to achieve symptom alleviation through some means other than insight and the related positive introjective identifications with the therapist. See *Misalliance,* an essentially synonymous term.

Therapeutic Relationship. A term that embraces all components, conscious and unconscious, pathological and nonpathological, of the interaction between patient and therapist. For the patient, the therapeutic relationship involves both transference and nontransference components, while for the therapist it involves countertransference and noncountertransference elements. The term is strongly preferred to "transference" when describing the patient's relationship with the therapist, and equally preferred to "countertransference" when describing the therapist's or analyst's relationship to the patient. See *Transference, Nontransference, Countertransference,* and *Noncountertransference.*

Therapy, Lie. Any form of, or interlude in, psychotherapy or psychoanalysis in which the actual unconscious basis for the patient's symptoms, resistances, and the like are either not sought after or are sealed off. It entails both efforts at avoidance and attention to levels of meaning that in the therapeutic interaction serve primarily to create barriers and falsifications, to destroy more pertinent meaning, and thereby to seal off underlying chaotic truths.

Therapy, Truth. A form of therapy or analysis designed to foster the emergence and discovery, within the therapeutic interaction, of the unconscious processes, fantasies, memories, introjects, and transactions which are the basis for the patient's neurosis.

Transference. The pathological component of the patient's relationship to the therapist. Based on pathological unconscious fantasies, memories, and introjects, transference includes all distorted and inappropriate responses and perceptions of the therapist derived from these disruptive inner mental contents and the related mechanisms and defenses. These distortions may be based on displacements from past genetic figures, as well as on pathological interactional mechanisms. Unconscious transference fantasies and mechanisms are always communicated in some derivative form, while the manifest communication may allude to either the therapeutic relationship itself (disguised, however, in regard to the latent content) or to outside relationships. Transference responses are always maladaptive and can only be understood in terms of specific, indirect adaptive contexts (see Langs 1976c).

Transversal Communication. Associations from the patient that bridge, and therefore simultaneously express, both fantasy and reality, transference and nontransference, unconscious perception and distortion, truth and falsehood, self and object. Such communications are, on one level, entirely valid, while on another level, essentially distorted.

Transversal Intervention. A particular type of communication from the therapist or analyst to the patient which is shaped in keeping with the presence of a transversal communication. In essence, such interventions, usually in the form of interpretations, although sometimes developed through the playback of derivatives related to an unidentified adaptive context, take into account the dual qualities of transversal communications, and are stated in a manner that is open to the contradictory elements contained in the patient's associations.

Trial Identification. An aspect of the listening process especially developed by Fliess (1942) as an important means of empathizing with and cognitively understanding the communications from the patient. It entails a temporary merger with, or incorporation of, the patient and his material in the presence of distinct self-object boundaries in most other respects. It is a temporary form of being and feeling with the patient, and the cognitive-affective yield from such experiences must then be processed toward insightful understanding and subjected to the validating process.

Type A Field, the, and **Type A Communicative Mode, the.**
A bipersonal field and communicative style in which symbolism and
illusion play a central role. Such a field is characterized by the development of a play space or transitional space within which the patient
communicates analyzable derivatives of his unconscious fantasies,
memories, introjects, and perceptions, ultimately in the form of Type
Two derivatives. Such a field requires a secure framework, and a
therapist or analyst who is capable of processing the material from the
patient toward cognitive insights which are then imparted through
valid interpretations. Such endeavors represent the therapist's capacity
for symbolic communication. The Type A communicative mode is essentially symbolic, transitional, illusory, and geared toward insight.

Type B Field, the, and **Type B Communicative Mode, the.**
A bipersonal field characterized by major efforts at projective identification and action-discharge. The mode is not essentially designed for
insight but instead facilitates the riddance of accretions of disturbing
internal stimuli. It can, however, despite the interactional pressures it
generates, be used in a manner open to interpretation.

Type C Field, the, and **Type C Communicative Mode, the.**
A field in which the essential links between patient and therapist are
broken and ruptured, and in which verbalization and apparent efforts
at communication are actually designed to destroy meaning, generate
falsifications, and to create impenetrable barriers to underlying
catastrophic truths. The Type C communicative mode is designed for
falsification, the destruction of links between subject and object, and for
the erection of barriers designed to seal off inner and interactional chaos.

Type C Narrator, the. A patient who utilizes the Type C communicative mode through the report of extensive dream material or the
detailed description of events and experiences within his life or in regard
to the therapeutic interaction. Such material is characterized by the
absence of a meaningful adaptive context, the lack of analyzable
derivatives, and the use of these communications essentially for the
generation of nonmeaning and the breaking of relationship links. It is
not uncommon for the Type C narrator to interact with a therapist or
analyst who makes extensive use of psychoanalytic clichés, generating a
therapeutic interaction falsely identified as viable analytic work,

while its primary dynamic function falls within the Type C communicative mode.

Type One Derivatives. Readily available inferences derived from the manifest content of the patient's associations, without the use of an adaptive context. These inferences constitute one level of the latent content, arrived at in isolation and without reference to the dynamic state of the therapeutic interaction and to the adaptive-dynamic function of the material at hand.

Type Two Derivatives. Inferences from the manifest content of the patient's material that are arrived at through the abstracting-particularizing process when it is organized around a specific adaptive context. These disguised contents accrue specific dynamic-adaptive meaning when so organized, and are the main medium for the therapist's or analyst's interpretations, primarily in terms of the therapeutic interaction.

Unconscious Fantasy. The working over in displaced form of a particular adaptive context. The relevant contents are outside the patient's awareness and are expressed in derivative form in the manifest content of his associations. This is a type of daydreaming without direct awareness of the essential theme, and may be either pathological or nonpathological. The derivatives of unconscious fantasies are an essential medium of interpretive work and have important genetic antecedents. Among the most crucial unconscious fantasies are those related to the therapist, and when they are distorted they fall into the realm of transference, while those that are nondistorted belong to nontransference. These daydreams include representations from the id, ego, superego, self, and from every aspect of the patient's inner mental world, life, and psychic mechanisms.

Unconscious Interpretation. A communication usually from patient to therapist, expressed in disguised and derivative form, and unconsciously designed to help the therapist understand the underlying basis for a countertransference-based intervention. These interpretations can be recognized by taking the therapist's intervention as the adaptive context for the material from the patient that follows; hypothesizing the nature of the therapist's errors; and accepting the patient's material as reflecting an introjection of the error, and an effort to heal the disturbing aspects of that introject. Put in other terms, the patient's responses are viewed as a *commentary* on the therapist's intervention, and are found to contain unconscious efforts to assist the therapist in gaining insight in regard to the sources of his errors.

Unconscious Introject. A network of intrapsychic precipitants derived from interactions between the subject and object, in the past and present. They are derived from the process of introjective identification, and depend on the nature of the contents and mechanisms involved, as well as qualities within both subject and object. Introjects may be short-lived or relatively stable, pathological and non-pathological, incorporated into the self-image and self-representations or isolated from them, and may involve any of the structures of the mind, id, ego, and superego. In psychotherapy, an especially important form of introjection occurs in response to the therapist's projective identifications, either helpful or traumatic, nonpathological or pathological, which generate alterations in the inner mental world of the patient. Such a process is continuous with the therapeutic interaction and may, in addition, occur within the therapist as a result of projective identifications from the patient. See also *Introjects.*

Unconscious Memory. Derivative precipitates of past experiences—mixtures of actuality and distortion—expressed through indirect communication and inner representations of which the subject is unaware. Such reminiscences without awareness may be pathological or nonpathological, and the former are an important aspect of the genetic basis of the patient's psychopathology.

Unconscious Perception. A term used to describe evidence of valid perceptiveness of another person's (an object's) communications and cues of which the subject is unaware. These may be identified through a correct appraisal of the nature of an adaptive context, including an accurate understanding of the object's unconscious communications. While outside the subject's awareness, his derivative communications demonstrate an essentially veridical perception in terms of the prevailing underlying realities. When the adaptive context is known, unconscious perceptions are reflected in Type Two derivatives. They are the basis for nondistorted introjects.

Validated Hypothesis. A silent hypothesis that has been confirmed via Type Two derivatives, and especially an interpretation or management of the frame that has been communicated to the patient and which is affirmed through the development of Type Two derivatives and the appearance of a *selected fact*.

Validating Process, the. A term used to describe conscious and unconscious efforts within either patient or therapist to affirm, support, and substantiate conscious or unconscious formulations and hypotheses. It is a crucial component of the listening process, receives its ultimate test in the patient's responses to the therapist's interpretations and management of the framework, and must take the form of confirmation via Type Two derivatives and the development of a *selected fact* (see Langs 1976c, 1978g).

Validation, Indirect. See *Validation via Type Two Derivatives,* with which it is essentially synonymous.

Validation via Type Two Derivatives. A form of confirmation that is synonymous with the development of a *selected fact,* and with the modification of repressive barriers. This type of indirect, derivative validation is the essential proof of the truth of a psychoanalytic clinical formulation and intervention. Every clinical psychoanalytic hypothesis can be accepted as a general truth only if it has been subjected to this type of validation.

Vested Interest Deviation. A modification in the standard framework regarding which the therapist has a special investment. Examples are his having his office in his home and the signing of insurance forms in order to enable him to receive his fee. The concept draws its importance from the finding that deviations in which the therapist has an inordinate investment tend to generate silent sectors of misalliance with the patient. The responses of the latter tend to be highly disguised, and often appear in the form of embedded derivatives. As a result, the material related to such a deviation tends to be difficult to recognize and interpret. Often the therapist has a significant blind spot in this area, rendering the bastion and misalliance so generated difficult to identify and even more difficult to modify.

REFERENCES

Allen, S. (1956). Reflections on the wish of the analyst to break or change the basic rule. *Bulletin of the Menninger Clinic* 20: 192–200.

Arlow, J., and Brenner, C. (1966). The psychoanalytic situation. In *Psychoanalysis in the Americas,* ed. R. Litman, pp. 23–43. New York: International Universities Press.

Balint, M. (1968). *The Basic Fault: Therapeutic Aspects of Regression.* London: Tavistock.

Baranger, M., and Baranger, W. (1966). Insight in the analytic situation. In *Psychoanalysis in the Americas,* ed. R. Litman, pp. 56–72. New York: International Universities Press.

Bion, W. (1962). *Learning from Experience.* In W. Bion, *Seven Servants.* New York: Jason Aronson, 1977.

_____(1970). *Attention and Interpretation.* In W. Bion, *Seven Servants.* New York: Jason Aronson, 1977.

Bird, B. (1972). Notes on transference: universal phenomenon and hardest part of analysis. *Journal of the American Psychoanalytic Association* 20: 267–301.

Bleger, J. (1967). Psycho-analysis of the psychoanalytic frame. *International Journal of Psycho-Analysis* 48: 511–519.

Bouvet, M. (1958). Technical variations and the concept of distance. *International Journal of Psycho-Analysis* 39: 211–221.

Calogeras, R. (1967). Silence as a technical parameter in psychoanalysis. *International Journal of Psycho-Analysis* 48: 536–558.

Eissler, K. R. (1953). The effect of the structure of the ego on psychoanalytic technique. *Journal of the American Psychoanalytic Association* 1: 104–143.

_____(1958). Remarks on some variations in psychoanalytic technique. *International Journal of Psycho-Analysis* 39: 222–229.

_____(1974). On some theoretical and technical problems regarding the payment of fees for psychoanalytic treatment. *International Review of Psycho-Analysis* 1: 73–101.

Fliess, R. (1942). The metapsychology of the analyst. *Psychoanalytic Quarterly* 11: 211–227.

Frank, J. (1956). Indications and contraindications for the application of the standard technique. *Journal of the American Psychoanalytic Association* 4: 266–284.

Freud, A. (1954a). Problems of technique in adult analysis. *Bulletin of the Philadelphia Association for Psychoanalysis* 4: 44–70.

_____(1954b). The widening scope of indications for psychoanalysis, discussion. *Journal of the American Psychoanalytic Association* 2: 607–620.

Freud, S. (1900). The interpretation of dreams. *Standard Edition* 4/5.

_____(1905). A fragment of an analysis of a case of hysteria. *Standard Edition* 12: 109–120.

_____(1909). Notes upon a case of obsessional neurosis. *Standard Edition* 17: 3–122.

_____(1912). Recommendations to physicians practising psychoanalysis. *Standard Edition* 12: 109–120.

_____(1913). On beginning the treatment (further recommendations on the technique of psycho-analysis I). *Standard Edition* 12: 121–144.

_____(1915). Observations on transference-love (further recommendations on the technique of psycho-analysis III). *Standard Edition* 12: 157–171.

_____(1918). From the history of an infantile neurosis. *Standard Edition* 10: 153–320.

_____(1937a). Constructions in analysis. *Standard Edition* 23: 255–269.

_____(1937b). Analysis terminable and interminable. *Standard Edition* 23: 209–254.

Greenacre, P. (1954). The role of transference. *Journal of the American Psychoanalytic Association* 2: 671–684.

———(1959). Certain technical problems in the transference relationship. *Journal of the American Psychoanalytic Association* 7: 484–502.

———(1971). *Emotional Growth, Vols. 1 and 2.* New York: International Universities Press.

Greenson, R. (1958). Variations in classical psychoanalytic technique: an introduction. *International Journal of Psycho-Analysis* 39: 200–201.

———(1965). The working alliance and the transference neurosis. *Psychoanalytic Quarterly* 34: 155–181.

———(1967). *The Technique and Practice of Psychoanalysis.* Vol. 1. New York: International Universities Press.

———(1972). Beyond transference and interpretation. *International Journal of Psycho-Analysis* 53: 213–217.

Greenson, R., and Wexler, M. The non-transference relationship in the psychoanalytic situation. *International Journal of Psycho-Analysis* 50: 27–39.

Grinberg, L. (1962). On a specific aspect of counter-transference due to the patient's projective identification. *International Journal of Psycho-Analysis* 43: 436–440.

Gudeman, J. (1974). Uncontrolled regression in therapy and analysis. *International Journal of Psychoanalytic Psychotherapy* 3: 325–338.

Halpert, E. (1972). The effect of insurance on psychoanalytic treatment. *Journal of the American Psychoanalytic Association* 20: 122–133.

Hoedemaker, E. (1960). Psycho-analytic technique and ego modification. *International Journal of Psycho-Analysis* 41: 34–46.

Kanzer, M. (1963). Book review of *The Psychoanalytic Situation* by L. Stone. *International Journal of Psycho-Analysis* 44: 108–110.

———(1975). The therapeutic and working alliances. *International Journal of Psychoanalytic Psychotherapy* 4: 48–73.

Langs, R. (1972). A psychoanalytic study of material from patients in psychotherapy. *International Journal of Psychoanalytic Psychotherapy* 1: 4–45. In Langs 1978f.

———(1973a). The patient's view of the therapist: reality or fantasy. *International Journal of Psychoanalytic Psychotherapy* 2: 411–431. In Langs 1978f.

———(1973b). *The Technique of Psychoanalytic Psychotherapy.* Vol. 1. New York: Jason Aronson.

———(1974). *The Technique of Psychoanalytic Psychotherapy*. Vol. 2. New York: Jason Aronson.

———(1975a). The patient's unconscious perception of the therapist's errors. In *Tactics and Techniques in Psychoanalytic Therapy, Vol. 2: Countertransference,* ed. P. Giovacchini. New York: Jason Aronson. In Langs 1978f.

———(1975b). Therapeutic misalliances. *International Journal of Psychoanalytic Psychotherapy* 4: 77–105. In Langs 1978f.

———(1975c). The therapeutic relationship and deviations in technique. *International Journal of Psychoanalytic Psychotherapy* 4: 106–141. In Langs 1978f.

———(1976a). *The Bipersonal Field*. New York: Jason Aronson.

———(1976b). The misalliance dimension in Freud's case histories. I. The case of Dora. *International Journal of Psychoanalytic Psychotherapy* 5: 301–317. In Langs 1978f.

———(1976c). *The Therapeutic Interaction*. 2 Vols. New York: Jason Aronson.

———(1978a). Framework, misalliance, and interaction in the analytic situation: three encyclopedia articles. In Langs 1978f.

———(1978b). Interventions in the bipersonal field. In Langs 1978f.

———(1978c). *The Listening Process*. New York: Jason Aronson.

———(1978d). Misalliance and framework in the case of the Rat Man. In Langs 1978f.

———(1978e). Misalliance and framework in the case of the Wolf Man. In Langs 1978f.

———(1978f). *Technique in Transition*. New York: Jason Aronson.

———(1978g). Validation and the framework. In Langs 1978f.

———(1979). *The Supervisory Experience*. New York: Jason Aronson.

Levy, S. (1977). Countertransference aspects of pharmacotherapy in the treatment of schizophrenia. *International Journal of Psychoanalytic Psychotherapy* 6: 15–30.

Lipton, S. (1977a). The advantages of Freud's technique as shown in his analysis of the Rat Man. *International Journal of Psycho-Analysis* 58: 255–274.

———(1977b). Clinical observations on resistance to the transference. *International Journal of Psycho-Analysis* 58: 463–472.

Little, M. (1951). Counter-transference and the patient's response to it. *International Journal of Psycho-Analysis* 32: 32–40.

Loewald, H. (1960). On the therapeutic action of psycho-analysis. *International Journal of Psycho-Analysis* 41: 16–33.

Loewenstein, R. (1958). Remarks on some variations in psychoanalytic technique. *International Journal of Psycho-Analysis* 33: 181–195.

Lorand, S. (1963). Modifications in classical psychoanalysis. *Psychoanalytic Quarterly* 32: 192–204.

Milner, M. (1952). Aspects of symbolism in comprehension of the not-self. *International Journal of Psycho-Analysis* 33: 181–195.

Nacht, S. (1958). Variations in technique. *International Journal of Psycho-Analysis* 39: 230–234.

Racker, H. (1957). The meaning and uses of countertransference. *Psychoanalytic Quarterly* 26: 303–357.

———(1968). *Transference and Countertransference.* London: Hogarth Press.

Reich, A. (1958). A special variation of technique. *International Journal of Psycho-Analysis* 39: 230–234.

Rodgers, T. (1965). A specific parameter: concurrent psychotherapy of the spouse of an analysand by the same analyst. *International Journal of Psycho-Analysis* 39: 238–239.

Searles, H. (1959). The effort to drive the other person crazy: an element in the aetiology and psychotherapy of schizophrenia. *British Journal of Medical Psychology* 32: 1–18.

———(1965). *Collected Papers on Schizophrenia and Related Subjects.* New York: International Universities Press.

———(1975). The patient as therapist to his analyst. In *Tactics and Techniques in Psychoanalytic Therapy, Vol. 2: Countertransference,* ed. P. Giovacchini. New York: Jason Aronson.

Seitz, P. (1978). Book review of *The Bipersonal Field* by R. Langs. *Journal of Nervous and Mental Disease* 166: 374–375.

Stone, L. (1954). The widening scope of indications for psychoanalysis. *Journal of the American Psychoanalytic Association* 2: 567–594.

———(1961). *The Psychoanalytic Situation.* New York: International Universities Press.

———(1967). The psychoanalytic situation and transference. *Journal of the American Psychoanalytic Association* 2: 567–594.

Strachey, J. (1934). The nature of the therapeutic action of psychoanalysis. *International Journal of Psycho-Analysis* 15: 127–159.

Tarachow, S. (1962). Interpretation and reality in psychotherapy. *International Journal of Psycho-Analysis* 43: 377–387.

Viderman, S. (1974). Interpretation in the analytic space. *International Journal Review of Psycho-Analysis* 1: 467–480.

Wangh, M. (1962). The "evocation of a proxy": a psychological maneuver, its use as a defense, its purpose and genesis. *Psychoanalytic Study of the Child* 17: 451–469.

Winnicott, D. W. (1958). *Collected Papers*. London: Tavistock Publications.

———(1965). *The Maturational Processes and the Facilitating Environment*. New York: International Universities Press.

Zetzel, E. (1966). The analytic situation. In *Psychoanalysis in the Americas,* ed. R. Litman, pp. 86–106. New York: International Universities Press.

See Langs (1976c) for a comprehensive bibliography of writings on the therapeutic environment, and for an extensive discussion of the literature.

INDEX